William Kirk Dickson

The Jacobite Attempt of 1719

Letters of James Butler, Second Duke of Ormonde

William Kirk Dickson

The Jacobite Attempt of 1719
Letters of James Butler, Second Duke of Ormonde

ISBN/EAN: 9783337132972

Printed in Europe, USA, Canada, Australia, Japan

Cover: Foto ©ninafisch / pixelio.de

More available books at **www.hansebooks.com**

PUBLICATIONS

OF THE

SCOTTISH HISTORY SOCIETY

VOLUME XIX

THE JACOBITE ATTEMPT OF 1719

December 1895

THE JACOBITE ATTEMPT
OF 1719

LETTERS OF JAMES BUTLER, SECOND DUKE OF ORMONDE, RELATING TO CARDINAL ALBERONI'S PROJECT FOR THE INVASION OF GREAT BRITAIN ON BEHALF OF THE STUARTS, AND TO THE LANDING OF A SPANISH EXPEDITION IN SCOTLAND

Edited, with an Introduction, Notes and an Appendix of Original Documents, by

WILLIAM KIRK DICKSON
M.A., ADVOCATE

EDINBURGH
Printed at the University Press by T. and A. Constable
for the Scottish History Society
1895

PREFACE

THE Letter Book of the second Duke of Ormonde, now edited for the Scottish History Society, was acquired by the British Museum in November 1890, and is catalogued as No. 33,950 of the Additional Manuscripts. It is a thin vellum-covered volume, consisting of ninety folios, and containing copies, kept in the handwriting of two secretaries, of letters written by the Duke between November 4th, 1718, and September 27th, 1719. Twenty-three of the letters are addressed to Prince James Francis Edward Stuart, and fifty-seven to Cardinal Alberoni. They relate almost entirely to the Cardinal's projected invasion of this country in 1719 on behalf of the exiled Stuarts, which ended in the Earl Marischal's landing in the West Highlands and the Battle of Glenshiel. They are an important addition to our somewhat scanty sources of information regarding this enterprise.

In the Introduction I have tried to tell the story anew from contemporary authorities. A number of original documents relating to the undertaking are collected in the Appendix.

I have to record my humble gratitude to Her Majesty the Queen for the permission graciously accorded to me to make use of a portion of the Stuart Papers in the Library at Windsor.

My thanks are also due to the Earl of Kintore, for permission to reproduce the portraits of the tenth Earl Marischal and of Field-Marshal James Keith, in his possession at Keith

Hall; to the Council of the Society of Antiquaries of Scotland, for permission to reproduce Bastide's plan of the Battle of Glenshiel from the Proceedings of the Society; to Viscount Dillon, for access to General Arthur Dillon's papers at Ditchley; to the Bishop of Edinburgh, for the letter of Bishop Gadderar, printed in Appendix, p. 296; to the Rev. Roderick Morison, minister of Kintail, for information as to the traditions and place-names of Seaforth's country; and to Mr. Richard R. Holmes, Her Majesty's Librarian at Windsor, for his courteous assistance in the examination of the Stuart Papers. I am specially indebted to Mr. T. G. Law, Secretary of our Society, for much valuable advice and help. The Index is the work of Mr. Alex. Mill, of the Signet Library.

W. K. D.

EDINBURGH, *October* 15, 1895.

CONTENTS

	PAGE
INTRODUCTION,	xix

THE DUKE OF ORMONDE'S LETTERS:[1]—

I. To the King (James Stuart), Paris, Nov. 4, 1718,	1
II. To the Earl of Mar, Paris, Nov. 4,	2
III. To Cardinal Alberoni, Alcala, Dec. 1.	4
IV. To the same, Madrid, Dec. 4,	5
V. To the King, Madrid, Dec. 5,	6
VI. To General Arthur Dillon, Madrid, Dec. 8,	8
VII. To the Earl Marischal, Madrid, Dec. 8,	9
VIII. To Cardinal Alberoni, Guada Lama, Dec. 9,	10
IX. To General Arthur Dillon, Guada Lama, Dec. 9,	11
X. To Cardinal Alberoni, Valladolid, Dec. 17,	12
XI. To General Arthur Dillon, Valladolid, Dec. 17,	13
XII. To Cardinal Alberoni, Valladolid, Dec. 17,	13
XIII. To the King, Valladolid, Dec. 17,	15
XIV. To Cardinal Alberoni, Valladolid, Dec. 22,	17
XV. To the King, Valladolid, Dec. 22,	19
XVI. To the Earl of Mar, Valladolid, Dec. 23,	21
XVII. To Cardinal Alberoni, Valladolid, Dec. 24,	21

---

[1] In the Table of Contents the Letters are referred to by the real names of the persons to whom they are addressed. In the Manuscript they are often headed by fictitious or cipher names. These are in all cases explained by headnotes. A key to the cipher names used in the Letters is appended to the Manuscript. It is printed at page 189. It is not quite complete. The missing names have, so far as possible, been supplied from the Stuart Papers. Throughout the letters the expression 'the King' refers to James Francis Edward Stuart, called the 'Chevalier de St. George,' and the 'Old Pretender.' The same usage is for convenience generally followed in the Contents and the headnotes. Throughout the volume dates which refer to events happening or letters dated on the Continent are New Style; those referring to events in Great Britain are Old Style, nominally eleven days earlier.

THE DUKE OF ORMONDE'S LETTERS—*continued*

		PAGE
XVIII.	To Cardinal Alberoni, Valladolid, Dec. 25, 1718,	22
XIX.	To the Same, Valladolid, Dec. 31,	23
XX.	To the Same, Valladolid, Jan. 4, 1719,	25
XXI.	To Baron de Walef, Valladolid, Jan. 4,	27
XXII.	To Sir Peter Redmond, Valladolid, Jan. 7,	28
XXIII.	To Cardinal Alberoni, Valladolid, Jan. 7,	28
XXIV.	To the Same, Valladolid, Jan. 11,	30
XXV.	To the Prince of Campo Florido, Valladolid, Jan. 13,	32
XXVI.	To Cardinal Alberoni, Valladolid, Jan. 17,	33
XXVII.	To the Prince of Campo Florido, Valladolid, Jan. 17 (*Memorandum*),	35
XXVIII.	To the Prince of Campo Florido, Valladolid, Jan. 20,	35
XXIX.	To Cardinal Alberoni, Valladolid, Jan. 21,	36
XXX.	To the Same, Valladolid, Jan. 21,	39
XXXI.	To the Prince of Campo Florido, Valladolid, Jan. 24,	39
XXXII.	To Cardinal Alberoni, Valladolid, Jan. 25,	40
XXXIII.	To the Same, Valladolid, Jan. 26 (*Not sent*),	42
XXXIV.	To the Prince of Campo Florido, Valladolid, Jan. 26,	43
XXXV.	To Cardinal Alberoni, Valladolid, Jan. 26,	44
XXXVI.	To the Same, Valladolid, Jan. 27,	45
XXXVII.	To the Prince of Campo Florido, Valladolid, Jan. 27,	48
XXXVIII.	To Cardinal Alberoni, Valladolid, Jan. 30,	49
XXXIX.	To the Prince of Campo Florido, Valladolid, Jan. 31,	50
XL.	To the Rev. Ezekiel Hamilton, Valladolid, Jan. 31,	50
XLI.	To Toby Mathews, Valladolid, Jan. 31,	51
XLII.	To Cardinal Alberoni, Valladolid, Feb. 1,	52
XLIII.	To the Duke of Liria, Valladolid, Jan. 25,	53
XLIV.	To the Prince of Campo Florido, Valladolid, Feb. 7 (*Not sent*),	53
XLV.	To the Rev. Ezekiel Hamilton, Valladolid, Feb. 7,	54

CONTENTS

THE DUKE OF ORMONDE'S LETTERS—*continued* PAGE

XLVI. To Toby Mathews, Valladolid, Feb. 7, 1719	55
XLVII. To the Prince of Campo Florido, Valladolid, Feb. 7,	55
XLVIII. To Cardinal Alberoni, Valladolid, Feb. 8,	56
XLIX. To the same, Valladolid, Feb. 10,	59
L. To the same, Astorga, Feb. 13,	60
LI. To General Crafton, Astorga, Feb. 13,	62
LII. To the Duke of Gordon, Astorga, Feb. 13,	63
LIII. To the Marquis de Risbourg, Foufrien, Feb. 17,	63
LIV. To the Same, Betanzos, Feb. 23,	64
LV. To the Same, Sada, Feb. 24,	65
LVI. To the Same, Sada, Feb. 24,	65
LVII. To Baron de Walef, Sada, Feb. 24,	65
LVIII. To Sir Timon Connock, Sada, Feb. 24,	66
LIX. To Cardinal Alberoni, Sada, Feb. 26,	67
LX. To the Earl Marischal, Sada, Feb. 26,	69
LXI. To Glengarry, Sada, Feb. 26,	69
LXII. To MacLean of Brolas, Sada, Feb. 26,	70
LXIII. To 'Clanronald's cousin' (Donald MacDonald of Benbecula), Sada, Feb. 26,	70
LXIV. To the Marquis de Risbourg, Sada, Feb. 27,	71
LXV. To the Same, Sada, March 1,	72
LXVI. To the Same, Sada, March 2,	73
LXVII. To the Same, Sada, March 2,	73
LXVIII. To Don Balthasar de Guevarra, Sada, March 3,	74
LXIX. To Baron de Walef, Sada, March 3,	75
LXX. To the Same, Sada, March 6,	76
LXXI. To the Marquis de Risbourg, Sada, March 6,	77
LXXII. To Baron de Walef, Sada, March 9,	78
LXXIII. To the Marquis de Risbourg, Sada, March 12,	78
LXXIV. To Cardinal Alberoni, Sada, March 12,	79
LXXV. To Baron de Walef, Sada, March 12,	80
LXXVI. To the Marquis de Risbourg, Sada, March 15,	81
LXXVII. To Baron de Walef, Sada, March 15,	82
LXXVIII. To Sir Timon Connock, Sada, March 16,	82
LXXIX. To the Marquis de Risbourg, Sada, March 16,	83

THE DUKE OF ORMONDE'S LETTERS—*continued*

PAGE

LXXX. To Cardinal Alberoni, Corunna, March 17, 1719,   84
LXXXI. To the King, Corunna, March 17, . . 86
LXXXII. To the Earl of Mar, Corunna, March 17, . 87
LXXXIII. To the Marquis de Risbourg, Corunna, March 19, 88
LXXXIV. To the Same, Corunna, March 20, . . 88
LXXXV. To Don Balthasar de Guevarra, Corunna, March 20, 89
LXXXVI. To Cardinal Alberoni, Corunna, March 22, . 90
LXXXVII. To the King, Corunna, March 22, . . 93
LXXXVIII. To the Same, Corunna, March 27, . . 95
LXXXIX. To Cardinal Alberoni, Corunna, March 27, . 96
XC. To Messrs. Crean & Company, Bankers, Madrid, Corunna, March 27, ... 98
XCI. To Cardinal Alberoni, Corunna, March 31, . 99
XCII. To the King, Corunna, March 31, . . 101
XCIII. To the Same, Corunna, April 4, . . . 101
XCIV. To Cardinal Alberoni, Corunna, April 5, . 102
XCV. To the King, Corunna, April 5, . . . 104
XCVI. To Cardinal Alberoni, Corunna, April 9, . 104
XCVII. To the King, Corunna, April 11, . . 108
XCVIII. To the Same, Corunna, April 12 (*Not sent*), . 109
XCIX. To the Same, Corunna, April 13, . . 110
C. To Cardinal Alberoni, Corunna, April 13, . 111
CI. To the King, Corunna, April 14, . . 112
CII. To Cardinal Alberoni, Corunna, April 17, . 112
CIII. To the Same, Corunna, April 21, . . 113
CIV. To the Same, Corunna, April 28, . . 115
CV. To the Prince of Campo Florido, Corunna, April 28, 115
CVI. To Sir Timon Connock, Corunna, April 29, . 116
CVII. To Cardinal Alberoni, Corunna, April 30, . 117
CVIII. To the Marquis de Risbourg, Sobrado, May 6, . 117
CIX. To Sir John Healy, Sobrado, May 6, . 118
CX. To the Earl Marischal, Lugo, May 9, . 119
CXI. To the Marquis de Risbourg, Lugo, May 9, 120
CXII. To Sir John Healy, Lugo, May 12, 121
CXIII. To Admiral Cammock, Lugo, May 15, . 122
CXIV. To Sir Peter Redmond, Lugo, May 15, . 122

CONTENTS

THE DUKE OF ORMONDE'S LETTERS—continued

		PAGE
CXV.	To Sir Redmond Everard, Lugo, May 15, 1719,	123
CXVI.	To the Marquis de Risbourg, Lugo, May 18,	123
CXVII.	To Sir John Healy, Lugo, May 18,	124
CXVIII.	To Colonel Owen, Lugo, May 18,	125
CXIX.	To Sir John Healy, Lugo, May 20,	125
CXX.	To Cardinal Alberoni, Lugo, May 23,	126
CXXI.	To Sir Timon Connock, Lugo, May 23,	126
CXXII.	To the Marquis de Risbourg, Lugo, May 26,	127
CXXIII.	To Sir John Healy, Lugo, May 26,	128
CXXIV.	To Cardinal Alberoni, Lugo, June 12,	128
CXXV.	To Sir Timon Connock, Lugo, June 12,	129
CXXVI.	To the Duke of Liria, Lugo, June 12,	130
CXXVII.	To the Prince of Campo Florido, Lugo, June 12,	130
CXXVIII.	To the Marquis de Risbourg, Lugo, June 14,	131
CXXIX.	To Sir John Healy, Lugo, June 14,	131
CXXX.	To Cardinal Alberoni, Lugo, June 16,	132
CXXXI.	To the Marquis de Risbourg, Lugo, June 16,	132
CXXXII.	To Sir Timon Connock, Santiago, June 26,	133
CXXXIII.	To M. Seminati, Santiago, June 26,	134
CXXXIV.	To the Marquis de Risbourg, Santiago, June 26,	134
CXXXV.	To Mr. Joyes, Santiago, July 2,	135
CXXXVI.	To Sir Peter Redmond, Santiago, July 3,	136
CXXXVII.	To Cardinal Alberoni, Santiago, July 4,	136
CXXXVIII.	To the Queen (Maria Clementina), Santiago, July 4,	137
CXXXIX.	To Sir Timon Connock, Santiago, July 4,	138
CXL.	To the Marquis de Risbourg, Santiago, July 4,	138
CXLI.	To the Same, Lugo, July 8,	139
CXLII.	To Sir Timon Connock, Lugo, July 8,	140
CXLIII.	To Cardinal Alberoni, Lugo, July 9,	140
CXLIV.	To Mr. Joyes, Lugo, July 9,	141
CXLV.	To Sir Timon Connock, Lugo, July 9,	141
CXLVI.	To Cardinal Alberoni, Lugo, July 15,	143
CXLVII.	To the Marquis de Franclieu, Lugo, July 15,	143
CXLVIII.	To Lady Arthur, Lugo, July 15,	144
CXLIX.	To Sir Timon Connock, Lugo, July 12,	144

THE DUKE OF ORMONDE'S LETTERS—*continued*

		PAGE
CL.	To the Count of Castelblanco, Lugo, July 21, 1719	145
CLI.	To Sir Timon Connock, Lugo, July 23,	146
CLII.	To the Same, Lugo, July 24,	147
CLIII.	To the Marquis de Risbourg, Lugo, July 24,	147
CLIV.	To Cardinal Alberoni, Lugo, July 26,	148
CLV.	To Sir Timon Connock, Lugo, July 26,	150
CLVI.	To the Earl of Mar, Lugo, July 26,	150
CLVII.	To the Hon. James Murray, Lugo, July 26,	151
CLVIII.	To the King, Lugo, July 29,	151
CLIX.	To the Queen (Princess Maria Clementina), Lugo, July 29,	152
CLX.	To the Hon. John Hay, Lugo, July 29,	152
CLXI.	To the King, Lugo, July 30,	153
CLXII.	To the Same, Lugo, July 31,	153
CLXIII.	To Sir Timon Connock, Lugo, July 31,	153
CLXIV.	To M. de Clancostrum, Lugo, Aug. 4,	154
CLXV.	To Mr. Morgan, Lugo, Aug. 4,	155
CLXVI.	To General Echlin, Lugo, Aug. 4,	155
CLXVII.	To the Marquis de Risbourg, Lugo, Aug. 6,	156
CLXVIII.	To Cardinal Alberoni, Lugo, Aug. 7,	157
CLXIX.	To Admiral Cammock, Valladolid, Aug. 18,	157
CLXX.	To Cardinal Alberoni, Valladolid, Aug. 19,	158
CLXXI.	To the King, Valladolid, Aug. 19,	159
CLXXII.	To Sir Timon Connock, Valladolid, Aug. 19,	160
CLXXIII.	To the Hon. John Hay, Valladolid, Aug. 19,	160
CLXXIV.	To Baron Walef, Valladolid, Aug. 19,	160
CLXXV.	To Sir Timon Connock, Valladolid, Aug. 23,	161
CLXXVI.	To Cardinal Alberoni, Valladolid, Aug. 23,	163
CLXXVII.	To Lady Arthur, Valladolid, Aug. 23,	163
CLXXVIII.	To the King, Valladolid, Aug. 23,	164
CLXXIX.	To the Prince of Campo Florido, Lugo, Aug. 5, (Sent from Valladolid, Aug. 26, *Memorandum*),	164
CLXXX.	To Cardinal Alberoni, Valladolid, Aug. 30,	164
CLXXXI.	To the King, Valladolid, Aug. 30,	165
CLXXXII.	To Admiral Cammock, Valladolid, Sept. 1,	166
CLXXXIII.	To Cardinal Alberoni, Valladolid, Sept. 2,	166

CONTENTS

THE DUKE OF ORMONDE'S LETTERS—*continued*   PAGE

CLXXXIV. To Lady Arthur, Valladolid, Sept. 2 (*Memorandum*), 1719, ... 167
CLXXXV. To the Duke of Perth, Valladolid, Sept. 2 (*Memorandum*), ... 167
CLXXXVI. To Cardinal Alberoni, Valladolid, Sept. 5, . 168
CLXXXVII. To the King, Valladolid, Sept. 6, . 170
CLXXXVIII. To Bishop Atterbury, Valladolid, Sept. 8, . 171
CLXXXIX. To Cardinal Alberoni, Valladolid, Sept. 9 (*Not sent*), ... 171
CXC. To Baron Walef, Valladolid, Sept. 9, . . 172
CXCI. To the Duke of Perth, Valladolid, Sept. 9 (*Memorandum*), . . . 173
CXCII. To Captain Esmonde, Valladolid, Sept. 9 (*Memorandum*), ... 173
CXCIII. To Cardinal Alberoni, Valladolid, Sept. 9, . 173
CXCIV. To Sir Timon Connock, Valladolid, Sept. 9, . 174
CXCV. To Cardinal Alberoni, Valladolid, Sept. 13, . 175
CXCVI. To the King, Valladolid, Sept. 13, . 176
CXCVII. To Sir John Healy, Valladolid, Sept. 13, . 176
CXCVIII. To Cardinal Alberoni, Valladolid, Sept. 16, . 177
CXCIX. To the King, Valladolid, Sept. 20, . 180
CC. To Cardinal Alberoni, Valladolid, Sept. 20, . 180
CCI. To the Same, Valladolid, Sept. 22. . 181
CCII. To the Same, Valladolid, Sept. 23, . 184
CCIII. To Don Blas de Loya, Valladolid, Sept. 26, . 185
CCIV. To the King, Valladolid, Sept. 26, . 185
CCV. To the Queen, Valladolid, Sept. 26, . 186
CCVI. To the Hon. John Hay, Valladolid, Sept. 26, . 186
CCVII. To Sir Timon Connock, Valladolid, Sept. 26, . 186
CCVIII. To Cardinal Alberoni, Valladolid, Sept. 27, . 187

KEY TO CIPHER NAMES, ... 189

APPENDIX

I. PAPERS RELATING TO EVENTS ABROAD:—

	PAGE
1. The Duke of Ormonde to James Stuart, Oct 3, 1718,	193
2. Ormonde to the Earl of Mar, Oct. 3,	194
3. Ormonde to Mar, Oct. 17,	195
4. Ormonde to James, Oct. 17,	196
5. Ormonde to James, Oct. 21,	197
6. James to William Dicconson, Nov. 2,	198
7. James to Ormonde, Nov. 2,	199
8. James to Ormonde, Nov. 27,	200
9. Mar to Ormonde, Dec. 2,	202
10. Mar to the Earl Marischal, Dec. 6,	204
11. Mar to Lord Panmure, March 21, 1719.	206
12. James to Pope Clement XI., Feb. 7,	216
13. James to Dicconson, March 11,	217
14. James to Dicconson, March 22,	217
15. The King of Spain (Philip V.) to James, March 16,	218
16. The Queen of Spain (Elizabeth Farnese) to James, March 16,	218
17. Cardinal Alberoni to Ormonde, March 18,	219
18. James to Dicconson, March 31,	221
19. Alberoni to Ormonde, April 4,	222
20. The Abbé Dubois to Secretary Craggs, Jan. 16,	223
21. Dubois to Craggs, March 8,	224
22. Dubois to Craggs, March 11,	227
23. Report from St. Malo to the Conseil de Marine, March 3,	228
24. Report from Marseilles to the Conseil de Marine, Feb. 26,	228
25. The Earl of Stair, British Ambassador in Paris, to Craggs, March 11, 12,	229
26. Stair to Craggs, March 15,	232
27. Stair to Craggs, March 18,	232
28. Craggs to Stair, March 9/20,	234

CONTENTS

PAPERS RELATING TO EVENTS ABROAD—*continued*   PAGE

29. Report from British Envoy at Lisbon, March 7, 1719 . 236
30. Stair to Craggs, March 22, . 236
31. Craggs to Stair, March 16/27, . 237
32. Stair to Craggs, April 2, . 238
33. Alberoni to James, April 4, . 240
34. The King of Spain to James, April 9, . 241
35. The Queen of Spain to James, April 9, . 242
36. Report as to the Dispersion of the Spanish Fleet, April 9, ... 243
37. Report as to the Dispersion of the Spanish Fleet, April 10, ... 245
38. Report as to the Dispersion of the Spanish Fleet, April 13, ... 246
39. Alberoni to James, April 16, . . . 246
40. The King of Spain to James, April 25, . . 248
41. The Queen of Spain to James, April 25, . 249
42. Alberoni to James, April 26, . . . 250
43. Sir Timon Connock to James, April 28, . 252
44. Alberoni to James, June 7, . . 253
45. The King of Spain to James, June 8, . . 254
46. The Queen of Spain to James, June 8, . 255
47. Alberoni to James, June 28, . . 255
48. Alberoni to James, Aug. 12, . . 257
49. The King of Spain to James, Aug. 15, . 257
50. The Queen of Spain to James, Aug. 16, . 258
51. Alberoni to James, Aug. 20, . . 258
52. James to the King of Spain, Sept. 5, . 259
53. James to Ormonde, Sept. 5, . . 259
54. Princess Clementina to Ormonde, Sept. 11, 260
55. James to Alberoni, Sept. 14, . . . 261
56. James to the King of Spain, Sept. 14, . . 263
57. Princess Clementina to the Queen of Spain, Sept. 14, . 263
58. James to Ormonde, Sept. 14, . . . 264
59. James to Ormonde, Oct. 3, . . . 265
60. James to Ormonde, Oct. 14, . . . 267

II. PAPERS RELATING TO EVENTS IN SCOTLAND:—

	PAGE
61. The Marquis of Tullibardine to Mar, April 29, 1719,	269
62. Tullibardine to Mar, June 16 (*Account of the Battle of Glenshiel*),	269
63. The Earl of Seaforth to James, Aug. 10,	273
64. General Lord Carpenter to Charles Delafaye, Secretary to the Lords Justices, June 27,	274
65. Lord Justice-Clerk Cockburn to Delafaye, June 27,	275
66. Major-General Wightman to Delafaye, June 30,	276
67. Carpenter to Delafaye, July 4,	277
68. Carpenter to Delafaye, July 7,	278
69. Carpenter to Delafaye, July 21,	279
70. Carpenter to Delafaye, July 28,	280
71. Wightman to Delafaye, Aug. 4,	280
72. Carpenter to Delafaye, Aug. 18,	281
73. Carpenter to Glengarry, July 29,	282
74. Wightman to Delafaye, Sept. 1,	282
75. Return of the Troops in Scotland for July 1719,	284
76. Wightman to Delafaye, Sept. 17,	285
77. Carpenter to Delafaye, Sept. 12,	286
78. Glengarry to Carpenter, Aug. 24,	287
79. Enclosure from the Earl of Findlater to Carpenter, Aug. 24,	288
80. Gordon of Glenbucket to Carpenter, Aug. 29,	288
81. Carpenter to Delafaye, Sept. 19,	290
82. Wightman to Delafaye, Sept. 29,	290
83. Account of Expenditure on the Spanish Prisoners,	292
84. Return of the Troops in Scotland for September 1719,	294
85. Brigadier Preston to Delafaye, Oct. 22,	295
86. Bishop Gadderar to Bishop Campbell, Nov. 7,	296

INDEX, ... 299

ILLUSTRATIONS

I. PORTRAIT of the second DUKE OF ORMONDE, from a mezzotint after Kneller, by J. Smith, . *Frontispiece*

II. MAP illustrating the landing of the Expedition and the Battle of Glenshiel, ... *at p.* xliv

III. PLAN of the BATTLE OF GLENSHIEL, by Lieut. John Henry Bastide, ... *at* p. lii

IV. PORTRAIT of George Keith, tenth EARL MARISCHAL, from the original by Pierre Parrocel, in the possession of the Earl of Kintore at Keith Hall, *at* p. 1

V. PORTRAIT of Field Marshal JAMES KEITH, from the original by Francesco Trevisani, at Keith Hall, *at* p. 193

INTRODUCTION

JAMES BUTLER, second Duke of Ormonde, is one of the most notable figures in the history of the reigns of William III. and of Queen Anne. Born in Dublin Castle in 1665, he succeeded his grandfather, the famous first Duke, in 1688. At the Revolution he attached himself to the cause of the Prince of Orange, acted as High Constable at the coronation of William and Mary, and was rewarded for his services with the Garter, and a colonelcy in the Life Guards. He was present at the Boyne, took an active part in the Irish campaign of 1690, and served at Steinkirk and at Landen. Under Queen Anne he commanded the troops in the Vigo expedition of 1702, was twice Lord Lieutenant of Ireland, and in 1712 succeeded Marlborough in the post of Captain General of the army, and in the conduct of the campaign in Flanders, which ended so ignominiously, thanks to Bolingbroke's double-dealing.

The close of Anne's reign found Ormonde one of the leaders of the Tory party, many of whose members were then casting their eyes towards the king over the water. Ormonde was deeply implicated in the plots which were formed for bringing over James Stuart on his sister's death. With his great name and immense personal popularity, Ormonde might have played the part of Monk, and been the leader of a counter-revolution. But the opportunity was too great for him. 'Pour exécuter un pareil projet, il falloit un autre génie:' writes the Duke of Berwick, 'de si grands desseins ont besoin d'un Héros, et c'est ce que le Duc d'Ormond n'étoit pas.'[1]

---

[1] *Mémoires du Maréchal de Berwick* (ed. 1778), vol. ii. p. 144. Berwick gives a most interesting account of the Jacobite plots at the time of Anne's

On the 21st of June 1715, Secretary Stanhope moved his impeachment. It seemed at first that he meant to stay and weather the storm, but on the 8th of August he followed the example which had been set by Bolingbroke and fled to France, where he openly entered James's service. On August 20th he was attainted, his estates declared forfeited, and his honours extinguished.

At the time of the rising of 1715 Ormonde endeavoured to land with a small force on the coast of Devonshire, to raise the Jacobites of the West of England, but finding that his confidential agent, Colonel Maclaine, had betrayed his plans to the Government, he returned to France without having disembarked.[1]

James returned from his ill-fated expedition to Scotland in February 1716. Immediately afterwards his insane quarrel with Bolingbroke deprived him of the only minister he ever had who could be called a great statesman.[2] Ormonde and Mar now remained his chief advisers, the latter, notwithstanding his disastrous mismanagement in Scotland, retaining the greater share of the Prince's confidence.

---

death, of which he was himself the mainspring. *Ibid.* pp. 126 *et seq.* See p. 3, note 1.

Field-Marshal Keith gives the following pithy sketch of Ormonde's character: 'He was a man of a very easy temper, and of an ordinary understanding, so diffident of himself that he often followed the advice of those who had a smaller share of sense than himself; he was as irresolute and timorous in affairs as he was brave in his person, and was apt to lose good opportunities by waiting to remove difficulties which naturally attend great designs, and of which a part must always be left to fortune in the execution; he was a man of entire honour, a good friend, and a strict observer of his word.'—*Memoir*, Spalding Club, 1843, p. 3. There is an excellent sketch of his life by Professor A. W. Ward in the *Dictionary of National Biography.*

[1] Berwick, vol. ii. p. 165.

[2] 'May my arm rot off if I ever use my sword or my pen in their service again!' said Bolingbroke.—Macknight's *Life of Bolingbroke* (London, 1863), p. 494. 'I believe,' wrote Lord Stair to Horace Walpole, 'all poor Harry's fault was that he could not play his part with a grave enough face; he could not help laughing now and then at such kings and queens.'—*Ibid.* p. 488. For an account of his dismissal see his Letter to Sir William Windham, *Works* (ed. 1754), vol. i. p. 74, and Berwick, vol. ii. p. 174. Berwick speaks very strongly of James's folly in quarrelling with his most valuable servant.

The death of Louis XIV., which took place on September 1st, 1715, was a serious misfortune to the Jacobites. After the suppression of the rising of 1715, the Regent Orleans showed a desire to form friendly relations with the British Government. He was actuated not only by motives of public policy, but by a regard to his personal interests. In the event of the death of the young king he was the next heir to the throne, the claim of Philip V. of Spain to the Crown of France having been formally renounced. It was well understood, however, that Philip would not hold himself bound by this renunciation, and Orleans saw how strong an ally Britain would be in the event of a disputed succession. Friendship with King George's government meant, of course, the discontinuance of all countenance to the Stuart cause. James was compelled to leave Bar-le-Duc in Lorraine, where he had resided since the Peace of Utrecht.[1] He went first to Avignon, then he crossed the Alps, and settled down in the Papal dominions, where he spent the rest of his life, first at Urbino and afterwards at Rome. When he went to Italy his pension of 50,000 crowns was stopped by the Regent.

France could no longer be looked to either as a base of operations or as a source of supply.

It was to Sweden that the Jacobites next turned for support. Charles XII. hated King George, and had a very tangible grievance against him. At the Peace of Westphalia the Bishoprics of Bremen and Verden had been secularised and ceded to Sweden. In 1712 they were, along with Sleswick and Holstein, wrested from Sweden by Frederick IV. of Denmark. They had long been coveted by the Electors of Hanover, and in July 1715 Frederick ceded them to George, the price paid being £150,000 and the support of a British fleet against Sweden. After this Charles was naturally very willing to push the

---

[1] An interesting article on James's residence at Bar-le-Duc, by Mr. H. W. Wolff, appeared in *Blackwood's Magazine* for August 1894.

Elector from his British throne, and lent a ready ear to the proposals of the Jacobites. At the time of the rebellion of 1715 it had been proposed that a Swedish force should be landed in Scotland, and Berwick had been in communication with Baron Spaar, the Swedish Minister at Paris, on the subject.[1] Charles was then closely besieged in Stralsund, and had something else to think about. An invasion of Great Britain in the Stuart interest remained, however, a fixed object with him, and had the support of his chief Minister, Baron Gortz.

In the winter of 1716-17 Gortz was at the Hague as Swedish Envoy. From Holland he corresponded with Count Gyllenborg, the Swedish Minister in London, with Spaar at Paris, with James, and with Ormonde. His schemes included a general Jacobite rising in England, and the invasion of Scotland by 12,000 Swedish troops, headed by Charles in person. The enterprise had the support of Spain; Cardinal Alberoni sent a subsidy of 1,000,000 French livres. Had it been carried out the House of Hanover would certainly have been in far greater danger than it ever was in 1715.

It came to nothing. Some of Gyllenborg's letters were intercepted and deciphered by the British Government, and on January 29th, 1717, Stanhope laid the matter before the Council, and proposed the extreme measure of seizing the person and papers of the Swedish Minister, on the ground that he had violated the law of nations by conspiring against the Sovereign to whom he was accredited. On the same night Gyllenborg's house was surrounded by a detachment of the Guards, and General Wade arrested his person and secured his papers. So startling a step required the fullest justification; it was amply furnished when Gyllenborg's correspondence was laid before Parliament. Gortz was at Calais on his way to England when he heard of Gyllenborg's arrest; he at once returned to Holland, and a few days afterwards was taken into

---

[1] Berwick, vol. ii. p. 147.

custody at Arnheim at the instance of the British Cabinet. The King of Sweden neither owned nor disowned the action of his Ministers. After some months of negotiation they were both released, but all hope of Swedish help to the Jacobites was over for the time.[1]

In the autumn of 1717 Ormonde went on a mission to the north, accompanied by Sir Henry Stirling, a nephew of Dr. Erskine, the Czar's physician, and Messrs. Daniel O'Brien, Jerningham, and Wogan. The object of the mission was twofold, to arrange a marriage between James and one of the daughters or nieces of the Czar Peter, and to endeavour to adjust the differences between Peter and Charles XII. with the view of obtaining their help against George I. It failed in both objects. Ormonde was not received at either the Swedish or the Russian Courts. He spent the winter and spring months at Mittau in Courland, and returned to Paris in June 1718, bitterly chagrined at the futile issue of his long and toilsome journey.[2] Mar wrote to him from Urbino on the 26th of May announcing that a bride had been found for James in the person of Princess Maria Clementina Sobieski, third daughter of Prince James Sobieski, and granddaughter of John Sobieski, King of Poland.[3]

---

[1] Lord Mahon's *History of England from the Peace of Utrecht* (ed. 1858), vol. i. pp. 256-261; Tindal's *Continuation of Rapin's History* (ed. 1763), vol. vii. pp. 48-56. Gyllenborg's correspondence was published by authority at the time (London, folio, 1717). A selection is printed in the *Parliamentary History*, vol. vii. pp. 396-421, and in Tindal, vol. vii. pp. 55 *et seq.*, note. His letters to the Swedish Chancery are preserved in the Royal Archives at Stockholm; they were examined by Mr. W. Bliss in 1882 for the Record Office. See his MS. Report to the Master of the Rolls, Record Office, Bliss's Transcripts, Stockholm, Portfolio 108.

[2] Mar to Sir Hugh Paterson, Urbino, June 23, 1718.—Intercepted Jacobite Correspondence, Hanover Papers, Brit. Mus., Stowe MSS. 232, f. 117.

[3] *Ibid.* ff. 149-50. Mar describes the Princess as 'Jolie, pas fort grande, mais d'une age a croître encore; elle a beaucoup d'esprit, de bonne humeur et de discretion.' The volume of the Stowe MSS. cited contains interesting details as to Ormonde's journey. For an account of the numerous attempts to find a suitable match for James see the *Letters of Bishop Atterbury*, edited from the Stuart Papers by Mr. J. H. Glover (London, 1847), p. 15.

In the summer of 1718 the affairs of the Jacobites were in a bad way. Their exchequer was very low, and one of its main sources of supply was cut off by the death, on May 7th, of James II.'s widow, Mary of Modena, whose French pension died with her. No foreign power seemed disposed to help them. The British Government, which was most capably represented at the Paris Embassy by Lord Stair,[1] was bringing strong pressure to bear on the Regent to drive them out of France. Orders were actually issued for their expulsion,[2] Ormonde himself was threatened with arrest;[3] according to Stair, he had to feign sickness in order to be allowed to remain in France.[4] He seems to have paid a flying visit to Italy in the course of the autumn,[5] but was back in the neighbourhood of Paris before the end of October. Then came the offer of help from Spain, which opened a new chapter in the Stuart story, and was the beginning of the enterprise which is the subject of this volume.

To understand the motives which led to this offer it is necessary to refer to the relations existing between England and Spain at the time.[6] Cardinal Giulio Alberoni, Philip of Anjou's famous minister, was then at the zenith of his extraordinary career. From the humblest circumstances—he was the son of an Italian gardener, and had begun life as a village curate—he had in a few years risen to be a prince of the Church, and one of the most powerful ministers in Europe. Since 1715 he had been absolute master of Spain, and had raised her to some semblance of her ancient greatness. At first he was disposed to be friendly to England, but the relations of the

---

[1] John Dalrymple, second Earl of Stair, grandson of Lord President Stair, was British Ambassador at Paris from 1715 to 1720.
[2] Stair to Robethon, Private Secretary to George I., May 4 and 31, 1718.—Hanover Papers, Stowe MSS., 231, ff. 79, 92.
[3] Stair to Robethon, Aug. 4, 1718.—*Ibid.* f. 114.
[4] Stair to Robethon, Aug. 22, 1718.—*Ibid.* f. 126.
[5] Stair to Robethon, Oct. 28, 1718.—*Ibid.* f. 196.
[6] For a full account of the foreign affairs of the period see Mahon, vol. i., *passim*.

two countries had become more and more hostile, and in the summer of 1718 they had reached a critical condition. In 1717 war broke out between Spain and the Emperor Charles VI. The first scene of operations was Sardinia, which was occupied by a Spanish force. Early in 1718 a great armament was fitted out at Barcelona. Its obvious destination was either Italy or Sicily. England was bound by the Treaty of Utrecht to guarantee the neutrality of Italy, and by that of Westminster, concluded with the Emperor in May 1716, to maintain the integrity of the imperial dominions, of which Naples formed a part. Diplomatic remonstrance was fruitless, and things rapidly drifted towards hostilities. Before Parliament rose in March, the House of Commons, in answer to a royal message, undertook to make good any necessary excess of expenditure on the sea service for the year. On the 4th of June Sir George Byng sailed from Spithead with twenty ships of the line.

Byng's orders were precise. On reaching the Mediterranean he was to intimate his arrival to the King of Spain, and to state that he was instructed to use all means to promote peace. If, however, the Spaniards persisted in attacking imperial territory in Italy, or occupying Sicily, ' in such case,' the orders ran, ' you are, with all your power, to hinder and obstruct the same.' [1]

On the 30th of June, N.S., Byng reached Cape St. Vincent, and sent his secretary with a letter to Colonel Stanhope, the British envoy at Madrid, detailing his orders. Stanhope showed the letter to Alberoni, who, on reading it, absolutely refused to recall the Spanish troops, or consent to a cessation of arms. Stanhope used his powers of persuasion in vain. Alberoni was obdurate; all he would consent to do was to lay Byng's letter before the king. Nine days later he returned it with a note appended: ' His Majesty has done me the honour to tell me that the Chevalier Byng may execute the

---

[1] The text of these orders is printed in Tindal, vol. vii. pp. 208-211.

orders which he has from the king his master. Escurial, 15th July 1718.'

Byng proceeded to do so. On the 23d of July he reached Port Mahon. On the 1st of August he anchored in the Bay of Naples. Here he learned that a Spanish army of 30,000 men, under the Marquis de Lede, had landed on the 2d of July in Sicily, taken Palermo and Messina, and overrun a great part of the island. Byng made one more effort to preserve peace. He sent Captain Saunders, his senior captain, with a letter to the Spanish commander, urging him to consent to a cessation of arms for two months, that matters might be adjusted, otherwise, he said, 'he should hope to merit his Excellency's esteem by the execution of the other part of his orders.' De Lede answered that he had no powers to treat, and could not agree to any armistice. Byng at once put to sea. On the 11th of August he engaged the Spanish fleet, under Don Antonio de Castaneta, off Cape Passaro, and utterly defeated it. Most of the Spanish ships were captured or burnt, and the Admiral was made a prisoner.[1]

Alberoni was furious. Monteleone, the Spanish Ambassador in London, was at once ordered to present his letters of recall. British ships were seized in Spanish ports; British Consuls were ordered to leave Spanish territory; and it was determined to strike the British Government in what was believed to be its weakest point by an invasion on behalf of the exiled Stuarts.[2]

---

[1] It was after this action that Captain Walton, who had been detached in pursuit of a number of Spanish ships which had escaped under Rear-Admiral Mari, wrote his famous despatch:—'SIR,—We have taken and destroyed all the Spanish ships and vessels which were upon the coast, the number as per margin. —I am, etc., G. WALTON.' He had taken six ships and burnt six others. See the account of the battle in Tindal, vol. vii. pp. 216 *et seq*.

[2] According to St. Philippe the project was originally suggested by the Pope, Clement XI.—*Mémoires* (French edition, Amsterdam, 1756), vol. iii. p. 354. St. Philippe's information about the whole affair is, however, very inaccurate.

That some such enterprise would be undertaken seems to have been generally regarded as likely after the rupture between England and Spain. Ormonde certainly anticipated it (Letters to James and to Mar, Oct. 3, 1718), and Cardinal Aquaviva, writing to James on October 1, suggested that it might be well to send

For such an enterprise Ormonde, with his military reputation and his great personal popularity in England, was the obvious leader. He was accordingly invited to Madrid. The invitation, which was sent through Cellamare, the Spanish Ambassador at Paris, reached him there in the beginning of November.

It is at this point that our Letters begin. On November 4, 1718, Ormonde wrote from Paris to James announcing his immediate departure for Spain,[1] and expressing his indignation at the news, which he had just received, that Princess Clementina, when passing through the Imperial territories on her way to join her betrothed husband, had been arrested at Innspruck; 'a favour of the Emperor to the English Government,' as Lord Mahon justly says, 'unworthy of them to solicit and base in him to grant.'[2] On the evening of the following day he set out for the Spanish frontier.[3] He was accompanied by his aide-de-camp, George Bagenal, and by General Crafton, an Irish officer in the Spanish service, and was followed at a short interval by Colonel Owen with a number of the servants who had been in Ormonde's employment in Paris.[4] According to Stair, orders for his arrest had been given at Bayonne and at Roussillon;[5] Dubois afterwards wrote to Lord Stanhope that he crossed the Pyrenees *déguisé en valet*.[6] Alberoni, on the

---

a representative to the King of Spain to arrange matters in view of possible contingencies.—Stuart Papers.

Alberoni seems to have greatly overestimated the amount of disaffection, considerable as it was, which existed in England.

[1] Letter I.
[2] This 'hellish contrivance,' as one of Mar's correspondents calls it, excited general indignation on the Continent. Even at Vienna people were shocked. The Pope remonstrated vigorously with the Emperor—wrote him a 'thundering letter,' says Mar.—Mar to Dillon, Dec. 6, 1718. Stuart Papers.
[3] Dillon to Mar, Nov. 15, 1718.—Stuart Papers.
[4] Stair to Robethon, Dec. 29, 1718.—Hanover Papers, Stowe MSS., 231, 253.
[5] Stair to Robethon, Nov. 9, 1718.—*Ibid.* f. 225.
[6] Dubois to Stanhope, March 15, 1719.—Hardwicke Papers, cited by Lord Mahon, vol. i. p. 333, note.

other hand, anxious to sow discord between England and the Regent, caused it to be stated that he had left France openly with the connivance of the Government.[1] The secret of the invitation was well kept; not even Crafton knew it. It was given out that Ormonde's object was to seek in Spain the asylum denied him in France. Alberoni denied all connection with the journey. On December 13th the Marquis de Beretti Landi, Spanish Ambassador in Holland, acting on instructions, expressly stated to the States-General that the reports of Ormonde's going to the Spanish Court were groundless, and that the King of Spain would never concern himself with the affairs of the Pretender.[2] A statement to the same effect had been made personally by Cellamare to Stair.[3]

On the 1st of December Ormonde had arrived at Alcala, whence he wrote informing Alberoni of his arrival. Within the next two days he reached Madrid, and received a warm welcome from the Cardinal.

The interviews which took place between Ormonde and Alberoni at Madrid, and the plans which were then concerted, are detailed in a long letter sent to James at Rome on the 17th of December.[4] At their first meeting Alberoni stated that he had sent Sir Patrick Lawless, an Irish officer in the service of Spain, to Sweden to engage Charles XII. to enter into an alliance with Spain for the purpose of dethroning George I. When they next met the Cardinal asked what force Ormonde thought sufficient to attempt a restoration

---

[1] Stair to Craggs, Jan. 3, 1719.—State Papers, Foreign, France, 353.

[2] *Political State*, vol. xvi. p. 532. Their High Mightinesses seem to have taken the statement for what it was worth, as on the following day we find them remitting to their deputies for Foreign Affairs to examine and report as to its accuracy.

[3] 'J'en ay parlé dimanche dernier au Prince de Cellamare à la toilette de Madame la Duchesse de Berri, il m'a dit qu'il n'etoit pas vray que la cour avoit invité le duc d'Ormonde de passer en Espagne, mais qu'on recevroit la comme on le pourroit recevoir ailleurs, il me dit qu'il pouvoit me dire cela avec certitude.' —Stair to Craggs, Nov. 29, 1718, State Papers, Foreign, France, 352.

[4] Letter XIII.

of the Stuarts. Ormonde suggested 7000 or 8000 men, with 15,000 muskets to arm the English Jacobites, and a proportionate supply of ammunition. Alberoni answered that in view of the great number of Spanish troops in Sicily, and the prospect of a war with France, it was impossible to spare a man, but that the arms and ammunition should be forthcoming, and that funds should be supplied to Sweden for the invasion of Britain. At the same time he produced a memorial which had been sent by the King of Sweden, expressing his willingness to enter into an alliance with Spain against King George. At a third meeting the Cardinal announced that he had decided to furnish 5000 men, 4000 foot and 1000 troopers, with 300 horses, two months' pay for the men, ten field guns, 1000 barrels of powder and 15,000 muskets, together with suitable transport. With these Ormonde was to land in the west of England, the stronghold of Jacobitism, where it was expected that there would be no difficulty in raising a great army in support of the Stuart cause, and attempt an attack on London.[1]

Ormonde then pointed out the importance of making a diversion in Scotland to raise the Highland clans. Alberoni asked if he could suggest a suitable leader for such an expedition, and he mentioned the name of the young Earl Marischal, who had been out in the '15, and was now at Paris. It was decided that he should be sent for.

It was also decided that James should be invited to come to Spain, to accompany the expedition if possible, or, at all events, to follow it. Alberoni expressed the opinion that in view of the number of Imperial troops in Italy, and the animus which the Emperor had shown in the arrest of Princess Clementina, James's person was no longer safe in Rome.

---

[1] According to Dubois's information it was expected that 26,000 men could be raised.—Dubois to Craggs, March 8, 1719, Stowe MSS., 247, f. 38. Appendix, No. 21, p. 225.

Bagenal was to follow Lawless to Sweden, to represent to Charles the importance of invading England before the spring.

The expedition was to be fitted out at Cadiz, and it was arranged that while it was preparing Ormonde should go to Valladolid, and remain there as privately as possible. Every effort was of course used to keep the destination of the fleet a secret. Ormonde remained for nearly two months at Valladolid, busying himself in sending messages to the adherents of the Stuarts in England to warn them of what was afoot. On December 22d he wrote again to James, urging him to come to Spain with all possible secrecy and despatch.

In the meantime grave events had been happening in Paris. There was in France a strong party, or rather congeries of parties, who hated the Regent Orleans and his minister Dubois, and who bitterly resented the great changes of policy which had followed the death of Louis XIV. The leader of the malcontents was nominally the Duc du Maine, son of Louis XIV. by Madame de Montespan, but really the Duchesse du Maine, the granddaughter of the great Condé. In the winter of 1718 a plot was organised to seize the person of the Regent in one of his parties of pleasure near Paris. The States-General were to be convoked, and the King of Spain as next in blood proclaimed the rightful Regent, with the Duc du Maine as his deputy. The conspiracy was fomented by Alberoni through the ambassador Cellamare. A hint from London put the Regent on his guard. In the beginning of December Cellamare sent an account of his proceedings to Alberoni by the hands of a young Spanish abbé, Don Vincente Portocarrero. The messenger was stopped at Poitiers, and his papers seized and forwarded to Dubois, who laid them before the Regent. Cellamare was arrested and conducted to the frontier. The Duc and Duchesse du Maine, Cardinal Polignac, and the other leaders of the conspiracy were exiled or imprisoned. The plot was effectually crushed. The Duc de St. Aignan, French Ambassador at

Madrid, only saved himself from Alberoni's clutches by a hasty flight.[1]

At a meeting of the Council of Regency on the 3rd of January 1719, war with Spain was resolved on,[2] and was declared on the 9th. England had declared war on the 17th of December, o.s.

On the 25th of January, a piece of very bad news reached Ormonde at Valladolid.[3] On the 11th of December Charles XII. had been shot through the head in the trenches before Frederickshall in Norway. His death meant an entire change in the policy of Sweden. His sister Ulrica was proclaimed his successor; his ministers were dismissed; all his projects, including that of invading Britain, were abandoned. Gortz, who had been the chief instigator of this enterprise, and who was cordially hated by the people, was brought to trial before a specially constituted court, found guilty of high misdemeanours in administration, and beheaded at Stockholm on March 3d, 1719.[4] So again the prospect of help from Sweden vanished.

Ormonde's letter to James, of December 17th, reached Rome on January 26th. It was the first intimation which the people there had received of the project which was afoot. In Ormonde's former letters he had said nothing of Alberoni's invitation; Mar, writing to General Arthur Dillon[5] on December 27, was still ignorant whether he had gone to Spain by invitation or not. The news was received with joy by the little Stuart

---

[1] Mahon, vol. i. pp. 320-324. There is a detailed account of the plot in the *Political State*, vol. xvi. pp. 506-527. St. Simon tells very dramatically the story of its discovery.—*Memoirs*, St. John's English edition, vol. iii. chap. 20.

[2] Stair to Craggs, Jan. 3, 1719.—State Papers, Foreign, France, 353.

[3] Letter XXXII.

[4] It appeared from Gortz's papers that Charles had definitely undertaken to Alberoni to invade Great Britain after he had reduced Frederickshall.—*Political State*, vol. xvii. p. 41.

[5] As to Dillon, see p. 31, note 3.

Court,[1] and James decided to proceed to Spain at once, all the more readily as he had reason to believe that he was no longer safe in Italy.[2] It was necessary that he should go by sea, as a land journey through France was out of the question. It was of the utmost importance that Alberoni's project should, if possible, be kept secret to the last moment, and Byng was cruising in the Mediterranean. Every precaution was accordingly taken to conceal James's departure. It was

---

[1] Mar's intimation of the news to Dillon is a curious specimen of the mystic language with which the Jacobite correspondence of the period abounds : 'Now for something to divert you. You must know that your old love Phillis had one sent to her t'other day from her friend Sara w^t proposalls from her admirer, that old doting fellow 3^k for her liveing w^t him, and that he is impatient for her company. The proposalls he makes her are very advantageous, wch are needless to repeat, and behold what the charms of an old rich lover are, for she has not had vertue enough to resist the temptation, and is actually to set out to him in a very few dayes. She takes but a chambermaid and the person who brought her the message along w^t her, and they go by her Unckle Stanlyes. Her two women, Philips and Frank, go by her Cousin Griffin's, who is to help them on their way ; and when once she is w^t her lover, she is to give orders to the rest of her family as she thinks fittest, and they are to continue at her house with her landlord Prichard until she do, not knowing where she is gone, she haveing consulted nobody upon it but one or two of us who chanced to be in her good graces at this time. Y^r absence may have cured y^r love, but if it has not, let me advise you not to break y^r heart, for the old fellow cannot live long, and you may have the richer love of her afterwards. She is in some concern that she will not be able to write to her friend David soon, but she will as soon as it is in her power. She is now looking for a chair in such a way that it may not alarme her admirers, and has the promise of one wch if it hold and the weather be favourable she will likely set out this week, but strong as her love is she cannot think of traveling in cold. This is not worth y^r answering, tho' I wou'd be glad to know the temper you'll be in upon it.

'I am heartily sory for the sad accident of honest Mother Kemp's breaking up house (*i.e.* the death of the King of Sweden), and it could never have hapned in a worse time, for she could have got you something to consol you for loosing y^r love, but I hope some of her Nimphs will go on w^t her trade in the same way, but alace it may take some time e'er that be, and the want will be for the present, wch I fear may make that rake Amorslie go to some other house in the mean time, and tempt you and others of old Kemps customers to follow his example, so that the poor house will never recover its trade again. But enough of this stuff.'—Mar to Dillon, Jan. 30, 1719, Stuart Papers.

[2] James had been at Bologna in the beginning of the winter, and had come into Rome professedly on account of his health, but really for safety, on account of the nearness of large bodies of Imperial troops.—James to Ormonde, Nov. 9, 1718, Stuart Papers.

skilfully arranged. On the 8th of February James apparently set out from Rome to the northward, accompanied by the Dukes of Mar[1] and Perth. The wildest rumours were circulated in the city as to the object of his journey; he was gone to be mediator in the peace between the Emperor and the King of Spain; he was to be Regent of Sweden; King George was dead, and he had been sent for by the English Ministry.[2] In reality the person who accompanied Mar and Perth was a member of the household named Paterson. The party pursued their journey northwards on their way to Genoa. On entering Imperial territory, they were arrested at Voghera and conveyed to the Castle of Milan. Davenant, the British resident at Genoa, wrote to Stair at Paris with the good news that the Pretender was taken, which Stair exultingly sent on to London.[3] The prisoners were civilly treated, and after a short confinement were set at liberty and returned to Rome.[4]

Early in the morning of the same day on which the party left Rome, the real James had quietly set out for Nettuno, a little coast village some thirty miles south from Rome. There he went on board a small French vessel, carrying Genoese colours, which had been provided by Admiral George Cammock, an Englishman in the naval service of Spain, who had been intrusted by Alberoni with this important service. He got safely out to sea. Not even the Pope knew of his destina-

---

[1] James made Mar a titular Duke in 1715.
[2] James Murray to Mar, Rome, Feb. 11, 1719.—Stuart Papers.
[3] Stair to Craggs, March 4, 1719.—State Papers, Foreign, France, 353.
[4] The journey, arrest, and imprisonment are fully described by Mar in a long and interesting letter to Lord Panmure, in the Stuart Papers, printed in Appendix, No. II, p. 206. The arrest seems to have caused some consternation among the Jacobites, as Mar was known to carry important papers and ciphers.—James Murray to Sir Hugh Paterson, March 5, 1719, Intercepted Jacobite Correspondence, Hanover Papers, Stowe MSS., 232, f. 194. These, however, he managed to destroy. Among the intercepted Jacobite letters is one from a certain Captain Geddes, a Scots officer in the Imperial Navy, to a friend in London, dated Vienna, March 10, 1719, in which he says that the Emperor entirely repudiated the arrest, threw the whole responsibility of it on the local officers, and ordered the prisoners to be released at once. He was very angry indeed, says Geddes: 'Jamais on ne l'a veu en telle rage.'

tion, a lack of confidence at which His Holiness seems to have been much displeased.[1]

In the meantime the equipment of the fleet was being rapidly pushed on at Cadiz, where it was given out that it was intended for Sicily. Ormonde was still at Valladolid. His original intention was to go to some place in the neighbourhood of Cadiz, and wait there till the expedition was ready;[2] but in compliance with Alberoni's wishes, it was arranged that he should go to Corunna, and there be picked up by the fleet as it passed. The news of the death of the King of Sweden seems to have caused Alberoni to hesitate for a day or two as to the prudence of going on with the enterprise,[3] but the hesitation did not last long. On the 4th of February he wrote to Ormonde directing him to set out for Corunna. Ormonde received the letter on the 7th, and started on the 10th.[4]

After Ormonde's meeting with Alberoni at Madrid, he had written to the Earl Marischal asking him to come to Spain, but saying nothing of the intended enterprise.[5] The invitation found the Earl in Paris towards the end of December, on the point of leaving for Avignon, where he was to have spent the winter.[6] On December 30th he started for Spain,[7] accompanied by his younger brother, James Keith, afterwards the famous Field Marshal. They travelled to Marseilles, and thence by sea to Palamos in Catalonia. Here they told the Commandant that they were English officers going to Madrid to seek employment in the army. Coming from an enemy's country, and giving so lame an account of themselves, they were sent on under arrest to Gerona, where they were recognised and vouched

---

[1] Murray to James, March 6, 1719.—Stuart Papers. James's farewell letter to the Pope is printed in Appendix, No. 12, p. 216.
[2] Letter XXIII.   [3] Letters XL, XLI, XLII.   [4] Letter XLIX.   [5] Letter VII.
[6] Mar to the Earl Marischal, Dec. 6, 1718.—Stuart Papers.   Appendix, No. 10, p. 204.
[7] Letter XXIX. The journey is narrated in James Keith's *Memoirs*. He gives an amusing account of the profound respect with which the brothers were received by Prince Pio of Savoy at Barcelona, under the impression that one of them must be James himself, travelling incognito.

for by the Duke of Liria, Berwick's son, who was stationed there in command of his regiment.

The Duke knew nothing of the expedition against England, and the Keiths concluded that they had been sent for merely to enter the King of Spain's service. They accordingly proceeded leisurely towards Madrid, which they reached about a fortnight later. On their arrival they reported themselves to Alberoni, who explained the nature of the service for which they were wanted. The Earl Marischal at once set out for Valladolid, to receive Ormonde's instructions. He found that Ormonde had left for Corunna, followed him, and on the evening of the 12th of February overtook him at Astorga.[1] On the following day he left to return to Madrid, and the Duke pursued his journey towards Corunna. Marischal reached Madrid after five days' absence, and Alberoni agreed to give him two frigates and two thousand muskets, with a supply of money and ammunition, also a small body of Spanish regular troops to form a nucleus for the army of Highlanders who were expected to flock to James's standard. With these the Earl sailed for Scotland from Passage, the port of San Sebastian, on the 8th[2] of March. He carried with him letters from Ormonde to the Duke of Gordon, Glengarry, Maclean of Brolas, and Donald Macdonald of Benbecula, Clanranald's cousin.[3] We shall see later how the expedition fared.[4]

Ormonde reached Sada, close to Corunna, on the 24th of February, and reported his arrival to the Marquis de Risbourg, Viceroy of Galicia. There he waited anxiously for news of the

---

[1] Letter L.

[2] The evidence as to the date of the Earl Marischal's sailing is contradictory. The date in the text is that given to Lord Carpenter by a Spanish lieutenant taken prisoner at Eilean Donan.—*London Gazette*, June 2, 1719; *Hist. Reg.*, vol. iv. p. 281. Apparently, after sailing, the ships had to put into Santander on account of the weather.—Letters LXXXVIII, LXXXIX, XCI.

[3] Letters LII, LXI, LXII, LXIII.

[4] P. xli *et seq*. According to Stair, the money for the expedition to Scotland was found by the Count of Castelblanco, Lord Melfort's son-in-law.—Stair to Craggs, May 7, 1719, State Papers, Foreign, France, 353.

Cadiz fleet. After many delays the fleet was at last ready for sea. It sailed from Cadiz on the 7th of March, under the command of Don Balthasar de Guevarra.[1]

The force consisted of five ships of war, the Admiral's, carrying sixty-four brass guns, two of fifty guns, one of twenty, and a smaller vessel, with twenty-two transports, besides two ships bound for the West Indies, in all twenty-nine sail.[2] There were 5000 troops on board, with arms for 30,000 more.[3] Ormonde, who was to come on board at Corunna, was to command the troops as Captain-General of the King of Spain. On landing in England he was to publish a declaration in the name of His Catholic Majesty announcing his resolution to use all his power for the restoration of James, and promising that in the event of ill success all who had joined the enterprise should find a secure retreat in his dominions, and that all land or sea officers should be employed in his service with the same rank which they had held in Great Britain.[4]

James landed at Rosas in Catalonia on the 9th of March,

---

[1] Letter LV.

[2] An Irish skipper, who reached Cork on March 28th, gives us a vivid glimpse of the embarkation. 'The Transports were extreamly crowded,' he says, 'abundance of men being forced to lie on the Deck; and the cut straw for the Horses being packed up in Bags they were obliged to lash these Bags a long side the Ships exposed to the Weather. A great many of the men shipped for Soldiers had been pressed in the Streets of Cadiz and immediately hurried on board. The Horses were ill stowed, and had been shipped 20 days before they left Cadiz; and no more than 21 Days Provisions were put on board with these Forces.'—*Political State*, vol. xvii. p. 399. Captain Cavendish, of H.M.S. *Dover*, wrote from Gibraltar that the Spaniards had pressed at least 1500 men to complete their regiments, and were in such want of seamen that they pressed all the boatmen they could find to man their two largest ships of war.—*Ibid.* p. 400. 'Tout le monde est d'accord que leur Infanterie est quelque chose de très pitoyable,' writes Stair to Craggs, March 18, 1719.—State Papers, Foreign, France, 353. Appendix, No. 27, p. 232.

[3] The evidence as to the strength of the expedition is somewhat conflicting. The figures in the text are given by Richard Spartman, an English ship's mate, who was impressed at Cadiz, and compelled to navigate one of the Spanish transports. After the dispersal of the fleet he brought his ship into the Tagus.—*Political State*, vol. xvii. p. 409.

[4] Tindal, vol. vii. p. 256.

after an adventurous and most unpleasant voyage. He had
been caught in storms and chased by British cruisers. He had
suffered from sea-sickness and from fever. More than once he
had been compelled to go ashore and lie in hiding. At the
Iles d'Or, off Hyères, he had had to share the accommodation
of a miserable inn with an unsavoury crowd, and, as it was
carnival time, the unlucky Prince, '*quoique incommodé de la
mer*,' was obliged to dance with the hostess.[1] Now, however,
his troubles were over for the time. He was delighted with
his reception in Spain. 'I am very much made of in this
country,' he writes to Dicconson from Saragossa.[2] At Madrid
he was received with royal honours, lodged in the Palace of
Buen Retiro, and furnished with an escort of the King of
Spain's life-guards.[3]

In the meantime Ormonde at Corunna was waiting eagerly
for tidings of the fleet. He knew that every hour was precious,
for by this time the secret of the expedition had been discovered.[4] The whole chance of success depended on taking the
British Government by surprise. It was mere madness to talk
of invading England with 5000 men if the Government had
time to make their preparations, and to take precautions
against a rising of the Jacobites at home. Alberoni had given
Ormonde to understand that the fleet would be ready by the
10th of February;[5] as we have seen, it did not leave Cadiz till
the 7th of March; it was not till the 16th that the news of its
departure reached Corunna.[6] A small vessel was sent to watch

---

[1] Alberoni to Ormonde, March 18, 1719.—Stuart Papers. Appendix, No. 17, p. 219.

[2] March 22, 1719.—*Ibid.* Appendix, No. 14, p. 217.

[3] *Political State*, vol. xvii. p. 5. On March 20, 1719, Alberoni wrote to Count Rocca:—'Il Re Giacomo sbarcò a Roses il giorno 9 del corrente, ed havrà preso ieri il viaggio per questa Corte, ove sarà ricevuto da queste Maestà con quelle dimostrazioni adattate all' infelice stato d'un povero Principe abban-donato e perseguitato da tutto il mondo. Infine, grazie a Dio, dopo havere uscito da mille pericoli, è in salvo; e certamente quanto li è successo nel viaggio fa vedere cheè un miracolo se sia giunto in Porto.'—*Lettres Intimes de J. M. Alberoni*, Paris, 1892, p. 627.

[4] Letter LXXII.   [5] Letter XLV.   [6] Letter CX.

for it off Cape Finisterre. The frigate in which Ormonde was to sail was ready for sea, and he was ready to go on board. As the days of March slipped past, and there was still no news of the fleet, his anxiety grew intense. At last he despaired of success. On the 22d of March he wrote to Alberoni, and to James, to say that he thought the enterprise, as originally planned, was now hopeless, and proposed that the project of invading England should be abandoned, and that the expedition should endeavour to effect a landing in Scotland, where they were sure to find plenty of recruits among the clans, and where they might hold out in the Highlands, and trust to the chapter of accidents.[1] Alberoni seems to have agreed to the idea of a change of plan, as a *pis aller*, but it was given up in obedience to James's wishes.[2]

King George's Government had ample warning of the danger. So early as January 16th Dubois had written to Secretary Craggs warning him that Alberoni was meditating some enterprise against Great Britain.[3] The French Government had abundant information as to events in Spain, all of which was communicated to Stair, by whom it was sent on to London. At first it was thought that the Cadiz fleet was meant for Ireland, but on March 4th Stair wrote informing Craggs of its true destination.[4] On the 8th, and again on the 11th, Dubois wrote giving details as to Alberoni's preparations, and offering the help of the Regent to the British Government.[5]

---

[1] Letters LXXXVI, LXXXVII.

[2] Alberoni to Ormonde, April 4, 1719, Stuart Papers, Appendix, No. 19, p. 222; Letters XCIV, XCV.

[3] Dubois to Craggs, Jan. 16, 1719.—State Papers, Foreign, France, 358, Appendix, No. 20, p. 223.

[4] Stair to Craggs, March 4, 1719.—State Papers, Foreign, France, 353. In a private letter to Craggs on March 12th, Stair expresses the opinion that Ormonde's intention probably was to land at Liverpool, seize Chester, march down the Severn, and raise the west country.—*Ibid.* The State Papers contain numerous other letters from Stair, with further information as to the expedition.

[5] Craggs Papers, Stowe MSS. 247, ff. 35-40 b, 64-68. Appendix, Nos. 21, 22, pp. 224, 227. He wrote to Stanhope on the 15th, *cit. supra*, p. xxvii, note 6. A list of the troops offered by the Regent, amounting to eighteen battalions of infantry

INTRODUCTION xxxix

In England the threatened invasion caused no great alarm, but prompt measures were taken to meet it. The Government's information was communicated to Parliament by a Royal message on March 10th,[1] and the House of Commons undertook to make good whatever expense might be necessary for the defence of the country. A proclamation was issued offering a reward of £5000 for the capture of Ormonde. A Commissioner was sent down into the west country to report as to any movements among the disaffected gentry there.[2] All diligence was used in fitting out and manning the fleet. On the 11th of March Sir John Norris sailed from Spithead with seven ships, to cruise off the Lizard, on the 12th he was followed by two more ships, and on the 24th by Lord Berkeley with seven more. Three frigates were sent across the Bay of Biscay to watch for the Spanish fleet. The troops in the west of England were

---

and ten squadrons of cavalry, is in the State Papers, Foreign, France, 353. At the same time the services of 1500 sailors were offered (Craggs to Stair, March 9th, 1719, *ibid.* 351a. Appendix, p. 234). The troops were declined with thanks, but 600 sailors were actually sent over to Portsmouth (Conseil de Marine to Dubois, April 6th, 1719, *ibid.* 354 a). However, as Craggs wrote at the time, 'Our navy pride themselves on doing their own service without any obligation to foreign helps,' and the Frenchmen were sent home with a month's pay in their pockets.—Craggs to Stair, April 9th, o.s. *Ibid.* 351 a.

Stair thoroughly distrusted the French. In a private letter to Craggs on March 20th, he says :—'To tell you ye truth I have no manner of taste to be assisted by French troops in England, ye byass of all this nation towards ye Pretender is inconceivable; however, ye Regents good disposition, and his succours being ready at Havre, Calais and Dunkirk, will have a very good effect, and help to keep our Jacobites in awe, who, upon ye whole matter, I believe, are much better disposed to drink ye Pretender's health than to fight for him.' He writes again on the 26th :—' If you want to be assisted by France you must take care not to need it, for if ever you doe need it, you may be well assured you will have no help from thence.' . . . 'In one word, my dr. Craggs, as long as you stand firm upon yr leggs you'll lead France, whenever wee come to be obliged to lean upon her for support she'll help to tumble us down.'—Craggs Papers, Stowe MSS., 247, ff. 96, 107.

[1] The dates in this paragraph are Old Style.

[2] According to his reports nothing of any importance was being done.—S. Buckley to Craggs, Dorchester, March 11th and 14th; Bridgewater, March 18th; Bath, March 21st, April 1st, 1719.—Craggs Papers, Stowe MSS., 247, ff. 98, 102, 103, 117, 119, 120.

reinforced by several regiments. Four battalions were brought over from Ireland. King George's foreign allies were desired to get in readiness the contingents with which they had undertaken to furnish him in case of rebellion or invasion, and about the middle of April two Swiss battalions in the service of the States-General landed in the Thames, and three Dutch battalions in the north of England.[1]

As the event happened, these precautions were needless. The unfailing ill-luck of the Stuarts had not deserted them. Guevarra's fleet never doubled Cape Finisterre. As at the time of the Armada, the winds and waves had fought for England against the Spaniard.

After leaving Cadiz on the 7th of March, the fleet steered west-south-west to the latitude of 34° 50′, and then changed its course to the north-north-east. On the night of the 28th it was about fifty leagues west of Cape Finisterre. About one in the morning of the 29th it encountered a terrible storm, which lasted for forty-eight hours. The fleet was scattered to the four winds. Horses, guns, stores, and arms had to be thrown overboard. Many men died of hardship and privation. The flagship was dismasted and lost most of her guns. All the ships were more or less crippled. They made their way to port as best they could, some back to Cadiz, some into the Tagus, some into the ports of Galicia.[2] On the 10th of April five ships reached Corunna with the bad news; five more had arrived by the 13th.[3] The tidings of disaster met James on his way from Madrid. He arrived at Corunna on the 17th[4] to find that the armament which had carried such great hopes was utterly ruined. The enterprise had failed. On April 24th, Stair wrote from Paris to Craggs, 'I think we're

---

[1] *Political State*, vol. xvii. pp. 336, 337; *Hist. Reg.*, vol. iv. pp. 138, 155-163; Craggs to Stair, March 30, 1719.—State Papers, Foreign, France, 351a. These authorities conflict as to some details.

[2] St. Philippe, vol. iii. p. 364; Reports from Corunna, Appendix, Nos. 36, 37, 38, pp. 243 *et seq.*; Spartman's narrative, *cit. supra*, p. xxxvi, note 3.

[3] Letter XCVI.   [4] Letter CII.

intirely out of danger from ye Spanish invasion for this year.'[1]

We have now to follow the fortunes of the Earl Marischal's expedition to Scotland.[2] As we have seen, he sailed from Passage on the 8th of March. The Spanish force which accompanied him consisted of a detachment of twelve men per company from each of the twenty-four companies of Don Pedro de Castro's regiment of foot, under the command of a lieutenant-colonel, with six captains, six lieutenants, and six ensigns, three hundred and seven in all, including officers.[3]

---

[1] Private, Craggs Papers, Stowe MSS., 247, f. 148. Lord Berkeley, in a private letter to Craggs, dated on board H.M.S. *Dorsetshire*, ten leagues from the Lizard, April ½, 1719, says, 'I think the Spaniards have made an end of their expedition, for should they have the good luck to get into the Groine, when they know the preparations we have made for them, which they must do by this time, they'l hardly come out again to trouble us.'—*Ibid.* f. 144.

[2] The principal authorities for the history of the expedition to Scotland are Keith's *Memoirs*, and the naval and military despatches, which were printed at the time in the *London Gazette*, and are reprinted in the *Historical Register*, vol. iv. pp. 279-285. St. Philippe gives a detailed but inaccurate account, *Mémoires*, vol. iii. p. 360 *et seq.* A valuable source of information as to the battle of Glenshiel is the plan drawn by Lieutenant J. H. Bastide, of which there is one copy in possession of the Queen at Windsor, and another in that of the Duke of Marlborough at Blenheim. The Blenheim copy was the subject of an interesting paper read to the Society of Antiquaries of Scotland by Mr. A. H. Millar in 1882 (*Proceedings*, 1882-83, p. 57). An anonymous contemporary account of the battle, in the possession of Mr. C. S. Home-Drummond-Moray of Abercairney, was communicated by Mr. Millar to the Society in 1885 (*ibid.* 1884-85, p. 64). By the courtesy of the Council of the Society I am permitted to reproduce from their *Proceedings* a reduced facsimile of Bastide's plan (at p. lii). A 'Distinct Abridgement of some Materiall Poynts relateing to Scotts Affairs,' giving a full account of the expedition, was sent by Mar to Lord Nairne in August 1719, and is printed in the Appendix to Mr. T. L. Kington Oliphant's *Jacobite Lairds of Gask*. Mar's account of the battle is evidently taken from Tullibardine's letter to him of June 16th, which is in the Stuart Papers, and is now printed for the first time. Appendix, No. 62, p. 269. The Stuart Papers also include letters from Glendaruel and Glengarry, but they contain no additional information of importance. See also letters printed in Mr. Murray Graham's *Stair Annals*, chap. xv.

[3] Statement by a Spanish lieutenant, taken prisoner at Eilean Donan, to Lord Carpenter, *cit. supra*, p. xxxv, note 2. The uniform of the Spaniards is described as 'white lined with yellow.'—*Original Weekly Journal*, May 30, 1719.

Young James Keith—he was only twenty-two—was intrusted with the perilous duty of warning the Jacobite exiles in France, now an enemy's country, of the intended expedition. Furnished with credentials from Ormonde, and supplied by Alberoni with a sum of about 18,000 crowns, he set out from Madrid on the 19th of February. He went first to San Sebastian, where he handed over 12,000 crowns to the Prince of Campo Florido, for the equipment of the two frigates destined for Scotland. With the remainder he crossed the frontier, and about the end of February arrived at Bordeaux. Here he met General Gordon, Brigadier Campbell, and some others, to whom he delivered his message, and left them some money to hire ships to transport themselves to Scotland.[1] Brigadier Campbell went to Spain to join the Earl Marischal. On the 3rd of March Keith arrived at Orleans. There he found the Marquis of Tullibardine, by whom he was accompanied to Paris, where he arrived next day.

At Paris there took place a deplorable exhibition of that fatal jealousy which was the curse of most Jacobite enterprises, and which proved the ruin of this one. Keith may tell the story himself: 'Howsoon I got there, I advertised the Marquess of Seafort, who immediatly came to the house where I was, and brought along with him a brother of Lord Duffus's, and some whille after came in Campbell of Glenderuel. I told them the reason of my coming, and showed them the short credentials I had brought from the Duke of Ormonde. Glenderuel smiled at reading them, and told me that that billet wou'd have been of little weight with them, had they not been already advertised by the Duke of Marr, to obey what orders the Duke of Ormonde shou'd send. This plainly let me see that we had two factions amongst us, and which proved the occasion of our speedy ruin when we landed in Scotland. However,

---

[1] Clanranald and Lochiel were among those who crossed to Scotland. General Gordon was too ill to go.—Distinct Abridgement. Compare, however, Alberoni's letter to James, Appendix, No. 39, p. 246.

they agreed to obey the orders, and I went away next day to Rowen to provide a ship for them, which in ten days I got fitted out by the help of a merchant there, and ready to put to sea. Howsoon this was done I wrote to them to come down with all hast, the ship being already at Havre de Grace. When they arrived Glenderuel asked me if I had seen General Dillon whille I was at Paris. I told him I had not; that General Dillon being at St. Germains, I durst not venture to go there, being too well known not to be discover'd; and that tho' the interest of those there was the same with ours, yet their imprudence was so great that they were not to be trusted with a secret which, shou'd it take vent, must occasion our being stopt at the instance of the Earl of Stair, then Embassador from the Court of England; that besides, having no instructions to communicate anything to him, I made no doubt but he had been advertised by some other canal.

'Glenderuel declared he did not think those reasons valid, and that Dillon shou'd be advertised of this, and desired to let us know if the King (whose affairs he was then intrusted with at Paris) had given him no particular instructions on this head. This was the pretence; the true reason was, to get a commission which they knew he had in his hands, and was design'd for the King of Sweden's expedition in the year 1717, by which the King constituted the Marquess of Tullibardine Commander in chieff of his forces in Scotland. This Glenderuel thought absolutly necessary for his own private ends, being surer to govern the easy temper of the Marquess than of those who otherwise wou'd naturally have the command of the army, and particularly to prevent its falling into the hands of General Gordon, with whom he was not in very good intelligence.

'The day before we embarked, the express they had sent to Paris returned with a pacquet from General Dillon, of which they showed a letter full of common place advices relating to the conduct we shou'd hold in Scotland, but not a word of the commissions, which they keept to be drawn out on proper occasions.'[1]

On the 19th of March the party left Havre in a small ship of twenty-five tons,[2] and after sailing round the west coast of Ireland, and narrowly escaping capture by the British fleet, reached the Isle of Lewis on April 4, N.S., March 24, O.S.[3] Here they found that the Earl Marischal had arrived, and that his two frigates were at anchor in the harbour of Stornoway with the men still aboard. Keith went at once to join his brother, and warned him of what had happened at Paris, and of the difficulties which might arise as to the command. Next day Seaforth and Tullibardine came to Stornoway, and in the evening a council of war was held. Tullibardine said nothing of the commission which he had received from Dillon, and the command accordingly remained in the Earl Marischal for the time, as senior Major-General. It was then discussed whether an attempt should be made to land at once on the mainland, or whether the expedition should remain in the Lewis till news arrived of Ormonde's landing in England. Tullibardine and Glendaruel advised the latter course, but Marischal determined to land as soon as possible in Scotland, and at once make a dash for Inverness, the garrison of which was not more than three hundred strong. There it would be possible to hold out until a sufficient force had been collected to attempt a march to the south. It was accordingly decided to sail for the main-

---

[1] Keith, pp. 42-44. Mar says that Seaforth was at first unwilling to go, and that he allowed Tullibardine and Glendaruel to leave Paris without him, and only followed them on the advice of a 'person of distinction,' evidently Dillon.—Distinct Abridgement.

[2] Mar gives the date as the 20th. Their departure from Paris did not escape the vigilance of Stair. On March 15 he writes to Craggs : 'Tous les Ecossois qui etaient ici sont partis subitement depuis 4 jours, entre autres Ld. Seaforth, Mr. Sutherland frère de Lord Duffus, Campbell de Kellendarouel et quelques autres, on croit qu'ils ont pris le chemin des Pays Bas ; les autres qui etoient en Guienne et en Languedoc sont tous eclipsez ; on croit qu'ils passent en droiture dans les Isles et dans le Nord d'Ecosse sans passer en Espagne.'—State Papers, Foreign, France, 353.

[3] The dates from here to p. liv. are Old Style.

MAP TO ILLUSTRATE THE LANDING OF THE EXPEDITION AND THE BATTLE OF GLENSHIEL

At p. xliv

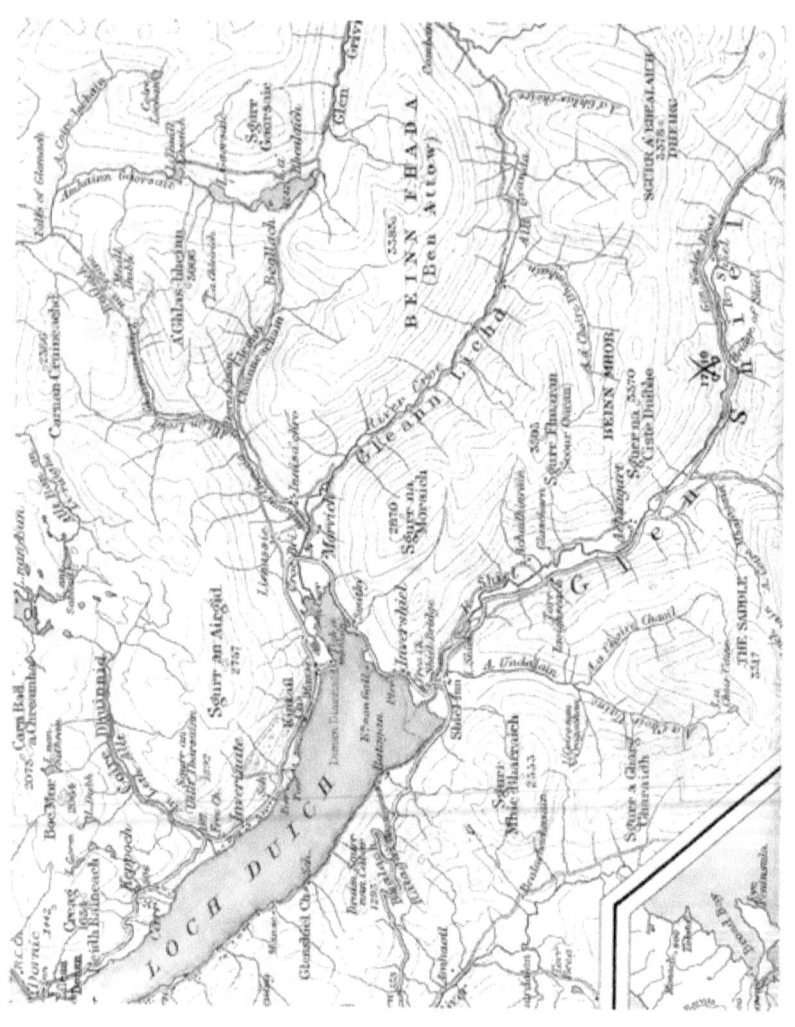

land three days after. In the meantime the Spanish troops were landed in order to refresh themselves after their long voyage.

Next morning, however, Tullibardine requested that a council of war might once more be assembled, and 'after having,' says Keith, 'made a sort of speech which nobody understood but himself,' he produced his commission of Lieutenant-General. Marischal accordingly resigned the command of the troops, reserving that of the ships, which had been expressly committed to him by Alberoni. Tullibardine and Glendaruel still wished to remain in the Lewis, but the others so strongly protested against this course that they acquiesced in the Earl Marischal's views. Accordingly the expedition again put to sea, on April 4th. Their intention was to land in Kintail, which was part of Seaforth's own country, but owing to contrary winds they were only able to reach Gairloch. From Gairloch Glendaruel was despatched with letters to a number of the Highland chiefs, announcing the arrival of the expedition. The ships left Gairloch on the 6th, but a storm which rose that night drove them back to the Lewis. It was not till the 13th that they effected a landing on the shores of Loch Alsh.

Next day Glendaruel returned with news that James's adherents were ready to rise as soon as there was any certain news of the landing of Ormonde's expedition.[1] On the 17th

---

[1] Intimation of the intended invasion from Spain had been sent to the leaders of the Jacobite party in the Lowlands, but they had determined that no movement should be made until they were sure that Ormonde had landed. On hearing of the Earl Marischal's arrival, Lockhart of Carnwath sent him a memorial expressing his views as to what ought to be done. The main point emphasised in the memorial is the universal hatred with which the Union was regarded in Scotland, and the importance of making its repeal a chief article of the Jacobite policy. It does not appear that the document ever reached its destination. A catastrophe was very nearly caused by an 'unknown fellow' who came to Mr. Milnes, tutor to young Macdonell of Glengarry, representing that he was a servant of Lochiel's, that Ormonde's fleet had arrived, and that he had been sent ashore to warn his master's friends to be ready to take up arms. In consequence of this news, which was confirmed by a letter from Lord Stormont,

an informal council of war was held. The Earl Marischal and Brigadier Campbell proposed marching straight to Inverness with the Spaniards and 500 men whom Seaforth undertook to raise, but Tullibardine and Glendaruel were still in favour of a Fabian policy. 'The same demone,' says Keith, 'who had inspired them with the design of staying in the Lewis hindered them from accepting this proposition.' Clanranald and Lochiel arrived on the 20th. Clanranald also counselled delay. Several days passed, and there came on news of Ormonde. Tullibardine was with difficulty dissuaded from re-embarking and returning to Spain. This made Marischal resolve to burn his boats. He determined to send the two frigates back to Spain. Tullibardine tried to detain them, but they obeyed Marischal's orders and put to sea on the 30th, just in time, for within a week after their departure there arrived on the coast a British squadron consisting of five ships: the *Worcester*, 50 guns; *Assistance*, 50; *Dartmouth*, 50; *Enterprise*, 40; and *Flamborough*, 24, under the command of Captain Boyle. The *Assistance* and the *Dartmouth* sailed round the north of Skye and anchored in Loch Kishorn. Boyle with the *Worcester*, *Enterprise*, and *Flamborough* came through Kyle Rhea, and on May 9th anchored at the mouth of Loch Alsh.

The Jacobites had fixed their headquarters at Eilean Donan Castle, the ancient stronghold of the Mackenzies. The castle, now a picturesque ivy-covered ruin, is situated on a little island close to the shore, opposite the village of Dornie, at the point where Loch Alsh branches into Loch Duich and Loch Long.

---

then at his house in Annandale, to the effect that Ormonde's fleet had been seen off the coast, Lords Nairn and Dalhousie prepared to take the field. Lockhart, however, was satisfied that the messenger was either a common swindler or a Government spy, and succeeded in preventing Nairn and Dalhousie from committing themselves. 'As for my Lord Stormont's information,' says he, ' I gave it the less credit when I perceived his Lordship's letter was dated at one in the morning, about which time I knew he was apt to credit any news that pleased him.'—*Lockhart Papers*, vol. ii. pp. 17-23.

It consists of an ancient and massive keep some fifty feet square, surrounded by courtyards and out-buildings. Here most of the ammunition and provisions of the expedition were stored under the guard of a garrison of forty-five Spaniards, the main body of the troops being encamped on the mainland close to the shore.

On the 10th of May Boyle with his three ships came up the loch to Eilean Donan, and sent an officer with a flag of truce to demand the surrender of the Castle. The boat was fired upon and not permitted to land. At eight o'clock in the evening the ships opened fire upon the Castle. The old stone fortress, impregnable in Highland warfare, could not be held under artillery fire, and when a storming party of two boats' crews landed, they met with little resistance. The Spanish garrison were taken prisoners, and afterwards sent round to Leith in the *Flamborough*, and three hundred and forty-three barrels of powder and fifty-two barrels of musket bullets were captured. The buildings in which the provisions had been stored for the use of the Jacobite camp were set on fire, and the Castle was blown up.[1] The *Flamborough* went up Loch Duich in search of another magazine which had been formed near the head of the loch, under a guard of 30 Spaniards, who blew it up as she approached.[2]

The invaders were now in a sorry plight. Their retreat by sea was cut off. The coast was vigilantly patrolled by the boats of the British squadron. It was impossible even to cross to Skye. They had lost nearly the whole of their ammunition

---

[1] Boyle's despatch, *Historical Register*, vol. iv. p. 280. According to Mar's account the bombardment began in the morning and lasted all day, and in the evening the Spaniards surrendered at discretion, without any resistance, and without a man killed or wounded. A considerable number of roundshot have from time to time been found in and about the ruins of the Castle. Two of these are now in the possession of the Rev. Roderick Morison, minister of Kintail.

[2] According to local tradition, the site of this magazine was beside the small fresh-water lake called Loch nan Corr, close to where the Manse of Kintail now stands. Musket bullets, some of them fused together as if by an explosion, have been found in the manse garden.

and provisions, and were in one of the wildest and most desolate parts of Britain, with no base of operations from which it was possible to draw any further supplies. The Government troops in Scotland were being rapidly reinforced from the south. Tullibardine now determined to do what he ought to have done at first, namely to endeavour to raise a force from among the clans. By this time the fatal news of the dispersion of the Cadiz fleet had reached the Highlands, and naturally recruits were not very plentiful. 'Not above a thousand men appeared,' says Keith, 'and even those seemed not very fond of the enterprise.' Lord George Murray, Tullibardine's brother, had already arrived with what forces he could muster from Perthshire, and those which Rob Roy had collected in Stirlingshire and in the north part of Argyllshire. On May 23d they marched to the head of Loch Duich. On the 5th of June Lochiel, who had gone home to raise what forces he could, came in with 150 men; on the 7th, Seaforth brought in about 500 of his men; and on the 8th, arrived a son of Rob Roy's with some 80 more recruits.[1]

In the meantime the garrison from Inverness had been largely reinforced, and on the 5th of June Major-General Wightman, who had commanded part of Argyll's troops at Sheriffmuir, marched from Inverness with a force of about 850 infantry, besides 120 dragoons and some 130 Highlanders, and a battery of four Cohorn mortars.[2] He marched to the head of Loch Ness, where he halted for a day, and thence over by Glenmoriston towards Kintail.

It was decided to await Wightman's attack in Glenshiel, the

---

[1] Details as to the discussions in which so much time was wasted, and as to the comings and goings of the Highland chiefs, will be found in Mar's Distinct Abridgement. His narrative does not always agree with Keith's; the latter is probably the more trustworthy, written as it was by an eyewitness, a very competent observer of military events, who at the time of writing had long ceased to have any connection with Scottish affairs.

[2] The light bronze mortar for field use was introduced by Baron van Cohorn, the famous Dutch military engineer, at the siege of Grave in 1674.

grand and desolate glen which runs inland in a south-easterly direction from the head of Loch Duich, skirting the vast southern slopes of Scour Ouran. The position selected for defence was at the place where the present road crosses the river Shiel by a stone bridge, some five miles above Invershiel.[1] Here a shoulder of the mountain juts into the glen on its northern side, and the glen contracts into a narrow gorge, down which the Shiel, at this point a roaring torrent, runs in a deep rocky channel, between steep declivities covered with heather, bracken, and scattered birches. Above the pass the glen opens out into a little strath. Then, as now, the road ran through the strath on the north side of the river and entered the pass along a narrow shelf between the river and the hill, from which it was entirely commanded. This position was occupied by the Jacobite forces on the 9th of June. They were joined in the course of the day by another hundred recruits, and next day by about a hundred more.

On the evening of the 9th Lord George Murray, who commanded the outposts, reported that the enemy were encamped within four or five miles, at the head of Loch Clunie.[2] Next morning he reported that they had struck their camp and were marching over the watershed into Glenshiel. As they advanced Murray retired before them, keeping at a distance of about half-a-mile. About two in the afternoon the armies came in sight of each other, about half-a-mile apart. Wightman halted, and deployed his troops for the attack.

The great natural strength of the Jacobites' position had

---

[1] Wightman, in his despatch of June 11th (*London Gazette*, Special, June 19, 1719; *Hist. Reg.* vol. iv. p. 283), calls the site of the battle the Pass of Strachell, a name which still appears in guide-books, though it is not known in the district. Tullibardine calls it Glenshielbeg. The local Gaelic name is Lub-innis-na-seangan, 'the bend of the river at the island of ants.'

[2] Wightman gives the name of his camping-ground on the night of the 9th as Strachlony, probably Strathloan, about a mile to the west of where Clunie Inn now stands. This would agree with the distance given by Murray.

d

been increased by hasty fortifications. A barricade had been made across the road, and along the face of the hill, on the north side of the river, entrenchments had been thrown up. Here the main body was posted, consisting of the Spanish regiment, which now only paraded some 200 strong,[1] under its Colonel, Don Nicolas Bolano; Locheil with about 150 men; about 150 of 'Lidcoat's'[2] and others; 20 volunteers, 40 of Rob Roy's men, 50 of M'Kinnon's, and 200 of Lord Seaforth's commanded by Sir John Mackenzie of Coul. Seaforth himself was on the extreme left, up on the side of Scour Ouran, with 200 of his best men. The hill on the south bank of the river, the right of the position, was occupied by about 150 men under Lord George Murray.[3] Tullibardine commanded in the centre, accompanied by Glendaruel. Brigadier M'Intosh of Borlum was with the Spanish Colonel. The Earl Marischal and Brigadier Campbell were with Seaforth on the left.

Wightman's right wing was composed of 150 grenadiers, under Major Milburn; Montagu's regiment, commanded by Lieut.-Colonel Lawrence; a detachment of 50 men under Colonel Harrison; Huffel's Dutch regiment, and four companies of Amerongen's. On the flank were 56 of Lord Strathnaver's men under Ensign Mackay. The whole wing was commanded by Colonel Clayton. The left wing, which was deployed on the south side of the river, consisted of Clayton's regiment, commanded by Lieut.-Colonel Reading, and had on the flank about 80 men of the Munroes, under

---

[1] Forty-five had been taken prisoners at Eilean Donan, and about fifty, some of whom were invalided, had been left in the rear with the baggage.

[2] 'Lidcoat,' the name used in Tullibardine's letter to Mar of June 16th, is evidently a pseudonym; it may mean Glengarry. Mar, in his Distinct Abridgement, speaks of these men as 'a friend's'—'out of the neighbouring bounds.'

[3] These figures, taken from Tullibardine's letter to Mar, make the total Jacobite force about 1120. Wightman gives the figures as '1640 Highlanders, besides 300 Spaniards, and a Corps apart of 500 Highlanders who were posted on a Hill in order to make themselves Masters of our Baggage.' His own force amounted, as we have seen, to about 1100.

Munro of Culcairn.¹ The dragoons and the four mortars remained on the road.²

The engagement began between five and six o'clock, when the left wing of the Hanoverians advanced against Lord George Murray's position on the south side of the river. The position was first shelled by the mortar battery, which, escorted by the dragoons, had advanced along the road to within 400 yards of the Jacobite centre. It was then attacked by four platoons of Clayton's with the Munroes. The first attack was repulsed, but the attacking party was reinforced, and Lord George's men, who were badly supported, were driven from their position and retreated beyond the burn, which, coming down from Frioch Corrie, descends towards the Shiel in rear of the ground which they had occupied. The precipitous banks of the burn effectually checked pursuit. After the right wing of the Jacobites had been dislodged, Wightman's right began to move up the hill to attack their left. The detachment commanded by Lord Seaforth was strongly posted behind a group of rocks on the hillside, and it was against them that the attack of Montagu and Harrison's troops was directed. Seaforth was reinforced from the centre by the remainder of his own men under Sir John Mackenzie. Finding himself hard pressed, Seaforth sent down for further support. Another reinforcement under Rob Roy went to his aid, but before it reached him the greater part of his men had given way, and he himself had been severely wounded. Rob Roy's detachment next gave way, and retired towards the mountain. They were followed by 'Lidcoat's' men and others. The whole force of Wightman's

---

[1] Captain George Munro of Culcairn, younger brother of Sir Robert Munro of Foulis, had, in the absence of his elder brother, assembled a number of the clan to conduct the regular troops through the mountains to Glenshiel. He was severely wounded in the action. See Appendix to Doddridge's *Life of Colonel Gardiner*, p. 251.

[2] See Plan. Bastide's drawing is rather a reconnaissance sketch than a plan properly so called. The scale of feet only applies to the direction from east to west.

attack was now directed towards the Jacobite centre, against which the fire of the mortar battery had by this time been turned. The Spanish regulars stood their ground well, but finding that most of their allies had deserted them, they also at last began to retire up the hill to the left. The whole of Tullibardine's little army was now in retreat. The retreat soon became a flight. The victorious Hanoverians pursued their defeated enemies over the shoulder of Scour Ouran, and only halted as darkness fell, when they had nearly reached the top of the mountain.[1] Far up the hill there is a corrie which to this day the shepherds call Bealach-na-Spainnteach, the Spaniards' Pass.[2]

The action had lasted some three hours. The loss of the English troops amounted to 21 men killed, and 121 wounded, officers included.[3] That of the Jacobites is difficult to esti-

---

[1] Sir Walter Scott, in the *Tales of a Grandfather*, says that at Glenshiel the Government troops were compelled to retreat, and Dr. Hill Burton speaks of the result of the action as doubtful. The accounts given by Keith and Tullibardine entirely confirm Wightman's despatches. The Jacobites were routed. It was a sorry celebration of James's birthday.

[2] Just above the bridge the Shiel falls into a deep pool, into which it is said that many of the Jacobites threw their arms as they retreated. The waterfall is known as Eas-nan-arm (the Fall of Arms). Weapons have been found in the bed of the stream. Only last year (1894) a bayonet was found imbedded in the shingle some distance below the Fall, by a shepherd named Alexander Findlayson. It is now in the possession of Mr. Mitchell, Ratagan.

[3] These are the official numbers. *London Gazette*, June 20-23, 1719. An officer who was present gives the following list of casualties: 'Mountague's Regiment, 1 Capt., 1 Lieut., 1 Sergeant, 7 Corporals and Cent. kill'd; 2 Lieut., 1 Serg., 35 Cent. wounded. Clayton's, 2 Serg., 1 Corp. kill'd; 2 Captains, 1 Serg., 21 Centinels wounded. Harrison's, 3 Corporals and Centinels kill'd; 1 Capt., 1 Lieut., 1 Serg., 14 Centinels wounded. General Huffel's (Dutch), 1 Lieut., 3 Corporals and Centinels killed; 1 Capt., 1 Ensign, 2 Serg., 6 Cent. wounded. Col. Amerongen's (Dutch), 1 Serg. kill'd; 1 Lieut., 9 Cent. wounded. Total, 21 kill'd, 119 wounded, besides Highlanders.'—*Weekly Journal*, July 4, 1719. On the 13th of June, Provost Hossack of Inverness wrote to Duncan Forbes of Culloden: 'Colonel Montagu, and some horse having this forenoon come in from Killichnimman, brought a great number of Letters from our Army, which goe by this Post, and will confirm that the Troops attacked the Rebels in their most advantageous post, beat them from it not without loss, and were in pursuite of them next day; the Spaniards having capitulated to surrender on the afternoon thereof. Captain Downes and two Lieutenants of Montagu's were killed; Captains Moor and Heighington of Clayton's wounded; as is Cullairn on the

LIEUT. BASTIDE'S PLAN OF
THE BATTLE OF GLENSHIEL

At p. lii

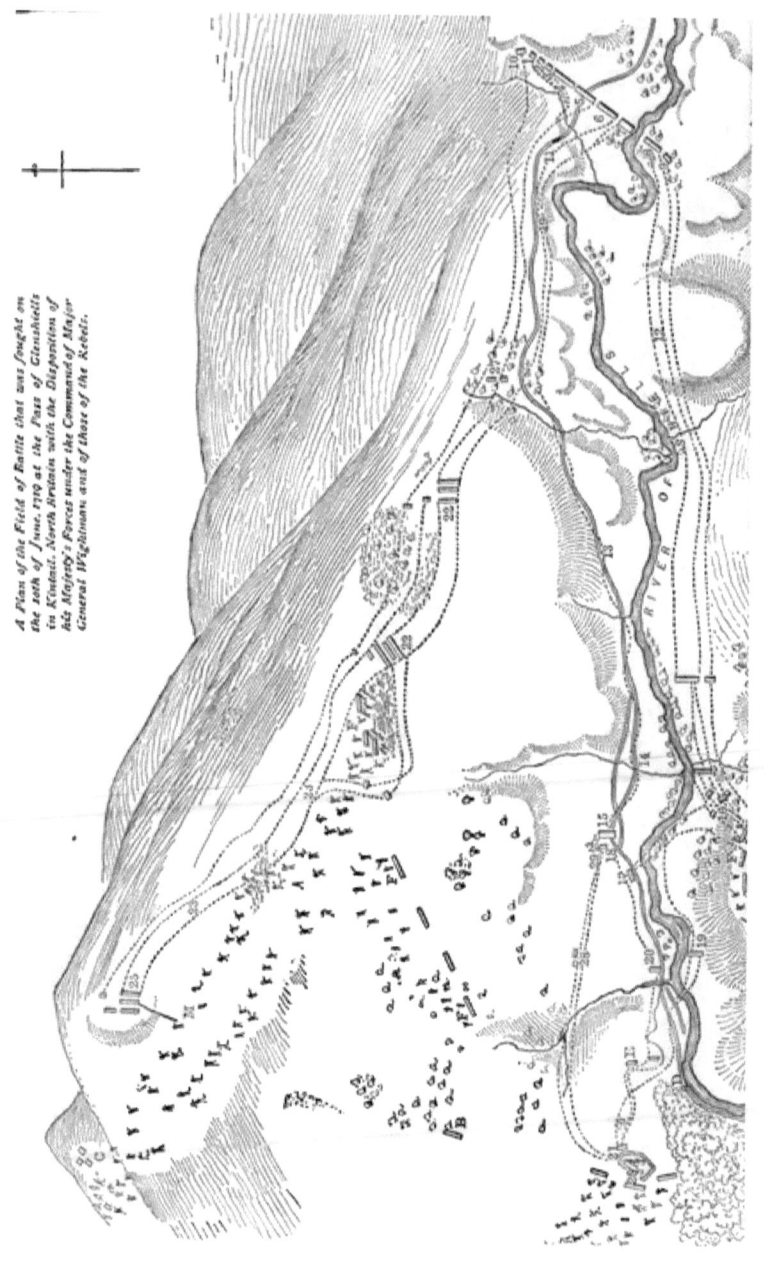

REFERENCES TO THE PLAN

1. A Sergt. and 12 Grenadiers.
2. An Officer and 24 do.
3. Main Body of Grenadiers, 120 in Num.
4. Col. Montagu's Regmt.
5. Col. Harrison's Detacht Battalion.
6. Huffel's Regmt. and 4 Companies of Amerongen's.
7. Dragoons.
8. Col. Clayton's Regiment.
9. The Monro's Highlanders.
10. The Sutherland's Right.
11. The first march by ye Right.
12. Clayton's march by the Left.
13. The Dragoons march to the Plain.
14. The Dragoons Halt.
15. The Dragoons advance to the middle of the Plain.
16. Clayton's four Plottoons and the Monro's making ye First Attack on ye Rebels' Right.
17. Cohorn Mortars throwing Granades at the Rebels where ye First Attack was Ordered.
18. Cohorn Mortars throwing Granades at ye Spaniards in their Entrenchments.
19. Part of Clayton's attacks the Barricade of the Pass.
20. 35 Dragoons on Foot attack the Spaniards Breast Works.
21. The Dragoons mount the Hill.
22. Our March in line of Battle to the Rock where the Attack began under ye command of Col. Clayton.
23. Our Right pursue the Rebels.
24. The Plottoons and the Monro's halt upon the Hill, having putt the Ennemy to the Flight.
25. Our Right halts upon ye Mountain.
26. Part of Clayton's takes possession of ye Hill that commanded the Pass.
27. Guard for the Baggage and place for the Hospital.
28. The Bagage advanced with the wounded men for their security.
29. Majr.-Genl. Whightman giving his directions during the Action.

REFERENCES TO THE ENNEMY

A. A Spanish Regiment posted on the Hill that commanded the Plain and the Pass.
B. Spaniards march to ye Mount and Halt.
C. The Spaniards retire to the Top of the mountain.
D. The Barricade that defended the Pass on the River Side.
E. The Breastworks on the Side of the Hill.
F. The Highlanders drawn up before the attack.
G. A straggling number of Highlanders fire upon the Plottoons of Clayton's and the Monro's behind them in the time of the attack.
H. A Body of Highlanders going to sustain their Right.
M. The Flight of the Rebels. The Mount called Skururan the highest in Scotland except Benevis.

mate; it could not have been great, as Keith thought at the time that not more than a hundred men on both sides had been killed or wounded. Besides Seaforth, Lord George Murray was wounded. One English officer was killed, Captain Downes, of Montagu's regiment. He was buried on the field of battle; his resting-place is still pointed out, on the south side of the river, just above the Pass. Local tradition has transformed it into the 'Dutch Colonel's Grave.' If all tales are true, his ghost still walks the glen o' nights.

On the night after the battle, the Jacobite chiefs, seeing that they had neither provisions nor ammunition, and that their few troops had not behaved so as to give much encouragement to try a further action, resolved that the Spaniards should surrender, and that the Highlanders should disperse as best they could. Accordingly next morning the Spanish commander delivered his sword to General Wightman, and 'everybody else,' says Keith, 'took the road he liked best.'

A week later, Wightman writes to say that he is 'taking a tour through all the difficult parts of Seaforth's country to terrify the Rebels by burning the houses of the Guilty and preserving those of the Honest.'[1] On June 30th he writes from Inverness, 'I have used all possible means to put a Dread upon those who have been more immediately concerned in this late unnatural Rebellion, and by all just accounts am assured the Rebells are totally disperst.'[2]

---

thigh, and the bone safe. It said Seafort is wounded on the shoulder, and Gordon in the Legg. This is what occurs for news now.'—*Culloden Papers*, p. 73. Captain Downes is the only officer mentioned in Wightman's despatch of June 11 as having been killed.

[1] *London Gazette*, June 27-30, 1719.—The despatch is dated on June 17, 'from the Camp of Aderhanon.' Aderhanon is rather a puzzle. By the change of a letter it becomes a fairly good phonetic rendering of Edracharon, the now obsolete name of the place in Strathcarron, where the farm of New Kelso now stands. It is in the very middle of Seaforth's country, in a sheltered strath, close to the river Carron, and to the road to Inverness—an ideal site for a camp.

[2] Wightman to Charles Delafaye, Secretary to the Lords Justices, June 30, 1719. Home Office Papers, Record Office, Scotland, Bundle 14, No. 60. Appendix, No. 66., p. 276.

The rising was over. Its leaders, after lurking for a while, with a price on their heads,[1] in Knoydart and in Glengarry's country, effected their escape to the Continent.[2]

The Spanish prisoners, two hundred and seventy-four in number, were marched to Inverness, and on the 27th they set out for Edinburgh.[3]

'When the Spanish battallion were brought prisoners to Edinburgh,' says Lockhart, 'the officers, who had the liberty of the town, were used by the loyall party with all the civility and kindness imaginable; but the Government for a long time refused to advance subsistance money to them, by which in a little time they were reduced to great straits, which appeared even in their looks tho' their Spanish pride would not allow them to complain. As I was well acquainted with Don Nicolas who commanded them, I took the liberty to ask him if he wanted money; and finding it was so, I told him it was unkind in him to be thus straitned, when he knew our King, for whose cause he suffr'd had so many friends in town that would cheirfully assist him; so I immediatly gott him credit for as much money as was necessary for himself and his men, till he gott bills from the Marquis de Beretti-Landi the Spanish embassadour in Holland, when he thankfully repay'd what was advanced to him.'[4] In October the Spaniards were sent home to their own country.

James and Ormonde were still in Spain, hoping that their

---

[1] A reward of £2000 was offered for the capture of Tullibardine, Seaforth, or the Earl Marischal.—Douglas's *Peerage*.

[2] Stair had prophesied the speedy end of the expedition. On May 16 he wrote to Robethon: 'Je ne suis pas en peine de ce peu de Rebelles qui sont débarqués en Ecosse, ils mourront bientôt de faim dans ces montagnes, et s'il y a des Espagnols qui échappent, cela ôtera l'envie aux autres de se promener de nouveau en Ecosse.'—Hanover Papers, Stowe MSS. 231, f. 313.

[3] Wightman to Delafaye, June 30, 1719, *cit*.

[4] *Lockhart Papers*, vol. ii. pp. 23-24. For details as to the treatment of the Spanish prisoners and the measures taken for quieting the country, see documents in Appendix, pp. 274 *et seq*.

enterprise might yet be renewed. Alberoni at first professed his intention of going on with it, but the thing was hopeless.[1] The fleet would have taken three months to refit, and Alberoni soon found his hands full enough of affairs nearer home. He put a stop even to the project which Ormonde had formed of sending assistance to the Earl Marischal in Scotland.[2] The remnant of the Cadiz fleet was employed in an abortive expedition for the purpose of raising the malcontents in Brittany. Ormonde himself took part in this affair. Craggs, writing to Stair, on November 2nd, describes it as 'an ill-concerted project, fit for the Cardinal to contrive, and the late Duke of Ormonde to execute.'[3]

During the summer the war with France had become sufficient to occupy all the energies of the Spanish Government. The campaign on the Pyrenean frontier was energetically conducted by the Duke of Berwick. In April, the Marquis de Silly passed the Bidassoa and captured the arsenal at Port Passage, where he destroyed six ships of war which were on the stocks. On the 18th of June Fuentarabia was reduced. The naval station at Santona was destroyed. The city of San Sebastian was taken on the 2nd of August, and the citadel on the 17th. James began to find that he was outstaying his welcome. It was evident that before long the French would be able to dictate terms of peace to Alberoni, and it was certain that one of the conditions of peace would be the departure of James from the dominions of the Catholic King. It was better that he should go now of his own accord than that

---

[1] 'Cardinal Alberoni still pretends to carry on the enterprise against Great Brittain. He has given orders for victualling the ships anew, and for reassembling the Troops, but evry body in Spain laughs at that Project, and indeed they do so pretty much in France, excepting our Jacobites, who have faith enough to believe evry thing that makes for them, let it be ever so impossible.'—Stair to Craggs, May 24, 1719, State Papers, Foreign, France, 353.

[2] Letter CXIX.

[3] State Papers, Foreign, France, 354a. For an account of this affair see St. Philippe, vol. iii. pp. 366-368.

he should be compelled to do so later. A pretext for suggesting his departure was all that was wanted, and one was easily found.¹

During the months of the winter and spring, Princess Clementina had remained in captivity at Innspruck. She had been able to write to James. Her sad little letters, written in an unformed school-girl hand—she was just sixteen—turn up with pathetic frequency among the Stuart Papers. In April she escaped from her prison. The escape, which had been long and carefully planned, was effected with great skill and daring by Charles Wogan, who had accompanied Ormonde to Russia in the winter of 1717.² Wogan's companions in the enterprise were three officers of Dillon's Irish Regiment in the French service, Major Gaydon, and Captains Misset and O'Toole, with Misset's wife and her French maid. The party made their way to Innspruck. Jeanneton, the maid, was told that the object of the journey was to carry off an heiress as a bride for O'Toole. She was introduced into the house in which the Princess was lodged. The Princess changed clothes with her, and succeeded in passing the sentry. Wogan had a carriage in waiting. They fled over the Brenner, and succeeded in reaching Venetian territory. At Bologna, Clementina was married to James by proxy, James Murray, afterwards titular Earl of Dunbar, acting as his representative.

---

¹ 'The Marshal [Berwick] now begins to think the Court of Spain is in earnest for peace, and looks upon the Pretender's being gone for Italy as a proof of it, judging that the Cardinal sends him away now to avoid being obliged to do it with a worse grace as a condition of the Peace.'—Colonel William Stanhope to Craggs, Mont Louis, September 19, 1719, State Papers, Foreign, Spain, 163. Colonel Stanhope accompanied Berwick's headquarters. His numerous letters from the front to Lord Stanhope and to Craggs, accompanied by sketches, lists of troops, etc., are preserved among the State Papers, and give detailed information as to the campaign.

² The contemporary narratives of the escape have been collected by Dr. J. T. Gilbert in a most interesting volume, *Narratives of the Detention, Liberation, and Marriage of Maria Clementina Stuart*, Dublin, 1894. The story, which reads like a chapter from Dumas, is told by Mr. Andrew Lang in a recent magazine article, 'The Escape of Maria Clementina,' *Macmillan's Magazine*, February, 1895.

On arriving at Rome she was lodged in the convent of the Ursulines, and was received by the Pope as Queen of England.

It was at first proposed that she should be sent to join James in Spain, and the Pope offered his galleys to convey her,[1] but as matters now stood the sooner James was back in Italy the better. He sailed from Vinaros on the 14th of August. On the 25th he landed at Leghorn, and on September 3rd met Clementina at Montefiascone.[2]

So the curtain falls on this luckless enterprise. On the 10th of September James wrote from Rome to Sir Hugh Paterson in Holland: 'Il viendra s'il plaist a Dieu des tems plus heureux,' he says sadly, 'en attendant nous devons prendre patience, sans nous laisser decourager par nos malheurs passez, mais plustost avoir bon courage et pousser nostre pointe quand l'occasion s'en offrira. Le bonheur dont je jouis a present dans mon domestique doit estre une consolation a mes amis, je vous prie de les assurer de mon amitié, estant sincerement à eux et à vous.—TRUEMAN.'[3] The 'tems plus heureux' never came for poor Mr. Trueman. Even the domestic happiness was short-lived. Prince Charlie was born in 1720, Henry in 1725. Then came an ugly story of jealousy, quarrels, separation. For a generation longer the adherents of the lost cause struggled and schemed, cherishing hopes which grew fainter year by year, till they vanished for ever in the smoke of Cumberland's guns at Culloden.

The subsequent fate of the chief actors in the story may be shortly noted. Alberoni fell from power in December 1719, and in the following month King Philip announced his accession to the Quadruple Alliance. The Cardinal retired to

---

[1] Stair to Craggs, June 17, 1719, State Papers, Foreign, France, 353.
[2] A second ceremony of marriage was celebrated at Montefiascone. As to the validity of the previous ceremony at Bologna, see James's letter to Ormonde, Appendix, No. 53. p. 259.
[3] Intercepted Jacobite Correspondence, Hanover Papers, Stowe MSS. 232, f. 219.

Italy, where he died in 1752.¹ Ormonde stayed on in Spain. He accepted a pension of 2000 pistoles from the King, and was concerned in some of the later Spanish projects, none of which came to anything, for the restoration of the Stuarts. In 1725 he went to France. His later years were spent at Avignon. Lady Mary Wortley Montagu saw him there in 1743. 'To say truth,' she says, 'nobody can be more insignificant. He keeps an assembly where all the best company go twice in the week, lives here in great magnificence, is quite inoffensive, and seems to have forgotten every part of his past life and to be of no party.'² He died in 1745. Seaforth made his peace with King George in 1726, and spent the rest of his days at home. Tullibardine unfurled Prince Charlie's standard in Glenfinnan in '45, and died next year in the Tower. Both the Keiths, after many vicissitudes, entered the service of Frederick the Great. The Earl Marischal went as Prussian Ambassador to France and Spain, and became Governor of Neuchatel. He died at Potsdam in 1778, a man greatly

---

¹ The Keiths met him at Sestri Levante in 1720. 'The Earl Marischal,' says James Keith, 'began to give him an account of what had passed in Scotland; to which the other answer'd, that having now no more interest in the affairs of Spain, and resolving never more to have any, he desired to be excused hearing it any further than what concerned himself, whom he was glad to see safely return'd.'—*Memoirs*, p. 56.

² To Wortley, June 1, 1743, cited by Lord Mahon, vol. i. p. 128. There were some pretty scandals circulated about Ormonde's life at Madrid and at Avignon, for which the curious may consult the Marquis d'Argens's *Memoirs of Count du Beauval* (English translation, London 1754), and the spurious *Mémoires de la Vie de Mylord Duc d'Ormond*, published at the Hague in 1737, and purporting to be translated from an English original written by himself. (English translation, London 1741.) Two pamphlet biographies of Ormonde were published during his exile: *Faithful Memoirs of the Life of James Butler, late Duke of Ormonde*, etc. London: Printed for W. Shropshire over against the Duke of Graftons in New Bond Street, 1732, pp. viii. 47; and *The Life and Character of James Butler, Late Duke Marquis and Earl of Ormond*, . . . by T. B., *with a particular account of all his Battles*, etc. London: Printed for R. Walker at the White Hart, without Temple Bar, and sold by the Booksellers of London and Westminster, 1739, pp. viii. 35. A larger work is *The Life of James, late Duke of Ormonde*. London: Printed for M. Cooper at the Globe in Paternoster Row, 1747, pp. vi., 544. The last describes Ormonde's earlier career in great detail, but dismisses his thirty years of exile in a few pages.

beloved, even Jean Jacques Rousseau has a good word for him. James Keith was the most fortunate of all. He wrote his name large in history as one of the greatest of Frederick's Marshals, and died a soldier's death at Hochkirchen in 1758. His statue stands in the Wilhelmsplatz at Berlin. Only six years ago (1889), the present German Emperor, 'to commemorate Field Marshal Keith's glorious services, and to the end that they should be for all time honoured and kept in memory,' ordered that the 22d Silesian Regiment should be named the Keith Regiment.

GEORGE KEITH,
10th Earl Marischal

SAM'S LETTERS

BEGINNING IN NOVEMBER 1718

Sam, *Duke of Ormonde.*

I

To PETER[1]

Peter,	*The King (James Stuart).*[2]	Mrs. Phillis,	*The King.*
Simon,	*Duke of Ormonde.*	Dutton,	*General Arthur Dillon.*[3]
Elmore,	*The Emperor Charles VI.*	Otway,	*The Regent Orleans.*
Barnaby,	*The Elector of Hanover (George I.).*	Herne,	*The Elector of Hanover.*
		Kerr,	*The King of Spain (Philip V.)*
Sorrell,	*Spain.*		
		Martel,	*Earl of Mar.*[4]

PARIS, NOVEMBER 4, 1718.

I WAS not a little Surprized at the receiving of Mr. Peter's Letter of the 9th October, and am very heartily concern'd

---

[1] The original of this letter, signed 'L. Sangston,' is in the Stuart Papers. Received at Rome, Nov. 25.

[2] See p. vii, note.

[3] Arthur, Count Dillon, younger son of Theobald, seventh Viscount Dillon, born 1670, outlawed as a Jacobite 1690; went to France in command of a body of men which his father had raised in Ireland for the service of Louis XIV., and which became the famous Régiment de Dillon. He saw much service in the French army, acted as Lieutenant-General under Tessé in Provence in 1707, and under Berwick in Dauphiné in 1709, and commanded the siege of Kaiserslautern in 1713. For many years he was James's chief agent in Paris. During the Regency his activity in the Stuart cause got him into serious trouble with the French authorities. He just escaped being sent to the Bastille. In 1721 James made him a titular earl. He died at St. Germains in 1733. A letter of condolence from James to his son, expressing the highest esteem for the General, is in the possession of Lord Dillon at Ditchley.

[4] John Erskine, eleventh Earl of Mar of the Erskine line, the famous 'Bobbing John,' who headed the rising of 1715. He accompanied James in his flight from Montrose, and remained his chief adviser till 1724, when he was succeeded in the Prince's confidence by John Hay. In the following year he severed his connection with the Stuarts. He died at Aix-la-Chapelle in 1732, aged fifty-seven. James made him a titular duke in 1715, and gave him the Garter in 1716.

at the news you sent to Mr. Simon.¹ It is sure the most barbarous Action that has been done for many ages. This subject is too Disagreeable to dwell upon, but I cannot but be impatient to know if that Elmore will persist in this inhuman way of acting. I own I fear it considering his strict friendship with Mr. Barnaby. I wish I may be mistaken. Pray God give Mr. Peter patience to bear this Mortification, and in his own time restore him to his Estate.

I must now inform you that I saw Mr. Simons. He told me that he hoped to set out to morrow Morning for Mr. Sorrell's where he hopes in God he may be able to serve Mrs. Phillis in her Law-suit. He says that as soon as it pleases God that he arrives there he will let Mrs. Phillis hear from him, with an account of her suit, but he desires that Mrs. Phillis shou'd not speak of this to any one.

Poor Dutton I fear may be clapt up for Debt by Mr. Otway at Hern's suit; I suppose he gives you a full account of his affairs. I shall obey your orders concerning the Factors you mention. I have no news to send you, only that every body here believes that Otway will begin a Lawsuit with Kerr. Simon desires that none but Martel may know of his design. Pray God preserve Peter. I am with all truth, etc.

II

To MARTEL ²

Martel,	*Mar.*	Martilla,	*Countess of Mar.*³
Paul,	*The King.*	Dutton,	*Dillon.*
Elmore,	*The Emperor.*	Otway,	*The Regent Orleans.*
Phillis,	*The King.*	Ker,	*The King of Spain.*

---

¹ The arrest of Princess Clementina. See Introduction.

² Original, signed 'L. Simpson,' in Stuart Papers. Received at Rome, Nov. 25.

³ In 1713 Mar married as his second wife Lady Frances Pierrepoint, second daughter of the Duke of Kingston, and sister of Lady Mary Wortley Montagu. She joined him at Rome in the winter of 1718. Her letters in the Stuart Papers show that she had some share of her sister's literary talent.

Belson, *Duke of Berwick*.[1] Simon, *Ormonde*.
Egan, *Sir Redmond Everard*.[2] Peter, *The King*.
Panton's, *Paris*. Amorsley, *Cardinal Alberoni*.

PARIS, NOVEMBER 4, 1718.

I HAVE been a good deal mortifyed at the Disagreeable News I had from Paul in his to me of the 19th October, and cannot but fear that Elmore will persist in what he has begun for the same reasons that have made him act so very inhumanly. I heartily wish that I may be mistaken. I must referr you to mine to Mrs. Phillis.

I hope before this time that Martilla is safely arrived; give me leave to desire you to make my compliments to her. Dutton gives you all the news that is stirring. It is not

---

[1] James Fitz-James, Duke of Berwick, Marshal of France, the natural son of James II. of England by Arabella Churchill, Marlborough's sister, was born at Moulins, Aug. 21, 1670, and educated in France. He served first in the British Army, but after the Revolution joined his father in France. He entered the French service, and in 1702 became a naturalised Frenchman. He became one of the most famous of French commanders, his greatest achievement being his campaign against the Anglo-Portuguese army in Spain in 1707, which culminated in the victory of Almanza. He was killed at the siege of Philipsbourg, June 12, 1734.

Berwick was a good friend to James, and rendered him invaluable service, though, naturally enough, he had no very great respect for his half-brother's character. Every effort was used to induce him to take the military command in Scotland in 1715, but he answered, with perfect justice, that he was a French subject and a Marshal of France, and that it was impossible for him to go to Scotland in face of the positive orders of the Regent. ' 'Tis neither consisting with my honour, my duty, my oaths, nor even with the King's interest or reputation, that I should desert like a trooper. It was with his Majesty's leave that I became a Frenchman, and I cannot depart from the vast obligations I now have incumbent upon me without breach of faith and public gratitude.'—Berwick to Mar, Feb. 12, 1716; Stuart Papers, printed in appendix to Mr. Percy M. Thornton's *Stuart Dynasty*. See also Berwick's *Mémoires*, vol. ii. p. 167. A study of Berwick's career entirely confirms the opinion of a certain Colonel Henry Esmond, whom most of us know: 'He was the sword and buckler indeed of the Stuart cause: there was no stain on his shield except the bar across it, which Marlborough's sister left him. Had Berwick been his father's heir, James the Third had assuredly sat on the English throne. He could dare, endure, strike, speak, be silent. The fire and genius perhaps he had not (that were given to baser men), but except these he had some of the best qualities of a leader.'—Thackeray's *Esmond*, book iii. chap. viii.

[2] Sir Redmond Everard was an active and confidential partisan of the Stuarts, and an intimate friend of Atterbury and of Ormonde. He went to Paris to meet Ormonde on the return of the latter from his Russian mission.

doubted but that Otway will go to law with Ker. Belson is to manage the suit.

Mrs. Egan left Mr. Panton's ten days ago, but Simon has not heard any thing of her or from her since her departure. I am still of the same opinion that I was in when I wrote last to Martel that if Ker does not begin the Law suit before Hilary term next that I fear and with reason that Mrs. Phillis' cause may be very desperate if not quite lost. If that Mr. Peter has had any dealing with Ker or Amorsley it is absolutely necessary that Simon shou'd be informed of it that he may take his measures accordingly. Do me the favour to make my Compliments to my friends, and believe me, etc.

III

Au CARD. ALBERONI

ALCALA, DECEMBRE LE PREMIER, 1718.

J'AY l'honneur d'informer votre Eminence par Monsieur de Crafton de mon arrivée. Il ne sçait rien de ce que vous avez mandé à monsieur le Prince de Chelamar, il croit seulement que je viene dans ce Pais en esperance de pouvoir servir le Roy mon Maitre en ce conjuncture ou il y a apparence de Guerre, et d'avoir azile ce que m'etoit refusé en France. Il m'etoit necessaire pour faciliter mon Sortir de ce pais là.

Je vous supplie Monseigneur de me faire sçavoir ce que je dois faire, et quels mesures je dois prendre. Monsieur de Crafton sçait que je n'ay pas envie d'etre connu. J'attends vos ordres avec impatience, et je suis avec tout le respect imaginable, etc.

[To CARDINAL ALBERONI. *Alcala, December* 1, 1718.

I HAVE the honour to inform your Eminence by M. de Crafton[1] of my arrival. He knows nothing of what you have told the Prince de Cella-

---

[1] General Crafton, who accompanied Ormonde to Spain, commanded an Irish regiment of dragoons in the Spanish service, raised in 1705. His name occurs frequently in the letters of Sir Toby Bourke, Jacobite representative at the Spanish Court in 1706, to Lord Caryll, which are among the Carte Manuscripts in the Bodleian Library.

mare;[1] he merely believes that I have come into this country in the hope that I may be able to serve the King my Master at this juncture when things look like war, and to obtain the asylum which was refused to me in France. He was necessary to me to facilitate my departure from that country.

I beg you, Monseigneur, to let me know what I ought to do and what steps I ought to take. M. de Crafton knows that I do not wish to be known. I eagerly await your orders, and I am with all imaginable respect, etc.

IV

Au CARD. ALBERONI

MADRID, DECEMBRE 4^{IEME}, 1718.

J'AY l'honneur de vous renvoyer les papiers que votre Eminence m'a donné hier au soir. Il me semble que l'on est trop enteté sur la Conquete de Norvegue, et que l'on ne songe ni propose aucun projet pour une Descente en Angleterre qu'après la reduction de Norvegue, ce que peut tirer en longeur, mais les Instructions que votre Eminence a donné a Monsieur de Lawless j'espere auront un si bon effet qu'ils reviendront de leur Entetement de poursuivre leurs desseins sur la Norvegue.

Touchant l'article de la France, je croy qu'ils se trompent, *p. 4.* car pendant l'autorité du duc d'Orleans et la bonne Correspondence entre l'Espagne et la Suede, La France ne sera jamais en amitié avec elle. Je oubliois hier au soir d'informer votre Eminence que j'ay raison de croire que je verois bien tot la personne qui a donné le Memoire. Par la premiere Poste j'en serois mieux informe. J'ay l'honneur d'etre avec toute la reconnoissance et le respect imaginable etc.

Si Monsieur de Lawless ne peut trouver Monsieur Guillemberg en Hollande, il pourra s'addresser à Monsieur Price qui estoit Resident de la part du Roy de Suede, et comme je croy il est encore, il est attaché à Monsieur de Gortz et tres bien Intentionee.

[To CARDINAL ALBERONI. *Madrid, December* 4, 1718.
I HAVE the honour to return the papers which your Eminence gave

---

[1] Antonio Giudice, Duke of Giovenazzo and Prince of Cellamare, went as Spanish Ambassador to France in 1715, and was expelled after the discovery of the plot narrated in the Introduction, p. xxx.

me last night. It seems to me that they¹ are too obstinately set on the conquest of Norway, and that they neither think of nor propose any project for an invasion of England till Norway has been reduced, which may be a long affair; but I hope that the instructions which your Eminence has given to M. de Lawless² will have so good an effect that they will give up the infatuation of pursuing their designs on Norway.

As regards France, I think they are mistaken, for during the rule of the Duke of Orleans, and the good understanding between Spain and Sweden, France will never be friendly with her (Sweden). I forgot last night to inform your Eminence that I have reason to believe that I shall very soon see the person who brought the memorial. By the first post I will be better informed as to this.—I have the honour, etc.

If M. de Lawless cannot find M. Gyllenborg³ in Holland he might address himself to M. Price, who was, and I understand still is, resident on behalf of the King of Sweden; he is attached to M. de Gortz,⁴ and very well disposed.]

V

To PETER⁵

Peter,	*The King.*	Andrew,	*Princess Maria Cle-*
Simon,	*Ormonde.*		*mentina.*
Mr. and Mrs. Ker,	*The King and Queen*	Amorsley,	*Alberoni.*
	of Spain.	Evans,	*England.*
Sangston,	*Ormonde.*	Mrs. Onslow,	*Duchess of Ormonde.*⁶
Paul,	*The King.*	Simson,	*Ormonde.*
Mrs. Phillis,	*The King.*	Kemp,	*The King of Sweden.*

MADRID, DECEMBER 5TH, 1718.

SIMON arrived at Mr. Ker's the first of December as Mr.

---

¹ Charles XII. of Sweden and his ministers.

² Sir Patrick Lawless was an Irish officer in the service of Spain. He had been Spanish agent in London in 1714, and had been obliged to withdraw to Holland on account of his connection with Jacobite intrigues. Alberoni had at this time sent him on a mission to Sweden, as to which see Letter XIII. He afterwards received orders to go to Amsterdam in order to join Ormonde in the event of his effecting a landing in England.—Stair to Craggs, March 29, 1719; State Papers, Foreign, France, 353.

³ Charles, Count Gyllenborg, born 1679; Swedish minister in London from 1703 to 1717; afterwards Councillor of State, President of the Council of Ministers, and Chancellor of the University of Upsala; died 1746. See Introduction, p. xxii.

⁴ George Henry, Baron de Gortz, became Minister of Finance to Charles XII. in 1715; executed March 3, 1719. See Introduction, p. xxii. He wrote his own epitaph: *Mors Regis, Fides in Regem est Mors mea.*

⁵ Original, signed 'L. Sangfield,' in Stuart Papers. Received at Rome, Jan. 17, 1719.

⁶ Ormonde's second wife, Lady Mary Somerset, daughter of the first Duke of

Sangston told me, where he received Mr. Paul's of the 2d of November. He told me, y[t] Mr. Paul assured him that he and Mrs. Phillis[1] were in good health which I am heartily glad of, and pray God to keep them so. I am very glad to see by Mr. Peters that he has heard from his Cousin Andrew[2] and that he and his Partners keep to their resolution of going on with their joynt Trade, and that their losses do not in the least dishearten them.

Since my Cousin[3] arrived he told me that he has been very kindly received by his friend Mr. Amorsley who was so kind as to invite him to come to pass some time with him, and assures him that he and his Bro[r] Ker are very willing to do every thing that reasonably can be expected or asked of them to forward the Match between Mrs. Phillis and Mr. Evans. Mrs. Phillis's Compliments were made to Mr. and Mrs. Ker and to my friend Amorsley who wou'd acquaint the above mention'd persons with it.

p. 5.

By the next Poste I shall be able, I believe, to inform Mrs. Phillis of some things concerning her affairs that will be satisfactory to her. Mrs. Onslow shall be acquainted with Mrs. Phillis's Goodness to her. Simson has not seen Sir P. Redmonds, nor does not designe it. Simson is private by his Cousin Amorsley's desire. I believe Ker and Kemp will joyn stocks; by my next I shall say more on this subject. I have the Paper of News Mr. Paul mentions, but have not shown it where it can do any harm. I wish Mrs. Phillis all imaginable happyness, and that she may soon see her Brother Andrew. —I am, etc.

Beaufort. By her he had two daughters, Elizabeth, who died unmarried in 1750, and Mary, who in 1710 married the first Earl of Ashburnham, and died *s. p.* in 1712. His first wife was Lady Anne Hyde, daughter of the Earl of Rochester.

[1] Marked in original, 'Princess.' Phillis elsewhere means James.
[2] 'Anderson' in original.
[3] Ormonde himself. So marked in original.

VI

To DUTTON [1]

Dutton,	*Dillon.*	Sorrell,	*Spain.*
Simons,	*Ormonde.*	Ker,	*The King of Spain.*
Amorslye,	*Alberoni.*	Phillis,	*The King.*
Digby,	*Dillon.*	Onslow,	*Ormonde.*

MADRID, DECR. 8TH, 1718.

My niece Simons has been very kindly received by her Aunt Amorslye. The Good old woman is ready to do her all the Kindness that she can reasonably expect. Mrs. Simons talked to her of her old friend Mrs. Digby, whom she remembers with all the Affection and Esteem that is possible, and to be short, desired me to propose to her that if she will come and live with Mrs. Sorrell she will give her a commission of Captain General, the pay of which is two thousand Pistoles a year; she will also give her a Government, and a Commanderie; she will also provide for her eldest son in the Army, and for her younger children in the Church. Mrs. Ker and Mrs. Amorslye desired Mrs. Simons to assure Mrs. Digby that they will have a particular care of her whole family. They desire that if Mrs. Digby approves of this that she will not lose any time in coming to them.

My Unckle Simons desires the same of you: it will be I am sure for my sister Phillis's Good, and I must press you not to delay coming, for reasons which I cant venture to inform you of.

p. 6. It was designed and Endeavoured that Onslow's being being here shou'd be a secret, but the Indiscretion of Sir Peter Redmans [2] will spoil that design; he has little credit with my Aunt Amorslye. What you may believe to be the reason of

---

[1] Copy, in Dillon's handwriting, in Stuart Papers, partly in cipher.

[2] Sir Peter Redmond was an officious ass who pestered the Jacobite leaders at this time with offers of his services. James wrote of him to Ormonde on Nov. 2, 1718: 'I find that one Sr. Peter Redmond hath a great vocation to be my man in those parts (Spain). I am sure I never promised him he should be so, and tho' I think few people more honest I know few more unfitt, all things considered, for such a nice business.'—Stuart Papers.

Redmond's letters to Mar in the Stuart Papers quite bear out this opinion. It

your being desired to come without delay keep to yourself. Mrs. Ker and her Sister Amorslye are very Affectionately my niece Phillis's friends, and I am sincerely your's.

VII

To CHARPENTIER

Charpentier, *The Earl Marischal.*[1]

MADRID, DECEMBER 8TH, 1718.

I DESIRE you will give yourself the trouble to come and meet your humble servant. Pray ask the Bearer for an Address how to write to me, and he will give you one that will inform you where you may find me. If you please to bring your Brother[2] with you he will be welcome. Pray keep your Journey a Secret, let not any one know where you are going. Believe me S^r, very sincerely, etc.

---

will be seen that Ormonde snubs him persistently. His pertinacity, however, was not altogether unrewarded, as James made him a titular baronet in 1717, and a baron in 1721. List of Jacobite Honours, *Notes and Queries*, third series, vol. ix. p. 71.

[2] George Keith, tenth and last Earl Marischal. As a lad he served under Marlborough. He was out in the '15, after which he escaped to the Continent, and was attainted, and his estates forfeited. As we have seen, he commanded the expedition to Scotland in 1719. After its failure he returned to Spain, where he lived for many years, being from time to time employed in negotiations on behalf of James. After 1745 he went to Prussia. He gained the high esteem of Frederick the Great, who sent him as ambassador first to Paris, and afterwards to Madrid, gave him the Black Eagle, and made him governor of Neuchatel. In 1759 he received a pardon from George II. and returned to Scotland. An Act having been passed enabling him to inherit, notwithstanding his attainder, any estate which might descend to him, he succeeded to the Kintore estates on the death of the fourth Earl of Kintore in 1761. Ultimately, at Frederick's urgent request, he went back to Prussia. He died at Potsdam in 1778.

[3] The Earl's younger brother, James Keith, has left a more famous name. He also was in the '15, and at Glenshiel. He then entered the Spanish service, which he quitted in 1728 for that of Russia. In 1747 he offered his services to Frederick the Great, who recognised his worth, made him almost at once one of his marshals, and bestowed on him his highest confidence. His subsequent biography is part of the history of Prussia. He fell at the head of his men on the disastrous day of Hochkirchen, Oct. 14, 1758, aged sixty-two. His unfinished Memoir is one of the most readable of autobiographies. The story of the brothers is well told by Dr. Hill Burton in *The Scot Abroad*. See Introduction, pp. xlii *et seq.*, lix.

VIII

Au CARD. ALBERONI

Guada Lama, Decembr. 9ieme, 1718.

Je viens de recevoir les Paquets que votre Eminence m'a envoyé. J'ay la les nouvelles de Londres et ne suis pas surpris de ce que le Parlement vient de faire. Je croy qu'il y a plus de Fanfaronade en leur manière de procedé que de vray courage, et ils croyent que leurs menaces de faire le Guerre intimideront la Cour d'Espagne et la feront soumettre à des conditions telles qu'ils voudront imposer.

J'ay avis de Londres que l'on a cassé douze Regiments, ce qui n'a pas l'apparence de Guerre. Je viens de recevoir une lettre de Paris du 2ieme Novembre qui m'assure que la personne en question devoit partir pour venir à Madrid en trois semaines ou plutot. Nous n'avons donc rien a craindre sur son compte.

Je croy que votre Eminence sera d'opinion que la personne que j'ay laissé devoit etre depeché sans perdre du tems. J'ay oublié de demander à votre Eminence que vous vouliez donner vos Ordres pour quatre ou cinque cens Granades. J'ai l'honneur d'etre avec tout le respect imaginable, etc.

[To Cardinal Alberoni. *Guada Lama, December 9, 1718.*

I have just received the packets which your Eminence has sent me. I find in them news from London, and am not surprised at what Parliament has done. I think there is more bluster than real courage in their way of acting. They think that their threats of war will intimidate the Court of Spain, and make it submit to such conditions as they choose to impose.[1]

I hear from London that they have disbanded twelve regiments, which does not look like war. I have just received a letter from Paris dated November 2, which assures me that the person in question should leave for Madrid in three weeks or less. We have then nothing to fear on his account.

I think your Eminence will be of opinion that the person I have left ought to be set on his way without delay. I forgot to ask your Eminence to give orders for four or five hundred grenades.—I have the honour, etc.

---

[1] Parliament met on Nov. 11, o.s. The debate on the Address produced a warm discussion on Spanish affairs. Stanhope and Craggs resolutely defended

IX

To DUTTON

Dutton,	*Dillon.*	Mrs. Phillis,	*The King.*
Kemp,	*The King of Sweden.*	Frank,	*Mar* (?)
Mrs. Ker,	*The King of Spain.*	Evans,	*England.*
Mrs. Gregory,	*The King of Sweden.*	Mrs. Digby,	*Dillon.*

GUADA LAMA, DECEMBER 9TH, 1718.

I HAVE just received your obliging letter of the 29th Novr. I find you have seen or are to see one of Kemp's friends that is to come lately from him. I hope and have great reasons to believe that Mrs. Ker and Mr. Gregory will be marryed, but I think there is no need of acquainting Mrs. Phillis of it yet, for if she knows it, it will not be a secret. Frank will certainly inform his friends of it, which may make it publick and break the match. I do not acquaint her with some things that relate to Mr. Ker and Evans; they are for her Good; but my aunt Amorsley desires me not to be too hasty in informing my niece of it.[1] I wrote to you last night, and am still of the same opinion as to Mrs. Digby. I am faithfully your's.

I expect Mrs. Kemp's friend.

---

the action of the Government. Stanhope said in the House of Lords that it was high time to check the growth of the naval power of Spain, in order to protect the trade of British subjects, who had been violently oppressed by the Spaniards, that he thought it an honour to have been amongst those who advised Byng's instructions (see Introduction, p. xxv.), and that he was ready to answer for them with his head. The Government had substantial majorities in both Houses—thirty-three in the Lords and sixty-one in the Commons. See Mahon, vol. i. p. 325.

[1] James was not very good at keeping a secret. In January 1719 we find Forman M'Mahon, one of his adherents in Paris, imploring him not to write to the notorious Olive Trant about affairs of State. 'She has but too many acquaintances of both sexes,' he says, 'and I fear that her Vanity and Indiscretion will always get the better of her duty.'—Stuart Papers. This was the lady immortalised in Bolingbroke's well-known picture of the exiled court in 1715: 'Care and hope sat on every busy Irish face. Those who could read and write had letters to show, and those who had not arrived to this pitch of erudition had their secrets to whisper. No sex was excluded from this ministry. Fanny Oglethorpe, whom you must have seen in England, kept her corner in it, and

X

Au CARD. ALBERONI

Mon Parent, *Bagenal*.

VALLADOLID, DECEMBRE 17ᴱᴹᴱ, 1718.

J'ay receu ce matin les Paquets qui etoient destinées pour mon Parent. J'ay lu des copies des lettres, et je ne doute pas que les Originaux n'auront les effets desirés.

p. 8 Je suis bien sensible à l'honneur de votre Souvenir, et des Civilités que je recois icy par les ordres de votre Eminence. J'attends avec impatience l'arrivée de mon Parent pour luy pouvoir parler avant que de Cacheter mon Packet, mais il est passé sept heures, et monsieur le President demande mes lettres devant huit. J'ay l'honneur d'etre avec tout le respect imaginable, etc.

[To CARDINAL ALBERONI. *Valladolid, December* 17, 1718.

I HAVE received this morning the packets which were intended for my kinsman. I have read copies of the letters, and I have no doubt that the originals will have the desired effect.

I am very sensible of the honour of your remembrance, and of the courtesies which I receive here by your Eminence's orders. I await with impatience the arrival of my kinsman, so as to be able to speak to him before sealing my packet, but it is past seven o'clock, and the President asks for my letters before eight.—I have the honour, etc.]

Olive Trant was the great wheel of our machine.'—Letter to Sir William Windham, *Works*, vol. i. p. 34.

James quite understood that he was kept in the dark. Just before receiving Ormonde's letter of December 17, detailing Alberoni's project (Letter XIII. *infra*), he had written from Rome to Dillon: 'It is very manifest to me that a *mistery is made to me*, but it being *almost as clear* that *that reserve must be for a greater good*, I have no other uneasiness upon that score but the *want of knowing positively what I wish and guess is a doing*, for I know *Onslow* (Ormonde) too well to suspect him of being wanting to me in anything, and not to be perswaded that he always dos what lyes in his power to *serve me* in the most essential manner.'—James to Dillon, Jan. 24, 1719, Stuart Papers.

XI

To DUTTON[1]

Dutton,	*Dillon.*	Phillis,	*The King.*
My Niece Simons,	*Ormonde.*	Mrs. Frances,	*Mar* (?)
My Bror. Samson,	*Ormonde.*	Peter,	*The King.*
Mrs. Sangston,	*Ormonde.*	Marsfield,	*The King's Marriage.*
Mrs. Digby,	*Dillon.*	Mrs. Simson,	*Ormonde.*
My Aunt,	*Alberoni.*	My Niece,	*The King.*

VALLADOLID, DECEMBER 17TH, 1718.

I HAVE just received your's of the 6th December. I have little to trouble you with but to thank you for your concern for my niece Simons. My Bror. Samson told me he shou'd be very glad to see the two young Students[2] you mention, and to do them all the good he can. I referr you to Mrs. Sangston's that she wrote to Mrs. Digby of the 8th Instant, and hope that Mrs. Digby will not delay what is desired of her. My Aunt is truly very kind to my sister Phillis, depend on it. I am glad your Creditors do not pursue you with that violence they did, but I hope you will not compound with them. I have receiv^d Mrs. Frances's and the Copys of Peter's account. I am sorry the poor man had not better luck with his friend Marsfield. I hear Mrs. Simson writes to him by this Poste. Pray do not delay what Mrs. Simons desires of you, it is for my Niece's Service, and you are willing to do the Girl all the Good you can. Believe me Sincerely, etc.

XII

Au CARD. ALBERONI

Mon Parent, *Bagenal.*

VALLADOLID, DECEMBRE 17^{IEME}. 1718.

JE viens de recevoir les Paquets que vous aviez eu la bonté de m'envoyer par un Courier Extraordinaire. Je voy les reso-

---

[1] Copy in Dillon's writing in Stuart Papers.

[2] Probably the two Keiths. Even before the receipt of Ormonde's letter to the Earl Marischal (*ante*, p. 9) they had thought of seeking service in Spain. James Keith was advised to offer his services for the Sicilian expedition of 1718, but at that time, he candidly says, he was 'too much in love to think of quitting Paris.'—*Memoir*, p. 35.

lutions du Parlement qui ne m'ont pas surpris non plus que les Mensonges atroces qui sont dans l'harangue. C'est un procedé dont on doit s'attendre d'un tel Gouvernenent. Je suis bien aise qu'ils méprisent tant leurs enemys qu'ils n'augmentent point leurs Troupes depuis la grande reforme qu'ils ont fait, il faut agir avec vigueur et ne point perdre la Saison, la fin de Mars sera trop tard. Mon Parent doit appuyer sur ca : il n'est pas encore arrivé, d'abord qu'il vienne je le depescheray.

p. 9.

Je n'ay point eu des lettres de mon Pais. Je suis averti de Paris qu'il y a deux Messieurs qui viennent me trouver et qu'ils ont des Paquets pour moy. Le Chevalier s'en est allé a Rome etant averti qu'il n'etoit pas en Seureté ailleurs. J'ay l'honneur d'etre, etc.

[To CARDINAL ALBERONI. *Valladolid, December* 17, 1718.

I HAVE just received the packets which you have been good enough to send me by a special courier. I see the resolutions of the Parliament, which have not surprised me, any more than have the atrocious falsehoods which the speech contains.[1] It is what one might expect from such a Government. I am very glad that they so despise their enemies that they have not increased the number of their troops since the great reduction [2] which they have made. We must act with energy and not lose the season; the end of March will be too late. My kinsman ought to press this. He has not yet arrived; as soon as he comes I will send him.

I have had no letters from home. I am informed from Paris that two gentlemen are coming to find me, and that they have letters for me. The Chevalier has gone to Rome, being warned that he was not safe elsewhere.—I have the honour, etc.]

---

[1] See p. 10, note.
[2] *Réforme* is here used in its obsolete military sense.

XIII

To PETER[1]

14/a,	Alberoni.	165,	England.
21/l,	Sir Patrick Lawless.	475,	Scotland.
507,	The King of Sweden.	9/m,	The Earl Marischal.
496, 497,	The King of Spain.	14/e,	Brigadier Campbell.[2]
249,	The Elector of Hanover.	23/b,	Bagenal.
289,	The King.	508,	Sweden.
Elmore,	The Emperor.	Morpeth,	James Murray.[3]

VALLADOLID, DECEMBER 17TH, 1718.

ACCORDING to my Promise in my last I must now inform you of the Situation of your affairs, which, I hope, will be satisfactory to you.

14/a came to me privately and informed me that he had sent 21/l to 507 to engage him to enter into an Alliance with 497, that the Chief Article was to endeavour to dethrone 249 their common enemy, that he carryed Bills with him to enable 507 to make the attempt with promises of an Annual Subsidy provided he enter'd into the Allyance.

The next time I saw 14/a he asked me what I demanded as necessary to make an attempt to restore 289. I told him seven or eight thousand men with 15,000 arms and Ammunition proportionable. He answered that 496 wou'd be willing to grant that number if he were in a condition, but considering that the greatest part of their Troops are in Sicily, and that they are threat^{ned} with an Invasion from France in two Places, *p.* 10

---

[1] Original in Stuart Papers, entirely in cipher. Received at Rome January 26, 1719.

[2] Brigadier Campbell of Ormidale. He went to Scotland at the time of the '15, and was one of the Jacobite prisoners taken to Carlisle. Bishop Nicolson, of Carlisle, writing to the Archbishop of York on Dec. 17, 1716, says of him: 'This unfortunate man was in no engagement, and had not been four days in Scotland, when he was taken in one of the Western Islands. He has been in foreign service (under the Czar, the Venetians, etc.), from his youth; and I dare parole for him, if the Government sends him back to the Adriatick Coast, he'l never petition for another return into his native country.' Ten days later the Bishop writes that the Brigadier has 'slipp'd thro' the gaolers fingers, and is gone off.'—*Miscellany of the Scottish History Society*, vol. i. pp. 531, 535. He was at this time at Bordeaux.—Brigadier Campbell to Mar, Bordeaux, December 14, 1718, Stuart Papers.

[3] The Hon. James Murray, second son of the fifth Viscount Stormont, and

that is, by the way of Roussillon and Navarre, they cou'd not spare a man, but that they wou'd give 15,000 arms and Ammunition proportionable, and that money shou'd not be wanting to enable 507 to invade 165.

He also shew'd me a Memorial sent him by the Prince de Chelamar from a Minister of 507 who is come to Paris; in that 507 desires to enter into a Strict Alliance with 497, and the Chief Article is to depose 249, others relate to Germany, which are too long to be inserted here. The person that brought the Memorial arrived at Paris the Evening that I left it, as I have been since informed. He was very desirous to see me, and has sent me a Copy of the Memorial by an Express by Sea, which I expect every day, and he was to follow it in a few days.

I made 14/a another visit at his desire, and after some discourse he told me that 497 wou'd give five thousand men, of which four thousand are to be foot, a thousand Troopers, of which three hundred with their horses, the rest with their Arms and Accoutrements, and two months pay for them, ten field Pieces, and a thousand Barrels of Powder and fifteen Thousand Arms for foot, with every thing necessary to convoy them.

I told 14/a that it wou'd be necessary to have a Diversion made in 475, and since he cou'd not spare any more men I desired him to let us have two or three thousand arms to send thither. He asked me if there was any man of consideration, to go with them. I told him of 9/m who was in Paris, and he desired me to write to him to come with all despatch and as privately as possible. I will write to 14/c to come hither as soon as I know where he is. As to the Gentlemen at Bordeaux they shall have timely notice.

I am now in Valladolid, where 496 thought fitt I shou'd reside. 14/a desired me to let him have one in whom I cou'd confide to send to 507 to press him to invade England before the Spring, especially since 496 had come to a resolution of

p. 11.

---

brother of Lord Chief-Justice Mansfield. He was admitted to the Faculty of Advocates in 1710, was for some time M.P. for the Elgin Burghs, and under Queen Anne was one of the Commissioners for settling the trade with France. In 1718 he joined James at Urbino, and became one of his confidential advisers. He negotiated the marriage with Princess Clementina, and acted as the Prince's proxy at the marriage ceremony at Bologna. James, in 1721, created him titular Earl of Dunbar. He died at Avignon in 1770.

sending Troops, which he had not done when 21/*l* was despatched. 23/*b* is the person I left with 14/*a*. I expect him here every hour in his way to 508, and his Instructions are to tell 507 that no money will be given by 497 unless he consents to make an Attempt upon 165 in the time proposed.

23/*b* will have Instructions to propose to 507 to send two Thousand men to 475 with five Thousand Arms.

14/*a* seem'd very uneasy at your Situation in Italy. He fears that your person is not in Safety considering the late inhuman Proceedings against the Princess. He thinks Rome the worst place for you to be in because of Elmore's Spys, and the Difficulty you will have of getting privately from thence, and he does not think your person safer there than elsewhere. Upon what he says, and the letter I received from Morpeth of the ninth November, it is my humble opinion that you ought to come to 497 with all expedition, that you may be out of Elmore's power, and your presence is necessary here either to Embark with the Troops if you can arrive in Time, or to follow as soon as possible, for 14/*a* is of opinion that the Opportunity must not be lost tho' you shou'd not arrive in *p.* 12. due time, and if it be possible you ought to be here to go to 165 with the Troops.

14/*a* desires that this design may be the Strictest Secret, and I beg of you not to acquaint Cardinal Aquaviva [1] with it, and when you come away to give it out that it is for your own Safety.

XIV

Au CARD. ALBERONI

Maître Pierre, *The King.*   Une personne, *Ezekiel Hamilton.*[2]
Mon Parent, *Bagenal.*

VALLADOLID, DECEMBRE 22, 1718.

J'AY receu, Monsieur, l'honneur de la votre hier au soir avec les Incluses, et suis ravi que vous avez pris la resolution d'envoyer

---

[1] Cardinal Acquaviva was in charge of Spanish affairs at Rome.

[2] The Rev. Ezekiel Hamilton, formerly attached to James's household, and for some time private secretary to Ormonde. He had carried messages between Bolingbroke and Ormonde and the English Jacobites in 1715. See Bolingbroke's Letter to Sir William Windham, *Works*, vol. i. p. 57.

B

chercher Maitre Pierre au plus tot. Je vous avoue que je Craignis fort pour sa Seureté etant dans un pais ou il est environne d'enemis.

J'envoye selon vos desirs une personne de qui je reponds et une que Pierre m'a depeché quand j'etois dans le Nord, c'est une persone sage et discrete et que j'ay connu long tems.

Je suis de votre opinion, Monsieur, qu'il est impracticable qu'il puisse venir par terre, mais en quel lieu il doit s'embarquer, et de quelle maniere il faut faire le voyage c'est une chose si delicate et de telle consequence que je n'ose prendre sur moy de le conseiller; il faut qu'il en decide lui meme, mais je lui supplieray de bien garder le secret, qu'il se derobe avec deux ou trois personnes tout au plus, et qu'il se deguise en homme de livrée.

p. 13.

Vous avez eu la bonté de me dire que vous aviez dessein que Monsieur de Cammock le meneroit. Il n'y a que deux moyens de s'embarquer ou dans un vaisseau de Guerre ou de prendre un petit batiment qui est neutre; il y a de risque dans tous les deux. Un Officer de mer peut mieux en juger, et ne sachant pas ou est l'Escadra de Monsieur Bing, j'aurois encore plus de Difficulté à donner mon opinion.

Dans la relation des nouvelles de Londres vous voyez la raison pourquoi tant de Toris se sont absenté du Parlement, mais quand les Subsides seront en question je suis seur qu'ils seront assidues, et qu'avec les Whigs mecontents ils embarasseront si fort la Cour qu'ils auront beaucoup de peine a lever de l'argent pour fournir aux depens de la guerre.

Mon Parent arriva icy Dimanche et partit Lundi. Il m'a rendu l'honneur de la votre, je croy que son voyage est tres necessaire, et qu'il aura un bon effet. J'ay l'honneur d'etre.

[To Cardinal Alberoni. *Valladolid, December 25,* 1718.

Sir,—Last night I had the honour to receive your letter, with its enclosures. I am delighted to hear that you have decided to send for Mr. Peter as soon as possible. I confess that I fear much for his safety, as he is in a country where he is surrounded by enemies.

I send as you desire a person for whom I can answer, one whom Peter sent me when I was in the North; he is a judicious and discreet person, and I have known him a long time.

I am of your opinion, sir, that it is impossible for him to come by land, but at what place he ought to embark, and how he ought to make the voyage, are matters so delicate and of such consequence that I dare not take it upon myself to advise him. He must decide himself; but I shall beg him to keep the secret well, to escape with two or three persons at the most, and to disguise himself as a man in livery.

You have been good enough to tell me that you intended that M. de Cammock[1] should bring him. There are only two ways of making the voyage, either to come in a ship of war or to take a little vessel which is neutral. There is some risk in either way. A naval officer would be the best judge, and as I do not know the whereabouts of Byng's[2] fleet, I should have all the more difficulty in giving an opinion.

You see in the account of the news from London how it is that so many of the Tories have absented themselves from Parliament; but when the taxes come on for discussion, I am sure that they will be assiduous in their attendance, and that with the discontented Whigs they will embarrass the Court so much that they will have great difficulty in raising money to meet the expenses of the war.

My kinsman arrived here on Sunday, and left on Monday. He delivered your letter to me. I think his journey is very necessary, and will have a good effect.—I have the honour, etc.]

XV

To PETER[3]

Peter, *The King.*   14/a, *Cardinal Alberoni.*
         496, *The King of Spain.*

VALLADOLID, DECEMBER 22, 1718.

14/a sent me by express yours of November 27th with the Enclosed Copy of yours of the 23d November to Cardinal

---

[1] George Cammock, or Camocke, had been a captain in the British navy, from which he was dismissed in 1715 for gross breaches of discipline. He entered the Spanish service, and was made a rear-admiral. At the battle of Cape Passaro (see p. xxvi), he held a junior command. He tried to bribe both Byng and Walton to betray their trust, and take their ships into a Spanish port. It may be recorded to his credit that he was kind to James Keith when the latter was in great poverty in Madrid in 1720.

[2] Admiral Sir George Byng, the victor of Cape Passaro, created Viscount Torrington in 1721. It was he who chased the French fleet out of the Firth of Forth at the time of the Jacobite attempt of 1708. He was the father of the unfortunate Admiral who was shot at Portsmouth in 1757, '*pour encourager les autres,*' as Voltaire said.

[3] Original in Stuart Papers, entirely in cipher. Received at Rome, January 24, 1719.

Aquaviva. In mine of 17th December I gave you a full and particular account of your affairs here, of which I now send you a Duplicate.

p. 14.
By 14/a advice I send you the Bearer to acquaint you that it is 496's desire that you shou'd come away Immediately and as privately as possible, and not to bring above two or three persons at most. I suppose 14/a will write himself. He says you cannot be too cautious: that he is afraid you have spys in your house, and the shorter warning you give those who come with you the better. It is his opinion and mine that you ought to disguise yourself even in a Livery if it be necessary.

14/a desired me to give my opinion as to the place and manner of Embarkation. He thinks it impracticable for you to come by land. He told me that he designed that Cammock shou'd attend you if you pleased to make use of him.

There are but two ways of going, either in a Ship of War or in a Small Vessel. There is danger in either way; and this is so nice a point, and of so great importance, that I can't take it upon me to give my advice, and therefore you will be pleased to decide it yourself, especially since you will certainly know whether Bing's squadron be in your parts, which is more than I do.

As to Sir Peter Redmonds,[1] I never saw him, and never had any Correspondence with him. I believe he is very honest, but I fear he is Indiscreet, which proceeds from his zeal.

p. 15.
There cannot be too much care taken to keep the Secret. Shou'd any account of it be sent to England, and the letters be intercepted, the Cypher may be easily found out.

Be pleased not to acquaint even Cardinal Aquaviva with the contents of my Letter of the 17th December, for I believe that 14/a has not informed him of it. 14/a insists upon the Strictest Secrecy, all depending upon it.

I desire that the Bearer may be sent back to me, unless you have use for him. God give Peter a Good Journey.

---

[1] See James's letter in Appendix, p. 199, which Ormonde had evidently received.

XVI

To MARTEL

Martel, *Mar.* Martilla, *Countess of Mar.*
Dutton, *Dillon.* Morpeth, *James Murray.*

VALLADOLID, DECEMBER 23, 1718.

I HAD the favour of yours of the 2d December, which I shall more fully Answer by the Poste, because I have not time to put it now in Cypher, and if it were not so, it might discover that the Bearer is Charged with. I expect the Pacquet you mention to be sent by Dutton. My Compliments pray to Martilla and Morpeth. I am Glad the former is safely arrived. I have not heard of the foolish Pamphlett you mention.[1]

XVII

Au CARDIN. ALBERONI

Pierre, *The King.*

VALLADOLID, DECEMBRE 24, 1718.

JE viens, Monsieur, de recevoir l'honneur de la votre ce matin, et je croy qu'a l'heure qu'il est le courier vous a rendu la mienne, et que la personne que je vous ay envoyé avec des Depesches pour Pierre est arrivée aussi.

Il est absolument necessaire que Pierre vienne sans perdre du

---

[1] This probably refers to an anonymous pamphlet entitled *A Letter from a Gentleman at R(ome) to a Friend at L(ondon)*, printed in London in 1718. (French translation, Amsterdam, 1718). It purports to give an account of affairs at the exiled Court, and describes James's blind zeal for Popery, and his bias towards the Scotch. According to the author, Mar had gained James's entire confidence, had filled the household with Scotch hangers-on of his own, and had sent Ormonde on his futile mission to Russia merely to get him out of the way. The pamphlet was attributed to the Abbé Strickland. Mar affected to despise it, but it evidently annoyed him. In a letter to Campbell of Glendaruel on December 20, 1718, he speaks of the author as a 'little conceited, empty, meddling prigg.'—Stuart Papers. Copies of the pamphlet in English and French, with contemporary manuscript annotations, are preserved in the Hanover Papers.—Stowe MSS., 231, ff., 161-171. See Appendix, p. 203.

tems a fin qu'il ne soit plus au pouvoir de ses enemis, et qu'il soit à Porté ou d'aller avec ou de Suivre selon qu'on Jugera à Propos. Comme le Succès depend du Secret et de la Promte execution que Pierre fasse, toute la Diligence qu'il puisse faire il ne sera pas ici trop tot.

Puisque une bonne Partie de l'affaire doit etre Executee à Cadiz, je croy qu'il vaut Mieux de ne la point Separer, car la Jonction est tres incertaine, et sujette à bien des accidens. Il est vrai qu'etant dans ce lieu là couvrira mieux le Jeu, mais le Trajet est bien plus grand, pour ce qui me regarde il faut que j'aille avec ; dans l'autre endroit il y a bien des accidens qui pourront m'empecher de les Joindre. J'ay l'honneur d'etre, etc.

[To CARDINAL ALBERONI. *Valladolid, December* 24, 1718.

SIR,—I have just had the honour to receive your letter this morning. I suppose that by this time the courier has given you mine, and that the person whom I sent to you with despatches for Peter has also arrived.

It is absolutely necessary that Peter should come without loss of time, so that he may be no longer in the power of his enemies, and may be in a position either to accompany or to follow (the expedition), as may be thought expedient. As success depends on secrecy and on promptitude of action, Peter will not with all possible diligence be here too soon.

Since a good part of the work must be carried out at Cadiz, I think it would be better not to divide it, for meeting is very uncertain and very liable to accidents. It is true that being in that (other) place will hide the game better, but the journey is much longer. So far as I am concerned, I must go with them ; in the other place there are many accidents which might prevent me from joining them.—I have the honour, etc.]

XVIII

Au CARD. ALBERONI

VALLADOLID, DECEMBRE 25, 1718.

JE viens, monsieur, de recevoir l'honneur de la votre du 24 Decembre par le Courier, et je suis bien faché d'apprendre les Nouvelles que vous me mandez. J'espere que ca n'a point de rapport à notre Affaire.

Ce que vous dites d'une Passeport est une chose assez delicate, et aussi ce que vous proposez de publier parce que ca pourroit avoir un mauvais effet dans mon Pais. Je ne croy pas que ma demeure ici peut Decouvrir le Dessein puisque l'affaire doit etre executée à Cadiz. Si vous croyez le passeport necessaire il faut que Monsieur de Lawless soit informé de le verité aussi bien que mes amis. Les Lettres ecrites pour la Passeport arriveront à Paris bien plutot que les avis puissent etre Donné au Nord et à mon Pais. Les Lettres par la Poste seront apparemment plus incertaines qu'elles n'etoyent, et la voye de la mer etant aussi bien incertaine peut tirer en Longueur, Pour ce qui regarde Pampelone je croy que c'a n'auroit pas l'effet proposé. J'attends vos ordres et je vous souhaite les bonnes Fetes. J'ay l'honneur d'etre, etc.

[To CARDINAL ALBERONI. *Valladolid, December* 25, 1718.

I HAVE just had the honour to receive by the courier your letter of December 24, and I am very sorry to learn the news which you tell me.[1] I hope that it will not affect our enterprise.

What you say about a passport is a somewhat delicate matter, and also what you propose to publish, because it might have a bad effect in my country. I do not think that my stay here can reveal the project, because the work must be carried out at Cadiz. Should you think a passport necessary, M. de Lawless must be informed of the truth, as well as my friends. Letters written for the passport will get to Paris long before the news could reach the north or my country. Letters sent by post will apparently be more uncertain than they were, and the sea route being also very uncertain, might lead to delay. As regards Pampeluna, I think that that would not have the effect proposed.

I await your orders, and I wish you a happy feast.[2]—I have the honour, etc.]

XIX

Au CARD. ALBERONI

VALLADOLID, DECEMBRE 31, 1718.

JE viens, Monsieur, de recevoir l'honneur de la votre du 28, avec l'incluse, qui ne peut pas manquer d'avoir un tres bon Effet. Je suis bien faché d'apprendre qu'il y a tant de Gens Arrestes. Je suis fort en peine pour celui qui est de ma connoissance, il

---

[1] Evidently the discovery of the conspiracy against the Regent Orleans, referred to in Introduction, p. xxx. Cellamare was arrested on December 9.

[2] 'A happy feast'—*buona festa*—a phrase still in common use among Catholics.

n'etoit pas auparavant trop bien avec le Gouverneur, à qui cette affaire donnera bien à penser, voyant qu'il y a tant de Gens de distinction, et le Mecontement si General.

Je suis trop interessé en toutes manieres pour manquer en la moindre part qui depend de moy. J'attends avec impatience l'arrivée des personnes que me doivent informer de l'etat de nos amis, et les resolutions qu'ils ont pris de nous seconder selon ce que je leurs ay mandé. Je leurs ay bien recommandé le Secret.

p. 18. Il n'y a guere d'apparence d'avoir l'homme que vous avez nommé pour chef. J'aurois été bien aise qu'il fut de la Compagnie, mais j'espere qu'on ne manquera pas des Gens qui savent le Chemin parce que j'ay prié mes amis d'envoyer des personnes bien entendues et bien informées de tout ce qus regarde cette affaire.

J'ay receu une lettre de 4^{ieme} de ce mois du Capitaine du petit vaisseau qui doit venir. Il me mande que le tems etoit si orageux qu'il n'osoit pas se mettre en mer, mais qu'il ne manqueroit pas de faire voile à la premiere occasion. Pour l'autre on ne pouvoit pas avoir des nouvelles car le Passeport n'etoit envoyé que le 19 de ce mois. Vous pouvez etre assuré, monsieur, que d'abord que je recoive des nouvelles je vous le manderay par un Courier. Je suis ravi qu'on travaille à force de votre Coté, car le tems est precieux.

Pour Monsr. le Baron de Walef je le connois pour un fort Galant homme, et un à qui je crois on se peut fier, un officier de son caractere est utile en toutes occasions.

J'ay receu, Monsieur, des Lettres de Monsieur le Chevalier Redmonds, qui me pressent fort de consentir qu'il me vienne voir. Je ne voulus pas lui donner response jusqu'à ce que fut votre Sentiment la dessus. Je ne le connois pas, mais on dit qu'il est fort zelé ; pour la reste je n'en repond pas.

J'espere que la personne que je vous ay envoyé est parti. J'ay l'honneur d'etre.

[To CARDINAL ALBERONI. *Valladolid*, *December* 31, 1718.

SIR,—I have just had the honour to receive your letter of the 28th with the enclosure, which cannot fail to have a very good effect. I am very sorry to hear that there have been so many people arrested. I am very anxious about my acquaintance. He has not hitherto stood very well with the Governor, to whom this affair will give much matter for thought, seeing that there are so many persons of distinction concerned, and that the discontent is so general.

I am in every way too much interested to fail in the smallest part which depends on me. I await with impatience the arrival of those who can inform me of the state of our friends, and the resolutions which they have taken to support us according to what I have told them. I have strongly urged secrecy upon them.

There is not much prospect of getting the man whom you mentioned as leader. I should have been glad if he could have gone with the expedition, but I hope that we shall not lack people who know the way, as I have begged my friends to send persons skilful and well-informed with regard to all that concerns this matter.

I have received a letter of the 4th of this month from the captain of the little vessel which is to come. He tells me that the weather has been so stormy that he dared not put to sea, but that he will not fail to set sail on the first opportunity. As to the other, one could not have news, for the passport was only sent on the 19th of this month. You may rest assured, sir, that as soon as I receive news I shall inform you of it by a courier. I am delighted that on your side they are working with such energy, for time is precious.

As to M. le Baron de Walef,[1] I know him as a man of honour, and one on whom I believe we can rely; an officer of his character is always useful.

I have received letters from Sir Peter Redmond, in which he strongly urged me to let him come to see me. I did not wish to give him an answer until (I knew) your opinion, and I do not know him, but they say he is very zealous; beyond that I do not answer for him.

I hope that the person whom I have sent to you has left.—I have the honour, etc.]

XX

Au CARDINAL ALBERONI

Maitre Pierre, *The King.*   Mon Parent, ?

VALLADOLID, JANVIER 4, 1719.

J'AY receu, Monsieur, par l'ordinaire d'hier l'honneur de la

---

[1] Blaise Henri de Corte, Baron de Walef, a Belgian literary and political adventurer. He seems to have been in the British military service about 1714. He was concerned in the Duc du Maine's conspiracy, in connection with which he was at this time on a mission to Spain. See the article on his life by M. Daunou in the *Biographie Universelle.* He acted also as a Jacobite agent. According to Mr. Edward Armstrong, it was probably through him that the secret of the Cadiz expedition was discovered.—*Elisabeth Farnese,* p. 120.

votre du 31 Decembre avec l'incluse de Maitre Pierre, qui n'est qu'une copie de la Lettre que vous m'avez envoyé il y a dix Jours.

Je suis fort en peine pour mes Lettres n'ayant point eu par le derniere ordinaire, et comme vous remarquez, je crains fort qu'elles ne soyent ouvertes comme sont toutes celles qui vont d'une pais à l'autre ; j'ay pris toutes les precautions possibles, et je suis bien seur qu'elles ne pourront pas etre Dechifrées.

Je vous envoye une Lettre que j'ay receu ce matin de mon Parent. Je connois Deux des ces messieurs dont il fait mention, et je suis seur qu'ils sont chargé de quelque commission pour moy.

Je veux envoyer une personne en mon pais au plutot, et je vous supplie, monsieur, d'avoir la bonté de donner vos ordres pour avoir un vaisseau pret ou à Bilbao ou à St. Sebastian comme vous jugerez à propos et que le maitre soit aux Ordres de celui que j'envoyeray. Je suppose qu'il ne sera un batiment Espagnol. Il faut que l'equipage croit que le vaisseau soit destiné pour l'Hollande, mais quand il sera au mer le Patron peut gagner quelque Rade d'Angleterre et mettre la personne à terre, ca seroit à souhait. Si non, il faut qu'il aille en Hollande, d'ou il pourra passer en Angleterre en vingt-quatre heures. Le petit batiment n'etant pas arrivé, il n'y a d'autre moyen.

Je suis bien aise de Scavoir que tout sera pret à la fin du mois. Faites moy le plaisir de m'informer du tems que vous proposez que les voitures se mettrent en Chemin a fin que la personne que j'envoye puisse en informer les Gens de Confiance, et qu'ils puissent prendre leurs mesures pour nous seconder.

Je ne connois pas les deux messieurs dont vous faites mention ; apparemment je les verray bientot. Je suis impatient de Scavoir s'il y a des Nouvelles de Monsieur de Lawless. J'ay l'honneur d'etre, etc.

[To Cardinal Alberoni. *Valladolid, January* 4, 1719.

Sir,—I had the honour to receive by yesterday's post your letter of December 31, with the enclosure from Mr. Peter, which is merely a copy of the letter which you sent me ten days ago.

I am very anxious about my letters. I had none by the last post, and, as you observe, I greatly fear that they may be opened, as all letters are which go from one country to the other. I have taken all possible precautions, and I am quite sure that they cannot be deciphered.

I send you a letter which I have received this morning from my kinsman. I know two of those gentlemen whom he mentions, and I am sure that they are intrusted with some commission for me.

I wish to send some one to my own country as soon as may be, and I beg you, Sir, to have the goodness to give orders to have a vessel ready either at Bilbao or at St. Sebastian, as you think best, and that the master may take his orders from the person whom I will send. I suppose that it will not be a Spanish ship. The crew must think that the ship is bound for Holland, but after she is at sea the captain can make for some English roadstead, and land my messenger. That will be all one could desire. If not, he must land in Holland, whence he can reach England in twenty-four hours. The little vessel not having arrived, there is no other way.

I am very glad to know that all will be ready at the end of the month. Do me the kindness to inform me of the time at which you propose that the ships should sail,[1] so that my messenger may be able to tell our friends, and that they may be able to take their measures to help us.

I do not know the two gentlemen whom you mention, apparently I shall see them soon. I am anxious to know if there is any news from M. de Lawless.—I have the honour, etc.]

XXI

Au BARON DE WALEF

VALLADOLID, JANVIER 4, 1719.

J'ay receu la votre du 27 du mois passé, je vous suis bien obligé d'interet que vous prenez en ce qui me regarde.

J'espere que vous reussirez en ce que enterprenez puisque vous me mandez c'est pour les interets de mon Roy.

Je serois toujours bien aise de vous voir et de vous rendre Service en ce que dependera de moy etant tres parfaitement votre tres, etc.

Ne vous donnez pas la peine de venir ici.

[TO BARON DE WALEF. *Valladolid, January* 4, 1719.

I HAVE received your letter of the 27th of last month. I am greatly obliged to you for the interest which you take in the matter which concerns me.

---

[1] Throughout the letters *voiture* is used in its obsolete sense of a ship or vessel.

I hope that you will succeed in what you are undertaking, since you tell me that it is for the interest of my king.

I shall always be very glad to see you, and to be of service to you so far as it is in my power, being very much your, etc.

Do not take the trouble to come here.]

XXII

To SIR P. REDMONDS

VALLADOLID, JANUARY 7TH, 1719.

I HAVE had the favour of two of yours, and shou'd be very glad to have seen you, but no body comes to me here, nor can I abuse the retreat that I am allowed here, therefore I hope you will not take it ill that I cannot have the satisfaction of receiving the visit you designed me. I am very sensible of your zeal for the King's Interest, and also of your personal merit, which makes me regrett the not having it in my power to see you here. Believe me very much, etc.

XXIII

Au CARD. ALBERONI

VALLADOLID, JANVIER 7^{ieme}, 1719.

J'AY receu, Monsieur, hier au Soir l'honneur de votre Lettre par le Courier avec l'incluse pour St. Sebastien, et ce Matin j'ai eu la votre du 4^{ieme} par l'ordinaire avec les deux Paquets et les imprimées qui sont tres bien ecrites. Il n'en avoit point de mon Pais, dont je m'etonne, mais j'etois bien aise de voir par une de mon Correspondent à Bordeaux du 24^{ieme} Decembre qu'il avoit receu les miennes du 5 et 12eme Decembre, et qui les avoit envoyé à Paris. Les autres etoient des imprimés des Copies des Lettres du Prince de Chelamar au Cardinal Alberoni.

J'envoye une personne avec la lettre à St. Sebastian que est qualifié en toutes manieres, et dont j'en reponds de la fidelité et de la discretion, et qui sera chargé d'avertir nos amis de tout ce que nous faisons, et d'etre informé lui meme des Mesures qu'ils ont pris pour nous seconder, et qui reviendra à la Courogne avec des Gens Capables de gouverner la Barque. Il ne portera point de lettres.

Quand j'ay pensé d'aller du coté de Cadiz ce n'etoit point avec dessein d'entrer dans la place, mais de rester à quelques lieues de là a fin de n'etre pas connu, et d'etre à porté de me mettre dans la voiture quelques heures avant qu'il seroit pret a marcher. Mais je me Conforme à votre Sentiment et tacheray de me rendre au premier lieu autant en Cachet que je puisse, mais j'aurai de la difficulte ne Connoissant pas le Pais ni la Langue, et il n'y a pas un de mes Gens qui Savent l'Espagnol ; j'attendray encore de vos Nouvelles la Dessus. Je crois qu'il vaut mieux que je ne parte d'ici trop tot ni de m'arreter en Chemin de peur d'en donner l'alarme. Je suis bien aise que la Personne est Embarquée. J'espere qu'il pourroit etre arrivé si les vents soyent favorables, et que Pierre gardera bien le Secret, et se depeschera, car il y va de son tout.

A ce qui regarde monsieur le Chevalier Redmonds, je feray comme vous le Souhaitez, et je vous Supplie de m'envoyer les Messieurs Irlandois de qui mon Parent fait mention dans sa lettre, s'ils viennent à Madrid. J'ay l'honneur d'etre, etc.

Je vous envoye le nom que vous demandez, c'est Jacques.

[To CARDINAL ALBERONI. *Valladolid, January 7*, 1719.

SIR,—I had last night the honour to receive your letter by the courier, with the enclosure for St. Sebastian, and this morning I have had by post yours of the 4th, with the two packets and the printed documents, which are very well written. There was nothing from my country, at which I am surprised, but I was very glad to see by a letter of my correspondent at Bordeaux, of December 24th, that he had received mine of December 5th and 12th, and that he had sent them to Paris. The others were prints of the copies of the letters of the Prince of Cellamare to Cardinal Alberoni.

I send with the letter to St. Sebastian a person who is in every way qualified, and for whose fidelity and discretion I will be responsible. He is charged to inform our friends of all that we are doing, and to make himself acquainted with the measures they have taken to support us, and he will return to Corunna with people capable of taking charge of the ship. He will carry no letters.

When I thought of going towards Cadiz, I did not intend to enter the place, but to remain at a few leagues distance, so as not to be known, and to be at hand to go on board a few hours before the expedition was ready to leave. But I defer to your opinion, and shall try to reach the formerly arranged place as secretly as I can. I shall have some difficulty, however, as I know neither the country nor the language, and not one of my household knows Spanish; I shall still wait to hear from you as to this. I think it would be well that I should neither start from here too soon nor stop on the way, for fear of giving the alarm. I am very glad that the person[1] has sailed. I hope that he may have arrived if the winds are favourable, and that Peter will keep the secret well, and make haste, for his all is at stake.

As regards Sir P. Redmond, I will do as you wish, and I beg you to send me the Irish gentlemen whom my kinsman mentioned in his letter, if they come to Madrid. I have the honour to be, etc.

I send you the name you ask,—it is James.]

XXIV

Au CARD. ALBERONI[2]

Dutton, *Dillon*.   Melchior, *M. Seminati*.

DE VALADOLIDE, JAN. YE 11TH, 1719.

J'AY eu hier au Matin, Monsieur, l'honneur de la votre du 7me. Ce que vous fait mention touchant la voiture couvrira bien le jeu. Il est absolument necessaire que j'ay quelques Aids de camps qui parle francois ou Anglois, autrement je ne pourois pas me faire entendre; ayez la bonté d'y penser.

J'ay envoyé mon Secretaire et un autre Monsr nommé Lesly qui a eu l'honneur de vous faire la reverence; c'est un Garçon du bien de merite de qui j'en repond des toutes manieres. J'ay envoyé deux de peur que un pouroit manquer par quelque accident.

Je suis faché que vous n'avez pas eu des Nouvelles encore de Monr de Lawles. J'espere que mon Parent sera arrivée a bon port. Je vous envoy un papier que j'ay receu de mon Amy Dutton par la main de un des ces deux Messieurs qui ont eu l'honneur de vous rendre leurs devoirs. C'este d'une vielle date. Il n'osoit pas l'envoyer par la poste.

J'ay encore receu par l'ordinaire d'hier, du 15 du passé, du Maitre de la petite voiture que le tems a continué si orageux depuis qu'il a ecrit sa premiere lettre qu'il n'osoit pas ce mettre en mer, mais qu'il ne perdra pas la premiere occasion. J'ay

---

[1] Probably Cammock, who was to arrange for James's voyage from Italy.
[2] The hand changes here.

avis de Paris que la Personne qui vous a envoyé la memoire devoit partir le 9me du mois passé, mais qu'il se trouve bien embarassé coment passer la frontiere.

J'ay receu une lettre d'un amy de Dutton, qu'il a prié me faire scavoir que mes lettres etoient arrivées. Il n'osoit pas ecrire de peur que ses lettres ne furent ouvertes, pendant ce Vacarme.

Mon Correspondant a Bordeaux me mande du 31me Decembr qu'il a receu le passeport, et qu'il depeschera son Voiture. Je suis etonné que j'ay ne pas des Lettres de mon pays. Je suis avec beaucoup de respect, etc.

P.S.—J'ay envoyé une memoire à Melchior pour vous presenter. J'ay le receu de Paris. Si vous avez a faire de la personne qui s'ofre, vous aurez la bonté de me le faire scavoir. Il est de mon Pays, et fort habile en son metier.

Vous aurois la bonté de bruler la memoire que j'ay l'honneur de vous envoyer en cette lettre.

[To CARDINAL ALBERONI. *Valludolid, January* 11, 1719.

SIR,—I had the honour to receive your letter of the 7th yesterday morning. What you mention about the vessel will hide the game well. It is absolutely necessary that I should have some aides-de-camp who speak French or English, otherwise I shall not be able to make myself understood. Be so good as to keep this in mind.

I have sent my secretary and another gentleman named Lesly, who has had the honour of paying his respects to you. He is a young man of much merit, and I will answer for him in every way. I have sent two in case one of them should fail by any accident.

I am sorry that you have still no news of M. de Lawless. I hope that my kinsman has landed safely. I send you a paper which I have received from my friend Dutton by the hand of one of these two gentleman who have had the honour of paying their respects to you. It is of old date. He dared not send it by the post.

I have received by yesterday's post another letter, dated the 15th of last month, from the master of the little vessel, who says that since he wrote his former letter the weather has continued so stormy that he has not dared to put to sea, but that he will not lose the first opportunity. I have news from Paris that the person who sent you the memoir[1] was to leave on the 9th of last month, but that he is much at a loss as to how he is to pass the frontier.

I have received a letter from a friend of Dutton's, whom he had asked

---

[1] See Letter XIII.

to let me know that any letters had arrived. He dared not write himself for fear his letters should be opened during these troubles.

My correspondent at Bordeaux, writing on December 31, tells me that he has received the passport, and that he will despatch his vessel. I am surprised that I have no letters from my own country.

I am with much respect, etc.

P.S.—I have sent a memorial to Melchior to present to you. I have received it from Paris. If you have any employment for the person who presents himself, be so good as to let me know. He is a countryman of mine, and very skilful in his business.

You will have the goodness to burn the memorial which I have the honour to send you in this letter.]

XXV

Au PRINCE de CAMPO FLORIDO[1]

Stamfort, *Ezekiel Hamilton.*

De Valadolide, Jan. ye 13, 1719.

J'ay receu l'honneur de la votre et vous suis infinim^t obligé de la bontés que vous avez en vous donnant le peine de trouver les moiens pour faciliter le voyage de mon Amy, et que vous voulez bien avoir la bontés de tachér de procurer un Vaisseau pour Monsr Stamfort, que a l'heur qu'il est a l'honneur de vous faire la reverence et de vous assurer de mes tres humbles Respects et de ma reconnoissance des toutes vous Civilitez, dont je ne puis jamais perdre la Souvenir.

J'espere qu'on trouvera une Batiment prête et la personne qui est allé à Bilbao j'espere qu'il peut etre a cet heur en Hollande.

Vous verres, Monsieur, un autre personne qui a eu l'honneur de vous faire la reverence. Il doit aller avec Monsieur Stamfort; il sont destinés pour la meme Pays, mais j'ay laissé en leurs pouvoirs de s'accorder entre eux de quell maniere ils iront, etc.

---

[1] The Prince of Campo Florido, Captain-General at San Sebastian, was a Sicilian, and had been General of the Galleys in Sicily. On the transfer of Sicily to the House of Savoy at the Treaty of Utrecht, he elected to remain in the service of the Catholic king, and came to Spain.—St. Philippe, vol. iii. p. 99.

[To the Prince of Campo Florido. *Valladolid, January* 13, 1719.

I have had the honour to receive your letter, and am infinitely obliged to you for your kindness in having taken the trouble to facilitate my friend's voyage, and that you should have the kindness to try to procure a vessel for M. Stamfort, who now has the honour to pay his respects to you, and to assure you of my profound respect, and of my gratitude for all your courtesies, which I can never forget.

I hope that a vessel will be found ready, and as to the person who went to Bilbao, I hope he is at this moment in Holland.

You will see, Sir, another person who has had the honour of paying his respects to you. He ought to go with M. Stamfort; they are bound for the same country, but I have left it to them to arrange between them how they are to travel.]

XXVI

Au CARD. ALBERONI

Amorsley, *Alberoni.*   Un de mes Parens, *Everard.*
Mon Secretaire,   *David Kennedy.*

De Valadolide, le 17me Janvier 1719.   *p. 25.*

J'ay eu, Monsieur, l'honneur de la votre du 14me du courant ce matin, et par cette Ordinaire une Lettre de mon Amy a Paris du 31me X^{bre}, qui me mande qu'il a receu et envoyé toutes mes Lettres, et qu'il y avoit une personne arrivé de mon pays que mes Amis m'ont envoyé selon ce que j'avois desirée, mais voyant l'impossibilité de passer la Frontiere il toit obligée d'aller en Bretagne pour s'enbarquer sur la petite Barque, ou de trouver quelque autre moyen de me venir joindre. La même personne a fait scavoir a mes amis qu'a l'avenir il ne falloit plus Songer a envoyer par la ffrance. Il me mande aussi que la personne qui a donné la memoire au P. Chelamar etoit parti le 30me du passé pour la Bretagne pour tascher de joindre et d'accompagner celuy de qui J'ay ci dessus fais mention.

Dutton m'ecrit au 3me de ce mois qu'il avoit receu toutes mes Lettres et qu'il a toute la reconnaissance imaginable des bontez que ses Amis ont pour lui, et particulierment a Monsr Amorsley. Il mande qu'il prend ses mesures pour etre en Etat de jouir de leur bontez. Ce Seigneur Ecossois qui vous maves fait envoyer chercher et [*sic*] parti de Paris le 30me du passé pour se rendre a Madrid.

Quand J'ay receu vos ordres de Monsieur de Chelam{}^r J'ay renvoyé un des mes Parens qui m'etoit venus Joindre de la part de mes Amis, pour leur faire Scavoire que je vous allé trouver par votre desir, et prié de bien garder le Secret, que vous maviez mandé par le Prince, et que Je les ay desirée de m'envoyer au plus tot quelques Officiers de la Marine bien qualifiés de Commander et a minformer des mesures qu'ils preneroient pour nous seconder, et des toutes choses qui seroient necessaires en cas que vous auriez quelque projet. Si vous en aviez, l'execution ne pouvoit etre retardé plus long tems que le Commencement du Fevrier. Comme sa [sic] J'espere qu'il n'aura pas tant de Risques, car si nous pouvons debarquer les peuples sont si generallement bien disposés que nous ne manquerons point du Monde.

Monsieur de Crafton est tres brave homme et j'aurai assez du credit pour lui humanizer. Il me sera utile, mais il n y a pas a faire de lui confier le Secret.

Le President facilitera mon Voyage et pourroit le cacher mieux que personne.

Je souhaiterai d'avoir mon Secretaire; il est homme de Confiance, j'en reponde; mais il n'a pas sceu que vous m'aviez envoyé chercher.

J'ay un Parent, Cornette dans le Regiment de O'driscoll, il se nomme Monsieur de Esmonde; je serois bien aise de l'avoir avec moi.

J'ay l'honeur d'etre avec respect, etc.

[To CARDINAL ALBERONI. *Valladolid, January* 17, 1719.

SIR,—I have this morning had the honour to receive your letter of the 14th inst., and by the same post I have a letter, dated December 31, from my friend in Paris, who tells me that he has received and sent all my letters, and that a person had arrived from my country whom my friends had sent according to my desire; but as it is impossible to pass the frontier, he has been obliged to go into Brittany so that he may embark in a small vessel, or to find some other means of joining me. The same person has informed my friends that in future they must not think of sending by France. He tells me also that the person who has given the memorial to the Prince of Cellamare left for Brittany on the 30th of last month to try to join and accompany him whom I have mentioned above.

Dutton writes to me on the third of this month that he had received all my letters, and that he feels all imaginable gratitude for the kindness of his friends, and particularly to Mr. Amorsley. He says that he is taking measures to be in a position to benefit by their kindness. That Scottish lord whom you made me send for left Paris for Madrid on the 30th of last month.

When I received your orders from M. de Cellamare, I sent back one of my kinsmen,[1] who had come to join me on behalf of my friends, to let them know that I have gone to meet you by your desire, and to beg them to keep the secret which you had told me through the Prince, and have also asked them to send me some naval officers well qualified to command, and to inform me of the measures which they are taking to support us, and of everything which may be necessary in case you have any plan. If you have, its execution could not be postponed beyond the beginning of February. Thus I hope that there will not be so much risk; for, if we are able to land, the people are generally so well disposed that we shall not lack men.

M. de Crafton is a very worthy man, and I have influence enough to make him tractable. He will be of use to me, but it will not do to trust him with the secret.

The President will facilitate my voyage, and will be able to conceal it better than any one.

I should like to have my Secretary; I will answer for him as a trustworthy man; but he does not know that you have sent for me.

I have a kinsman named Esmonde, who is a Cornet in O'Driscoll's regiment; I should be very glad to have him with me.—I have the honour, etc.]

XXVII

NOTE.—His G. wrote to ye P. of Campo Florido ye 17th Jan., but there was no Copy taken of it, it being only Complim^t.

XXVIII

AU P. DE CAMPO FLORIDO

Mon Secretaire, *David Kennedy.*

DE VALADOLIDE, JAN. YE 20TH, 1719.

MONSIEUR,—J'ay l'honneur de la Lettre que votre Excellence me fait l'honneur de m'ecrire du 12me par la derniere poste, et vous suis je infiniment obligé des attentions qu'il vous a plût

---

[1] Sir Redmond Everard, who had come to Paris before Ormonde left.

d' avoir pour les Messieurs qui vous ont été recomendes. J'espere qu'ils sont partis et bien avancez en leur Chemins. J'ay mille remercim^ts a vous rendre aussi, Monsieur, pour la peine que vous avez d'avoir Soin des lettres, et pour ce qui regardoit mon Secretaire. Il est arrivé a Madrid apres avoir été Prisonier 5 Semaines.

Je vous Supplie, Monsieur, d'etre tres persuadé que je suis penetré des vos bontez, et que je seray ravi d'avoir des occasions pour vous temoigner ma reconnoissance, ayant l'honeur [sic] d'etre avec beaucoup de Respect, de votre Excellence, etc.

(Signed)   LE D. D'ORMONDE.

J'entends un peu L'italien.

[To PRINCE OF CAMPO FLORIDO. *Valladolid, January* 20, 1719.

SIR,—I have had the honour to receive by the last post the letter of the 12th, which your Excellency did me the honour to address to me, and I am infinitely obliged to you for the courtesies which you have been pleased to show to the gentlemen who were recommended to you. I hope they have left, and that they are well on their way. I also owe you a thousand thanks for your trouble in taking care of the letters, and with regard to my secretary. He has reached Madrid, after having been a prisoner for five weeks.[1]

I beg you, sir, to rest assured that I greatly appreciate your kindness, and that I will be delighted to have an opportunity of showing my gratitude to you.—I have the honour, etc.

(Signed)   THE DUKE OF ORMONDE.

I understand Italian a little.]

XXIX

AU CARD. ALBERONI PAR UN COURIER

Stamfort, *Ezekiel Hamilton*.   Mon Parent, *Sir R. Everard*.
Dutton, *Dillon*.

DE VAL. LE 21me JANVIER 1719.

CE Matin, Monsieur, J'ay eu l'honneur de vos deux lettres du 18me et du 20me. Je n'ay pas des nouvelles de la personne que vous en faits mention qui par Mepris a eté renvoyé pour

---

[1] David Kennedy, Ormonde's secretary, had been arrested on the French frontier.—Brigadier Campbell to Mar. Bordeaux, Dec. 14, 1718.—Stuart Papers.

venir icy. Je ne voye pas coment cette mesentendus est arrivé car j'avois eu l'honneur d'ecrire a Monsr le P. de Campo Florido pour lui Expliquer mes desirs touchant Monsr Stamfort mon Secretaire et l'autre persone. N'ayant point des nouvelles de la derniere j'espere qu'ils sont partis ensemble.

La persone qui est alle joindre mon Ami en la Bretagne pour tascher de se rendre en ce pays est celui qui est venu du pays ou Monsr de Lawles est destinée. Je suis bien faché que vous n'avez pas des nouvelles du dernier. Il sera a Souhaiter qu'on eut quelque response de ce qu'il a proposé en cas qu'il soit arrivé. J'espere que Mon Parent arrivera au bon port.

J'attend le Compte de Mareschall avec impatience, affin qu'il peut partir avec les outils pour son Pays. Il est parti de Paris le 30me X^{bre}. Il y a beaucoup des Messieurs de son Pays a Paris et aux Environs de Bordeaux. J'avois pensé qu'il sera necessaire de les avertir affin qu'ils se tient prête pour passer, mais Je craignois que sa [sic] peut decouvrir l'affaire et des deux inconvenients il faut prendre le moindre. Il sera a Souhaiter qu'ils furent en leur pais, mais il y aura beaucoup de difficultés a les y faire passer.

J'attend Mon Secretaire cet Soir et suis bien impatient pour l'arrivé du petit Batiment.

Apparament Monsieur le Baron Walef sera icy dans un jour ou deux. Je vous suis bien obligé de la bonté, Monsr, que vous avez d'avoir envoier cherché Monsr d'Esmonde et d'avoir Songé aux Aides de Camp.

J'ecriray a la persone qui s'offert de venir au plus tot. Il est fort entendus en son metier. Je crois que Dutton est embarrassé comment se tirer de l'affaire cette vacarme le rendra difficile.

Il y a trois Officiers Ecossois a Madrid que je prend la liberté de vous recommender. Ils ont du merite mais ils sont aux Abois n'ayant point d'argent. Si j'etois en Etat de les fournir je ne vous dirai rien de leur necessités.

J'espere de vous rendre bonne Compte de Monsieur de Crafton quand je l'auray aupres de moy. J'ay l'hon^r, etc.

P.S.—J'espere qu'on metra une bonne Quantité des pierres a fusil. Il fera bon qu'il y a des Armuriers.

[To Card. Alberoni by a Courier. *Valladolid, January* 21, 1719.]

Sir,—I had this morning the honour to receive your two letters of the 18th and the 20th. I have no news of the person whom you mention, who by mistake has been sent back to come here. I do not see how that misunderstanding has arisen, for I had had the honour to write to the Prince of Campo Florido to explain to him my wishes regarding Mr. Stamfort, my secretary, and the other person. As I have no news of the latter, I hope they have set out together.

The person who has gone to join my friend in Brittany to try to reach this country is the same who has come from the country to which Sir Patrick Lawless is bound. I am very sorry that you have no news of the latter. It is to be hoped that there will be some response to the proposals which he has made, supposing him to have arrived. I hope that my kinsman will arrive in safety.[1]

I am eagerly awaiting the Earl Marischal, in order that he may set out for his country with the arms. He left Paris on the 30th December. There are many gentlemen of his country in Paris and in the neighbourhood of Bordeaux.[2] I had thought that it would be necessary to warn them so that they could hold themselves ready to cross, but I feared that that might reveal the project, and of two evils we must choose the less. It will be desirable that they should be in their own country, but there will be much difficulty in getting them over.

I expect my secretary this evening. I am very impatient for the arrival of the little vessel.

Apparently Baron Walef will be here in a day or two. I am greatly indebted to you, sir, for your kindness in having sent for Mr. Esmond, and in having thought about the aides-de-camp.

I shall write to the person who offers his services to come as soon as possible. He knows his business well. I think Dutton is puzzled how to withdraw from the affair.[3] This disturbance will make it difficult.

There are three Scotch officers at Madrid whom I take the liberty of recommending to you. They have merit; but they are in great straits as they have no money. If I were in a condition to supply them I would not mention their necessities to you.

---

[1] *i.e.* that Everard will arrive in England.

[2] Among the Scottish exiles in France were Seaforth and Campbell of Glendaruel, at Paris; Tullibardine at Orleans; and at Bordeaux, General Gordon, who took command of the Jacobite army in the '15 after Mar's departure; Brigadier Campbell, Lord George Murray, Lochiel, Keppoch, M'Dougall of Lorn, and M'Kenzie of Avoch. Many of the exiles were in great poverty. A letter from Robert Gordon to Mar (Bordeaux, Feb. 7, 1719, Stuart Papers) gives the names of some who were in urgent need, including Brigadier Campbell, Lord George Murray, Keppoch, and M'Dougall of Lorn.

[3] *i.e.* from the French service.

I hope to give you a good account of M. de Crafton when I have him beside me. I have the honour, etc.

P.S.—I hope that a good quantity of gun-flints will be supplied. It will also be well to have some armourers.]

XXX

Au CARD. ALBERONI, par l'ordinaire

Val., le 21me Janvier 1719.

Je viens, Monsieur, de recevoir une Lettre du Duc de Liria, dont j'ay l'honneur de vous envoyer une Copie traduite de l'Anglois en Francois, mot a mot. Je Souhaiteray de scavoir votre Sentiment avant que je fasse reponse. Je l'attendrai et suis avec Respect plus que personne, Monsieur, votre, etc.

[To Card. Alberoni, by post. *Valladolid, January 21, 1719.*

Sir,—I have just received a letter from the Duc de Liria,[1] of which I have the honour to send you a copy translated from English into French, word for word. I would like to know your opinion before answering it. I shall wait for it.—I am, etc.]

XXXI

Au PRINCE CAMPO FLORIDO

Stamfort, *Ezekiel Hamilton.*

Val., 24th Janvier 1719.

Monsr,—J'ai eu l'honneur de recevoir la lettre que v. E. m'a ecrite le 19re (comme elle est datee). Je suis ravi d'apprendre que Mr Lesley estoit arrivé. Je vous suis infiniment obligé de la peine que V. E. s'est donné pour faciliter l'embarquement de ces trois Messieurs, et la maniere que V. E. a prise aura j'espere l'effet desirée, et que par ce moien nous pourrons avoir des Nouvelles. Mes lettres ne doivent etre remplis que de

---

[1] The Duke of Liria, Berwick's eldest son, commanded an Irish regiment in the Spanish service, which was at this time stationed at Gerona. He was an ardent Jacobite. He had written to James on Jan. 10, expressing his zeal and devotion (Stuart Papers), and seems to have offered his services for Ormonde's expedition. See Letter XLIII.

emoignages de reconnoissance des attentions qu'il vous a plus avoir pour cet affaire. Permettez que je prends la liberté d'envoyer l'incluse p^r Mr Stampfort ; en cas qu'il soit parti, je Souhaiterai avoir la lettre renvoyée. J'espere que V. E. me fait la justice d'etre tres persuadé que j'ai l'honneur avec beaucoup de respect et plus que personne de V. E, le tres, etc.

[To the PRINCE OF CAMPO FLORIDO. *Valladolid*, 24*th Jan*. 1719.

SIR,—I have had the honour to receive your Excellency's letter, dated the 19th. I am delighted to hear that Mr. Lesley has arrived. I am infinitely obliged for the trouble which your Excellency has taken to assist the embarkation of these three gentlemen, and I hope that the way which your Excellency has taken will have the desired effect, and that by these means we will be able to get news. My letters ought to be full of nothing but expressions of gratitude for the trouble which you have been pleased to take about this affair. Allow me to take the liberty of sending the enclosed for Mr. Stamfort ; in case he has left I should like to have the letter returned.

I hope your Excellency will do me the justice to be assured that I have the honour, etc.

XXXII

Au CARD. ALBERONI P^R COURIER

Pierre, *The King*.

VALADOLIDE, LE 25IER JANVIER 1719.

CE moment, Monsr, je viens de voir Monsr le Baron de Walefe. Il m'a dit une Nouvelle que j'espere ne se trouvera pas veritable, qui est la morte du Roy de Suede ; mais je crains puis qu'elle vient de vous.

Il m'a aussy dit que La France estoit declarée qu'est la cause que la poste n'estoit pas arrivée. Je suis tres impatient pour l'arrivé de la petite Voiture avec les personnes qu'elle doit mener, mais j'aprehende forte que la voiture ne poura sortir du Lieu ou Elle est. J'espere que mes Soupsons sont mal fondes. Monsr le Baron m'a dit que vous aviez dessein de donner une Voiture a Monsr de Macdonnell. C'est un bon Garçon, mais il n'a jamais mené aucune Voiture, ny ne scait pas la Route ; il peut etre utille dans un autre Metier.

Mon Secretaire m'a dit qu'il n'y avoit que cinq pieces. Je

croyois que vous estiez d'accord d'en donner dix et 15,000 Outils avec tout ce que leurs estoit necessaire, mais la meme personne m'a dit qu'il n'y avoit que douse. J'espere qu'il s'est trompé. Monsr Le Baron m'a dit qu'il y aura 25 mille pistolles, Vous m'aviez dit qu'il y aura pour deux mois de gages. Il sera bon d'avoir quelque somme en cas de necessité au commencement, mais j'espere qu'il n'i aura pas besoin de la toucher. Vous aurez la bonté de me faire Scavoir votre sentiment et vos intentions sur ce que j'ai l'honneur de vous écrire.

Je ne veux pas hazarder cette lettre par la poste. Pour les outils il faut s'il est possible avoir des Bayonettes.

Je suis impatient d'avoir des Nouvelles de Pierre. Je m'etonne qu'il n'y en a pas de Mr de Lawless. J'ay l'honneur d'etre avec respect et plus que personne, etc.

(Sig^d) Le Colonel Comerfort.

P.S.—Le Baron est-il informé de l'affair de Monsr Lawless et de mon parent?

[To Card. Alberoni, by courier. *Valladolid, January 25, 1719.*

Sir,—I have this moment seen Baron de Walef. He has told me a piece of news which I hope will not turn out to be true—the death of the King of Sweden; but I am afraid it may be so, as the news comes from you.[1]

He also told me that France has declared war, which is the reason why the post has not arrived. I am very impatient for the arrival of the little vessel and the people whom she ought to bring; but I am very much afraid that she will not be able to leave the place where she is. I hope that my suspicions are ill-founded. The Baron tells me that you thought of giving a ship to M. de Macdonnell. He is a good fellow; but he has never commanded a ship, and does not know the course. He might be useful in another capacity.

My secretary tells me that that there are only five guns. I thought that you had agreed to give ten, and fifteen thousand muskets and their appurtenances, but the same person tells me that there are only twelve thousand. I hope he is mistaken. The Baron tells me that there will be twenty-five thousand pistoles. You told me that there would be enough for two months' pay. It will be well to have some money in case of need at the beginning; but I hope there will be no need to use it. Be so good as to let me know your views and your intentions on the matter on which I have the honour to write to you.

---

[1] See Introduction, p. xxxi.

I do not wish to risk this letter by the post. It will be desirable to have bayonets for the muskets if possible.

I am anxious to have news of Peter. I am surprised that there is none of M. de Lawless. I have the honour, etc.

(Signed) COLONEL COMERFORT.[1]

P.S.—Does the Baron know of the affair of M. Lawless and my kinsman?]

XXXIII[2]

Au CARDINAL ALBERONI p^r COURIER

Stamfort, *Ezekiel Hamilton.*   Mon Parent, *Bagenal.*

N.B.—This following letter was changed and not sent.

LE 26IE JANVIER 1719.

JE suis bien Surpris, Monsr, de voir arriver les deux Messieurs que je croyois estre bien avancés en leur voyage. Monsr Stamfort a eu l'honneur a ce qu'il m'a dit de vous ecrire de Burgos, pour vous informer des ordres qu'il a reçu de prince de Florido. Cecy est un misentendu bien a contretemps, car sens [*sic*] les ordres qu'ils ont reçu ils allerent s'embarquer le vent estant devenu favorable, ce qu'il n'avoit este de Six Semaines. Ces Messieurs partiront demain au grand Matin. Je souhaite qu'ils pouront trouver un Batiment pret, et un vent favourable. Vous aurez reçu une lettre de mon Parent; il a parti Samdy derniere a quatre heures aprez midy, et je croi que le vent a continué favourable de dedepuis. Je les ai fort recommandé de faire leurs possible pour nous envoyer des Pillotes et des jens [*sic*] a notre recontre pour nous informer s'il y a des Vesseaux de guerre en mer, et ou ils doivent croiser; voila tout ce qu'on peut faire.

Le vent a esté favourable a ce que ces Messrs croyent qu'ils esperent que mon Parent est arrivé en hollande. Monsr Stampfort m'a dit qu'il croyoit qu'il y avoit des Irlandois a Bilbao qui pouroient servir des Pillottes. Il y en a un qui s'appelle Allexandre Tullo. Il a esté employe dans la derniere affaire d'Ecosse pour transporter des Armes, et depuis de ramener plusieurs Seigneurs et Officiers qui estoient obligez de se sauver

---

[1] Ormonde frequently passed under this name in France.
[2] This letter is crossed out in the manuscript.

en France. Je croy qu'il sera bon de luy faire venir a la prem^{re} Endroit sens qu'il sent pour quel Service il sera destine. Il y a un autre a St. Sebastien qui s'appelle Robert Lambert. On dit que c'est un honest homme, et habil en son metier. Le Prince de Florido pourra s'informer de son charactere, et s'il repond a ce que l'on souhaite, je croy qu'il sera bon qu'il fut envoyé au premier lieu. Je croi qu'il y a a Cadix un qui s'appelle le Chevalier Sherlock. Il sera bon de s'informer de sa capacité. Je sçai qu'il est fort honest homme.

J'ai appris par ces Messieurs que la guerre estoit declaré en France, c'estoit le Bruit a Bilbao. J'ai l'honneur d'etre avec beaucoup de respect, Monsr, etc.

(Signé) Le Col. Comersfort.

[This letter (written, but not forwarded) is practically the same as No. xxxv *infra*, dated the evening of the same day.]

XXXIV

Au PRINCE de FLORIDO

Val., Le 26ier Jan^r 1719.

Monsr,—Je suis tres fache de misentendu qu'est arrivé; mais il n'y a point de remede. J'espere que V. E. aura la bonté de continuer ses attentions pour hater, et faciliter l'Embarquement de ces Messieurs qui auront l'honneur de vous presenter cette lettre, et de me croire avec beaucoup de respect de votre Excellence Le tres humble, etc.

(Signé) Le Duc D'Ormonde.

[To the Prince of Campo Florido. *Valladolid, January 26, 1719.*

Sir,—I am very sorry for the mistake which has occurred; but it cannot be helped. I hope that your Excellency will have the goodness to continue your services to hasten and facilitate the departure of these gentlemen who will have the honour to present this letter to you, and to believe me with great respect your Excellency's, etc.

(Signed) The Duke of Ormonde.]

XXXV

Au CARD. ALBERONI by yᴱ P. of Campo Florido's courier

Stamfort, *Ezekiel Hamilton.*   Mon Parent, *Bagenal.*

Val., Jan. 26th au Soir.

Je suis bien surpris, Monsieur, de voir arriver a ce moment les deux Messʳˢ que je croyois bien avancés en leur Voiage, Monsieur Stamfort a eu l'honneur a ce qu'il m'a dit de vous ecrire de Burgos pour vous informer des Ordres qu'il a receu du Prince de Florido. Cecy est un misentendu bien a Contretems. car sans ses ordres ils allerent s'embarquer, le vent etant devenu favourable ce qu'il n'avoit eté de Six Semaines.

Ces Messʳˢ partiront demain au Grand matin. Je souhaite qu'ils pourront trouver un Batiment prest et un vent favourable. Vous aurez receu, Monsʳ, une Lettre de mon Parent qui partit Samedie dernier après Midy, et j'espere qu'il pouroit etre arriveé en Hollande, le vent ayant continueé favorable.

J'ay recommendé a ces Messʳˢ de fair leur possibles pour m'envoyer des Pilottes et des Gens a notre rencontre pour nous informer s'il y a des Vaisseaux de Guerre en Mer, et ou ils sont destinés a Croiser; voila tout qu'on peut faire.

Monsʳ Stamfort m'a dit qu'il y avoit a Bilbao un Capitain de Vaiseau qui s'apelle Alexandre Tullo. Il a eté employée dans la derniere Affaire D'Ecosse, pour transporter des armes et depuis pour ramener des Seigⁿʳˢ et Officʳˢ qu'etoient obligés de se sauver en France. Je crois qu'il sera bon de luy fair venir a la premier Endroit sans qu'il scait pour quelle service il sera destiné. Il y a un Lambert a Sᵗ Sebastⁿ. On dit qu'il est honéte homme et habille en son metier. Le Prince de Florido pourra s'informer de son Caractere, et s'il repond a ce qu'on souhaite il sera bon qu'il fut aussi envoyé au premier lieu.

p. 31.   Le Chevalier Sherlock est a ce que je crois a Cadix. C'est un honete homme, mais je ne scais s'il est Capable; il sera bon de s'informer. J'ay l'honʳ d'etre avec beaucoup de Respect, Monsʳ, etc.

[To Cardinal Alberoni, by the Prince of Campo Florido's Courier.
Valladolid, January 26, evening.

Sir,—I was greatly surprised to see arrive just now the two gentlemen who I thought were by this time well on their journey. Mr. Stamfort has had the honour, as he tells me, to write to you from Burgos to tell you of the orders which he received from the Prince of Florido. This is a most unfortunate mistake; for had it not been for his orders they were going to embark, the wind having become favourable, which had not been the case for six weeks.

These gentlemen will set out to-morrow morning early. I hope they may find a vessel ready and a favourable wind. You will have received a letter from my kinsman who left last Saturday afternoon. I hope that he may have arrived in Holland, as the wind has continued favourable.

I have recommended these gentlemen to do what they can to send us pilots, also men to meet us to let us know if there are men-of-war at sea, and where they are ordered to cruise. That is all one can do.

Mr. Stamfort told me that there was at Bilbao a ship-captain called Alexander Tullo. He was employed in the last affair in Scotland to take over arms, and afterwards to bring back the gentlemen and officers who had to take refuge in France. I think it would be well to make him come to[1] the first place without knowing the service for which he is intended. There is one Lambert at San Sebastian. They say he is an honest man, and skilful in his profession. The Prince of Florido might inquire as to his character, and if the result is satisfactory, it would be well that he also should be sent to the first place.

The Chevalier Sherlock[2] is, I believe, at Cadiz. He is an honest man, but I do not know if he is capable; it would be well to inquire.

I have the honour, etc.]

XXXVI

Au CARD. ALBERONI BY Yᴇ SAME COURIER

Stamfort, *Ezekiel Hamilton.*   Mon Parent, *Everard.*
         Dutton, *Dillon.*

VAL., JAN. YE 27TH, MORNᴺᴳ.

JE viens de recevoir ce matin, Monsieur, par votre Courier l'honneur de la votre du 25ᵐᵉ avec la facheuse Nouvelle de la mort du Roy de Suede, que en ce conjoncture est une tres grande perte ; mais il faut non obstant ce malheur poursuivre notre Projet. S'il etoit possible d'augmenter le mecontentement en Angleterre, se [*sic*] seroit les nouvelles que vous m'envoyé, de ce qui se passe dans le Parlement a l'instigation de votre Amy Stanhope touchant les Noncomformists et les Universités

---

[1] In?   [2] Peter Sherlock, created a baronet by James in 1716.

qui fera enrager nonseulement tous les Anglicains mais deplaira aussi aux Moderez.

J'espere que Monsr Lawless poursuivra son voyage pour tacher de persuader le Nouveau Gouvernement d'entrer dans le meme projet. Mr Stamfort m'a dit que mon Parent avoit apris la meme nouvelle avent son depart, et qu'il estoit resolu de continuer le sien pour voir ce qu'il peut faire, comme il est connu de Monsr Gortz. S'il a encore du credit peut estre que le Voyage de mon Parent ne sera pas inutile, mais il ne faut point defferer le Notre pour attendre cet Evenement.

J'espere que les Cinq Vaisseaux Anglois dont vous faites mention n'attraperont point votre Flotte d'Hollande. Nous ferons notre possible pour tacher les eviter.

Le Comte de Marishall est le Seigneur Ecossois que vous m'avez prié d'envoyer chercher pour mener les Armes en Ecosse, dont je n'ai point d'autre Nouvelle que celles que je vous ai mandé. Je le croy en Bretagne tachant de venir avec la petite Barque, mais je croy que ce Vacarme a causé un embargo generale qui l'empeche de Sortir, avec la personne qui m'a esté envoyé d'Engleterre, et celui qui a donné le Memoir a M^r le Prince Chelamare.

Je vous suis bien obligé de la bonté que vous avez pour ces Messrs Ecossois.

J'ai fait mention dans me dern^{re} lettre qu'il sera bon d'avoir une Somme d'Argent en cas de besoin. Pour ce qui regarde la personne de Gironne je me conforme a vos Sentiments.

Je serai bien aise si vous le trouvez a propos d'avoir les Noms des Regiments, et une liste particuliere de toute, pour voir cy elle accorde avec celle que j'ay.

J'espere que toutes les Armes sont de meme Calibre avec des Bayonnettes.

Je suis persuadé que Monsr Dutton fera son possible mais ce Vacarme l'aura beaucoup embarassé.

Je prends la liberté que vous me donnez d'ecrire par mon Secretaire. J'ai l'honneur d'etre avec beaucoup de respect, etc.

P.S.—J'avois dessein d'envoyer un Courier ce matin avec ma lettre d'hier au soir, mais je me sers de cette Occasion.

J'envoy un Courier aprez Monsr Stamfort pour l'informer de la mort du Roy de Suede, et je luy mande de dire a nos amis que non obstent cet malheur, que nous poursuivrons notre projet. J'ai cru qu'il estoit necessaire de leur donner cette information, de peur qu'ils n'eussent crû que cella auroit apporté du changement. Ce courier le doit joindre a Burgos.

[To CARDINAL ALBERONI, by the same courier.
Valladolid. January 27, morning.

SIR,—I have just received this morning the honour of your letter of the 25th, with the sad news of the death of the King of Sweden, which, in the present state of affairs, is a very great loss, but notwithstanding this misfortune we must follow out our enterprise. If anything could increase the discontent in England, it would be the news which you send me of what has taken place in Parliament, at the instance of your friend Stanhope,[1] about the Nonconformists and the Universities, which will not only enrage the Anglicans, but also displease the Moderates.

I hope that M. Lawless will pursue his journey, and try to persuade the new Government to undertake the same enterprise. Mr. Stamfort has told me that my kinsmen had heard the same news before his departure, and that he was determined to go on with his journey to see what he could do, as he is known to M. Gortz. If he has still any power perhaps my kinsman's journey will not be useless, but it will not do to put off our expedition to await this event.

I hope that the five English ships which you mention will not catch your Holland fleet. We shall do what we can to keep out of their way.

The Earl Marischal is the Scottish lord whom you asked me to send for to take the arms into Scotland. I have no news of him beyond what I have told you.[2] I believe he is in Brittany, trying to come by the little vessel, but I think this disturbance has caused a general embargo, which prevents him from leaving, as well as the person who has been sent to me from England, and the person who gave the memorial to the Prince of Cellamare.

I am much indebted to you for your kindness to these Scotch gentlemen.

---

[1] James, first Earl Stanhope, who in 1717 succeeded Lord Townshend as First Lord of the Treasury and Chancellor of the Exchequer. He had commanded the British army in Spain from 1708 to 1710; and when a prisoner at Saragossa, after the disaster of Brihuega, had made the acquaintance of Alberoni, then a humble attendant of the Duke of Vendôme. They formed a personal friendship which lasted many years. On December 13, 1718, Stanhope introduced into the House of Lords a bill for the relief of Protestant Dissenters, which gave great offence to the Church party. It was carried by narrow majorities after important concessions had been made. See Mahon, vol. i. pp. 283, 326 *et seq.*

[2] In Letter XXIX.

I said in my last letter that it would be well to have a sum of money in case of need. As to the person of Gironne, I agree with your views.[1]

I should be very glad if you find it expedient to have the names of the regiments, and a detailed list of all, to see that it agrees with the one which I have.

I hope that all the muskets are of the same calibre, with bayonets.

I am sure that Mr. Dutton will do what he can, but this disturbance will have hampered him greatly.

I take the liberty which you gave me of writing by my secretary.—I have the honour, etc.

P.S.—I meant to send a courier this morning with my letter of last night, but am making use of this opportunity.

I send a courier after Mr. Stamfort to let you know of the death of the King of Sweden, and I am telling him to say to our friends that notwithstanding this misfortune, we will go on with our enterprise. I thought it necessary to tell them this for fear they might have thought that it would have caused a change. The courier ought to overtake him at Burgos.]

XXXVII

Au PRINCE de CAMPO FLORIDO

Val. p^r Express.   27th Janvier 1719.

Monsr,—Ce matin j'ai l'honneur de la lettre que votre Excellence m'ecrit du 24re par le Courier que vous envoyez au Pardo. Ce matin Monsr Stamfort et Monsr Lesley sont partis pour vous aller faire la reverence, et pour s'embarquer sens perdre un moment si le Batiment est pret et le vent favorable. J'ai l'honneur d'etre avec beaucoup de respect de V. E. Le tres, etc.   Sig^d Le Col. Comersford.

Excusé la liberté que je prends de l'incluse.

[To the Prince of Campo Florido. Val., by express. *January* 27, 1719.

Sir,—I have this morning the honour to receive your Excellence's letter of the 24th, by the courier whom you are sending to Pardo. Mr. Stamfort and Mr. Lesley left this morning to pay their respects to you, and to embark without losing a moment if the vessel is ready and the wind favourable. I have the honour, etc.

(Signed)   Colonel Comersford.

Excuse the liberty of the enclosed letter.]

---

[1] This probably refers to the Duke of Liria. See p. 39, note.

XXXVIII

A Mʀ ROBINSON ᴘʀ EXPRES

Robinson, *Alberoni.*

Val., le 30ʀᴇ Janvier 1719.

Je viens, Monsʳ, de recevoir l'honneur de la votre du 29ʳᵉ et Monsʳ le Barron partira dans un heur ou deux sens faute. J'attends avec impatience votre lettre du 28ʳᵉ pour etre informé de la raison du depart precipité du Barron. J'espere que ces nouveautez ne changera rien au projet. *p. 37.*

Ne sera t'il pas necessaire d'envoyer quelque un au lieu ou mon parent est allé pour tacher de faire entrer le nouveau Gouvernment dans le projet d'Alliance avec l'Espagne? Je croy qu'il n'y a point de temps a perdre, et qu'il faudra offrir une bonne Somme pour faire reussir ce dessein. Ne sera t'il point necessaire de tacher de gagner la personne le plus accredité dans la Nouvelle Cour par une bonne somme d'argent.

Je n'ai rien a ajouter que la parfaite reconnoissance de vos bontez et que je suis, etc.

P.S. Il n'y a point de relais pour cette route.

[To Mr. Robinson, by express. *Valladolid, January* 30, 1719.

Sir,—I have just had the honour to receive your letter of the 29th, and the Baron will leave in an hour or two without fail. I anxiously await your letter of the 28th, to be informed of the reason of the Baron's sudden departure. I hope that these new circumstances will not make any difference to the enterprise.

Will it not be necessary to send some one to the place to which my kinsman has gone, to try to get the new Government to take up the project of alliance with Spain? I think there is no time to lose, and that a good sum ought to be offered to effect this object. Will it not be necessary to try to gain the most influential person in the new court by a good sum of money?[1]

I have nothing more to add but my great gratitude for your kindness, and that I am, etc.

P.S.—There are no relays for this road.]

---

[1] 'Dans ces Cours du Nord tous les ministres s'attendent à de l'argent.' 'Hooker' (Jerningham) to Mar, Mittau, Sept. 23, 1718.—Intercepted Jacobite Correspondence, Stowe MSS., 232, f. 137. See Alberoni's letter to James, Appendix, No. 47, p. 255.

XXXIX

Au P. de CAMPO FLORIDO

Un Gentilhomme qui est mon Parent, *Toby Mathews.*

De Valadolide, Jan. ye 31st, 1719.

Monsieur,—J'ay l'honneur de vous envoyer un Gentilhomme qui est mon Parent. Il a l'honneur a ce qu'il m'a dit d'etre connus de votre Ex^{ce}. Je l'envoy pour Empecher les deux personnes qui devoient s'embarquer de partir jusque aux Nouvelles Ordres; mais en cas qu'ils sont deja parti je vous Supplie de tascher de trouver un Batiment pour ce Monsr qui a l'hon^r de vous presenter cette Lettre, pour lui transporter en mon Pais sans perdre un moment du tems.

J'ay eu l'honneur de la votre du 23me, et suis avec Grand respect de votre Ex^{ce}, etc. *P.S.*—Je prens la liberté de prier votre Ex^{ce} de fournir le Porteur avec la somme de 60 Pistoles en cas qu'il a besogne, et je la repaiera aux premiere lettres que je recois de votre Excellence. Je veus dire soissant pistoles.

[To the Prince of Campo Florido. *Valladolid, January* 31, 1719.

Sir,—I have the honour to send you a gentleman who is my kinsman. He tells me that he has the honour of being known to your Excellency. I send him to stop the two persons who are to sail from leaving until further orders; but in case they are already gone, I beg you to try to find a vessel for this gentleman who has the honour to present this letter to you, to take him out to my country without a moment's delay.

I have had the honour of your letter of the 23d. I am with great respect, etc.

P.S.—I take the liberty to beg your Excellency to supply the bearer with the sum of 60 pistoles in case he needs it, which I will repay as soon as I hear from your Excellency. Say sixty pistoles.]

XL

To the MAJOR wth a Copy of Robinson's

The Major, *Ezekiel Hamilton.* Robinson, *Alberoni.*

De Valadolide, Jan. ye 31st, 1719.

S^r,—The inclosed, which I received this morning from Mr Robinson, is ye occasion of my sending after you to desire you and your Companion to stay at St. Sebastien till you hear further from me. The bearer, Mr. Mathew, is a Relation of mine, a very honest Gentleman, but is not informed of y^e *p. 38.* contents, etc.

As soon as I hear further you shall be informed, and have directions how to proceed. My Complim^{ts} to your Companion, and believe me, etc. *P.S.*—In case you should be ordered back, it will be fit y^t H. L. should proceed to inform our friends what was doeing here, and y^o accidents that have put a stop to it. I have since thought it may be better to send Mr Mathew, because he runs no hazard, having never been in y^o King's service.

XLI

To TOBY MATHEWS

Major Stamfort, *Ezekiel Hamilton.*   Mr. Binet, *Ezekiel Hamilton.*

A Copy of Instructions by way of Letter, to Mr. Mathew, not to be opened by him, unless he found that y^o Maj^r (E. Hamilton) was gone from St Sebastian, dated Valladolid, Jan. ye 31st, 1719:

S^R,—If you find at your arrivall at St Sebastien y^t Major Stamfort and his Companion are certainly gone off for England, you are to endeavour to get thither after the best manner you can, and with as much privacy and Expedition as possible, make what dispatch you can for Londⁿ, and with great Caution find out Ld Arran,[1] Sir Red. Ev. or the Du^s of Orm^{de}, and inform them that since Mr. Binet (which is ye above mentioned Maj^r Stamfort) and his companion left Spain, accidents have happened hear [*sic*] which has altered the measures then aggreed upon, and that there is nothing now to be done. You will tell them that I desire Mr. Binet and his Companion may be sent back to me as soon as possible, and that I am much surprised that I have not seen any body from them since I left France. You'l burn this before you Embarque, and remember well the Contents. I am yours, etc.   OR^{DE}.

---

[1] Charles Butler, Earl of Arran, Ormonde's younger brother, born 1671, created Baron Cloughgrenan, Viscount Tullogh, and Earl of Arran in the peerage

XLII

MONS^R ROBINSON P^R L'ORDINAIRE

Robinson, *Alberoni*.

VAL., FIRST FEBRUARY 1719

J'AI recu hier, Monsieur, l'honneur de la votre du 27re avec la mauvaise nouvelle, touchant le Portugal. J'espere que c'est un bruit mal fondé, mais s'il est vrai, il faut avouer que voila bien des fasheuses accidents qui arrivent a la fois. Je vous supplie, Monsr, d'avoir la bonté de me faire sçavoir au plutot ce que vous estes resolu de faire parce que il n'y a pas un moment a perdre : si vous changer de sentiment il faut, j'envoy au plus vite pour en avertir mes Amis pour les empecher de se hasarder mal a propos.

Ne seroit il pas bon, Monsr, de tacher de faire entrer la Couronne de Suede dans nos projets. Si c'est le prince de Hesse qui succede, c'est un prince qui est fort entreprenant, et je croy qu'il ne sera pas difficile de lui faire entendre raison la dessus, et s'il est vray que le Barron de Gortz est arresté, il informera aparament le successeur des intentions du fû Roy, et il n'est pas de tout impossible que le Roy d'apresent les goutera ; ainsy le voyage de ces Messrs peut etre utille, le pis aller est qu'ils perdent leurs peines. Je suis impatient d'avoir de vos nouvelles et suis avec respect, etc.

[To MR. ROBINSON, by post. *Val., February* 1, 1719.

SIR,—I had yesterday the honour to receive your letter of the 27th with the bad news about Portugal. I hope that it is an unfounded rumour ; but if it is true, it must be admitted that many unfortunate accidents have happened together. I beg you, sir, to have the goodness to let me know as soon as possible what you have decided to do, for

---

of Ireland in 1693, died without issue 1758. In 1791 it was decided by the House of Lords in Ireland that Ormonde's English attainder had not affected his Irish dignities, and John Butler, then representative of the family, was restored to the honours of the house as seventeenth Earl of Ormonde. Lord Arran thus became fourteenth Earl *de jure* on the death of his brother without male issue in 1745, but he never bore the title. The present Marquisate dates from 1825.

there is not a moment to lose: if you change your intentions I must send at once to warn my friends, so as to prevent their endangering themselves uselessly.

Would it not be well to try to get the Swedish Government to join our enterprise? If it is the Prince of Hesse who succeeds, he is very enterprising, and I think it will not be difficult to get him to hear reason on this matter. If it is true the Baron de Gortz is arrested, he will be sure to inform the successor of the late king's intentions, and it is not impossible that the present king will like them: so the journey of these gentlemen will be of use. The worst that can happen is that they may lose their trouble.

I am anxious to have your news, and am with respect, etc.]

. . . .

XLIII

Au DUC de LERIA[1]

De Valladolid, le 25re Jan^r 1719

I HAVE had the honour of y^r grace's letter, and am infinitly obliged to you for the offers you are pleased to make me, of your house and Equipage at Madrid, but I do not yet know when I am to go thither. Shou'd there be at any time an attempt made towards the restoring of ye King, and that I shou'd have t'honour to be employed in it, y^r grace may be assured y^t I shou'd be glad of th' honour of y^r Company, and that I wou'd lay your pretensions before ye Cardinall, and be very ready on all occasions to shew the esteem and respect that I have for you, being with great truth and respect, etc.

XLIV[2]

Au PRINCE de CAMPO FLORIDO p^r express

Mr. Stamfort. *Ezekiel Hamilton.*

Le 7 Fevrier 1719.

J'ai receu l'honneur de la votre et prends la liberte de supplier V.E. de faire embarquer M^r Le Major Stamfort et Mr Lesley au plus tost, sens perdre un Moment de temps, si le vent est favourable.

---

[1] See Letter XXX. and note.
[2] This letter is crossed out in the manuscript.

Monsr Mathews a Ordre de venir me joindre. J'ai l'honneur d'etre avec tout l'Estime et respect imaginable de V.E., etc.

The above letter was not sent, but altered.

[To the Prince of Campo Florido, by express. *February* 7, 1719.

I HAVE had the honour to receive your letter, and take the liberty to beg your Excellency to hasten the departure of Major Stamfort and Mr. Lesley as much as possible, without losing a moment, if the wind is favourable.

Mr. Mathews has orders to join me. I have the honour, etc.]

XLV

To ye MAJOR from R^D. BUTLER

The Major,	*Ezekiel Hamilton.*	Rd. Butler,	*Ormonde.*
Robinson,	*Alberoni.*	Philips,	*Earl Marischal.*
Walton,	*Captain Morgan.*[1]	Obadiah,	*Mr. Wright.*
	Plunket's Clerk,	*M. Clancostrum*,[2]	*the King of Sweden's agent.*

De Valad., Feb. ye 7th, 1719.

You will find by ye Anex't Abstract of Robinson's Letter which his G. received this morning the reason of sending this Courier, his Gra. therefore desires that you and your Companion shou'd continue your intended journey for England with ye utmost diligence. He received a letter this day from Philips, who was safely arrived at Fraga. Instead of ye abstract I mentioned I believe it better to send you the heads of Robinson's letter of ye 4th instant received this morning. He desires that his Gr. w^d go as soon as possible to ye Groyne,[3] that ye ship for him left Cadiz ye 27th of Jan.[4] He says that he will send Ge^{ns} Gordon and Cambell as soon as possible for England; he has added to his former promisse 500

---

[1] Captain Morgan had been a Jacobite agent in England. Ormonde speaks of him as 'a great sufferer for the cause,' Letter CXLV. He apparently entered the Spanish navy; Colonel Stanhope, writing from Madrid in June 1722, mentions him as being in command of '3 small ships of 30 odd guns,' Stowe MSS., 250, f. 83 b.

[2] Otto Klinckowstrom (he signs so). [3] Corunna.

[4] The frigate *Hermione*, in which Ormonde was to embark at Corunna to join the fleet, left Cadiz with sealed orders to be opened forty miles at sea.

weight of powder so that he believes there is now enough to be disposed of elswhere as his Gra. thinks fit, but he thinks they dont want arms in Scotland. No news yet from Peter. He again presses his Grace to be gone and believes that ye designe is yet undiscovered. He has sent to his Gra. 80 Captains Comissions, and says he will send ye rest to the Groyne. He says that the Fleet will part from Cadiz before ye 10th inst. if the wind be not contrary, these are the most material points of his Letter. His Grace earnestly recomends it to you once more that he may have a positive account where the English fleet or Cruisers are and what Stations they are to keep. By Walton's of ye 13th Jan., received this day, we find that Obad^{iah} and Plunket's Clerke set sayle that day but as yet we have heard nothing further. Harry is to go with you, the other Gentleman has directions what he is to do, etc. If Mr. Mathew be gone you and Harry are to use ye utmost diligence to follow him and then to follow your first instructions.

XLVI

To Mr. MATHEWS

De Valadolide, Feb. ye 7th

S^r,—The Gentlemen you were sent to have just now received fresh directions to proceed on their Journey; you are therefore to go with as much speed and Secresy as possible to ye Corogne where you will meet me, but pray see none of your acquaintance on ye road nor do not mention me or what I now say to you on any occasion whatsoever. You may say at S^t. Sebastien that you are to this place, etc.

XLVII

Au PRINCE de CAMPO FLORIDO p^r express

Mr. Stamfort, *Ezekiel Hamilton*.

De Valad., le 7ro Fevrier 1719.

J'ai receu l'honneur de la votre et suplie V. E. d'avoir la bonté de faire embarquer Le Major Stamfort et Monsr Lesley au plus tost sens perdre un moment de tems si le vent est favourable.

Il faut que Monsr Mathew me vient joindre et qu'il ne embarque pas comme il avoit ordre, J'espere qu'il n'est pas party. J'ai l'honneur d'etre, etc.

[To the Prince of Campo Florido, by express.
Valladolid February 7, 1719.

I have had the honour to receive your letter, and I beg your Excellency to have the goodness to cause Major Stamfort and Mr. Lesley to embark as soon as possible, without losing a moment, if the wind is favourable.

Mr. Matthews must join me, and not sail as ordered. I hope he has not left. I have the honour, etc.]

XLVIII

A Mr. ROBINSON, p express

Robinson, *Alberoni.*   Peter, *The King.*
Dutton, *Dillon.*

Valad., February ye 8th, 1719.

Hier au matin, Monsr, j'ai receu l'honneur de la votre du 4re avec les Patentes, et Monsr le President m'a donné la Somme que vous avez la bonté de faire mention, et j'aurai soin de rendre Les vingte pistolles a Monsr de Hailly.

Monsr Le Baron est arrivé avec Monsr Hely. Le Baron m'a rendu les pacquets que vous lui eu avez chargé. Je vous supplie, Monsr, de me mettre au pied de leurs Majestés, et de les assurer de mes tres humbles, et tres respectueuses attachement, pour les honneurs qu'ils m'ont fait.

J'espere que le Ciel benira nos entreprises. La Cause est juste, et je suis persuadé que toutes les Troupes feront leur devoir.

Je suivrai vos ordres touchant Monsr de Crafton, et en tout ce que vous me marquez.

Monsr Le President fait tout ce qu'on peut desirer de luy. J'ai tous les raisons de monde de me louer de ces honnestetez dont je vous ay, Monsr, l'obligation comme en plusieurs autres choses dont je ne perdrai jamais un tres sincere et respectueuse reconnoissance. Je suis ravi, Monsr, que vous avez eu la bonté d'augmenter la quantité des poudres, mais je croy et je suis meme bien assuré qu'on manque des Armes en Ecosse comme j'avois l'honneur de vous dire. Pour ce qui est de ces Messrs Gordon & Campbell, je croy qu'ils auront des difficultes a se rendre en Hollande et de faire passer des Armes de la en Ecosse, par la meme raison qui a arresté ceux que vous aviez dessein de faire venir icy, mais s'il estoit possible d'en avoir de cet pays ou d'icy pour transporter en Ecosse ça sera fort a souhaiter. En tout cas s'ils ne vont pas en Hollande, il sera bon de les envoyer en Ecosse ou du moins de faire en sorte qu'ils nous joignent.

Pour M^r. Macdonell, si vous plait de me l'envoyer a la Courogne je serai bien aise de l'avoir.

J'ai eu une lettre du Comte de Marischal de Fraga du 28ro de Janvier. Il me mande qu'il sera a Madrid dans dix jours. J'espere, Monsr, que vous luy ferez l'honneur de lui donner audience. Il pourra vous informer de l'Estat de L'Ecosse, car il est bien informé et a beaucoup du Credit en ce pays. Si vous avez des Armes a luy donner pour L'Ecosse il aura soin de les mener.

J'ai receu une lettre d'une Ami en Bretagne du 13ro Janvier. Il me mande que le petit Batiment avec la personne qui m'a esté envoyé de mes amis, et celuy qui vient de Suede sont party de la le 13re. J'en suis bien en peine, n'aiant pas de leurs nouvelles, car ils devoient estre deja arrivez, mais les grands orages qu'il a fait me fait aprehendre pour Eux.

On me dit qu'il y a un Monsieur Connock[1] dans les Gardes. Je serai bien aise de l'avoir si vous le trouvez bon.

Permetez que je vous rende mille graces du Vin que vous avez eu la bonté de m'envoyer, et que j'ai toute la reconnoissance imaginable de vos bontez, et que je serai toute ma vie attaché a votre personne avec toute la sincerité imaginable aiant l'honneur d'etre tres parfaittement et plus que personne, Monsieur, etc.

P.S.—Je m'etonne qu'il n'y a point de Nouvelles de Maitre Pierre ny de Dutton. J'en suis bien en peine. Je tacherai s'il plait a Dieu de partir sens perdre du tems.

---

[1] At first written Connaugh, but corrected in another hand.

[To Mr. Robinson, by express. *Valladolid, February* 8, 1719.]

Sir,—Yesterday morning I had the honour to receive your letter of the 4th with the commissions. The President gave me the sum which you have the goodness to mention, and I shall be careful to pay the twenty pistoles to M. de Healy.[1]

The Baron has arrived with M. Healy, and has handed me the packets which you intrusted to him. I beg you, sir, to express my devotion to their Majesties, and to assure them of my most humble and respectful attachment for the honours they have done me.

I hope Heaven will bless our enterprise. The cause is just, and I am sure all the troops will do their duty.

I will attend to your orders about M. de Crafton, and in all that you tell me.

The President does all that can be desired. I have every reason in the world to be pleased with these kindnesses, for which I am indebted to you, sir, as for many other things, for which I shall always feel a very sincere and respectful gratitude. I am delighted, sir, that you have had the goodness to increase the quantity of powder, but I believe, and indeed am quite sure, that they are short of arms in Scotland, as I had the honour to tell you. As to Messrs. Gordon and Campbell, I think they will find it difficult to reach Holland and to get arms over from there into Scotland, for the same reason which stopped those whom you intended to bring here, but if it were possible to have some (arms) from that country or from here to take over to Scotland that would be very desirable. In any case, if they do not go to Holland it would be well to send them into Scotland, or at least to arrange for their joining us.

As to Mr. Macdonnel, if you please to send him to me to Corunna I shall be very glad to have him.

I have a letter from the Earl Marischal from Fraga, dated January 28. He tells me that he will be at Madrid in ten days. I hope, sir, that you will do him the honour to give him an audience. He will be able to tell you of the condition of Scotland, for he is well informed and has much influence in that country. If you have arms to give him for Scotland he will take charge of them for transport.

I have received a letter from a friend in Brittany dated January 13th. He tells me that the little vessel with the person whom my friends are sending to me, and him who is coming from Sweden, left there on the 13th. I am very anxious about them, as I have no news of them, and they ought to have arrived by this time, but the great storms which there have been make me fear for them.

I am told there is a Monsieur Connock[2] in the Guards. I should be glad to have him if you approve.

---

[1] John Healy or Hely was created a titular baronet by James in 1728.—List of Jacobite Honours.

[2] Sir Timon Connock received a commission in the Duke of Ossuna's troop of the Spanish life-guards in October 1705.—Sir Toby Bourke to Lord Caryll,

Let me offer you a thousand thanks for the wine which you have had the goodness to send me. I feel all imaginable gratitude for your kindness, and shall be all my life most sincerely attached to your person. I have the honour, etc.

P.S.—I am informed that there is no news of Mr. Peter nor of Dutton. I am very uneasy about them. I shall try, please God, to set out without losing time.]

XLIX

A MONS^R ROBINSON

Robinson, *Alberoni*.   Mon Parent, *Everard*.

VALLADOLIDE, LE 10RE FEVRIER, A 2 HEURES DU MATIN.

Je m'en vay partir en ce moment, et j'ai l'honneur de vous envoyer une Copie traduite en François de ce que mes amis m'ont envoyé par la personne qui est arrivé ce Matin de Madrid. Je vous envoy aussy la Copie d'une lettre qu'il m'a apporté de ce Monsr Suedois qui s'estoit embarqué avec lui. J'espere que si mon Parent et Monsr de Lawless poursuive leur voyage que ce ne sera pas inutille.

Je croy que vous aurez veu Mi Lord Marischall. Si vous ne l'employé pas pour mener des Armes en Ecosse, je vous prie de me l'envoyer.

Mes Amis m'ont mandé qu'ils m'envoyeroient quelques Officiers de Terre et de la Marine ; mais comme je n'ai pas de nouvelles apparamant ils ont esté empechez de venir pas des vents contraires ou quelque autre accident. Vous excuserez, Monsr, la liberté, je prends de vous ecrire p^r mon Secretaire. D'abord que serai arrivé au lieu ou je me dois rendre, j'aurai l'honneur de vous donner de mes nouvelles. Je vous prie de me croire avec beaucoup de respect, Monsr, etc.

P.S.—J'espere, Monsr, que vous n'aurez pas oublié Monsr Esmond.

Oct. 28, 1705, Carte MSS., 180, f. 120 b. Bourke says of him : 'He deserves anything, for he is a man of excellent principles, ye King and Queen of Spain have a true kindness for him, ye Princes and ye Ambassador do esteem him very much.'

[To Mr. Robinson. *Valladolid, February* 10, 2 *o'clock* A.M.

I am on the point of setting out, and I have the honour to send you a copy, translated into French, of what my friends have sent me by the person who arrived this morning from Madrid. I also send you a copy of a letter which he has brought me from that Swedish gentleman who embarked with him. I hope that if my kinsman and Mr. Lawless follow out their journey it will not be useless.

I suppose you have seen the Earl Marischal. If you do not employ him to take arms into Scotland, I beg you to send him to me.

My friends told me that they would send me some military and naval officers, but as I have no news of them, they seem to have been prevented from coming by contrary winds or some other accident. Pardon the liberty which I take in writing you by my secretary. As soon as I reach my destination I shall have the honour to give you my news.

I beg you to believe me, with much respect, etc.

P.S.—I hope, sir, that you have not forgotten Mr. Esmond.]

L

A Mr. ROBINSON par My Lord Marischall.

Robinson, *Alberoni*.

Astorga, le 13 Fevrier 1719.

Hier au soir, Monsr, My Lord Marischall m'a trouvé icy. Je suis bien aise que vous luy donnez deux mille fuzils et les poudres que vous faites mention. Il vous proposera de lui donner trois cents hommes. Si vous voulez bien les lui accorder, j'en suis seur que s'aura une tres bonne effet, car ce petite, nombre quand ils seront arrivez, le bruit du païs le diront trois mille, ce que obligera les Ennemis de garder beaucoup des Trouppes dans ce païs, et le bruit des Trouppes reglez en ce païs aura un tres bonne Effet, et le nombre est inconsiderable en cette pais mais sera d'une grande consequence en Ecosse.

Il sera bon d'envoyer le General Gordon et le Brig^r Campbell en Ecosse au plus vite aprez que nous aurons fait voille, et aussy d'en faire avertir plusieurs autres Seigneurs et Officiers qui sont a Paris et en France de s'y rendre sens perdre du temps. Mi Lord vous informera de leur noms.

Je vous prie, Monsr, d'avoir attention a ce qui Mi Lord vous proposera. Il y a beaucoup de Messrs Ecossois et Officiers en France, et en Hollande. Mais il faudra les faire donner de quoy se mettre en estat pour faire le voyage, aiant tout perdu, tout ce qu'ils avoient, et le Roy mon Maitre n'aiant pas de quoy leur paier leurs petites pensions qu'il leur donoit, depuis que le Regent a arresté ce qu'il estoit accoutumé de luy payer.

My Lord je croy par le moien de ses Amis en Hollande (quelques uns estant Marchands, les autres des Officiers) pourroit faire passer un petit nombre des Armes sens qu'on s'apperçut comme deux ou trois mille Fuzils, ce qui sera tres necessaire, et il me semble qu'il ne faudra pas epargner une petite somme pour une affaire qui sera de grande Consequence.

Mi Lord m'a dit que vous aviez la bonté de lui offrir une Commission du Roy, ce qui sera tres utille. Il aura besoin d'argent, ce que je suis bien assuré que vous ne lui refuserez pas.

p. 47.

My Lord prend avec lui les trois Messrs Ecossois qui sont avec Monsr Crafton. Ils seront plus utille avec lui qu'avec nous estant de ce païs, et My Lord en aura affaire quand il debarquera.

Le Maitre du petit Batiment qui est a St. Paul de Leon demande deux Commissions p^r deux Fregattes. Il faut si vous le trouvez bon que ces Commissions soient en Blanc. L'un des Fregattes a ce qu'il me mande est de 40 Cannons. Sy vous accordez cette demande que je croy ne sera pas inutille, Je tacherai de luy faire tenir ces Patentes. Je vous supplie, Monsr, de faire ce que vous pourez pour tacher d'avoir quelques Armes d'Hollande p^r L'Ecosse. Une diversion en ce pais sera d'une grande Consequence.

Je me donnerai l'honneur de vous faire sçavoir mon Arrivé quand je serai a porté de la Courogne, et suis avec beaucoup de respect, Monsr, etc.

[To Mr. Robinson, by the Earl Marischal.
Astorga, February 13, 1719.

Sir,—The Earl Marischal found me here last night. I am very glad that you are giving him two thousand muskets and the powder which you mentioned. He will propose that you should give him three hundred men. If you are pleased to agree to this, I am sure that it will have a very good effect, for when these few men have arrived, the talk of the country will make them three thousand, which will oblige the enemy to keep a large number of troops in that country, and the rumour of the regular troops being in that country will have a very good effect. The number is inconsiderable in this country, but will be of great importance in Scotland.

It will be well to send General Gordon and Brigadier Campbell into Scotland as soon as possible after we have sailed, and also to warn several other gentlemen and officers who are at Paris and in France to go there without losing time. The earl will tell you their names.

I beg you, sir, to consider what his lordship will propose to you. There are many Scotch gentlemen and officers in France and in Holland. But something must be given them to put them in a position to make the journey, as they have lost all, all that they had; and the king my master has no longer the means to pay the little pensions which he used to give them, now that the Regent has stopped what he was accustomed to pay him.[1]

His lordship could, I think, by means of his friends in Holland (some of whom are merchants and the others officers) get a small quantity of arms taken over without being discovered, say, two or three thousand muskets. This will be very necessary, and it seems to me that we should not grudge a small sum for a matter which will be of great importance.

His lordship has told me that you were good enough to offer him a commission from the king, which will be very useful. He will need money, which I am sure you will not refuse him.

His lordship is taking with him the three Scotch gentlemen who are with M. Crafton. They will be more useful with him than with us, as they belong to that country; and his lordship will need them when he lands.

The master of the small vessel which is at St. Paul de Leon asks for commissions for two frigates. These commissions should be blank, if you approve. One of the frigates, he tells me, carries forty guns. If you agree to this request, which I think will not be useless, I will try to make him keep these commissions. I beg you, sir, to do what you can to try to have some arms from Holland for Scotland. A diversion in that country will be of great importance.

I will do myself the honour to let you know of my arrival when I get within reach of Corunna. I am, with much respect, etc.]

LI

To Genl. Craffton

Astorga, 13th February 1719.

This is to desire you to order the three Scots Gentlemen that are with you to follow my Lord Marischall's orders. This is all I have to trouble you with at present, being very sincerely yours, etc.

---

[1] See Introduction, p. xxi, and p. 38, note 2.

LII

To the DUKE of GORDON[1]

Astorga, 13th February 1719.

My Lord,—I am so much convinced of y^r Grace's zeal and readyness for the King's Service that I make no doubt of your Grace's joining y^r interest with my Lord Marischall's for endeavouring the restoring of his Majesty. I hope in God to Land in England with a body of regular Troops, which will draw most of the Enemie's to oppose us, but y^r Grace and Lord Marischall's taking up Arms, with as many of y^r friends and well affected people, will make a great diversion, and contribute greatly to the hoped for Success, which the justice of our cause gives us reason to expect, and with the Blessing of God I do not doubt of. My Lord Marischall go's to you with Arms, and Ammunition. The King designs to go to England, his presence there being absolutely necessary.

p. 48.

Pray God send us a good meeting, and do me the justice to believe that I am with great truth and respect, my Lord, etc.

P.S.—This go's by my Lord Marischall, being the first that go's to Scotland; the rest of y^r Grace's Countrymen will follow as soon as possibly they can.

LIII

Au Marq^s de Risbourg[2] p Sr Timon Connock

De Foufrien, le 17re Fevrier 1719.

M^r.—Je suis ravi d'avoir cette occasion pour vous assurer de mes respects. J'espere d'avoir l'honneur et plaisir de vous ambrasser bientot, et renouveller notre ancienne Amitié.

Vous aurez la bonté, s'il vous plait, de me faire sçavoir par la personne qui aura l'honneur de vous presenter cellecy, si le Vaisseau que je dois monter est arrivé, et quelles nouvelles

---

[1] Alexander, second Duke of Gordon. He succeeded his father in 1716, and died in 1728. He was out in the '15, and was present at Sheriffmuir, but took no part in the affair of 1719.

[2] François Philippe de Melun, Marquis de Risbourg, Grandee of Spain, and Knight of the Golden Fleece, Viceroy of Galicia.

vous aurez receu de la Flotte, affin que je prends mes Mesures. J'attendrai avec impatience l'honneur de vos nouvelles, et je vous prie d'estre bien persuadé que j'ai l'honneur d'estre plus que personne, Monsr, etc.

[To the MARQUIS DE RISBOURG, by Sir Timon Connock.
Foufrien, February 17, 1719.

SIR,—I am delighted to have this opportunity of assuring you of my regard. I hope soon to have the honour and pleasure of embracing you, and of renewing our old friendship.

You will, if you please, have the goodness to let me know by the person who has the honour to deliver this to you whether the ship in which I am to sail has arrived, and what news you have received of the fleet, so that I may make my arrangements.

I shall anxiously await your news, and I beg you to believe that I have the honour, etc.]

LIV

Au MARQ^S DE RISBOURG P^R EXPRESS

DE BETANCOS, LE 23 FEVRIER 1719.

J'AI receu l'honneur de la votre p^r Mon^s le Major, et vous suis infiniment obligé des attentions que vous avez a mon Egard. Je me flatte d'avoir demain le plaisir et l'honneur de vous embrasser ; nous reglerons ce qu'il y aura a faire pour couvrir notre jeu.

Je crains beaucoup pour la Flotte si Elle est en Mer par le temps qu'il a fait depuis cinq ou six jours.

Je vous prie d'excuser que je ne fais pas ma lettre plus long, estant un peu fatigué du voyage, et estant justem^t arrivé. Croyez, Monsr, que j'aurai tout le plaisir au monde de vous assurer que personne ne vous honore plus parfaitement que, Monsr, etc.

[To the MARQUIS DE RISBOURG, by express. *Betanzos, February* 23, 1719.

I HAVE had the honour to receive your letter by the Major, and am infinitely obliged by your kindness towards me. I flatter myself that I shall to-morrow have the pleasure and honour of embracing you. We shall arrange what must be done to conceal our game.

I fear greatly for the fleet if it has been at sea in the weather which there has been during the last five or six days.

I beg you to excuse the shortness of my letter, as I am rather tired with my journey, having just arrived. Believe, sir, that it will give me the greatest pleasure to assure you that no one regards you with more honour than, etc.]

LV

Au MARQ^S de RISEBOURCQ

De Sada, le 24re Fevrier 1719, a 6 heur du Soir.

Je me donne l'honneur de vous envoyer cellecy pour vous assurer que je suis arrivé. Je suis impatient d'avoir le Plaisir de vous embrasser et de vous assurer que j'ai l'honneur d'etre plus que personne, etc.

[To the Marquis de Risbourg. *Sada, February 24, 1719, 6 p.m.*

I do myself the honour of sending you this to tell you that I have arrived. I am impatient to have the pleasure of embracing you, and of assuring you that I have, etc.]

LVI

Au MEME

Du 24 Fev^R, a 7½ du Soir.

Je viens a ce moment de recevoir l'honneur de la votre, Monsr, et vous suis bien obligé de ce que vous avez la bonté de me mander touchant la Flotte, et de l'interest que vous voullez bien prendre a ce que me regarde. Demain j'espere avoir l'honneur de vous assurer avec combien de respect j'ai l'honneur d'estre, Monsieur, etc.

[To the Marquis de Risbourg. *February 24, 7.30 p.m.*

Sir,—I have just this moment had the honour to receive your letter, and am greatly obliged to you for what you have the goodness to tell me about the fleet, and for the interest which you are pleased to take in what concerns me. To-morrow I hope to have the honour to assure you with how great respect I am, etc.]

LVII

Au BARON WALEF

De Sada, le 24 Fev^R, a 7 heur ½ du Soir.

Mons^R,—Je vous suis bien obligé de l'honneur de la votre et vous felecite sur votre arrivé.

J' avois dessein de faire ce que vous faites mention touchant Monsr Le Cardinal et aussy a l'egard de S^t. Sebastien. Je n'ai point de ce lieu, et cy je n'en reçois point, j'ai dessein d' envoyer le petit Batiment avec la personne qui est venu avec. Je suis ravy d'apprendre que les mariners sont d'oppinion que la Flotte ne pouroit sortir depuis dix jours. Je suis impatient de vous assurer de bouche combien je vous estime et que je suis tres parfaitement.

[To Baron Walef. *Sada, February 24, 7.30 p.m.*

Sir,—I am much obliged to you for your letter, and congratulate you on your arrival.

I meant to do what you mentioned about the Cardinal, and also with regard to St. Sebastian. I have no news from thence, and if I receive none, I intend to send the little vessel with the person who came by it. I am delighted to hear that the sailors think that the fleet could not have put to sea during the past ten days.

I am impatient to assure you by word of mouth how much I esteem you, etc.]

LVIII

To SIR TIMON CONNOCK

De Sada, le 24 Fevrier 1719.

S^r—I thank you for yours I receiv'd last night, and am much obliged to you for the trouble you have given yourself in providing the provisions that you sent me a list off. As to what the Marq^s de Risboureg proposes concerning my being supposed to be in arrest, will it not make a new noise about the country, and make my being here more talk'd off, but if the Marq^s thinks that it will cover any thing of our business, I consent to it. I hope to have the satisfaction of seeing you to morrow, and of assuring you of the true esteem and value that I have for you, being with great truth, Sir, etc.

LIX

Au Monsʀ Robinson, pʀ exprès

Robinson, *Alberoni.*   Pierre, *The King.*
Dutton, *Dillon.*

De Sada, 26 Fevrier 1719.

Je me donne l'honneur, Monsʳ, de vous informer que je suis arrivé icy avent hier au soir, aprez un voyage bien ennuiant. J'ai eu l'honneur de voir Monsʳ le Marqˢ de Risboureg hier au soir. Il fait tout ce qu'on peut desirer de lui. Il vous informera de tout ce que se passe. Nous sommes bien en peine pour la Flotte, si elle a esté en mer ces jours passés, car depuis dix jours il a fait un temps horrible, mais n'aiant pas de vos nouvelles, j'espere que la flotte n'a pas sorti du Port.

J'ai receu l'honneur de la votre par Monsʳ Connock, et vous suis infiniment obligé de l'avoir envoyé car assurement il me sera tres utile.

Vous aurez veu Mi Lord Marischal, et aussy recu ce que j'ai eu l'honneur de vous avoir envoyé le soir de mon depart. Je m'etonne qu'il n'y a point de Nouvelles de Maitre Pierre. J'en suis tres en peine. Dieu veuille qu'il n'a pas esté en mer pendant ces mauvais temps. Je suis de votre opinion, Monsʳ, qu'il sera le premier qui vous donnera de nouvelles de son arrivé.

Plut a Dieu que nous fussions arrivé en mon Païs, je crois que nous y trouverions beaucoup de brouilleries, ce que nous sera bien avantageux.

C'est presque un miracle qu'on n'a pas parlé de ce que s'y fait en dernier lieu.

Je n'ai point de nouvelles de Monsʳ de Matillion ny de l'Aid de Camp de Monsʳ Crafton.

Je souhaiterai fort d'avoir la liste des Regiments et les noms des Officiers qui commande les Trouppes, je veux dire des Espagnols. Il n'y a point de nouvelles du pilote Tullo: nous en avons deux icy qui appartenoit aux pacquet Boates et deux qui appartient au petit Batiment, mais on n'en Sauroit trop avoir

Monsʳ Dutton va ou vous faites mention. Je souhaite fort qu'il fut ou il souhaite d'estre, mais ce vacarme l'embarasse beaucoup; j'en suis tres assuré qu'il fera tout son possible pour quitter cette Famille.

Je crois que les Vaisseaux qui estoient arrestés en Hollande ont esté relachez et qu'ils sont en route. Monsr de Risbourcg vous informera des nouvelles qu'il vient de recevoir d'un Maitre de Vaisseau Hollandois qui est arrivé depuis deux jours. Le vaisseau est chargé de poudre p^r Barcellone. J'ai fait tout ce que je pourois pour n'estre pas connus, mais il y a des gens de Valadolide qui ont mandé a leurs amis que j'estois partis de là, et qu'ils croyient que je venois de ce cotté, et il n'y avoit pas moien d'empecher les voiturins de dire dans les Posades qui j'estois. J'attends, Monsr, avec impatience Monsieur de Macdonnell, et suis avec beaucoup de respect, etc.,

(Signed) De Comerfort.

[To Mr. Robinson, by express. *Sada, February* 26, 1719.

Sir,—I have the honour to inform you that I arrived here the evening before last, after a very tiresome journey. Last night I had the honour of seeing the Marquis de Risbourg. He is doing all that could be desired. He will inform you of all that happens. We are very anxious about the fleet, if it has been at sea these past days, for during the last ten days the weather has been dreadful, but as I have no news from you, I hope that the fleet has not left port.

I have had the honour to receive your letter by Sir T. Connock. I am exceedingly obliged to you for having sent him, for certainly he will be very useful to me.

You will have seen the Earl Marischal, and will have received what I had the honour to send you on the evening of my departure. I am astonished that there is no news of Mr. Peter. I am very anxious about him. God grant that he has not been at sea during this bad weather. I am of your opinion that he will be the first to give you the news of his own arrival.

Would to God that we were landed in my country. I think we shall find plenty of disturbances there, which will be a very good thing for us.

It is almost a miracle that what has been going on of late has not been spoken of.

I have no news of M. de Matillion, nor of Mr. Crafton's aide-de-camp.

I should much like to have the list of the regiments and the names of the officers in command of the troops—I mean the Spaniards. There is no news of the pilot Tullo. We have two here who belong to the packet-boats, and two who belong to the little vessel, but we cannot have too many.

Mr. Dutton is going to the place which you mention. I wish very much that he were where he wishes to be, but this disturbance impedes him much. I am very sure that he will do all that he can to leave that family.

I believe that the vessels which were stopped in Holland have been released and are now on their way. M. de Risbourg will inform you of the news which he has just received from the master of a Dutch ship which arrived two days ago. The ship is laden with powder for Barcelona.

I have done what I could not to be known, but there are some people in Valladolid who have told their friends that I had left there, and that they thought I was coming in this direction; besides it was impossible to prevent the drivers from saying in their inns who I was. I await Mr. Macdonnell with impatience. I am, etc.,

(Signed) DE COMERFORT.

LX

To the EARLE MARISCHALL PHILIPS

Mr. Robinson, *Alberoni.*

SADA, NEAR THE COROGNE, THE 26TH FEBRY 1719.

S^r,—I hope this will find you at St Sebastians ready to embarcke, and that you have had reason to be satisfied with our Friend Mr. Robinson. I came to this place the night of the 24th after a very tiresome journey.

I here enclose the letters that you thought necessary for the Persons you mentioned. I have no news of Tullo; we have had terrible bad weather these ten days, I hope in God the fleet has not been at Sea.

I have nothing more to trouble you with at this time but to wish you a safe passage, and that we may meet with the success y^t the justice of the cause deserves. I am with great truth, S^r, etc.,

(Signed) SADLER.

LXI

To GLENGARY [1]

p. 53.

SADA, NEAR THE COROGNE, THE 26TH FEBRY 1719.

S^r,—Though I have not the good fortune to know you personaly, yet I am no stranger to y^r character and personall

---

[1] Alastair Dubh Macdonell, eleventh Macdonell of Glengarry. He bore a distinguished part at Killiecrankie and in the '15, and commanded the right wing of the Jacobite army at Sheriffmuir. James made him a titular baron in 1716.

merit, and do not in the least doubt of y^r readyness to serve the King our master in the assisting my Lord Marischall to make a diversion in Scotland, whilst I am in England with a Body of Regular Troops of the King of Spain's Subjects. The King I hope is landed by this time, and will be ready to go with this Embarkation, or follow without any delay, I have hopes in God's blessing on our Enterprise from the justice of our Cause. Believe me with truth, Sir, etc.

(Signed)   ORMONDE.

LXII

To THE LAIRD OF BROLUS[1]

SADA, NEAR THE COROGNE, THE 26TH FEB^{RY} 1719.

S^r,—I hope you will be ready to show the same zeall for the King's service that you have hitherto done, and therefore I do not in the least doubt that you will use your interest to assist my Lord Marishall in making a diversion to employ ye Enemies' Troops, when I am in England with a Body of Regular Troops of the King of Spain's Subjects. I hope in God that we shall have the success that the justice of our Cause deserves. The King will be in England as soon as it is possible. I am with much truth, Sir, etc.

LXIII

To CLANRONALD'S COUSEN[2] (sent without direction to L^D Marischall)

SADA, NEAR THE COROGNE, THE 26TH FEB^{RY} 1719.

S^r,—My Lord Marishall comes to you with Arms and

He was not at Glenshiel, but after the battle he seems to have welcomed many of the fugitives. 'It's certain Your Majesty has not a braver nor better subject than this worthy old man,' wrote Tullibardine to James (Aug. 15, 1719, Stuart Papers). He died in 1724. See Appendix, pp. 281, 282, 287.

[1] Donald, third MacLean of Brolas. He served in the army under Queen Anne, was out in the '15, and was wounded at Sheriffmuir. Some arrangements seem to have been made for a gathering of the MacLeans in Mull at the time of the Earl Marischal's landing, but Brolas was warned by James Campbell, Sheriff-depute of Argyll, of the danger of engaging in any further Jacobite movements, and does not appear to have taken any part in the affair of 1719. He died in 1725. See J. P. MacLean's *History of the Clan MacLean*, pp. 215, 225.

[2] Donald MacDonald of Benbecula, Tutor of Clanranald, who commanded the

Ammunition and I am waiting for a fair wind to embarke with a Body of Spanish regular Troops, I know the zeall that you and y^r Family have shewn for the King's Interest, and I hope you will help my Lord Marischall in the making a diversion to employ some of the Enemies Forces, when I am in England. The King will be in this Embarkation or will follow as soon as is possible. We ought to hope for a Blessing to our Endeavours, considering the justness of our Cause. Believe me with truth, Sir, etc.,
                                                     OR——D.

p. 54.

N.B.—That the three above letters were sent under cover to the Earl Marischall.

LXIV

To the MARQ^S DE RISBOUR^CG

SADA, LE 27RE FEBRUARY 1719.

MONS^R,—Peut le Vaisseau Hermione sortir de la Ferole, si le vent vient au Sud West, et qu'il fait beaucoup de vent. Vous aurez s'il vous plait attention a cecy, si le Vaisseau vient a la Courogne ne sortiroit il pas plus facilement?

Apparament les lettres ne sont point arrivees. Je vous prie Monsr de me faire savoir votre Sentiment sur ce que j'ai l'honneur de vous demander et d'estre tres persuadé que j'ai toute la reconnoissance imaginable de vos honnestetes et que j'ai l'honneur d'estre, etc.

P.S.—J'espere que vous avez la bonté de donner une bonne quantite des Pierres a Fuzils.

[To the MARQUIS DE RISBOURG. *Sada, February* 27, 1719.

SIR,—Can the *Hermione* get out of Ferrol, if the wind goes to the south-west and blows hard? Please attend to this. If the ship were to go to Corunna would she not get out more easily?

Apparently the letters have not arrived. I beg you, sir, to let me

---

MacDonalds at Killiecrankie, was the cousin of Ranald, thirteenth MacDonald of Clanranald. Ranald was at this time in France. He went over from Bordeaux to take part in the Earl Marischal's expedition. He died at St. Germains in 1725, and Donald succeeded him as fourteenth MacDonald of Clanranald.—MacKenzie's *History of the MacDonalds,* p. 427.

know your opinion as to what I have asked you, and to believe that I am profoundly grateful for your kindness. I have the honour, etc.

P.S.—I hope that you will have the kindness to furnish a good supply of gun-flints.]

LXV

Au MARQ^S DE RISEBOURG, P^R LE CHEV^R HELEY

SADA, LE PREM^{RE} MARS 1719.

JE viens en ce moment de recevoir l'honneur de la votre je suis bien aise que L'Hermione est arrive pour les raisons que vous faites mention.

Monsr Le Chev^r de Helley aura l'honneur de vous voir, et vous informera Monsr de tout ce que je demande. Si vous avez des Chevaux de fraise, je vous supplie de me les donner.

Je vous suis infiniment obligé pour les pierres a Fuzil, et de l'attention que vous avez a tout ce que me regarde en particulier, Je vous supplie d'estre tres persuadé que j'en conserveray une eternelle reconnoissance.

Je suis impatient d'avoir des lettres, mais comme vous dites Monsr je croy que Monsr le Cardinal aura arresté tous les Courriers.

Je me remets a Monsr de Heley et vous supplie tres humblement d'estre persuadé du respect avec le quel j'ai l'honneur d'estre Monsr, etc.

[To THE MARQUIS DE RISEBOURG, per Sir John Healy.

Sada, March 1, 1719.

I HAVE just received your letter, and am very glad that the *Hermione* has arrived, for the reasons you mentioned.

Sir John Healy will have the honour to see you, and will inform you of all my requests. If you have any chevaux-de-frise I beg you will let me have them.

I am very greatly obliged to you for the gun-flints, and for your solicitude with regard to everything which concerns me personally. I beg you to rest assured that I shall always be grateful for it.

I am anxious to get letters; but, as you say, I think the Cardinal will have stopped all the couriers.

I refer to M. de Healy, and beg you to rest assured of the respect which I have the honour, etc.]

LXVI

Au MARQ^S DE RISBOURG

DE SADA, LE 2^D MARS 1719.

JE viens de recevoir l'honneur de la votre p^r Monsr de Hely, j'ai veu le Capitaine qui a ce qui me paroit est un Galant homme, je vous enverray demain Matin Monsr de Hely, et me remet au qu'il aura l'honneur de vous dire, je vous suis infiniment obligé des attentions qu'il vous a plu avoir pour faciliter ce que je vous demande.

Je vous supplie tres humblement d'estre persuadé que personne ne vous honore ni vous estime plus que Monsr, etc.

[To THE MARQUIS DE RISBOURG. *Sada, March 2, 1719.*
I HAVE just received your letter by M. de Healy. I have seen the captain, who seems to me to be a man of honour. I shall send M. de Healy to you to-morrow, and refer you to what he will say. I am very greatly obliged to you for all the trouble you have taken to meet my wishes.

I beg you to believe that no one honours or esteems you more than, etc.]

LXVII

p. 56.

Au MARQ^S DE RISBOUR^{CQ}

DE SADA, LE 2^D MARS 1719.

J'AI l'honneur de vous envoyer une lettre p^r Monsr L'Admiral, que je vous supplie de lui faire rendre quand il sera a la hauteur du Cap Finister. Cette lettre est pour lui prier de s'approcher de la Corogna, affin que s'il faisoit mauvais temps, que je puis avoir le moien de m'aboucher avec lui pour prendre nos mesures, ce qui sera impossible s'il tient la mer, et que le temps est si mauvais qu'une Chalouppe ne pourroit aller d'un navire a l'autre, nous ne pourrons pas pretendre ny songer de faire voile sens que nous nous voions car il ne sçauroit pas ou je destine d'aller et aussy il faut que nous ajustions les Signaux, et que nous soyons d'accorde d'un lieu de rendevous en cas que le mauvais temps separe la Flotte. Je vous supplie Monsr d'avoir la bonté de tacher de faire rendre ma lettre a Monsr de Gevare s'il est possible.

Monsr de Hely aura l'honneur de vous voir demain et vous informera de tout ce qui est necessaire, en attendant que j'ay l'honneur de vous voir, vous aurez s'il vous plait la bonté de me faire sçavoir vos sentiments par Monsr de Hely. Croyez qu'il est impossible d'estre avec plus de respect et de reconnoissance que j'ay l'honneur d'estre, etc.

[To the Marquis de Risbourg. *Sada, March 2, 1719.*

I HAVE the honour to send you a letter for the Admiral, which I beg that you will cause to be delivered to him when he is off Cape Finisterre. This letter is to request him to come into Corunna, in order that if the weather is bad I may be able to confer with him in order to adjust our plans, which will be impossible if he keeps at sea; and if the weather is so bad that a boat cannot go from one ship to another. We cannot possibly think of sailing until we have seen each other, for he will not know where I propose to go; besides which we must arrange as to the signals and agree as to a place of rendezvous in case the fleet should be separated by bad weather. I beg you, sir, to have the goodness to try to have my letter delivered to M. de Guevarra if possible.

M. de Healy will have the honour of seeing you to-morrow, and will inform you of all that is necessary until I have the honour of meeting you. Please be so good as to let me know your wishes through him.

Believe that it is impossible to be with more respect and gratitude than I have the honour to be, etc.]

LXVIII

A MONS^R DE GUEVARA[1]

De Sada, 3me Mars 1719.

M^R,—Je m'estime fort heureux d'avoir une personne de votre merite pour Commander la Flotte destinée pour cette entreprise ou j'ai l'honneur de Commander les Trouppes. Je vous prie, Monsr, d'estre bien persuadé que j'aurai bien du plaisir a trouver des occasions par où je pourrois vous temoigner l'estime que j'ai pour votre merite.

J'ai l'honneur, Monsr, de vous envoyer cette lettre pour vous prier de vouloir bien vous approcher de la Courogne aussy tot que vous pourrez affin que s'il faisse mauvais temps nous

---

[1] Rear-Admiral Don Baithasar de Guevarra. He held a junior command at the battle of Cape Passaro. His ship, the *St. Louis*, of fifty guns, was one of those which escaped.

pourrions nous aboucher avec plus de facilité car s'il faisoit mauvais temps il seroit impossible q'une chaloupe pourroit aller d'une navire a l'autre et nous ne pourrons continuer notre voyage sens que nous aions ajusté et reglé la routte que nous devons faire, ny estre d'accorde des signaux et d'un lieu de rendezvous eu cas que la flotte soit separée par du mauvais temps. Je suis tres impatient d'avoir l'honneur et plaisir de vous assurer combien j'ai l'honneur d'estre, etc.   (S^d) Or.

[To Monsieur de Guevara.   *Sada, March 3, 1719.*

Sir,—I think myself very fortunate in having a person of your merit in command of the fleet intended for this expedition, in which I have the honour to command the troops. I beg you, sir, to believe that it will give me great pleasure to find opportunities of proving to you the regard which I have for your merits.

I have the honour to send you this letter to ask you to come into Corunna as soon as you can, so that in the event of bad weather we may the more easily meet, for if the weather is bad it will be impossible for a boat to pass from one ship to another; and we shall not be able to proceed on our voyage without having arranged as to the course which we are to follow, and agreed as to the signals and as to a place of rendezvous in case the fleet should be separated by bad weather.

I am impatient to have the honour and pleasure of assuring you how much I have the honour to be, etc.]

LXIX

Au BARON WALEF

De Sada, le 3me Mars 1719.

J'ai receu la votre hier au soir, et j'ai ecrite a Monsr le Marq de Risbourg pour luy prier de vouloir bien envoyer ma lettre a Monsr Guevara d'abord qu'il pourra. Je prie l'admiral de s'approcher de la Courogne affin que nous puissions nous aboucher et regler tout ce que sera necessaire pour le voyage et decente, ce que ne pourra faire s'il faisoit un gros temps, et que l'admiral tient la mer car en ce cas il seroit impossible *p. 58.* qu'une chaloupe pourroit aller d'une navire a l'autre.

Monsr Le Cardinal m'a rien dit de ce que vous faites mention, mais j'aurai toujours beaucoup d'egarde pour vos sentiments, mais je ne crois pas qu'il est necessaire que j'aille a la ville.

Pour le memoire que vous m'avez envoyé c'est fort bon, mais vous pouvez estre assuré que j'ai bien pensé a toutes ces affaires, Dieu veuille que nous puissions debarquer, Je suis fache d'apprendre que vous estes indisposé mais j'espere que ce ne sera rien, croyez moy tres parfaitement, etc.

[To Baron Walef. *Sada, March* 3, 1719.

I received your letter last night, and I have written to the Marquis de Risbourg asking him to forward my letter to M. de Guevarra as soon as possible. I am asking the admiral to come into Corunna so that we may meet and arrange all that is necessary and befitting for the voyage, which cannot be done if the weather is bad and the admiral at sea, for in that case it will be impossible for a boat to go from one ship to another.

The Cardinal has told me nothing of what you mention, but I shall always have a great regard for your views. I do not think, however, that it will be necessary for me to go to the town.

As to the memorial you have sent me, it is very good, but you may rest assured that I have fully considered all these matters. God grant that we may be able to land. I am sorry to hear that you are ill, but I hope it will be nothing serious. Believe me, etc.]

LXX

Au BARON WALEF

Sada, le 6 Mars 1719.

Je viens ce moment de recevoir l'honneur de la votre, et suis bien en peine du retardement de la flotte, et je crains fort que le Cardinal ne change du sentiment. Je ne croys pas que les Whigs estoit dans l'interest du prince de Hesse ; J'ai eu une lettre du Cardinal datée le 13me Janvier par ou il me mande que ce Monsr et l'aid de Camp de Monsr Crofton, estoient partis le 12. Son Eminence m'avoit fait scavoir que les Estats Generaux avoient arresté les vaisseaux qu'avoient les armes, et deffense de faire passer aucune Munition de Guerre p^r L'Espagne. Je souhate que les vaiss^x qui ont esté veues du Cap soient les Fregates Anglois. Je vous prie Monsr de faire bien mes Compliments a Monsr le Marq^s de Risbourg, j'ai recu l'honneur de la siene avant hier, et soyez persuadé que je suis tres parfaitement Monsr, etc. Mes Compliments a tous vos Messrs.

[To Baron Walef. *Sada, March* 6, 1719.

I have just received your letter. I am very anxious about the delay of the fleet, and am much afraid that the Cardinal may change his intention. I do not think that the Whigs are on the side of the Prince of Hesse.[1] I had a letter from the Cardinal, dated January 13, in which he told me that that gentleman and Mr. Crafton's aide-de-camp had left on the 12th. His Eminence also informed me that the States-General had stopped the ships with the arms, and had laid an embargo on all warlike stores from Spain. I hope that the ships seen off the Cape are the English frigates. I beg you, sir, to present my compliments to the Marquis de Risbourg. I received his letter the day before yesterday. Rest assured that I am, etc.

My compliments to all your gentlemen.]

LXXI

Au MARQ^S DE RISBOURG

DE SADA, LE 6 MARS 1719.

Monsr,—Je me serve de cette occasion pour vous rendre mes tres humbles graces de l'honneur de la votre et vous suis bien obligé de ce que vous avez la bonte de m'assurer que vous tacherez de faire rendre ma lettre a l'admiral quand il sera arrivé a la hauteur du Cap. Je m'ettonne qu'il n'y a pas des nouvelles de Madrid, j'espere que nous en aurons demain. Il seroit a souhaiter que les gros vaisseaux qui ont esté veu du Cap furent ceux qui doivent venir d'Angleterre.

J'attends M^r D'Hely quand vous n'aurez plus affaire de luy. J'ai l'honneur d'etre plus que personne au monde, Monsr, etc.

[To THE MARQUIS DE RISBOURG. *Sada, March 6, 1719.*

Sir,—I take advantage of this opportunity to offer you my very humble thanks for the honour of your letter, and am greatly obliged that, as you have the kindness to assure me, you will try to have my letter delivered to the admiral when he is off the Cape. I am surprised that there is no news from Madrid; I hope we shall have some to-morrow. It is to be hoped that the large ships which have been seen off the Cape were those which are to come from England.

I expect M. de Healy when you have no further need of him. I have the honour, etc.]

---

[1] The Prince of Hesse-Cassel, husband of Ulrica Eleonora, the sister and successor of Charles XII., was a candidate for the Swedish throne.

LXXII

Au BARON WALEF

Sada, 9me Mars 1719.

Je viens de recevoir la votre ce moment, et suis faché de ce que vous m'apprenez du retardement de la flotte. Il paroit que le Cardinal a esté trompé, puisque vous dites qu'elle ne pouvoit avoir esté pret a fair voile que le prem^{re} de ce mois. Je suis faché et mortifié que l'on ait decouvert le secret. Je n'ai point des nouvelles du Cardinal, et je ne l'ecrirai point sur cet article que je n'ai quelque avis de luy sur la decouverte.

p. 60.

Si les Anglois on [*sic*] sceu le dessein ils ne manqueront pas des vaisseaux pour estre pret a metre en mer, il n'y a point de Courrier Extraordinaire arrivé. J'espere que ces nouvelles ne se trouveront pas toute a fait si mauvais que vous me mandez. Je croyois avoir eu l'honneur de voir Monsr le Marquis ce soir, mais j'ai appris qu'il ne vient pas. Je vous prie de me Croire tres parfaitement, etc.

Mes compliments S.V.P. a Monsr le Marq^{s} de Reisbourg.

[To Baron Walef. *Sada, March* 9, 1719.

I have just received your letter, and am sorry about what you tell me as to the delay of the fleet. The Cardinal seems to have been misled, since you tell me that the fleet could not have been ready to set sail before the first of this month. I am sorry and vexed about the discovery of the secret. I have heard nothing from the Cardinal, and I will not write to him on this subject, as I have no information from him as to the discovery.

If the English know of the project they will not lack ships to be ready to put to sea. No extraordinary courier has arrived. I hope this news will not turn out quite so bad as you tell me. I expected to have the honour of seeing the Marquis this evening, but I hear that he is not coming.

I beg you to believe me, etc. Please give my compliments to the Marquis de Risbourg.]

LXXIII

Au MARQ^{s} de RISBOURCQ

Sada, le 12re Mars 1719.

M^{r},—J'ai receu l'honneur de la votre, et vous suis bien obligé de la bonté que vous avez de me faire savoir que vous envoyez un Courrier a la Cour, Je me serve de cette occasion puisque vous voulez bien me le permettre, pour écrire au Cour, mais je n'ai rien a dire attendant avec impatience des nouvelles de Monsr le Cardinal, et le depart de la Flotte, le retardement est bien mortifiant, mais il faut avoir patience. Je suis fâché que je n'ai point joui de l'honneur de votre Compagnie ; mais il faut que je me prive de cet plaisir puisqu'il y a des mesures a garder.

Il faut attendre a tout moment le retour de votre Courrier. Quand vous aurez des nouvelles, je suis seur que vous aurez la bonté de me les communiquer.

Je vous supplie d'etre bien persuadé qu'on ne peut etre avec plus de respect que j'ai l'honneur d'etre, Monsr, etc.   OR.

[TO THE MARQUIS DE RISBOURG. *Sada, March* 12, 1719.

SIR,—I have had the honour to receive your letter, and am greatly obliged to you for your kindness in letting me know that you are sending a courier to the court. I take advantage of this opportunity, since you are good enough to allow me to do so, to write to the court, but I have nothing to say, as I am awaiting with impatience the Cardinal's news, and the departure of the fleet. The delay is very annoying, but one must have patience. I am sorry that I have not enjoyed the honour of your company ; but I must deny myself that pleasure, as there are arrangements to attend to.

The return of your courier must be looked for at any moment. When you receive news, I am sure you will have the goodness to communicate it to me.

I beg you to rest assured, etc.   OR.]

LXXIV

AU CARD. ALBERONI   *p. 61.*

Maître Pierre, *The King.*

SADA, LE 12RE MARS 1719.

MONS^R,—Je me serve de cette occasion pour vous assurer de mes tres humbles respects, Je n'ai rien de nouveau a vous mander d'icy, Je suis bien impatient de recevoir de vos nouvelles, je croy que le Courrier qui a esté depeché il y a quatorze jours est en chemain, Je souhaiterai de voir M^r le Chev^r Macdonnel, et suis bien en peine pour avoir de nouvelles de Maitre Pierre j'espere, Monsr, que vous en aurez eu, et que je les saurai par la prem^{re} occasion.

Le nommé Tullo est arrivé icy. Je croy qu'il y aura quelque lettre pour moy a Madride, s'il y en a j'espere les avoir par le prem^r Courrier. Soyez persuadé, Monsr, que j'ai l'honneur d'estre avec beaucoup de respect et plus que personne, etc.

(S^d) De Comerfort.

[To Cardinal Alberoni. *Sada, March* 12, 1719.

Sir,—I take advantage of this opportunity to assure you of my very humble respects. I have no news from here to tell you. I am very impatient to receive your news. I trust that the courier who was sent off a fortnight ago is on his way. I should like to see the Chevalier Macdonnel. I am in great anxiety to have news of Mr. Peter. I hope, sir, that you have news of him, and that I shall hear it on the first opportunity.

Tullo has arrived here. I think there will be some letters for me at Madrid. If that is so I hope to have them by the first courier.

Rest assured, sir, that I have the honour, etc.

(Signed) De Comerfort.]

LXXV

Au BARON WALEF

Sada, le 12me Mars 1719.

Je vous prie, Monsr, de me dire si vous vous souvenez ce que Monsr le Cardinal vous a dit touchant le temps que je devois donner la patente de Brigadier a Monsr le Chevalier Heley, si je ne me trompe vous m'avez dit que Monsr le Cardinal ne voulloit pas que je le luy donna que quand nous serions embarquez, Monsr d'Hely ne sçait pas que je vous ecris sur cette affair. J'espere que vous estes bien aprez votre voiage je suis tres impatient pour avoir des nouvelles comme vous pouvez croir, Dieu veuille qu'elles soient bonnes, quand j'en receverai, mes compl. S.V.P. a tous vos Messrs et soyez persuadé que je suis tres parfaitement Monsr etc.

[To Baron Walef. *Sada, March* 12, 1719.

Sir,—I beg you to tell me if you remember what the Cardinal said to you as to the time at which I ought to give Sir John Healy his commission of brigadier.[1] If I am not mistaken, you told me that the Cardinal did not wish me to give it to him until we had embarked. He does not know that I am writing to you about this. I hope that you are well after your journey. I am very anxious to have news, as you can believe. God grant that it may be good news when I do receive it. My compliments, etc.]

LXXVI

Au MARQ^s de RISBOURCQ

p. 62.

SADA, LE 15 MARS 1719.

Monsr,—Je vous suis bien obligé de la bonté que vous avez eu de m'envoyer les Gazettes je vous les renvoye.

Je croy que les vaisseaux qui ont estez veues allont la routte de Lisbonne, pourront estre ceux qui estoient destines pour la porte Mohan, ils doivent estre quatre vaisseaux de Guerre, mais sens doute ils auront beaucoup des vaisseaux marchands. J'espere que je ne me trompe pas, et qu'ils tiendront leur routte pour le Detroit, s'ils vont a Lisbonne Ils seront informez de l'armement que se fait a Cadix, ce que sera fort a contretemps, Je vous prie Monsieur d'estre persuadé que j'ai l'honneur d'etre avec beaucoup de respect Monsr, etc.

P.S.—On aura pris des gros vaisseaux marchands p^r des vaisseaux de guerre.

[To THE MARQUIS DE RISBOURQ. *Sada, March* 15, 1719.

SIR,—I am much obliged for your kindness in sending me the Gazettes, which I return.

I think that the ships which have been seen making for Lisbon may be those bound for Port Mahon. There should be four men-of-war, but no doubt they will have many merchant ships. I hope I am not mistaken, and that they will make for the Straits. If they go to Lisbon they will get news of the expedition fitting out at Cadiz, which will be a very bad business. I beg you to believe that I have the honour, etc.

P.S.—They will have taken some large merchantmen for men-of-war.]

---

[1] Under the old French monarchy a *brigadier* was an officer ranking between a colonel and a *maréchal de camp*. The word is now used for a corporal of cavalry.

LXXVII

Au BARON WALEF

SADA, LE 15 MARS 1719.

M^R,—Hier au soir j'ai receu l'honneur de la votre. Vous pouvez croire l'impatience que j'ay de ce retardement. Nous ne voyons que trop que la Flotte n'est pas arrivé, mais nous sommes tout a fait ignorant de ce que le retient, si c'est le vent contraire, ou manque de Matelots, mais il me semble assez extraordinaire que Monsr le Cardinal ne veut pas me donner de ces nouvelles. S'il avoit changé de sentiment quelle mistere y a-t-il a me le faire scavoir, enfin je ne comprend rien a tout cecy.

p. 63. A ce que vous faites mention touchant quelque jalouzie qu'il pourroit arriver, si nous allions en Ecosse sur le commandement, il n'y pourroit avoir, puisque la patente de mon Roy, de Capitaine General est de commander par mer aussy bien que par terre. Enfin il faut avoir patience car il n'y a point de remede, j'espere que demain ou aprez demain au plus tard, le Courrier sera de retour. Mes Complim^{ts} S.V.P. a vos Messrs Croyez moy parfaitem^t etc.

[To BARON WALEF. *Sada, March* 15, 1719.

SIR,—Last night I had the honour to receive your letter. You can believe my impatience at the delay. We see only too well that the fleet has not arrived; but we are entirely ignorant as to what is detaining it, whether contrary wind, or want of seamen. It seems to me, however, very extraordinary that the Cardinal does not think fit to give me this information. If he had changed his intention, what mystery is there about letting me know? In short, I do not understand this at all.

As for what you mentioned about some jealousy which might arise if we go to Scotland in command, there could not be any, as my King's commission as Captain General grants command by sea as well as by land.

In short, we must have patience, for there is no remedy. I hope that the courier will return to-morrow, or the day after to-morrow at latest. My compliments, etc.]

LXXVIII

To SIR TIMON CONNOCK

SADA, THE 16 MARCH 1719, at 12 at Noon.

S^R,—I have just now receiv'd yours, and wonder that there is no news of the Fleet, since the letters from Cadix of the 20th February mentions that all things was ready, and only waited for orders; it's surprising that we do not hear from the Cardinal. I own I cannot guess at the reason. I am sorry that it's talk'd off at Cadix that this expedition is for Scotland, and that it is your humble servant, that has the honour to command it; but there is no help for it.

I have told the Marquis my opinion in my letter to him last night, concerning the things that he inform'd me off, that you now mention, and it was the four ships designed for Port Mahon, with severall large merchant ships under their Convoy, which at a distance have been taken for ships of war. I own I know not what to think of the Cardinal's silence, but there is no remedy but patience. Pray believe me with great esteem etc.

My Comp. to Sr J. Haley and ye rest of your Company.

LXXIX

Au Marq^s de Risbourcq

Sada, le 16re Mars 1719.

M^r,—J'ai receu l'honneur de la votre p^r Monsr de Connock, et j'ai dessein s'il plait a Dieu de m'embarquer demain, J'espere que nous aurons bien tost nouvelle de l'arrivé de la Flotte. J'envoye avertir nos Messieurs qui sont a la Courogne de s'embarquer demain.

Je suis ravie que toute est prete. Je vous prie d'estre persuadé que je suis avec beaucoup de respect, etc.

P.S.—Par la lettre que j'ai receu de Monsr le Cardinal il est d'opinion qu'il sera necessaire d'envoyer un petit Batiment ou deux au Cap Finisterre pour nous avertir quand la Flotte paroitra, le Pacquet Boat qu'on vient d'equiper poura estre employé, Nugent doit le commander, Monsr De Connock aura l'honneur de vous rendre cellecy et de vous informer de tout ce que je croy estre necessaire.

[To the Marquis de Risbourg. *Sada, March* 16, 1719.

Sir,—I have had the honour to receive your letter by M. de Connock, and I intend, please God, to embark to-morrow. I hope that we shall very soon have news of the arrival of the fleet. I am sending to give our people at Corunna notice to embark to-morrow.

I am delighted that all is ready.

I beg you to believe me, etc.

P.S.—According to the letter which I have received from the Cardinal, he is of opinion that one or two small vessels should be sent to Cape Finisterre to let us know when the fleet appears. The packet-boat which has just been equipped might be employed. Nugent is to command her. M. de Connock will have the honour of delivering this to you, and of informing you of all that I think necessary.]

LXXX

Au CARDINAL ALBERONI, par exprès

Corogne, le 17re Mars 1719.

Hier au soir j'ai receu l'honneur de la lettre que V. Eminence m'envoya par Mr. Macdonnel avec l'agreeable nouvelle que la Flotte estoit parti le 7re du Courant. Je suis arrivé icy aujourd'hui avant diner, affin d'estre pret a m'embarquer d'abord que j'en aurai des nouvelles. Nous envoyons un petit Batiment a la hauteur du Cap Finisterre pour nous avertir de l'arrivée de la Flotte. Pendant que nous estions a Table j'ai reçu la lettre de V. E. avec la bonne nouvelle de l'arivée du Roy mon Maitre, c'est presque un miracle qu'il a si heureusement fait le voiage, j'espere que c'est une bonne augure, et que Dieu benira l'entreprise. Monsr le Marquis de Risbourcq, Monsr Walef et moy, avons parlé ensemble, et sommes tous d'accord qu'il est absolument necessaire que sa Majesté vient icy, affin d'estre prest pour s'embarquer quand l'occasion s'en presentera. J'ai veu la lettre que Monsr de Risbourcg envoye a V. Em. Il vous informa de tout ce que nous sommes Convenus, et je n'importunerai pas V. E. par des repetitions.

Je suis bien faché d'aprendre qu'on est alarmé en France et en Angleterre,—mais il faut faire de notre mieux, et esperer que la providence divine nous donnera un bon succes. Je suis du sentiment de V. E. de ce que vous faites mention touchant Monsr. Lawless et mon parent, et je ne doute pas que le Roy mon maitre ne l'aprouve, il est vray semblant que la Reine de Suede ne se melera pas des affaires etrangeres pour quelque temps. Je suis bien aise d'apprendre que votre Em. a fait acheter cinq ou six mille Fusils a Amsterdam, je me servirai de la permission que vous me donnez, selon que je trouverai occasion, aiant les addresses pour les Marchands ou Banquiers, et le nom de Monsr. Lawless. J'ai receu la Declaration de sa Majesté Catholique pour ce qui regard les sujets de mon Maitre, que ne pourroit qu'avoir un bon effet en cas de malheur, et celle pour estre lu a la tete de chaque Compagnie des sujets du Roy. A l'egard de ce que V. E. me mande touchant les officiers j'aurai attention, et je m'estime fort heureux d'avoir Mr. de Connock, et j'ai beaucoup d'estime p^r Mr. de Franlieu et les autres. Je m'etonne que V. E. n'a pas eu des nouvelles de Messrs de Gordon et de Campbell. Je suis seur que Dutton ne perdra pas un moment a venir quand il pourra. Je voy par les nouvelles que vous avez eu la bonté de m'envoyer, qu'il y a des grandes affaires sur le Tapis en Angleterre, touchant la succession et bien du changement dans la Cour s'il plait a Dieu il y aura beaucoup plus. J'ay l'honneur d'estre, etc.

P.S.—V. E. m'a envoyée une pacquet p^r My Lord Marischal —je vous le renvoye, je croy que c'estoit par mepris.

[To CARDINAL ALBERONI, by express. *Corunna, March* 17, 1719.

LAST night I had the honour to receive the letter which your Eminence sent me by Mr. Macdonnel, with the agreeable news that the fleet had sailed on the 7th of this month. I arrived here to-day before dinner, so as to be ready to embark as soon as I get any news. We are sending a small vessel to the latitude of Cape Finisterre to let us know of the arrival of the fleet. While we were at table I received your Eminence's letter with the good news of the arrival of the King my master. It is almost a miracle that he has made the voyage so successfully. I hope it is a good omen, and that God will bless the enterprise. The Marquis de Risbourg, Baron Walef, and myself have consulted together, and we are all agreed that it is absolutely necessary that His Majesty should come here, so as to be ready to embark when the opportunity occurs. I have seen the letter that M. de Risbourg is sending to your Eminence. He has told you of all that we have agreed upon, and I shall not trouble your Eminence with repetitions.

I am very sorry to hear that they have taken alarm in France and in England, but we must do our best, and hope that Divine Providence will give us good success. I am of Your Excellency's opinion as to what you say about M. Lawless and my kinsman, and I have no doubt that the King my Master will approve. It is not likely that the Queen of Sweden will meddle with foreign affairs for some time. I am very glad to learn that your Eminence has caused five or six thousand muskets to be bought in Amsterdam. I shall make use of the permission which you give me as I find opportunity, having the addresses of the merchants or bankers, and the name of M. Lawless. I have received the declaration of his Catholic Majesty regarding my Master's subjects, which cannot but have a good effect in case of misfortune, and that is to be read at the head of each company of the King's subjects. I shall attend to what your Eminence tells me about the officers. I consider myself very fortunate in having M. de Connock, and I have a great regard for M. de Franlieu and the others. I am surprised that your Eminence has not had news of Mr. Gordon and Mr. Campbell. I am sure that Dutton will not lose a moment in coming when he can. I see by the news which you have been good enough to send me that great events are happening in England as to the succession, and great changes about the Court.[1] Please God there will be many more.

I have the honour, etc.

P.S.—Your Eminence has sent me a packet for the Earl Marischal. I return it; I suppose it was sent by mistake.]

LXXXI

To the King, p^r express [2]

Corogne, 17 March 1719.

This day I receiv'd a letter from the Cardinal of the 13th Instant, with the agreeable news of your being landed at Roses, for which I do most heartily thank God, and do with all the sincerity and respect imaginable congratulate you on your safe arrivall into this Country, I was infinitly in pain for you during the bad weather that we have lately had, fearing that you might have been at sea, at that time, but thank God my fears are at an end. The Cardinal tells me that he has order'd relays on the Road for you, and desires to know my opinion, if it is best for you to come to this place, tho' I shou'd be gone.

---

[1] This probably refers to the quarrel between George I. and his son, which reached an acute stage in 1718, when the Prince of Wales, after having been placed under arrest in his own apartments, was ordered to quit St. James's. George wished to obtain an Act of Parliament to compel the Prince, on coming to the throne, to relinquish his German states. This project was given up on the strong remonstrances of Lord Chancellor Parker.

[2] The original of this letter is in the Stuart Papers.

I am entirely of opinion that you shou'd come hither, or in the neighbourhood, that you may be in a readyness to embarque, if that it pleases God I land in England, and meet with the success I hope for, in that case I will send back the men of war, and order them to make the best of their way to this place, if wind and weather permits, and, if not possible to come to this place, to endeavour to come to some port in the neighbourhood, for shou'd you stay at Madrid, or at a great distance from this place, it might so happen that you might lose an opportunity by being at so great a distance. *p. 68.*

I came to the Marq^s de Risbourcqe's this afternoon, to be ready to embarque but I have no news of the Fleet's being seen on the Coast, tho' I do expect every moment to hear of it's being seen off of the Cap Finisterre. It is very unlucky that the designe is discovered but it was almost impossible it shou'd not, the winds and weather having kept the Fleet from sailing after it had been ready to go to sea for some weeks. The Marq^s de Risbourg will have a Country house for you, near this Town, so that you will not be troubled with seeing Company, unless you pleas; tho' indeed there is but little here.—Mr. Bagnal is in Holland, the Cardinal will inform you of what he has mention'd to me of him and Mr. Lawles, concerning their being sent to Sweden, which I believe you will not think impropper, he will also inform you of arms that he has in Holland, and My Lord Marischall's going to Scotland, with arms, and ammunition, and also of everything that relates *p. 69.* to your service. I hope in God to see you where you ought to be, and pray to God to preserve you and give you all happyness. I am with great duty and respect y^r Majesty's, etc.

LXXXII

To the DUKE of MAR[1]

Zeky, Ezekiel Hamilton.

COROGNE, THE 17^{IE} MARS 1719.

MY LORD,—I am quite tired with writing, but would not

---

[1] Mar, as has been mentioned, had been made a titular duke by James. Ormonde evidently knew nothing of his arrest at Voghera (Introduction, p. xxxiii), and thought that he had accompanied James to Spain.

lose this opportunity of congratulating you on the king's safe arrivall, and on your own share of the good fortune in coming safe to this Country, after so hazardous a voyage ; I must refer you to mine to our Master, and to be sure the Cardinal will inform the king of everything that relates to his Interest. Zeky is now in England I believe, I sent him thither to inform our Friends of what was agreed on here, that they might be apprised of the undertaking, and send some small vessells to meet us, to give an account of y^r posture of affaires, and where the Cruisers were, and what ships might be in the soundings and chopps of the Channell. I had one from our Friends, I sent the Cardinal an abstract of what he brought me over. I hope you left all your friends well in Italy, and that we may have a happy meeting, God send it.

p. 70.

Believe me very, etc.

LXXXIII

Au MARQ^S DE RISBOURCQ

COUROGNE, LE 19^{IE} MARS 1719.

MONS^R,—Je vous prie de me donner Mille huit Cents Piastres, des Sept Mille Pistolles qu'il y a abord de L'Hermionne. J'ai l'honneur d'estre, etc.

N^{TA}—This order was Changed for one of Three thousand Piastres.

[To THE MARQUIS DE RISBOURG. *Courogne, March* 19, 1719.

SIR,—I request you to give me eighteen hundred piastres[1] of the seven thousand pistoles which are on board the *Hermione*. I have the honour, etc.]

LXXXIV

Au MARQ^S DE RISBOURG

COUROGNE, LE 20 MARS 1719.

MONS^R,—Aiant esté informé par le Capt de l'Hermionne que son Equipage n'est pas complete, et meme qu'elle n'est pas

---

[1] The old Spanish piastre or 'piece of eight' was worth about four **shillings**. The **gold** pistole was worth between fifteen and sixteen shillings.

composée des gens telles qu'il souhaiteroit avoir en cas de rencontre ; Je vous prie de donner vos ordres pour faire venir icy de Ponte a Vedre Le vaisseau nommé Le Prince des Asturies, appartenant au sieur Mahar, commandé p^r le s^r Nugent avec tout son Equipage, qui sera tres necessaire abord de l'Hermionne, estant des bons Matelots et des gens experimentés. Vous aurez aussy Monsr la bonté s'il vous plait, d'ordonner au Gouverneur de Ponte a Vedre de donner les provisions necessaires. J'ai l'honneur d'estre, etc.

[To the Marquis de Risbourg. *Courogne, March* 20, 1719.

Sir,—As I have been informed by the Captain of the *Hermione* that his crew is not complete, and that it is not composed of such men as he would like to have in the event of an engagement, I beg you to give orders to send here from Pontevedra the ship called *The Prince of the Asturias*, which belongs to M. Mahar, and is commanded by M. Nugent, with all her crew, who will be very necessary on board the *Hermione*, as they are good sailors and experienced men. You will also have the kindness, sir, if you please, to order the Governor of Pontevedra to supply the necessary provisions. I have the honour, etc.]

LXXXV

Au M. de GUEVARA

Corogne, le 20re Mars 1719.

Monsr,—Je m'estime fort heureux d'avoir une personne de votre merite pour commander la Flotte destinée pour l'entreprise ou j'ai l'honneur de commander les Trouppes. Je vous prie, M^r, d'estre bien persuadé que j'aurai bien du plaisir a trouver des occasions par ou je pourrai vous temoigner l'estime que j'ai pour votre merite. J'ai l'honneur de vous envoyer cellecy qu'est une copie d'une que j'ai envoyée déjà au Cape Finisterre, pour vous estre rendue, mais je me serve de cette occasion, de peur que l'autre pourroit manquer, pour vous prier de vouloir bien vous aprocher de la Corogne aussy tost que vous pourrez affin que nous pouvons nous aboucher avec plus de facilité, car s'il faisait mauvais temps il seroit impossible qu'une Chalouppe pourroit aller d'un navire a l'autre, et nous ne pourrons continuer notre voyage sens que nous aions ajusté et reglé la routte que nous devons faire, ny estre d'accord des signaux et d'une lieu de Rendezvous en cas que la Flotte soit séparée par le mauvais temps. Je vous prie, Mons\ufeffr, d'estre persuadé que j'ai l'honneur d'estre, etc.

p. 72.

[To M. DE GUEVARA. *Courogne, March* 20, 1719.

SIR,—I think myself very fortunate in having a person of your merit to command the fleet intended for the expedition in which I have the honour to command the troops. I beg you, sir, to believe that it will give me great pleasure to find opportunities of showing you the regard which I have for your merits. I have the honour to send you this letter, which is a copy of one which I have already sent to Cape Finisterre to be delivered to you, but I take advantage of this opportunity in case the other should fail, in order to beg you to come into Corunna as soon as you can, in order that we may the more easily confer, for if the weather is bad it will be impossible for a boat to pass from one ship to another, and we shall not be able to proceed upon our voyage without having adjusted and settled the course which we are to take, and agreed as to the signals and a place of rendezvous in case the fleet should be separated by bad weather.

I beg you, sir, to rest assured that I have the honour, etc.]

LXXXVI

Au CARD. ALBERONI, par exprès [1]

COROGNE, LE 22 MARS 1719.

J'AY l'honneur d'informer V. E. par ce Courier que nous n'avons pas des nouvelles de la Flotte, ce qui est un Contretemps tres facheux. Ce retardement de la Flotte causé par des Vents contraires rende notre Entreprise tres difficile et presque impossible, puisque je voy par la Lettre de V. E. a Mons\ufeffr le Marq\ufeffs de Risbourg que l'on est averti en France et en Angleterre de L'armement qui se faisoit a Cadix, du depart du Roy mon Maitre de Rome, et a l'heur qu'il est son arrivé en Espagne et le tems que j'ai demeuré en cet voisinage, ce qui les aura donné l'alarme et le tems de prendre leurs precautions pour nous opposer, V. E. se resouviendra que quand j'avois l'honneur de vous proposer ce projet que cetoit sur la supposition que nous la ferions par surprise, car autrement je naurois pas été si

---

[1] Copy in Stuart Papers.

imprudent que de proposer d'attacquer L'Angleterre avec cinq mille hommes quand on aura eté averti de notre desseins. Je ne veul pas dire par ceci qu'ils puissent diviner ou j'ai desseins de debarquer, cest a dire justement l'endroit, mais ils sim- *p.* 73. ageront bien que cest pour L'Angleterre ou pour L'Ecosse, car croyés moy Monseign^r ils ne prendront pas le change et ne croiront jamais que nous avons dessein d'aller en Irlande.

Permetté que je fasse sovenir V. E. de ce qui est dans le Papier que j'ai eu l'honneur de vous envoyer de Valladolid a mon de part de la. Cest l'abstracte de ce que mes amis m'avoient mandé et leur opinion en reponse de ce que j'ai les avois demandé en partant de Paris, la premiere article dit que si on peut surprendre les Hannoverians que le coup est immanquable mais autrement difficile et tres incertaine. Je suis en cette Voisinage depuis le 24me du Fevrier, cest les Vens et mauvais tems qui a fait ce Retardement, qui ait donné les tems aux Ennemis de prendre leurs precautions, V. E. jugera bien comme l'affaire est changé par cette retardement car ce qui a eté bon il y trois semaines ou un mois ne l'est pas a cet heur. Je crois qu'il sera bon d'aller en Ecosse ce que je nétois point d'opinion auparavant ce retardement ; on pourra eviter une Escadre que apparament nous attendra a l'entré de la manche, en allant au large par le Oüest de L'Irlande. Nous pourons avoir les armes et ammunitions de Hollande ; nous pourrons nous deffendre *p.* 74. et nous maintenir du Coté des Montagnes, mais il sera tres necessaire, si V. E. goute ce projet, que vous nous envoyez de la farine, du sel, vin, Brandevin, pour la subsistance, nous aurons du monde assez ; et je suis assuré que nos amis feront leur possible de nous joindre, c'est a dire ceux qui sont au nort d'Engleterre, et il est bon d'avoir un pied dans L'Isle, et il pourroit arriver des accidents a notre avantage, et il n'est pas impossible que les Troupes Angloises qui sont en ce pais pourront deserter. En cas que V. E. est du sentiment de ce que je propose, il faudroit que le Roy mon maitre vient pour aller sur la Flotte. Je n'ai pas voullu finir ma lettre jusques l'arrivé du petit Batiment que nous avons veu entrer en cette porte, nous crumes qu'il venoit de la Flotte, mais je viens de parler au patron. Il vient de St Sebastien, il dit que les deux Fregattes sont partis avec les trois cents soldats il y a onze jours, et que les vents ont estez sy contraires qu'il les croit a trente Lieux du Cap d'Ortegalle.

p. 75 Nonobstont ce que j'ai ecrit touchant le Roy mon Maitre, si la Flotte arrive nous nous embarquerons s'il plait a Dieu et continuerons la routte vers l'Engleterre, en esperance de rencontrer quelque Bastiment d'avis. Si je n'en trouve pas a la hauteur de l'endroit que nous appellons les soundings, je feray voille vers l'Ecosse et j'auray l'honneur de vous envoyer un petit Batiment pour vous informer de ce que J'ay dessein de faire. Je ne vous donne pas le detaille de ce que nos enemies peuvent faire, pour se fortifier contre nous; vous le sçavez, et Monsr de Risbourg vous informe aussy bien que Monsr de Walef. J'espere que nous aurons des nouvelles de V. E. si le vent demeure contraire. J'ay receu quatre cents pistolles de Monsr de Risbourcq par l'ordre de V. E. dont je vous suis bien obligé. Monsr de Risbourcq fait tout ce qu'on peut desirer de luy. J'ay l'honneur d'estre avec beaucoup de respect de Votre Eminence, etc.

[To CARDINAL ALBERONI, by express. *Corogne, March 22, 1719.*

I HAVE the honour to inform your Eminence by this courier that we have no news of the fleet, which is a very annoying mischance. This delay of the fleet, caused by contrary winds, makes our enterprise very difficult and almost impossible, since by your Eminence's letter to the Marquis de Risbourg I see that both in France and in England they are informed about the expedition fitting out at Cadiz, of the departure of the King, my master, from Rome, and now of his arrival in Spain, and the time that I have spent in this neighbourhood, all which will have given them the alarm and time to make arrangements to oppose us.

Your Eminence will remember that, when I had the honour to propose this enterprise to you, it was on the footing that it was to be carried out by surprise, for otherwise I should not have been so rash as to propose to attack England with five thousand men when they were informed of our intentions. I do not mean to say that they can find out where I propose to land, that is to say, the exact place, but they will understand quite well that the expedition is for England or Scotland, for, believe me, Monseigneur, they will not be taken in, and will never believe that we mean to go to Ireland.

Allow me to remind your Eminence of the contents of the paper which I had the honour to send you on my departure from Valladolid. It is the abstract of the information which I received from my friends and their opinion in reply to the inquiries which I made of them when I left Paris. The first article says that if we can surprise the Hanoverians the stroke is sure of success, but is otherwise difficult and very uncertain. I have been in this neighbourhood since the 24th of February; it is the winds and bad weather which have caused this delay, which has given the enemy time to take precautions. Your Eminence will judge how much the position of matters is changed by this delay; for what was good three weeks or a month ago is not so now. I think it would be well to land in Scotland, which I did not think before this delay; we could avoid a squadron which apparently is to be waiting for us at the mouth of the Channel by keeping well out to sea to the west of Ireland. We could get arms and ammunition from Holland, and could defend ourselves and hold out in the Highlands, but it will be very necessary, if your Eminence likes this plan, that you should send us meal, salt, wine, and brandy for provisions. We shall have plenty of men; and I am assured that our friends will do what they can to join us, that is to say, those who are in the north of England. It is well to have a footing in the island; accidents might happen to our advantage, and it is not impossible that the English troops in the country might desert. Should your Eminence agree to what I propose, the King my master ought to come to go on board the fleet.

I did not wish to finish my letter until the arrival of the little vessel which we saw enter this port. We thought that it came from the fleet, but I have just been talking to the master. He comes from St. Sebastian; he says that the two frigates with the three hundred soldiers sailed eleven days ago, and that the winds have been so contrary that he believes they will be thirty leagues from Cape Ortegal.

Notwithstanding what I have written with regard to the King my Master, if the fleet comes we shall go on board, please God, and proceed on our course towards England, in hope to meet some despatch vessel. If I do not find any at the latitude of the place which we call the soundings, I shall make sail for Scotland, and shall have the honour to send you a small vessel to let you know what I propose to do. I do not give you the details of what our enemies can do to fortify themselves against us; you know them, and M. de Risbourg can inform you, as well as M. de Walef. I hope that we shall have news of your Eminence if the wind remains contrary. I have received four hundred pistoles from M. de Risbourg by your Eminence's order, for which I am greatly obliged to you. M. de Risbourg does all that one could desire of him.—I have the honour, etc.]

LXXXVII

To the KING P^R EXPRES [1]

Corogne, 22d March 1719.

Sir,—I hope this will find you in good health, after your

---

[1] Original in Stuart Papers.

fatigue, and that you are satisfied with the Cardinal, I have not the least doubt of it. S^r I here enclosed send you a copy of mine to the Cardinal, which will inform you of my opinion concerning the enterprise, and the delays we have met with by the contrary winds, and bad weather, I do also enclose the opinions of your Friends in England in answer to some querries that I sent them from Paris, by a sure hand, you will see Sir that by them, they thought the attempt could not miscary, provided that we could surprise the enemies, therefore gave their reasons for not communicating of it but to a very few, they say at the same time, if that the attempt be discovered before the landing, it allmost will be impossible to suceed, I need not say any more on this subject refering to mine to the Cardinal. I have just now seen the Master of a ship from St Sebastiens that is just arriv'd from thence, he says that Lord Marishall I mean that the two Friggats with soldiers sail'd from St Sebastien eleven days ago, My Lord Marishall was with them, but this man did not mention him, Brig^r Campbell is with him, but the Master says that he do's believe that they are not above thirty leagues from the Cape Ortegall, the wind having been so contrary. You will see, Sir, my reason for what I mention concerning Scotland, occasion'd by our being detain'd so long by contrary Windes, which has given the Enemies time for to fit out a squadron, and to raise Troops, and send for Forreigners, what was good a month ago is not so now, I have been in this neighbourhood since the 24th of february expecting to have met the fleet when I arrived. In Scotland we may keep our ground in the Highlands, and waite for some occasion that may be advantageous, this is mention'd in mine to the Cardinal, and if we should embarke before I have the honour to kiss y^r hand, I will send you an advice Boat to informe you of what I designe to endeavour to do.

If wee go to Scotland you will be pleased to get the Cardinall to send by single ships, good sailers, Wines, Brandy, Meale, and Salt, with money for to help to pay your subjects that takes up arms for you. I have had one thousand Pistolles from the Cardinall, and Monsr de Risbourg lends me another thousand of his own, I do not intend to medle with this money of his should any accident hinder us to pursue our voyage, I expect a little money from my Relations and design to have it paid to him.

I will trouble you no longer at this time, but to beg of you to believe that I pray to God to give you success, and all happyness, I am with all duty and respect, etc.

LXXXVIII

To the KING, by express to yᴇ CARD.[1]

Corogne, yᴇ 27ᵗʜ Mar. 1719.

Sʳ,—On the 22ᵈ instant I had the honʳ to receive your Letter of yᵉ 11th from Girone and hope you came safe and in good health to Madrid. I am very glad the Princesse is at Rome, I heartily wish she were in this Country.[2] I have no News of the Fleet, there came to this place about two hours ago a little Privateer from Ponte Vedra, she had a Letter from me to yᵉ Spanish Admirall in case she shoud meet with him at sea—the Master of this Privateer had been here and I sent him back to his ship at yᵉ place I have mentioned to bring his Vessell hither with intention to take his Crew to recruit our Frigat who was not so well man'd as she ought to have been.

I suppose Sir that you will not make any stay at Madrid, I mean not above a day or two, but make the best of your way to this place that if the Fleet shou'd not be sailed from this Porte before you arrive you may take your measures as to goeing or otherwise as you will think most proper. You will have seen, Sʳ, by mine I had the honʳ to write of yᵉ 22ᵈ inst. what I propose and yᵉ uneasiness I am in at this delay which certainly was caused by the contrary Winds, and the ill consequences of the Enterprises being known in England, which must necessarily have put your Enemies on their Guard. I think there is nothing to be done but the goeing to Scotland, tho' to be sure they will not have neglected that kingdome. I hope you will have prevailed with the Cardinal to have given you a good

---

[1] Original in Stuart Papers.
[2] Princess Clementina was still at Innspruck.

summ of money for the uses I mentioned in my last, for when the troops are once landed and that there shoud be any insurrection in this kingdome when the French and German troops invade it, in that case I fear the troops that are in Scotland would be forgotten, and very little or no supplys sent them from Spain. I am in daily expectation of seeing somebody from England, but this is very uncertain the passage by Sea being lyable to so many accidents, shou'd any one come and bring good News which is hardly to be expected, then, I woud think of the first designe, whatever happens I will endeavour to inform you of what passes, shou'd you not arrive before we leave this place. My Lord Marischall with the two Frigats was put into St Andere as I was informed from a Master, that came from that place and arrived here two days agoe, I suppose he has acquainted the Cardinall with his being there. Coll. Owen [1] came hither last Night but brought no News.

I am with great Duty, S^r, etc,

LXXXIX

Au CARD. ALBERONI, par exprès

Major Stamfort, *Ezekiel Hamilton.*

Corogne, le 27me Mars 1719.

J'ay eu l'honneur de la Lettre de votre Eminence du 18me nous n'avons point des nouvelles de la Flotte ce qui m'ettonne beaucoup. Il est entré en cette porte une Corsaire de Ponte Vedre que nous avons fait venir icy pour se servir de son Equipage pour recruiter l'Hermione qui avoit besogne, Monsieur de Risbourg vous a donne le detaille de cecy aussi bien que de tous ce qui se passent, j'ay veu sa lettre et suis d'accord de tous ce qu'il mande a V. E. ce pourquoy je ne veul pas importuner V. E. d'un recit. J'ai fait donner une somme aux Officiers pour leur aider a avoir ce qui leurs etoit necessaire pour leur Voiage

---

[1] Colonel Owen, who followed Ormonde to Spain, had been dismissed from the British army. He was at Oxford in 1715, concerting measures with some of the Heads of Houses for an insurrectionary movement. His proceedings were discovered, and he only escaped arrest by a hasty flight. See Mahon, vol. i. p. 158.

ce que sera compté sur leurs Appointements. My Lord Marischall a eté relaché a St Ander apparament il aura informé V. E. de son arrivée. Le Coll. Owen arriva hier au soir. Jespere que le Roy d'Angleterre est arrivée en bonne santé a Madrid et qu'il ne restera pas plus long tems qu'il est absolument necessaire. Mon Secretaire le Major Stamforte partit de Bourdeaux le 26me de fevrier et je conte qu'il a eté en Angleterre il y a 15 jours, il me mande par Monsieur Lesley qu'il ne restera pas plus de deux fois vingt quatre heurs a Londres, qu'il partiroit sans perdre un moment pour me rencontrer, qu'il enveroit un Officier de la Marine dans un autre Batiment pour tasher de me joindre. Dieu veuille que l'un ou l'autre me rencontre. Sur ce que V. E. a ecrit touchant la Hermione il pourroit arriver des inconveniens, car si elle etoit au Cap il pouroit arriver que nous pourrions voir quelques Vaisseaux de guerre Angloises et la partie ne seroit pas egalle, s'il feroit quelque gros tems nous pourrions etre forcé en mer et manquer L'Escadre, la Fregate est preste a faire Voile, et je suis prêt a m'embarquer c'est pourquoi je crois quelle est mieux icy. Jespere que L'Escadre Angloise qui etoit a Lisbonne n'a pas taché de rencontrer la Flotte. J'ay l'honneur d'etre, etc.

p. 81.

[To CARDINAL ALBERONI, by express. *Corunna, March* 27, 1719.

I HAVE had the honour to receive your Eminence's letter of the 18th. We have no news of the fleet, which surprises me much. There has come into this port a privateer from Pontevedra, which we have brought here in order to make use of her crew to recruit the *Hermione* which needs men. M. de Risbourg has given you details as to this, as well as of all that is happening. I have seen his letter, and agree with all that he tells your Eminence, so I do not wish to trouble your Eminence with a narrative. I have advanced to the officers a sum to enable them to provide necessaries for the voyage, which will be deducted from their pay.

The Earl Marischal has apparently put in at Santander. He will have informed your Eminence of his arrival. Colonel Owen arrived here last night. I hope that the King of England has reached Madrid in good health, and that he will not stay longer than is absolutely necessary. My Secretary, Major Stamfort, left Bordeaux on the 26th of February, and I should think has been in England for a fortnight. He tells me by Mr. Lesley that he will not remain more than forty-eight hours in London, that he will set out to meet me without losing a moment, and that he will send a naval officer in another vessel to try to join me.

God grant that one or the other may meet me. As to what your Eminence has written about the *Hermione*, accidents might happen; for if she were at the Cape we might happen to meet some English men-of-war, and the match would not be equal; and if it were bad weather we might be driven out to sea and miss the fleet. The frigate is ready to sail, and I am ready to go on board. That is why I think she is better here. I hope that the English squadron which was at Lisbon has not tried to meet the fleet. I have the honour, etc.]

XC

Au MONS^R CREAN ET COMPAGNIE, PAR LE MESME EXPRES

MARS 27.

MONS^R,—Ayant receu avis des Messrs Sampson et Sandilanes de Bourdeaux qu'ils ont tirées sur le Sieur Vanbeque 220 pieces de huit en votre faveur, je vous renvoy par un Courier 55 pistolles d'Espagne pour payer la dite lettre, et en cas que la ditte lettre soit protestee ce que je n'ay pas lieu d'esperer par ce que ces Messrs me mandent vous aures la bonté de les remettre la ditte somme en leur mandant que cest pour le Compte de son Excellence le Duc D'Ormonde. Je suis, etc.

Vous estes prié Monsr d'avoir la bonté d'envoyer par le Courier qui vous donnera cette lettre 2 livres du meilleur Tea vert pour Monsr le Duc D'ormonde, addressé au Marquis de Risbourg.

N.B.—This Postscript belongs to ye last letter to ye Cardinal.

J'ay pris la liberté d'envoyer une petite somme d'argent a Monsieur Crean Banquier a Madrid. Je supplie V. E. de permettre que Maitre des Postes rend cette lettre avec L'argent.

[To MESSRS. CREAN and COMPANY, by the same express. *March* 27.

SIR,—Having been informed by Messrs. Sampson and Sandilanes of Bordeaux that they have drawn on M. Vanbeque for 220 pieces of eight in your favour, I send you by a courier 55 Spanish pistoles to meet the said bill; and in case the said bill should be protested, which I have no reason to believe from what these gentlemen tell me, you will be so good as to remit them the said sum, advising them that it is on account of his Excellency the Duke of Ormonde. I am, etc.

You are requested to have the goodness to send by the courier who will deliver this letter two pounds of the best green tea for the Duke of Ormonde, addressed to the Marquis de Risbourg.

N.B.—This Postscript belongs to the last letter to the Cardinal.

I have taken the liberty of sending a small sum of money to M. Crean, banker in Madrid. I beg your Eminence to allow the postmaster to deliver this letter with the money.]

XCI

Au CARD. ALBERONI, par exprès [1]

Stamfort, *Ezekiel Hamilton.*

COROGNE, LE 31ME MARS 1719.

La Lettre de V. E. j'ay eu l'honneur de la recevoir hier au Matin. Nous n'avons pas des nouvelles de la Flotte, et je vous prie d'etre persuadé que je suis bien eloigné de faire des difficultés puisque V. E. a veu par ma Lettre que nonobstant ceux qui se trouvent par le retardement causé par les vents contraires que j'etois prest a m'embarquer quand la Flotte arrivera, mais je voulois bien faire voir a V. E. que je n'etois point insensible ni ignorant de ces difficultes par ce malheureux retardement. Enfin je ferai tout mon possible pour que l'affaire reuisit etant un peu interessé moi mesme. Je crois que V. E. ne peut douter mais que les Enemis soient informés de l'Enterprise et j'espere que V. E. voudra bien m'envoyer une Somme pour etre employée ou l'occasion se presentera, car les Enemis apparament aura la precaution de fair venir a Londres toute L'argent que seroit dans les Doüanes, ce que j'avois compté de saisir d'abord que nous aurions eté a terre cest a dire si tot qu'il etoit possible, mais par la raison que j'ai l'honneur de dire je ne puis conter la dessus. Si la Flotte n'arrive pas plustot que V. E. me peut ecrire jespere que vous aurez la Bonté d'envoyer 50000 mille (sic) Ecus que ne sera employé qu'on il est absolument necessaire, mais je ne perdrai pas un moment de m'embarquer quand la Flotte arrive. Nous n'avons point de Chirurgien sur la Fregate, c'est a dire pas un qui est habille, ce pourquoi je supplie V. E. de vouloir bien donner permission au Chirurgien qui est icy nommé

---

[1] Copy in Stuart Papers.

Charier d'aller avec moi, et qu'il ne perd pas sa Charge qu'il ait icy, si la Flotte arrive je contera tant sur la bonté de V. E. que je lui prendra sur mon bord. J'espere que le Roi d'Angleterre est en chemin pour venir icy, j'attend a tous moments un Batiment d'Angleterre, Monsieur Stamfort mon secretaire m'a mandé de Paris du 2me du courant qu'il partoit le landemain matin pour L'Angleterre et qu'il demeureroit a Londres que deux jours au plus, qu'il viendroit a la Corogne s'il ne me rencontreroit pas en mer et qu'il y aura deux autres Messieurs qui feroient de même.

Je n'ai point des nouvelles de Compte, je ne scais s'il aura peu sortir de St Andere. V. E. peut croire que je scais toutes les inconvenients qui arrivera si cette Enterprise manque. Il est a cet' heur près de six heurs mais aucune nouvelle de la Flotte, l'on a veu des Vaisseaux a la hauteur du Ferolle nous croyons qu'il y auroit quelqu'un de la Flotte mais ils ne sont pas encore entrée. V. E. me permettra de lui recommender Monsieur le Marquis de Prado qui m'a faite milles honnetetez quand j'etois a Valladolid, je ne point eu de ses nouvelles depuis mon arrivée et vous pouvez etre bien assuré qu'il netoit point en ma Confiance. J'ai l'honneur avec beaucoup de Respect, etc.

[To CARDINAL ALBERONI, by express. *Corunna, March* 31, 1719.

I HAD the honour to receive your Eminence's letter of yesterday morning. We have no news of the fleet, and I beg you to believe that I am far from desiring to make difficulties, since your Eminence has seen that, notwithstanding those which exist on account of the delay caused by contrary winds, I am ready to go on board when the fleet arrives; but I wish to make it clear to your Eminence that I am not insensible to nor ignorant of the difficulties due to this unhappy delay. In short, I shall do what I can for the success of the undertaking, seeing that I have myself some interest in it. I think your Eminence cannot doubt that the enemy are informed of the enterprise, and I hope that your Eminence will have the goodness to send me a sum to be employed as occasion may arise, for it seems that the enemy will take the precaution to remove to London all the money in the custom-houses, which I had reckoned on seizing as soon as we landed, that is to say, as soon as possible, but for the reason which I mention I cannot count upon it. Unless the fleet should arrive sooner than it is possible for you to write to me, I hope that you will have the goodness to send me 50,000 crowns, which will not be used unless it is absolutely necessary; but I shall not lose a moment in going on board when the fleet arrives.

We have no surgeon on board the frigate, at least none who is capable.

I accordingly beg your Eminence to grant permission to a surgeon here named Charier to go with me, and that he may not lose the employment which he has here. If the fleet arrives I shall count upon your Eminence's kindness so far as to take him on board.

I hope that the King of England is on his way here. I expect every moment a vessel from England. Mr. Stamfort, my secretary, wrote me from Paris on the 2d of this month that he was to leave for England on the following morning, that he would remain in London two days at the outside, that he would come to Corunna if he did not meet me at sea, and that two other gentlemen would do the same.

I have no news of the Earl [Marischal]. I do not know if he has been able to leave Santander. Your Eminence may believe that I know all the ill consequences which will arise if this enterprise miscarries. It is now almost six o'clock, but no news of the fleet. Ships have been seen off Ferrol: we believe that they may be some of the fleet, but they have not yet come in.

Your Eminence will permit me to recommend to you the Marquis de Prado, who showed me much kindness when I was at Valladolid. I have had no news of him since my arrival, and you may be sure that he was not in my confidence. I have the honour, etc.]

XCII

To the KING, p^R express[1]

p. 84.

Corogne, the 31 March 1719.

S^R,—I cannot send you any news from this place. I have no account of the Fleet which is wonderfull. I send you, Sir, a copy of mine to the Cardinall, you see the reasons why I press for money, if this comes to you before you leave the Court, I hope you will do all you can to prevaill with him to comply with what I ask, it being absolutely necessary for your service, and I think the sum not unreasonable, considering the circumstances. Pray God direct you and give you all prosperity, I am with all submission, Sir, your most, etc.

XCIII

To the KING, p^R MR S^T Marie[2]

Corogne, 4th April 1719.

S^R,—This morning I had the honour of yours of the 30th,

---

[1] Original in Stuart Papers.
[2] Original in Stuart Papers. Received at Villafranca, April 10.

and am glad to find by it that you got safe to Madrid, and design'd to leave it on Monday. I hope in God that you will have a good journey hither. I have no news of the Fleet, but am in expectation, as I have been for these five weeks past to hear of its arrivall every moment. I find y^r Majesty do's not approve of what I mention'd concerning Scotland, which I meant only as a pise aller, I mention'd the difficultys that might reasonably be expected, by the unlucky delay of the Fleet's being detain'd by contrary winds, but shall not make any difficulty when the Fleet arrives, but do all that is possible to land in England. I shou'd think with submission that if it shou'd prove impracticable to land in England, it were better to attempt Scotland than to return to Spain, without attempting to land in Great Brittain, the Cardinal seem'd to be of this opinion in his to me of the 18th March. Monsr de Risbourg sends Monsr de St. Mary the King's Lieutenant of this Kingdome, to waite on you, he is a very honnest gentleman, and will do every thing he can to serve you; the Marquis desires me to assure your Majesty of his most profound respects, he is mortified he cannot be absent from this place that he might pay his duty to you on the Fronteers, but his presence is necessary here when ye Fleet arrives.

It would be of great consequence to hear from England that I might, according to what I hear from thence, take my measures, I do for the best and will venture as much as one can do to land in England, God send us good success: your Majesty do's not answer what I mention concerning mony. I hope my Lord Marischall will have a good passage. I do not know who has the honour to attend you, I thought the Duke of Mar had been one, but I see by the Gazette that he and the D. of Perth are stop'd in Italy which I am very sory for. I am with great duty and respect, S^r, etc.

XCIV

Au CA. ALBERONI, P^R EXPRES

COROGNE, LE 5RE AVRIL 1719.

HIER j'ai receu deux lettres de V.E. l'une au Matin du 31re et au soir celle du prem^{re} d'Avril. V.E. peut etre persuadé que je obeirai les ordres du Roy, et que je ne songerai plus a l'Ecosse, et qu'il ne sera pas ma faute sy nous ne debarquerons pas en Angleterre, car nous ferons tout ce qui est humainement possible pour aborder, et de faire reussir l'affair. Je suis interessé en toute maniere, et j'espere que je ne manquerai pas de fermeté pour ce qu'est mon devoir, l'honneur m'engage ceque j'estime plus qu'aucune chose au monde.

Je n'ai point de nouvelle de la Flotte, d'abord qu'elle arrive je ne perderai pas un moment a m'embarquer je n'ai jamais eu dessein de rester si la Flotte arrivoit pour attendre le Roy mon Maitre.

Selon les Nouvelles de Suede il me semble qu'il ne seroit pas inutile de tacher de faire un Alliance avec cette couronne, et V. E. a deux personnes en Holland qui pourront estre employez. Les affaires de Meclenbourg pourront bien brouiller les affaires au Nord, que L'Empereur ne trouvera pas son Conte. J'ai demandé de l'argent a V. E. et vous ai dit mes raisons, mais en meme temps vous ai mandé que je ne differeray pas un moment a m'embarquer pour l'attendre. J'ai l'honneur d'estre avec beaucoup de respect, etc.

[To Cardinal Alberoni, by express. *Corunna, April 5*, 1719.

Yesterday I received two letters from your Eminence, the one of the 31st in the morning, and in the evening that of April 1. Your Excellency may rest assured that I will obey the King's orders, that I will think no more of Scotland, and that it will not be my fault if we do not land in England, for we shall do what is humanly possible to land, and to make the enterprise succeed. I am interested in every way, and I hope that I shall not fail in constancy in my duty. I am bound by honour, which I value more than anything on earth.

I have no news of the fleet. As soon as it arrives, I shall not lose a moment in going on board. I never intended to remain, should the fleet arrive, to wait for the King my Master.

According to the news from Sweden, it seems to me that it would not be useless to try to make an alliance with that power, and your Eminence has two persons in Holland who might be employed. The affairs of Mecklenburg might very well throw the politics of the North into confusion, which the Emperor will not find to his account.[1] I have asked

---

[1] In 1716 difficulties had arisen between the Duke of Mecklenburg and his subjects, and the subsequent interference of the Czar with the domestic affairs of the Duchy had been warmly resented both by the Emperor and by the smaller German sovereigns. See Mahon, vol. i. p. 226.

your Eminence for money and have told you my reasons; but at the same time have let you know that I shall not delay my embarkation a moment to wait for it.

I have the honour, etc.]

XCV[1]

To the KING, by expresse

COROGNE, LE 5RE APRIL 1719.

S^R,—Last night I had the honour of y^r Majesty's of the first of April, and shall obey y^r orders, in doing all that is possible to land in England, and not mention Scotland any more.

The Cardinall preaches to me much on the subject of fermeté. I hope I shall not want it, and do my duty. I own I never was preach'd to on that subject before.

I shall do all that I can to serve you, being with great duty and submission, Sir, etc.

XCVI

To the CARDINAL.[2]

COROGNE, LE 9RE AVRIL 1719.

La lettre de V. E. du 4re J'ai eu l'honneur de la recevoir hier au matin, par laquelle je voye que sa Majesté a changé de sentiment, et contremandé les ordres que votre Em^{ce} m'avoit envoyé du prem^{re} du Courant. Je ne manquerai pas de faire tout ce qui me sera possible pour obeir aux ordres de sa Majesté, en tachant de debarquer en Angleterre, mais si cela se trouve impracticable, Je ferai tout ce que je puis pour mettre pied a terre en Ecosse ce qui ne sera que la derniere resource. Je croyois que aprez que le Roy et V. E. auriez reflechis que sa Maj. ny V. E. ne voudroient pas abandoner le Comte Marischall, et tant des Braves gens qui sont avec luy aussy bien que plusieurs autres qui ont taché de se rendre eu ce pays. Envers le midy il est arrivé un Batiment de transport chargé des Poudres et aiant a son bord deux Compagnies du Regiment de

---

[1] Original in Stuart Papers. [2] Copy in Stuart Papers.

Valance ; Monsr de Risbourcg envoya votre Eminence une relation de tout ce que le Capitaine du Vaisseau luy a informe, ce que n'est pas agreeable ; pour eviter une repetition je me rapporte a ce qu'il vous envoye, le vent est bon et nous attendons L'arrive de la flotte a chacque heure, Dieu veuille qu'elle arrive et en estat de se mettre en mer d'abord qu'elle aura pris de l'eau. Monsr de Risbourg fait ce qu'il peut pour avoir de quoy les fournir des vivres en cas qu'elle en manque, et je ne perderai pas un moment a m'embarquer quand elle sera pret a faire voille.

A L'Egard de ceque V. E. fait mention du Roy mon Maître, j'espere, et me flatte que l'on me fera la justice de croire que j ai pour sa personne, toute la plus respectueuse attachement qu'est possible, et qui me mette dans une grande inquietude en cette conjoncture, aiant autant a cœur son honneur et reputation que son interest, mais aprez avoir reflechy sur sa situation, j'ay pris la resolution de luy conseiller de ne se pas embarquer, et meme je feray mon possible pour luy empecher, il ne faut pas absolument que sa Majesté se hazarde asteur [*sic*], mais ce qui est embarassant, est quelle excuse faut il faire, car le publique juge avec malice des actions des princes aussy bien que des personnes des plus basse naissance, enfin il y a du pour et de contre, mais il ne faut pas hazarder sa personne. Je suis ravy que V.E. a eu la bonté de me faire avoir quarante Mille Ecus, et me mande qu'elle m'envoyera encore soixante. Monsr de Risebourg a envoyé hier au soir pour tacher d'en avoir de St Jacques, n'aiant pas toute la somme icy. J'ai dessein d'envoyer un Batiment qui appartient a un Irlandois qui est habitant de St Sebastien, et fort honnete homme, pour aller a Amsterdam avec la lettre pour Monsr de Sardy, avec un Autre pr Monsr de Clotau, et incluse une pour Monsr Gozzani avec l'ordre de V.E. pour les armes, et cinq cents quintaux de poudre, et de les envoyer en Ecosse a une Isle qui est prez des Montagnes d'Ecosse ou My Lord Marischall aura du Monde pour les recevoir, L'Isle s'appelle Wist ; J'envoy avec ce Batiment deux Officiers qui ont servy dans l'affaire du Duc de Mar, qui sont des gens d'honneur qui sont du païs des Montagnes qui connoissent le païs et qui parlent bien la langue de ce party de l'Ecosse, en cas que ce

Batiment rencontre une Escadre Angloise, ils rebrousseront chemain, et tachera de nous en avertir, s'ils sont bordé par une Navire Angloise, ils auront ordre d'avoir les lettres, et autres papiers pret a jetter dans la Mer avec du plomb, mais j'espere qu'ils n'auront pas affaire de cette precaution, le proprietair aiant avec luy une passeport Francoise, et les deux officiers seront deguisés en Matelauts, mais en cas des Accidents, V.E. ne trouueroit il pas a propos de tacher de faire tenir une lettre a Monsr Lawles (pour) Clautau pour lui ordonner d'envoyer ces armes, et poudres en Ecosse a l'endroit que Je fais mention. Cette Isle est situé a l'ouest d'Ecosse, et est une des Isles de Hebrides. Je croyois de finir ma lettre ce soir, pour l'envoyer a votre Em : mais Monsr Le Marq^a de Risbourg m'a prié d'attendre pour demain, croyant que nous verrions entrer quelque autre navires de la Flotte.

AVRIL, LE 10^{IE}

CE matin il est arrivé Cinq Vaisseaux de la Flotte, un qui S'appelle le Comte de Tholouse, est endomagé, Monsr de Risbourg vous envoy une dettaille de ce que les Patron de ces Navires lui ont informés. Je me referre a cette relation, et n'envoyerai pas le petit Batiment en Hollande, jusques a ce que je sçaurai les sentiments de V.E.

AVRIL., LE 11^{IE}

MONSIEUR LE MARQUIS DE RISBOURG envoye son Courrier a ce moment, nous n'avons pas veu aucune autre navire de la Flotte, Monsr de Risbourg fait mettre les Trouppes a terre, et aura toute la precaution possible pour les empecher de deserter. D'abord que nous aurons des Nouvelles du reste de la flotte, j'aurai l'honneur de vous ecrire, et je supplie V.E. d'estre persuadé que j'ay l'honneur d'estre avec beaucoup de respect, de V.E., etc.

P.S.—Le Patron du petit Batiment de St Sebastien s'appelle Jean Meaher, cet homme est connu de Prince de Campo Florido.

Ne serait il pas a propos que V.E. mande a Monsr Lawless, de faire acheter huit a dix mille Armes, avec des ammunitions pour estre pret pour estre envoyé ou on auroit besoigne.

[TO THE CARDINAL. *Corunna, April 9,* 1719.

I HAD the honour to receive yesterday morning your Eminence's letter of the 4th, by which I see that His Majesty has changed his mind and countermanded the orders which your Eminence sent me on the 1st. I shall not fail to do all that I can to obey His Majesty's orders by trying to land in England, but should that prove impracticable, I shall do what I can to land in Scotland, which will be only the last resort. I thought that after the King and your Eminence had reflected, neither His Majesty nor your Eminence would wish to abandon the Earl Marischal and so many brave men who are with him, as well as several others who have tried to reach that country.

Towards mid-day a transport ship arrived laden with powder, and having on board two companies of the regiment of Valencia. M. de Risbourg sends your Eminence an account of all that the captain of the vessel has told him,[1] which is not agreeable; to avoid repetition I refer to his letter.

The wind is fair, and we expect the arrival of the fleet every hour. Would to God that it would arrive, and in a condition to put to sea as soon as it has taken in water! M. de Risbourg does what he can to be able to supply the fleet with provisions if it needs them, and I shall not lose a moment in embarking when it is ready to sail.

As to what your Eminence says regarding the King my Master, I hope, and I flatter myself that people will do me the justice to believe, that I have all the most respectful attachment possible for his person. This gives me much anxiety at this time, as I have his honour and reputation at heart as much as his interest, but after having reflected on the situation, I have made up my mind to advise him not to embark, and indeed shall do what I can to prevent his doing so. It is not absolutely necessary that His Majesty should risk himself just now, but what is embarrassing is what excuse should be made, for the public judges with malice of the action of princes as well as of those of persons of the humblest birth; in short, there is something for and against it, but his person must not be risked.[2]

I am delighted that your Eminence has had the goodness to let me have forty thousand crowns, and that you promise to send me sixty thousand more. M. de Risbourg sent last night to try to get some from Santiago, as he had not the whole sum here.

I intend to send a vessel which belongs to an Irishman who lives at San Sebastian, a very honest man, to go to Amsterdam with the letter for M. de Sardy, another for M. de Clotau, and enclosed one for M. Gozzani

---

[1] Copy in Stuart Papers, Appendix, No. 36, p. 243.
[2] James's reputation for courage needed some nursing. As a lad he had behaved well in action; at Malplaquet he charged twelve times with the Maison du Roi, and was wounded in the arm; but his conduct in the '15 had not been such as to give his adherents much idea of his spirit. Bolingbroke said of him in the Letter to Sir William Windham: 'The spring of his whole conduct is fear, fear of the horns of the devil, and of the flames of hell,' but Bolingbroke is scarcely an unprejudiced witness.

with your Eminence's order for the arms and five hundred quintals of powder, and to send them to an island near the Highlands of Scotland, where the Earl Marischal will have people to receive them. The island is called Uist. I am sending with this vessel two officers who served in the Duke of Mar's affair, who are men of honour, who belong to the Highlands, who know the country, and who speak the language of that part of Scotland well. In case the vessel should meet an English squadron, they will come back and try to let us know. If they are boarded by an English ship, they have instructions to have the letters and other papers ready to throw into the sea with lead, but I hope that they will not have occasion for this precaution, as the owner has with him a French passport, and the two officers are disguised as sailors, but in case of accidents, would it not be well for your Eminence to try to forward a letter to M. Lawless, for Clotau, to order him to send these arms and powders to Scotland to the place I mention? This island is situated to the west of Scotland, and is one of the Hebrides.

I expected to finish my letter this evening and to send it to your Eminence, but the Marquis de Risbourg has asked me to wait till to-morrow, as he thinks that we may see some other ships of the fleet come in.

April 10.—This morning, five ships of the fleet arrived. One called the *Comte de Thoulouse* is damaged. M. de Risbourg is sending you a detailed account of the information which he has received from the masters of these ships. I refer to this report.[1] I shall not send the little vessel to Holland until I know your Eminence's views.

April 11.—The Marquis de Risbourg is now sending off his courier. We have not seen any other ships of the fleet. M. de Risbourg has caused the troops to be landed, and will take every possible precaution to prevent their deserting. As soon as we have news of the rest of the fleet, I shall have the honour to write to you, and I beg your Eminence to rest assured that I have the honour, etc.

P.S.—The master of the little vessel from San Sebastian is called John Meagher; he is known to the Prince of Campo Florido.

Would it not be well that your Eminence should instruct Mr. Lawless to buy from eight to ten thousand muskets, with ammunition, to be ready to be sent where they are wanted?]

XCVII

To the KING, by ye same express.[2]

Corogne, the 11th Apl. 1719.

Sir,—I have the honr to send your Majesty a Copy of a Letter that I received from the Cardinall the 8th instant, dated

---

[1] Copy in Stuart Papers, Appendix, No. 37, p. 245.
[2] Original in Stuart Papers.

the 4th.[1] You will see, Sir, that the King of Spain has changed his mind, and Countermanded the Orders I received from the Cardinall of ye 1st of this Month concerning Scotland. On Sunday Morning and Yesterday at Noon there came into this harbour five Ships from the Fleet. I send your Majesty a Copy of ye Information that ye Marquis de Risbourg has had from the Masters of each Ship,[2] and also from each Commanding Officer of ye troops on board each Vessell; we have not heard of any more Ships, but expect to see some arrive every hour. God grant that the rest of the Fleet come soon, and that they may be in a condition to put to Sea in a little time. The Cardinall has sent Orders to the Marquis de Risbourg to give me 40000 Crowns, and has promissed me three score thousand more.

This Embarkeation has been so unfortunatly delayed that I hope you will not think of goeing on board if that the ffleet shou'd be in a Condition to put to Sea in a short time; if my Opinion be of any consequence I shall be against your Embarking. Your Majesty will see in the Copy of mine to the Cardinal what I proposed concerning sending a ship to Amsterdam for to get yr Arms that are there to send them to Scotland. As soon as I hear what is become of ye rest of ye Fleet I will inform your Majesty of it. The Marquis de Risbourg has his little Country house ready for you, and has gotten a very good house in the Towne for your Majesty. I am with all submission, etc.

p. 92.

XCVIII

To the KING (*Not sent*)[3]

p. 93.

Corogne, the 12th April 1719.

Sr,—I wou'd not lose this opportunity of paying my duty to your Majesty, tho' I have no news to send you. We have not seen any more ships belonging to the Fleet, but the Marqs de Risbourcq had accounts to day, that there has

---

[1] This copy is in the Stuart Papers, Appendix, No. 19, p. 222.
[2] Appendix, No. 37.
[3] This whole page is crossed out.

arrived near the Cape in a little harbour, a Transport, with horses. She has been damag'd by the Storm, and lost nine horses out of two and twenty. He has had an account from Vigo of Sr Peter Sherlocke's Ship being put into that Port, with two hundred foot soldiers. The Master says in his letter, that they were four days without provisions, or Water; all the Commanding Officers of the Troops, and Masters of the Ships, that wee have seen, complain of want of Water and Victualls. The Lisbon gazette mentions that Mr Hardy with his Sqadron of five Ships, two of them being but frigates, sail'd the 16th of March from that Porte to endeavour to meet with the Spanish fleet, that was gone to Bristol, he must have had his share of the Storm.

I hope the fatigue of your Journey do's not affect y^r health.

XCIX

To the KING [1]

Corogne, the 13th April 1719.

Sir,—I have the honour to send your Majesty an abstract [2] of what the Marq^s de Risbourg is inform'd of from the Intendant of the Fleet, with the account that the rear Admiral gives of the condition of his own Ship, and some others that are put into Vigo, and also of two that are got into Muras. There is no news of the Commandant of the Fleet, who I fear is in a very bad condition, by the accounts we have had.

Mr. Macdonell will inform your Majesty of what I told him to inform you of, concerning the Lisbone Gazette, the Abstract mentions that two of the English Frigates were seen in the Mouth of the River of Vigo. I hope in God Hardies Squadron has not met with the fleet, for they must have had their share of the Bad Weather, having left the River of Lisbone the 16th last month.

I am heartily mortified to be obliged to send so ill news, but

---

[1] Original in Stuart Papers.
[2] In Stuart Papers. Appendix, No. 38, p. 246.

we must do all that is possible to put the fleet into a condition to go to Sea as soon as it is practicable.

I hope the fatigue of the journey do's not affect your health, which I pray God to preserve, and am with great duty and Submission y^r Majesty's, etc.

C

To ye CARDINAL by express

COROGNE, LE 13 AVRIL 1719.

MONSIEUR DE RISBOURG envoie a V.E. les avis qu'il a receu des Vaisseaux qui sont arrivés a Vigo et a Muros, il n'y a pas des Nouvelles de Monsieur de Guevarra, nous sommes fort en peine pour luy et son Navire, il n'y a que dix Vaisseaux arrivés encore, nous en attendons le reste avec beaucoup d'impatience, Dieu veuille qu'ils arrivent au bon Port.

Monsr de Risbourg a donné ordre pour payer une demie Mois de paye aux Troupes ce qui leurs sera fort aggreable après les fatigues qu'ils ont souffertes en Mer, ils leur est deu six Semaines au moins. Monsr le Marquis dit qu'il fera tout ce que dependra de lui pour fournir les Vivres et autres choses qui manqueront.

Je me remette a ce qu'il mande a V.E. etant Etranger en ce Paÿs. J'attend la reponse de V.E. sur ce que j'ay eu l'honneur de lui dire par le dernier Courrier touchant le petit Batiment que j'ay dessein d'envoyer a Amsterdam. J'ay l'honneur detre, etc. *P.S.*—L'intendant a vingt quatre milles Ecus de les quarant que V.E. lui a ordonné d'avoir pour me donner quand je lui demanderay. Je croyois qu'il etoit necessaire de prendre les precautions pour la sureté des Vaisseaux qui sont icy et a Vigo, de les faire entrer dans les lieux ou Monsieur le Marquis de Risbourg fait Mention, en attendant l'arrivée du reste de la Flotte.

[To THE CARDINAL, by express. *Corunna, April* 13, 1719.

M. DE RISBOURG is sending to your Eminence the information which he has received from the vessels which have arrived at Vigo and at Muros. There is no news of M. de Guevarra. We are very anxious about him and his ship. Only ten ships have arrived as yet; we await the others with much anxiety; God grant that they may come safe to port.

M. de Risbourg has ordered half a month's pay to be given to the troops, which will be very acceptable to them after the hardships which they have endured at sea. At least six weeks' pay is due to them. The Marquis says that he will do all that he can to supply victuals and the other things that are lacking.

I refer to what he writes to your Eminence, being a stranger in this country. I await your Eminence's reply as to what I had the honour to tell you by the last carrier about the little vessel which I propose to send to Amsterdam.

I have the honour, etc.

P.S.—The intendant has 20,000 crowns of the 40,000 which your Eminence ordered him to have to give to me on demand.

I thought that it was necessary to take precautions for the safety of the vessels which are here and at Vigo, to send them to the places which the Marquis de Risbourg mentions, awaiting the arrival of the rest of the fleet.]

CI

To the KING

Corogne, the 14th April 1719.

Sir,—This morning I have received the honour of your Majesty's of the 10th, 11th, and 12th. I am very glad you are come safe so far on your Way, and shall obey your Majesty's orders, and am impatient to have the honour to kiss your hand.

We have no further accounts of the Fleet. God grant they come safe into some of the Ports of this Kingdome. I have not any thing to informe you off, referring untill I have the honour to waite on your Majesty, being with great submission and duty, etc.

CII

Au CARDINAL

Corogne le 17ie Avril 1719.

Je me donne l'honneur d'informer V.E. que mon Maitre est arrivé ce matin en bonne santé aprez une voyage tres fatiguant tant par les mauuais temps que par les mechants chemains.

Depuis ma derniere lettre, du 13ie nous n'avons autres nouuelles des Vaisseaux de la Flotte, horsmis que la Fregatte

Andoulozie est arrivé a Vigo, Monsʳ. le Marqˢ. de Risbourg mande a V.E. l'Estat ou il est.

Monsʳ. le Major Stamforte est arrivé ce matin avec le Roy mon maitre qu'il a eu l'honneur de rancontrer a Betancos. Quand il partit de Londre, on n'en parloit point de notre affaire, c'estoit le 15ⁱᵉ de mars qu'it partit de cette Ville. Il dit que nos Amis estoient pret a nous joindre d'abord que nous serions debarquez.

Le Roy mon Maitre m'a dit qu'il vous envoyroit Monsʳ. de Connock et une detaile de ce que Monsʳ. le Major raporte. Je me donnerai l'honneur d'escrire a V.E. par cette occasion et suis avec beaucoup de respect.

[To the Cardinal. *Corunna, April* 17, 1719.

I HAVE the honour to inform your Eminence that my Master arrived this morning in good health, after a very fatiguing journey, as much from bad weather as from the wretched roads.

Since my last letter of the 13th, we have no further news of the ships of the fleet, except that the frigate *Andalusia*[1] has reached Vigo. The Marquis de Risbourg is writing to inform your Eminence as to her condition.[2]

Major Stamfort arrived this morning with the King my Master, whom he had the honour to meet at Betanzos. When he left London, nothing was being said about our affair. He left on the 15th of March. He says that our friends were ready to join us as soon as we landed.

The King my Master tells me that he will send you Sir T. Connock with a detailed account of what the Major reports. I shall do myself the honour of writing to your Eminence by that opportunity, and am with great respect, etc.]

CIII

Au CARDINAL ALBERONI pʀ. Sʀ. T. Connock.

Corogne, le 21 Avril 1719.

J'ai l'honneur de celle de V.E. du 16ⁱᵉ, et le Roy m'a montré celle que V.E. lui a ecrite.

Sa Majesté envoy Monsʳ. de Connock pour vous informer de

---

[1] The *Andalusia*, formerly called the *Greyhound*, was a twenty-gun ship which had been captured from the English.

[2] This seems to be what is meant.

ses sentiments depuis le malheur arrivé a la Flotte, et de ce qu'il pense estre necessaire pour la mettre en Estat de poursuivre le projet, a quoy je me refferre, et V.E. voirra par la, ce que sa Majesté fait mention a l'egard de My Lord Marischalle ce qui demande une prompte resolution, affin qu'il puisse prendre ses Mesures. J'ay le petit Batiment du Sieur Meagher, et encore un autre pour luy envoyer en mème temps en cas que l'un manque, et par eux j'envoyerai ce que V.E. me mande touchant le Marquis de Bereti Landi.

V. E. peut assurer sa Majesté que je n'ay pas donné aucune patante, ni n'en avois pas meme dessein d'en donner jusques a ceque nous fussions debarquez.

Ce qu'est arrivé a la Flotte est bien mortifiant, mais j'espere que votre Em: ne sera pas rebuté de poursuivre le projet, nous avons estés bien en peine pour Monsr. de Guevare, et pour le reste de la Flotte, c'est un bonheur qu'il n'y en a pas de perdu, il sera necessaire Comme V.E. fait mention qu'ils soient carénes.

J'ay l'honneur d'estre avec beaucoup de respect de V.E., etc.

[To CARDINAL ALBERONI, per Sir T. Connock. *Corunna, April* 21, 1719.

I HAVE had the honour to receive your Eminence's letter of the 16th, and the King has shown me that which your Eminence has written to him.

His Majesty is sending Sir T. Connock to let you know his views since the misfortune happened to the fleet, and what he thinks necessary to put it in a condition to follow out the enterprise. I refer to his letter, and your Eminence will see by it what His Majesty says as to the Earl Marischal. This demands prompt resolution, in order that he may take his measures. I have Meagher's little vessel and another to send to him at the same time, in case the first should fail, and by them I shall send what your Eminence tells me as to the Marquis de Beretti Landi.

Your Eminence may assure His Majesty that I have not granted any commission, nor did I ever intend to do so until we were landed.

What has happened to the fleet is very vexing, but I hope that your Eminence will not be deterred from following out the project. We have been very anxious about M. de Guevarra, and about the rest of the fleet. It is fortunate that none of them are lost. They will, as your Eminence says, need to be careened.

I have the honour, etc.]

CIV

Au CAR. ALBERONI P^R. EXPRES

COROGNE, LE 28^{IE} AVRIL 1719.

J'AI l'honneur d assurer Votre Eminence de mes tres humbles respects par le Courier que Monsr. Le Baron Walef nous envoy.

Le Roy ecrit a V.E. a quoi je me remette, aiant l'honneur d'estre avec beaucoup de Respect.

[To CARDINAL ALBERONI, by express. *Corunna, April* 28, 1719.

I HAVE the honour to assure your Eminence of my very humble respects, by the courier sent to us by Baron Walef.

The King is writing to your Eminence. I refer to his letter, and have the honour, etc.]

CV

Au PRINCE DE CAMPO FLORIDO

COROGNE, LE 28^{IE} AVRIL 1719.

MONSIEUR,—Je me donne l'honneur d'assurer V.E. de mes tres humbles respects, et de lui temoigner ma reconnoissance de toutes ses civilités, dont je ne puis jamais perdre le souvenir.

J'ay informé le Roy mon Maitre du zele et de l'attention que votre Excellence a temoigné en toutes occasions pour ses interests.

Votre Excellence aura appris la facheuse accident arrivé a La Flotte, ce qui est un terrible contre-temps mais il faut se soumettre avec patience a la volonté de Dieu et attendre une occasion favourable. J ay l'honneur d'estre, etc.

P.S.—Le pauvre Meagher est icy depuis le 18^{ie} de mars. *p.* 99. C'est un tres honête homme, et bien sensible de la protection donc [*sic*] votre Excellence l'honore.

[To THE PRINCE OF CAMPO FLORIDO. *Corunna, April* 28, 1719.

SIR,—I do myself the honour to assure your Excellency of my very humble respects, and to express my gratitude to you for all your courtesies, of which I can never lose remembrance.

I have informed the King my Master of the zeal and attention which your Excellency has on all occasions shown for his interests.

Your Excellency will have heard of the unhappy accident which has befallen the fleet. It is a terrible misfortune, but we must submit with patience to the will of God, and await a favourable opportunity.

I have the honour, etc.

P.S.—Poor Meagher has been here since the 18th of March. He is a very honest man, and very sensible of the protection with which your Excellency honours him.]

CVI

To SIR TIMON CONNOCK, BY EXPRESS

COROGNE, THE 29TH APRIL 1719.

I HAVE the favour of yours of the 26th this evening, and am very sorry to find by yours that you were indisposed, but I hope it proceeded only from your fatigue, and that rest will recover you, believe that I wish you all health and prosperity, being very sincerely your friend and servant.

I am glad the Cardinal do's intend to go on, and pursue the enterprise. God grant that his Catholick Majestie's affaires may have that success that he may able to persist in his generous intentions, but by y^r letter I much fear that his affaires, and situation are but in a bad way, which way soever they turn it must have a great influence on our Master's affaires.

I am sory we are not to have the satisfaction of your Company, but your being with the Court will be of great use for our Master's service. We have seen three large English men of War on Wednesday morning, they came to see what was in the harbour, and then sail'd to joyn the rest of their Squadron I suppose; from the Cap Finister they write that they have seen sixteen large Ships supposed to be English.

p. 100.   I am obliged to you for the trouble you will take in my private affaire, which I shall be glad to be inform'd off, because if it meets with difficulty I would try some other way to have the Bills negociated.

Our Master designs leaving this place in two or three days, and to go to Lugo, or to a Gentleman's house that is within four leagues of St. Jago.

The King designs to send one or two Small Ships to Lord Marishal, with Some provisions, and the orders for Monsr. de

Bereti Landi,[1] to send them Arms, and Ammunition, as they will have occasion for, or to bring him and his people off if they shou'd find it impossible to keep their ground. I believe I have quite tired you, so will end my letter with assuring you that I am with great truth, etc.

N^{ta}. Bené that Kennedy[2] wrot to Sir Timon by the same poste, to repay the Prince of Campo Florido the Sixty Pistoles that he gave M^r. Mathew at S^t. Sebastien, if the Prince did not place that money to the Publick acc^t.[3]

CVII

To the CARDINAL ALBERONI p^r. expres

CoROGNE, 30TH April 1719.

Hiere j'ai l'honneur de celle de Votre Eminence du 26me. Je suis ravi que Sa Majesté et V.E. continuent leur genereux dessein de poursuivre le projet. Pour ne point importuner V.E. je me remette a celle que le Roy mon maitre vous écrit, je souhaite toute sorte de succes a V.E. et suis avec beaucoup de respect, etc.

[To Cardinal Alberoni, by express. *Corunna, April* 30, 1719.

I had yesterday the honour to receive your Eminence's letter of the 26th. I am delighted that His Majesty and your Eminence continue your generous intention to follow out the project.

Not to trouble your Eminence, I refer to the letter which the King my Master is writing to you. I wish your Eminence all manner of success, and am with great respect, etc.]

CVIII

Au MARQUIS de RISBURG [4]

p. 101.

Sobrado, May 6^{ieme} 1719.

La Presse etoit si grande Monsieur quand le Roy partit que

---

[1] Lorenzo Vergiuso, Marquis de Beretti Landi, went as Spanish Ambassador to Holland in 1715.

[2] Ormonde's secretary.

[3] See Letter xxxix.

[4] From this point to the foot of p. 107 of the manuscript the hand is that of the first copyist, which ceased previously at p. 22.

Je ne pouvois pas avoir l'honneur de prendre Conge de vous, et de vous asseurer de ma reconnoissance de tous vos honnetetez dont Je suis penetré, Je vous supplie Monsieur d'etre bien persuadé que Je suis tres sensible des Marques d'Amitié que vous m'avez temoigné faites moy la Justice de Croire que J'ay l'honneur d'etre avec beaucoup de verité et de respect, etc.

[To THE MARQUIS DE RISBOURG. *Sobrado, May 6, 1719.*

SIR,—When the King left, the hurry was so great that I could not have the honour of bidding you farewell, and of assuring you of the gratitude which I feel for all your kindnesses. I beg you, Sir, to rest assured that I am very sensible of the marks of friendship which you have shown me. Do me the justice to believe that I have the honour, etc.]

CIX

Au CHEVALIER HEALY

SOBRADO, MAY 6^{ieme} 1719.

CE par ordre du Roy, Monsieur, que Je vous envoye Celleci, Sa Majesté est bien persuadée que vous ne negligerez rien qui dependra de vous pour faire equiper au plutôt les vaisseaux qui doivent aller en Ecosse, chaque Moment etant precieux.

Sa Majesté vous envoye une Lettre que vous auriez le soin de rendre à Monsieur Jones, et en meme tems vous l'aiderez de ce qu'il aura besoin pour le Mettre en etat de poursuivres on voyage sans perdre du tems, mais il faut qu'il prenne ses Precautions pour eviter L'Escadre Angloise.

Ayez la bonté de faire bien mes Complimens a tous nos Messieurs, et Soyez persuadé de la parfaite Estime avec laquelle J'ay l'honneur d'etre, etc.

On dit qu'il y a beaucoup de Brandevins a Redondella près de Vigo, Ca Seroit bon pour l'Ecosse.

[To SIR JOHN HEALY. *Sobrado, May 6, 1719.*

SIR,—I send you this by order of the King. His Majesty is well assured that you will neglect nothing which depends on you to get the fitting-out of the ships which are to go to Scotland completed as soon as possible, as every moment is precious.

His Majesty sends you a letter which you will take the trouble to deliver to Mr. Jones, and at the same time you will give him what help he needs to put him in a condition to pursue his voyage without losing time, but he must take precautions to avoid the English fleet.

Have the goodness to present my compliments to all our gentlemen, and be assured of the perfect esteem with which I have the honour, etc.

They say that there is plenty of brandy at Redondela, near Vigo. This would be good for Scotland.]

CX

To EARL MARESCHAL

LUGO, MAY 9TH, 1719.

I AM very much Mortifyed to be obliged to date my letter from this Country; when we parted I hoped to have dated my letter to you from a more agreeable place, but I must referr my self to the King's Letter, which will inform your Lordship of the misfortune happened to the fleet, and of every thing that concerns this affair.

It is a great happyness that his Majesty is Safely arrived in this Country after all the hazard he ran, and that he is in good health, having endured a great deal of fatigue. His Majesty Landed at Roses, and made all imaginable haste to come to the Groyne to Goe on board had it pleased God that the Fleet had been in a Condition to have pursued the voyage.

I came to the Neighbourhood of the Groyne the 24th February, expecting the Fleet, that the Cardinal informed me was to have Sett Sayl the 10th of the Same Month, the Frigate I was to have gone on board had been ready for some time. I had a letter from the Cardinal of the 12th March by Mr McDonel, which I received the 16th, which informed me that the fleet Sail'd from Cadix the 7th. I heard no account of the fleet from that time to the 9th of April when a Ship came in to Corunna giving us the disagreeable News of the fleet's having been dispersed the 27th of March, the Admiral having lost his Bow sprit and all his Masts. Some days after five Ships came in to Corunna disabled, and we have heard from Vigo and Several other places in this Kingdom that some of the fleet have been putt into their Ports. We have had also accounts of some Ships being in Lisbon, and of the Admiral and eight Ships being arrived in Cadix.

This a very Melancholy account, but no remedy against Storms: the King is in great Uneasyness for the Circumstances that your Lordship and those Gentlemen that are with you are in, and does all in his power to send you Succour by those two Ships commanded by Tullogh and Kays.

p. 103.

I send your Lordship a Packet that the Cardinal I suppose sent me by mistake, for you will see the Superscription, I sent it him back again, and yet again received it a second time, and now send it to your Lordship.

I have tired you too much with this long Letter, but cannot help expressing the Concern I am in for your Lordship and Company, and for the misfortune of this disappointment, but we must Submitt to the will of heaven.

Do me the favour to make my Compliments to my Lord Seaforth,[1] and to Mr Campbell, and to whom you think fitt not knowing who are with you.—I am, etc.

CXI

Au MARQUIS de RISBURG

Lugo, May 12^{ieme}, 1719.

Je vous suis bien obligé, Monsieur, de la Lettre que vous aviez eu la bonté de m'envoyer du 9eme de Courant, et vous prie d'etre persuadé que Je feray ce que dependra de moy pour meriter l'honneur de la Continuation de votre Amitié que J'estime comme Je dois. J'espere que les vaisseaux destinés pour la Grande Bretagne seront expediéz avec toute la Diligence possible, Je suis Seur que s'il dependoit entierement de vous, qu'ils partiront en tres peu de tems.

J'espere que Monsieur de Chacon[2] Sera utile où il est non obstant Monsieur l'Intendant. Continuez moy l'honneur de votre Amité, et croyez que J'ay l'honneur d'etre plus que personne avec respect, etc.

---

[1] William Mackenzie, fifth Earl of Seaforth, attainted after the '15, pardoned 1726, died 1740.

[2] Rear-Admiral Chacon of the Spanish navy. He held a command at the battle of Cape Passaro.

[To the Marquis de Risbourg. *Lugo, May* 12, 1719.

Sir,—I am greatly obliged to you for the letter which you had the goodness to send me, of the 9th inst., and I beg you to believe that I shall do what I can to deserve the honour of your continued friendship, which I value as I should.

I hope that the ships destined for Great Britain will be despatched with all possible diligence. I am sure that if it depended entirely on you they would sail in a very short time.

I hope that M. de Chacon will be useful where he is, notwithstanding the Intendant. Continue to honour me with your friendship, and believe that I have the honour, etc.]

CXII

To SIR JOHN HEALY

Lugo, May 12th, 1719.

This morning I received your's from Mr. M'Pherson, and am Sorry to find by it that the Marquis is still in the same way of Continuing to make Difficultys instead of obviating them.

I have little to trouble you with, the King writing to you by the Bearer. Mr. Tullogh I am informed wants some Guns for his Ship, which the King Would have you endeavour to Gett for him. I hope the Ship the Bearer is to go in will be ready to Sayl in a day or two after his arrival. Pray press the Marquis to dispatch Mr. Jones' Ship without the least delay, it wants but little to be in a Condition to goe to Sea, and for what is due to the Seamen I will answer for it rather than there shou'd be any delay in her going to Sea. I cannot imagine why the Intendant makes a Scruple of receiving to take the provisions that were putt on Shore from the Hermione; I do not care to give any orders concerning them, having nothing to do with what has been bought with the publick money. Pray let me hear from you when Opportunitys offerr, and do me the favour to make my Compliments to those Gentlemen that are with you, and Sir Peter Stafford in particular. I am heartily Sorry to hear that my poor Servant was in So ill a way when the bearer left you. Pray let him have all the help that can be, excuse this part of my letter, and believe me to be with great truth, etc.

CXIII

To Mr. CAMMOCK

Lugo, May 15th, 1719.

The King received your's of the 2d this evening, and has order'd me to let you know that he is very well assured of your zeal for his service, and thanks you for the repeated Assurances you give him. His Majesty is very Sorry for the Loss you have Sufferr'd in your voyage, but very glad that you escaped the Danger you were in, and wishes heartily that you had been in Spain when the Fleet was fitting out at Cadix. You may be assured y^t his Majesty will have you and your endeavour to serve him in remembrance if ever it pleases God to restore him.

I was very Sorry to hear at my Arrival in this Country that you were in Sicily, believing that if any thing was to have been undertaken for our Master's Service, that you were to have had the Command of the Fleet, and the Inspection of the Embarkation, which wou'd have been for the Good of the Service, and besides the particular Satisfaction it wou'd have given me to have had an old friend, and one so well qualifyed, to have gone with me. I am very truly Sorry for the Great Loss you have Sufferr'd in your Passage, and ready on all Occasions to Shew you how Sincerely, etc.

CXIV

To Sr PETER REDMONDS

Lugo, May 15th, 1719.

The King received your Letter, and has order'd me to give you his thanks for your repeated offers to serve him, and for your zeal for his Service.

His Majesty wou'd not have you think of going to Madrid or to the Court upon his Account, but will not forgett your willingness to undertake any fatigue for his Interest. I take this opportunity to assure you that I am very sincerely.

CXV

To Mr. EGAN

Mr. Egan, *Sir R. Everard.*
Mr. Allen, *Lord Arran.*
Mr. Fisher, *Ormonde.*
Tobacco, *money.*
Obadiah, *Wright.*
Binet, *Ezekiel Hamilton.*

Lugo, May 15th, 1719.

I DID not write to you at the same time I did to Mr. Allen, tho' this will go by the same Conveyance. You will see how uneasy Mr. Fisher is at the Disappointments of several particulars that you promised shou'd be performed, and that of sending an English Sea Officer to have care of the Spanish Fleet, and a land Officer to come and inform us of the State of the Army. This I assured the Cardinal wou'd be done, but not complyed with, which has vexed me extremely, for I am Cautious how I answer for any thing to the Cardinal. The next thing omitted which you promised was to send Tobacco, which is very necessary for Mr. Fisher's health, but that's neglected, tho' there were two ways of Conveyance, the one by Obadiah, the other by Binet. This Root is wanted, as you, who know his Constitution, may easily believe; and he could not have believed that his friends wou'd have so neglected him. My Compliments to them. Believe me with truth, etc.

p. 106.

CXVI

Au MARQUIS DE RISBOURG

Lugo, May 18ième, 1719.

MONSIEUR,—C'est avec beaucoup de plaisir que J'ay receu l'honneur de la votre, hier justement après que le Courier etoit parti. Les Assurances que que vous me donnez de la Continuance de votre Amitié m'est tres Sensible, et vous me ferez la Justice d'etre persuadé que Je l'estime Comme Je dois, et que Je Corresponderay avec bien du plaisir.

Le Roy mon Maître est bien assuré que vous ne negligez rien qui depend de vous pour equiper les Navires qui doivent aller en Angleterre et en Ecosse.

Je suis fâché d'apprendre que vous avez un Surcroit de difficultées par l'arrivée de Monsieur de Chacon, mais il faut avoir patience quand il n'y a pas de remede. Je suis fâché d'apprendre les Mauvaises Nouvelles de Passage. C'est la Prelude de la Guerre. Faites moy l'honneur de me croire.

[To the Marquis de Risbourg. *Lugo, May* 18, 1719.

Sir,—I received your letter with great pleasure yesterday, just after the courier had left. The assurances which you give me of your continued friendship are very pleasing to me, and you will do me the justice to believe that I value it as I should, and will reciprocate it with great pleasure.

The King my Master is well assured that you will neglect nothing which depends on you to fit out the ships which are to go to England and Scotland.

I am sorry to hear that your difficulties have been increased by the arrival of M. de Chacon, but one must have patience when there is no remedy. I am sorry to hear the bad news from Passage;[1] it is the beginning of war.

Do me the honour, etc.]

CXVII

To SIR JOHN HEALY

p. 107.

Lugo, May 18th, 1719.

Just after the Courier Passed I had your's and have but very little to trouble you with in Answer to it. I am Glad you seem to be better pleased with the Marquis than you used to be. The King is very well satisfyed that you do all that is in your power to dispose the putting of the Ships in a Condition to go to Sea, and his Majesty desires you to let Sir Peter Stafford know y^t he shou'd advance money for the Getting of Seamen for the Ships that Go to Scotland, and that his Majesty will reimburse him. You will See by the Enclosed what is desired by Monsr de Walef, who parted from hence this morning, it is order'd by the Cardinal, and the Intendant receiv'd the order by yesterday's Courier. My Compliments to the Gentlemen that are with you, and believe me.

---

[1] The destruction of the Arsenal by the French. See Introduction, p. lv.

CXVIII

To COL. OWEN[1]

LUGO, MAY 18TH, 1719.

LAST night I received your's of the 14, and will acquaint the King with what you propose concerning your being employed in the Guards, but I believe that in that Corps there is not any person received that is not a Roman Catholick, this you will consider before you take your resolution to go on board the Dutchman. You will let me hear from you, I think you had best come and attend the king who has not too much company with him. Believe me very sincerely your friend and ready to serve you when ever it is in my power being.

What can be done with your ship?

CXIX

p. 103.

To SIR JOHN HEALY[2]

LUGO, MAY 20TH, 1719.

S^R,—Last night at eight a clock I receiv'd your's, and was not a little surprised to find in it, that the Marquis had receiv'd orders from the Cardinal by the last Courier to put a Stop to the Ships going to Scotland. I could not but wonder his Eminence had not the Civility to have mention'd it to the King, but there is no help for it.

The King is very well pleased with your having kept Mr. Jones, he must stay till further orders.

Pray let Sir Peter Stafford know that what money is advanced by him for the Service of any of the Ships designed for Great Britain, must be placed to our King's account.

I am heartily concerned for the useage you have suffered, and wish it were in my power to shew you how much I am sincerely, S^r, etc.

---

[1] See p. 96, note.
[2] This letter is in the hand of the second copyist.

CXX

Au CARDINAL ALBERONI[1]

Lugo, May 23ᵉᵐᵉ, 1719.

Je Suis bien obligé à Votre Eminence de la bonté qu'elle a eu de m'envoyer mes lettres.

Votre Eminence sera informée par le Roy mon Maître qu'il a rapellé mon Parent que V. E. avoit envoyé pour accompagner Monsieur de Lawless ce qui lui sera une Grande Mortification. Je suis bien asseuré qu'il Seroit acquitté de sa Commission avec Addresse et avec fidelité, et puisque Sa Majesté ne veut qu'il ait l'honneur de la servir en ce pais là, Je Seray bien aise de l'avoir auprès de moy. Je m'etonne qu'il n'y a point de Nouvelles de ce qui Se passe en Ecosse. Je seray ravi de trouver des Occasions par où Je pourrois temoigner ma zele pour le Service de sa Majesté Catholique et de lui pouvoir etre utile. J'ay l'honneur d'etre avec bien de respect, etc.

[To Cardinal Alberoni.   *Lugo, May 23, 1719.*

I am greatly obliged to your Eminence for your kindness in forwarding my letters.

Your Eminence will be informed by the King my Master that he has recalled my kinsman,[2] whom your Eminence had sent to accompany Mr. Lawless, which will be a great mortification to him. I am quite sure that he would have discharged his commission with skill and fidelity, and since His Majesty does not wish that he should have the honour of serving him in this country, I shall be glad to have him with me.

I am surprised that there is no news of what is happening in Scotland.

I shall be delighted to find opportunities of showing my zeal for the service of His Catholic Majesty, and to be able to be of use to him.

I have the honour, etc.]

CXXI

To SIR TIMON CONNOCK

Lugo, May 23ᴅ, 1719.

I have had the favour of your's of the 30ᵗʰ April, and 4ᵗʰ, 8ᵗʰ and 14ᵗʰ Inst., and am extremely obliged for the account

---

[1] This letter is again in the hand of the first copyist, which continues till the middle of p. 114 of the manuscript.

[2] Bagenal.

you have given me concerning my private affairs. I am very sorry for the Mortification that poor Sir John Healy has met with, and for the bad news we have had of the Ships being destroyed that were a building at Passage, as well as for the ill posture the Affairs of Spain are in at this time. I do not doubt of your doing all y^t is in your power to do Good offices with his Eminence for those Gentlemen that the King has recommended to the Cardinal. Poor Meagher is ruined if not taken care of, and most of the rest but in a very bad condition if neglected.

I am ordered by his Majesty to send you the Enclosed, and he desires you to speak to the Cardinal for them. I have not yet heard from Mr. Joyse, but I suppose I shall soon. I am impatient to hear soon Good News from you, tho' by our Master's being to reside in this part of Spain I fear there is little hopes of it.

CXXII

Au Marquis de Risburg

p. 110.

Lugo, May 26eme, 1719.

C'est avec bien du plaisir Monsieur que J'ay receu l'honneur de la votre et J'espere que vous me continuerez l'honneur de votre Amitie ; J'y conte beaucoup. A l'egard de la Liste que vous me demandez Je vous envoye par ordre de sa Majesté Britannique, et c'est dans la forme que vous la desirez, Je serois bien aise que ces Messieurs Jouiront de la bonté du Roy, et Je suis bien asseuré qu'ils seront toujours Prets à temoigner leur zele pour le service du Roy. Je croy que les Poudres et les Armes que vous envoyez à Burgos n'arriveront pas de quelque tems puisque ils doivent etre chargé sur des mulets : Les trentes soldats sont arrivés ce matin. Faites moy la Justice d'etre bien persuadé que, etc.

[To the Marquis de Risbourg. *Lugo, May 26, 1719.*

Sir,—It is with much pleasure that I have received the honour of your letter, and I hope that you will continue to me the honour of your friendship. I value it greatly.

As to the list which you ask, I send it to you by order of His Britannic

Majesty, and it is in the form which you wish. I shall be very glad that these gentlemen should enjoy the King's bounty, and I am well assured that they will always be ready to testify their zeal for the King's service.

I suppose that the powder and arms which you are sending to Burgos will not arrive for some time, since they must be loaded on mules. The thirty soldiers arrived this morning.

Do me the justice to rest assured, etc.]

CXXIII

To SIR JOHN HEALY

Lugo, May 26, 1719.

I have receiv'd your's of the 23d, and send the Marquis the King's receipt for the money he had given his Majesty.

I send the Marquis also the list he desired, which I have signed by the King's order. I am sorry the Gentleman you have to do with continues his ill uneasy humour, but business with him will soon be at an end, and I shall have the satisfaction of seeing you here. The thirty men came hither yesterday. I have nothing to add, but that I am very sincerely, etc.

CXXIV

Au CARDINAL ALBERONI

Lugo, Juin 12, 1719.

J'ay receu l'honneur de celle de votre Eminence du 30eme de May, et vous suis bien obligé de la bonté que V.E. ait eu de me mettre aux pieds de sa Majesté en lui montrant ma Lettre du 24eme. Je conserveray toujours les sentimens de pouvoir tacher de lui etre utile. Il est bien mortifiant qu'on ne peut pas seconder les Gens en Ecosse puisque V.E. dit qu'il y a un bon nombre des Montagnards ensemble. V.E. voit par ce que les lettres de Londres marquent touchant la Flotte que Je ne vous ay pas trompé, quand J'assuray V.E. que si nous pourrions Debarquer en tems que le Coup etoit immanquable. Je suis faché de voir qu'il n'y a rien à faire du coté de la Suede, J'avoue J'etois un peu mortifié à l'egard de mon Parent. Je supplie V.E. d'etre tres persuadé que J'ay l'honneur d'etre plus que personne et avec bien du respect, etc.

[To CARDINAL ALBERONI. *Lugo, June* 12, 1719.

I HAVE had the honour to receive your Eminence's letter of May 30th, and I am greatly obliged for your Eminence's kindness in placing me at His Majesty's feet by showing him my letter of the 24th. I shall always retain the desire that I may be able to try to be of use to him.

It is very annoying that we cannot help the people in Scotland, since your Eminence says that there are a good number of Highlanders together.

Your Eminence sees by what the letters from London say about the fleet, that I did not deceive you when I assured your Eminence that if we could land in time the stroke could not fail. I am sorry to see that there is nothing to be done from the side of Sweden. I confess that I was a little annoyed about my kinsman.

I beg your Eminence to rest assured that I have the honour, etc.]

CXXV

To SIR TIMON CONNOCK

LUGO, JUNE 12TH, 1719.

I HAVE had the favour of your two Letters, one by Mr. M'Pherson, the other I had by the last Post, tho' of an older date. I Congratulate you on the honour the King has done you. His Majesty cou'd not have made a better choice, this without compliment to you. I am extremely obliged to you for your recommendation of Mr. Esmonds, and I do not doubt but that the Cardinal will provide for him. I am very glad that his Eminence will receive Monsieur de Magny; he deserves it from him, and is a very worthy honest Gentleman who loses a Considerable fortune.[1] I am in pain for him, for he left Rome above two months agon. I have heard from Mr. Joyce. Pray let me know how matters go with you, and believe me most sincerely.

The king bade me remember him kindly to you. He had your's by Mr. M'Pherson. By his Majesty's residing in these parts there is no likelihood of any thing for the common cause.

---

[1] The Marquis de Magny was concerned in the conspiracy against the Regent Orleans in December 1718, but had escaped.

CXXVI

To the DUKE of LIRIA

Lugo, June 12th, 1719.

I had the honour of your Grace's from Madrid, and was Glad to find by it that you gott safe and in good health to that place, where I hope you found her Grace[1] in perfect health. I am obliged to your Grace for the Goodness you had to take the trouble of bespeaking the Saddles. I wish your Grace all Prosperity, and am, etc. The King bade me remember him kindly to you, and His Majesty thanks you for the advice you give concerning Kelly.

CXXVII

Au PRINCE de CAMPO FLORIDO

Lugo, Juin 12eme, 1719.

J'ay l'honneur de recevoir Trois de vos lettres, et J'espere que votre Excellence me fait la Justice d'etre bien persuadé de ma reconnoissance pour toutes vos bontés. J'ay fait vos Complimens au Roy et sa Majesté m'ordonne de vous remercier de toutes les peines que vous aviez voulu prendre pour son service. J'envoyeray a Monsieur de Risbourg l'incluse touchant le pauvre Meagher qui est un tres honete homme. Je souhaite a votre Excellence un bon voyage, et toute sorte de Prosperité etant avec tout le respect Imaginable.

[To the Prince of Campo Florido. *Lugo, June* 12, 1719.

I have had the honour to receive three of your letters, and I hope that your Excellency will do me the justice to believe that I am grateful for all your kindnesses.

I have presented your respects to the King, and His Majesty directs me to thank you for all the trouble which you have been pleased to take in his service. I shall send to M. de Risbourg the enclosure relating to poor Meagher, who is a very honest man.

I wish your Excellency a pleasant journey, and all manner of prosperity, being with all respect, etc.]

---

[1] The Duke of Liria married the sister of the Duke of Veraguas.

CXXVIII

Au MARQUIS de RISBURG

Lugo, Juin 14, 1719.

C'est au desire du Sieur Meagher que J'ay l'honneur de vous envoyer l'incluse, c'est dommage qu'un pauvre homme plein de bonne volonté soit ruiné. Le Roy mon Maître m'a ordonné de vous prier de sa part que vous vouliez avoir la bonté de prendre le pauvre homme en votre Protection, et de lui rendre service : il souhaitera fort avoir une Attestation comment ses deux vaisseaux furent arreté ce qui me semble n'est que juste parceque c'est la verité. Je vous prie d'etre bien persuadé que J'ay l'honneur d'etre, etc.

[To the Marquis de Risbourg. *Lugo, June 14, 1719.*

At the desire of Mr. Meagher, I have the honour to send you the enclosed. It is a pity that a poor man, full of good will, should be ruined. The King my Master has directed me to request you, on his behalf, to have the goodness to take the poor man under your protection, and to be of service to him. He would much like to have a certificate as to how his two ships were seized; this seems to me only just, as it is the truth.

I beg you to believe that I have the honour, etc.]

CXXIX

To SIR JOHN HEALY

Lugo, June 14th, 1719.

I thank you for the Hungary water you sent me; pray do me the favour to pay for it, which I will repay when we meet. The King wou'd have you endeavour to get the Ste Marie putt on the King of Spain's Account, and that what is due to her Crew, and all other Expences since her Arrival in the Corunna may be defrayed by his Catholick Majesty. The King will have M^r O'Bryan and Mr Power putt on the List. Mr Power as Lieutenant, and the other as subl^t. His Majesty wou'd have you leave the 2000 Pistoles with Sir Peter Stafford, and that he shou'd deliver it to the Person who is Authorized to receive it, and that when you have given the Money to the Knight, you may come and wait on his Majesty.—I am.

CXXX

Au CARDINAL ALBERONI

Lugo, Juin 16, 1719.

Je prens cette occasion d'Asseurer votre Eminence de mes tres humbles respects. Sa Majesté Britannique vous ecrit, et Je ne veux pas vous importuner seulement de prier V. E. d'etre bien persuadé que J'ay l'honneur d'etre avec bien du respect etc.

[To Cardinal Alberoni. *Lugo, June 16, 1719.*

I take this opportunity of assuring your Eminence of my very humble respects. His Britannic Majesty is writing to you, and I do not wish to trouble you; only to beg your Eminence to rest assured that I have the honour, etc.]

CXXXI

Au MARQUIS de RISBURG

Lugo, Juin 16, 1719.

J'ay l'honneur Monsieur de recevoir hier au soir la votre par le Courier, et ce Matin deux des votres du 11eme, Je vous suis infiniment obligé de la bonté que vous avez de vous Interesser à ma Santé Je suis Dieu Merci retabli, et Je conserveray toujours une parfaite reconnoissance des vos Bontés. Apparement le Courier vous a informé de ce qui se passe d'ou il vient. Puisque l'Intendant ne peut avancer de l'argent pour les petits Batimens qui vinrent pour le service de sa Majesté Britanique il faut avoir patience. Le Capitain du St Jacques aura l'honneur de vous faire la reverence, et de vous rendre Celleci, J'espere que vous auriez la bonté de le laisser partir d'abord qu'il sera pret. Je m'etonne que l'Intendant ne veut pas recevoir les deux mille Pistoles, c'est une personne bien delicate, par la Gazette nous voyons que l'Escadre qu'etait sur vos Cotes soit arrivé dans la Manche. Faites moy la Justice, Monsieur, d'etre bien persuadé que J'ay l'honneur d'etre, etc.

[To the Marquis de Risbourg. *Lugo, June* 16, 1719.

Sir,—I had last night the honour to receive your letter by the courier, and this morning two of yours of the 11th. I am infinitely obliged for your kindness in interesting yourself about my health. I have recovered, thank God, and I shall always retain the utmost gratitude for your kindnesses. Apparently the courier has informed you of what is going on in the place from which he comes. Since the Intendant cannot advance the money for the small vessels which came for the service of His Britannic Majesty, we must have patience. The captain of the *St. Jacques* will have the honour of paying you his respects and of delivering this letter to you. I hope that you will have the goodness to allow him to leave as soon as he is ready.

I am surprised that the Intendant is not willing to receive the 2000 pistoles; he is a very scrupulous person.

I see by the 'Gazette' that the squadron which was off your coast has arrived in the Channel.

Do me the justice to believe me, etc.]

CXXXII

To SIR TIMON CONNOCK p^R expres [1]

S^T Jago, the 26TH June 1719.

By the laste poste I receiv'd the favour of yours of the 5th Instant, and am obliged to you for the agreeable acc^t you give me of Kelly's being arreasted at Pampelona, where I hope they will force him to make a discovery of the rest of his associates, that they may also be apprehended. The King bade me to remember him kindly to you, and thanks you for the concern you express for his safety. What you mention concerning this Place is very reasonable, and what I had already told his Majesty. I hop'd and do wish that he will go to Pont a Vedre, or to any other place, rather than to stay here; all imaginable precaution is taken to hinder or prevent any attempt or execution that may be design'd against his Person.

I am glad Sir Peter has had good success, and that Mon^r Patino is charged with what you mention concerning the Gentlemen recommended by the King, and that you will do all you can for poor Meagher. I give you many thanks for your

p. 115.

---

[1] The hand changes back again.

good offices to the Cardinal concerning My Cousen Esmond's promotion. I have heard from Mr Joyes, and am extremly obliged to him for his civilities. Mr Hamilton writes to you concerning Fitzgerald; if what is askt is reasonable, pray do me the favour to speak to the Cardinal for him. The Merchant that employes him is a very honest man, and a particular Friend of mine. When it is not inconvenient pray let me hear from you, and believe me sincerely, S^r, your, etc. My respects to his Eminence.

CXXXIII

A MONS^R SEMINATI

S^T JAGO, LE 26^LE 1719.

JE vous suis infiniment obligé Monsr de la peine que vous avez eu touchant les commissions que je pris la liberté de vous donner, et de toutes vos honetetez pendant mon sejour chez vous, J'en ay toute la reconnoissance imaginable et suis tres parfaitem^t.

[To M. SEMINATI. *Santiago, June 26, 1719.*

SIR,—I am infinitely obliged to you for the trouble you have had about the commissions which I took the liberty of giving you, and for all your kindnesses during my stay with you. I am extremely grateful for them, and am, etc.]

CXXXIV

AU MARQUIS DE RISBOURCG

S^T JAGO, 27TH JUNE 1719.

J'AI receu Monsr l'honneur de la votre 25^ie du Cour^t et voi que le Vaisseau que le Roy avoit envoyé en Escosse est arrivé et que le Capitaine ne dit rien de nouveau, mais seulement confirme ce que l'autre a informé sa Majesté Britanique; sa Majesté vous fait ses compliments. Je crois que les Portugais ne sont pas informé de ce que la Cour de L'Electeur d'Hanover a dessein de faire avec leur Flotte. Je vous prie, Monsr, d'estre bien persuadé que j'ai l'honneur d'estre, etc.

[To THE MARQUIS DE RISBOURG. *Santiago, June 27, 1719.*

SIR,—I have had the honour to receive your letter of the 25th current, and see that the ship sent by the King to Scotland has arrived, and that the captain says nothing new, but only confirms the information communicated by the other to His Britannic Majesty.

His Majesty sends you his compliments.

I do not think that the Portuguese have any information as to what the Court of the Elector of Hanover intend to do with their fleet.

I beg you, Sir, etc.]

CXXXV

To Mr. JOYES

S^T JAGO, 2^D JUNE [? JULY], 1719.

S^R,—I receiv'd yesterday your letter of the 21st June, and am much obliged to you for your civilities, and for the kind offers you make me, but I desire you may not be under any concern, for the uneasyness you had reason to be under, from the first letter you receiv'd from Mr Salvador, of no care being taken for the payment of the Bill you drew on my account, which I was Sure cou'd proceed from no other cause, than that of the Bills being sent before that advice cou'd come time enough to make provision for the payment, because of the Precaution that was necessary to be taken in an affair of that Nature. I am very glad on your account to find that you have since receiv'd advice that there is care taken to pay it, and I have thereupon receiv'd the Bill you return'd me of 400 Pistoles upon this Place. And as for the letter of Credit that you have sent my Cousen Butler for 400 Pistoles more on Lugo, I have wrote to Sir Peter Stafford about it, because (if his Bill of 250 Pistoles be paid upon account of that Bill 'tis more than I shou'd receive) I shall therefore expect his answer, and upon it, only take what remains to make up 900 Pistoles, leaving the other 100 to answer the dispursem^{ts} you have made, or may have occasion to make on my account.

p. 117.

Pray make my Compliments to my Lady Arther, with my thanks for the Tea she was so good to send me, which I have receiv'd, and is very good; I am sory that this place affords nothing fit for her acceptance. I shall be very glad of opportunities of shewing that I am so sensible of y^r civilities, that whenever it is in my power you will find me your most humble, etc.

CXXXVI

To SIR PETER REDMONDS

St. Jago, the 3ᴅ July 1719.

Sʀ,—I have the favour of yours, and obliged to you for the news you sent me in the Prints from London.

You have no reason to make any excuse for what you mention. The King our Master is very sensible of your good-will and zeall for his Service, and orders me to tell you so. I shall be very glad to hear from you, and of what you hear that may be for the King's service. I am much obliged to the Person you mention, that was so civill to enquire after me. If you think it proper, make him my compliments. You will remember who the Person is. I have no news of any kind, before this you will have heard of our Queen's being arriv'd at Rome.

Believe me with truth, etc.

I have receiv'd all your letters.

CXXXVII

Au CARD. ALBERONI, ᴘʀ Mʀ. Willoughby

St. Jago, le 4ᴇ Juillet 1719.

Votre Eminence verra par les lettres du Roy mon Maitre a sa Majesté, et a V.E. l'inquietude ou il se trouve a l'egard de la Reine D'Angleterre, depuis que le Comte de Gallas a parlé a sa Sainteté de la part de son Maitre, pour l'empecher de donner les Moyens a la Reine pour faciliter la jonction avec le Roy mon Maitre, qui est la chose que tous leur Fidels sujets souhaitent le plus ardament, et par consequent que l'Electeur D'Hanovre fera son possible pour l'Empecher. Plus cette affaire est differée, plus il y aura des difficultez a l'excuter, je suis bien persuadé que V.E. desire le rencontre de Mon Maitre avec la Reine d'Engleterre autant que je le puisse faire. Je ne scai pas quelle plie les affaires prendront, mais sy le Roy mon Maitre sera par malheur, obligé de sortir d'Espagne, Je serai ravi de pouuoir avoir l'occasion de temoigner mon zèle pour le service de sa Majesté, et trop heureux si je pouuois lui estre utille. Je supplie V.E de me faire l'honneur de me metre aux pieds de leurs Majestéz, et d'estre tres persuade que j'ai l'honneur d'estre plus que personne et avec bien de respect de V.E., etc.

[To CARDINAL ALBERONI, per Mr. Willoughby.
Santiago, July 4, 1719.

Your Eminence will see by the letters of the King my Master to His Majesty and to your Eminence, the anxiety which he feels with regard to the Queen of England,[1] since the Comte de Gallas[2] has spoken on behalf of his master to His Holiness, to prevent him from giving means to the Queen to facilitate her meeting with the King my Master the event which all their faithful subjects most ardently desire, and which accordingly the Elector of Hanover will do all he can to hinder. The longer this matter is delayed the more difficulties there will be in carrying it out. I am well assured that your Eminence desires the meeting of my master with the Queen of England as much as I can myself.

I do not know what turn affairs will take, but if the King my master should unhappily be compelled to leave Spain, I shall be delighted if I can have the opportunity of showing my zeal for the service of His (Catholic) Majesty, and too happy if I can be of use to him.

I beg your Eminence to do me the honour of placing me at the feet of their Majesties, and to rest assured that I have the honour, etc.]

CXXXVIII

To the QUEEN

ST. JAGO, THE 4TH JULY 1719.

VOTRE Majesté me permetra de temoigner ma joye sur son heureuse arrivé a Rome apres avoir souferte tant des fatigues, and courru tant des dangers. J'espere que le bon Dieu vous protegera, et que vous puissiez en peu de temps avoir la satisfaction de voir le Roy. Je souhaite a votre Majesté tout sorte de prosperité, et la supplie tres humblement de me faire l'honneur d'estre persuadee que je suis avec toute la submission et respect imaginable de Votre Majesté, etc.

[To THE QUEEN. *Santiago, July 4, 1719.*
Your Majesty will allow me to express my joy at your safe arrival at

---

[1] Princess Clementina.
[2] Imperial Ambassador at Rome. See Introduction, p. lvii.

Rome,[1] after having suffered so many hardships and passed through so many dangers.

I hope that the good God will protect you, and that you will soon have the satisfaction of seeing the King.

I wish your Majesty all manner of prosperity, and I humbly beg you to do me the honour to believe that I am, with all imaginable submission and respect, your Majesty's, etc.

CXXXIX

To SIR TIMON CONNOCK

St. Jago, the 4th July 1719.

I am glad of any occasion that offers to assure you of the continuance of my esteem and friendship which can never alter. We know not any thing that passes in your Parts, and if we did, I fear it would not be very agreeable. I here inclose send you Meaghers letter, and Mr. Smith's memoriall, both by the king's commands. They demand but what is just, and what I am sure you will do all can with the Cardinal to get them relief. I am extremly satisfied with Mr. Joyes's behaviour. Believe me with great truth, S^r, your, etc.

The King remembers him kindly to you.

CXL

Au MARQ^s de RISBOURCQ

St. Jago, the 4th July 1719.

C'est avec bien du plaisir Monsieur que je recois l'honneur de vos nouvelles. J'ai fait vos compliments a sa M. Britanique. Elle m'a ordonné de vous faire les siennes, il part demain p^r Lugo. Il est assez vraisemblable ce que vous dites des Portugais, mais je suis bien aise que cela manque confirmation, nous n'avons aucune nouvelle de ce qui se passe a Fontarabie, apparament qu'elle est prise, faite moi tonjours la justice d'estre persuadé que j'ai l'honneur d'estre avec bien du respect, etc.

[To the Marquis de Risbourg. *Santiago, July 4, 1719.*

Sir,—It is with much pleasure that I receive your news. I have presented your compliments to His Britannic Majesty; he has directed

---

[1] Princess Clementina arrived at Rome on May 15.

me to send you his. He leaves to-morrow for Lugo. What you say about the Portuguese is probable enough, but I am glad that it is not confirmed. We have no news of what is happening at Fontarabia. Apparently it is taken.[1]

Do me always the justice to believe that I have the honour, etc.

CXLI

Au Marq^s de RISBOURG

p. 122.

Lugo, the 8th July 1719.

Hier au soir Monsr J'ai eu l'honneur de recevoir la votre par Monsr Le Chevalier et suis bien fâché de son malheur. J'ai parlé a sa Majesté, et lui ai montré votre lettre, le Roy ecrira au Cardinal en sa faveur, et j'en ecrirai a Monsr de Conock pour soliciter le Cardinal de tacher de lui rendre des bonnes offices auprez de son Eminence. Sa Majesté m'ordonne de vous remercier de sa part de ce que vous temoignez sur l'heureuse arrivée de la Reine a Rome, et pour la grace que vous avez a sa consideration donné aux Deserteurs. Nous avons la nouvelle de la reduction de Fontarabie, aprez une vigoureux deffence, et a l'heur qu'il est je croy qu St Sebastien est attacqué. Je crains fort que les Portugais ne se rendent aux instances de l'Engleterre et des alliez, j'ai l'honneur d'estre avec bien de respect, Monsr, etc.

[To the Marquis de Risbourg. *Lugo, July 8, 1719.*

Sir,—Last night I had the honour to receive your letter by the Chevalier.[2] I am very sorry about his misfortune. I have spoken to His Majesty, and have shown him your letter; the King will write to the Cardinal in his favour, and I shall write to Sir T. Connock to solicit the Cardinal and try to do him some service with his Eminence.

His Majesty desires me to thank you on his behalf for your expressions regarding the Queen's happy arrival at Rome, and for the indulgence which you have on his account shown to the deserters.

We have news of the capture of Fuentarabia, after a vigorous defence, and I believe that now San Sebastian is attacked.

I am much afraid that the Portuguese will yield to the solicitations of England and the allies.

I have the honour, etc.]

---

[1] Fuentarabia surrendered on June 18.
[2] Francisco, see next Letter.

CXLII

To SIR TIMON CONOCK

Lugo, the 8th July 1719.

Sr,—The King has order'd me to desire you, to endeavour to prevail with his Eminence to restore Monsr Le Chevalier Francisco to the command of his ship the Hermione, he has been superseded and this disgrace he attributes to the Intendant of the Coruña. The King writes to his Eminence in his favour, everybodey gives him a very good Character, and I found him very willing to do all that was demanded of him. It is pity a young Gentlemen shou'd be ruin'd if he has not deserv'd it. I am sure your good Nature will make you do all you can to serve this poor Gentleman. Believe me with great truth, etc.

CXLIII

Au CARD. ALBERONI

Lugo, 9le Juillet 1719.

Je supplie Votre Eminence d'estre bien persuadé que je suis penetré de sa bonté envers mon Paren, Monsr D'Esmonde.

Monsr de Connock m'a informé de la maniere que V.E. a eu la generosité d'agir et que je me puisse flatter, que ce a esté en part a ma consideration, dont je conserverai une eternelle reconnoissance, trop heureux si je puis avoir des occasions pour temoigner combien Je suis sensible a tous vos bontez et veritablement attaché a votre Personne.

Je n'aurai pas recommendé Monsr D'Esmonde quoy qu'il fut mon Parent, mais que j'estois bien assuré qu'il est homme d'honneur, qu'il s'acquitera de son devoir, comme un honnète homme doit. Je supplie V.E. d'estre assuré de la plus parfaite respect avec laquelle j'ay l'honneur d'estre de V.E., etc. Postscript below.

[To Cardinal Alberoni. *Lugo, July* 19, 1719.

I beg your Eminence to believe that I am deeply sensible of your kindness to my kinsman, Mr. Esmonde.

Sir T. Connock has told me of what your Eminence has had the generosity to do, and that I may flatter myself that this has been partly on my account, for which I shall be always grateful, too happy if I can have any opportunities of proving how sensible I am of all your kindnesses, and how truly attached to your person.

I would not have recommended Mr. Esmonde, though he is my kinsman, unless I had been satisfied that he is a man of honour, and will do his duty as an honest man should.

I beg your Eminence to believe, etc.]

Postscript (below).

I suppose that your Eminence will have seen Mr. Morgan who landed at Santander, and that he will have informed your Eminence that the Swedish gentleman arrived at Santander with him. I do not know what he has proposed, nor even if he has credentials, but surely he will not have made the voyage without being furnished with them.]

CXLIV

To Mr. JOYES

Lugo, the 9th July 1719.

S^R.—This is to give you thanks for the care and trouble you have had in my little affair, and to assure you that I am very sensible of your good Will to me, believe that I shall never be forgetfull of y^r friendship, and that I shall be glad of opportunities to shew you that I am, etc.

P.S.—Au Car. Alberoni. Je croy que V.E. aura veu le Sr Morgan qui debarqua a St Andere, et qu'il aura informé V.E. que le Monsr Suedois est arrivé avec luy a St Ander, Je ne scay ce qu'il a a proposé ni meme s'il a des lettres de credence, mais apparament il n'aura pas fait le voyage sens en estre muny.

CXLV

To SIR TIMON CONNOCK

p. 125.

Lugo, the 9th July 1719.

I have receiv'd the favour of two of yours of the 20th and 22d. I want words to express how sensible I am of your goodness, and the attention you have had for whatever I have recommended to you, particularly in my Cousen Esmonde's affair, he and I are both of us infinitely obliged to you, and I hope you do me the justice to be persuaded that I can never forget your friendship and the marks you so frequently give me of it. I am most sensible of his Eminency's goodness, and particularly in this affair of my cousen's, the manner of doing it adds to the Obligation, and he shall allways find me very sensible of it, and very gratefull, and whatever his fortune may be, he will have a very sincere friend of me, tho' I fear a

p. 125. very useless one. I am very sory to hear your affaires are in so bad a Posture, I see that when you have gotten all your Troops together, you will not be able to hinder the French from attacking St Sebastien, and I believe that you are of opinion that it will be very difficult to hinder the Duke of Berwick from being Master of it.

I am very glad the King our Master has so good a Friend in Monsr de Patino,[1] and that tho' the List you mention is lost, yet that it shall not be any Prejudice to the Gentlemen concerned, but that they shall be paid from the first date of the List; I here send you enclosed the Copy of the List as you desire, and also a Memorial from Col. Owen, this by his Majesty's orders, which he desires you to speak to the Cardinal about, and if no inconvenience in it, that it may be granted.

p. 127. You will remember what I mention'd in my last concerning the poor Gentleman that Commanded the Hermione. I hope Kelly will discover the rest of his accomplices, if so to be sure you will let me know it. Pray give me the pleasure of hearing from you, when it is convenient, and believe me, with great truth, etc.

My compliments to Monsr Patino.

You will have seen before this comes to you a very honest Gentleman, Mr. Morgan, who has been a very great sufferer for the Cause; do him what service you can, I desire it of you. He sent Mr. Wright from Morlaix in his own ship, which has been a great charge to him, as you will find by his Nephew's Memorial that I sent from St Jago.

---

[1] Don Jose Patiño, Alberoni's naval intendant.

CXLVI

Au CARD. ALBERONI

Lugo, le 15 Juillet 1719.

La lettre de V.E. du 28^{le} du juin, j'ai eu l'honneur de recevoir hier. Je ne puis pas m'empecher de temoigner ma reconnoissance des bontez de V.E. pour Monsr D'Esmonde, c'est une repetition qui j' espere ne sera disagreeable a V.E.

Je suis bien faché de voir le progres des armes de France, il faut avouer que Monsr le Duc Regent est bien servi, et qu'il a mis les Francois sous la fereulle. Je supplie V.E. d'estre bien persuadé que j'ai l'honneur d'estre avec toute la verité imaginable, et tout le respect possible de V.E., etc.

p. 128.

[To Cardinal Alberoni. *Lugo, July* 15, 1719.

I had yesterday the honour of receiving your Eminence's letter of the 28th of June.

I cannot refrain from expressing my gratitude for your Eminence's kindness to Mr. Esmond, a repetition which I hope will not be disagreeable to your Eminence.

I am very sorry to see the progress of the French arms; it must be admitted that the Regent is well served, and that he has got the French under his thumb.[1]

I beg your Eminence to believe, etc.]

CXLVII

Au MARQ^s de FRANCLIEU

Lugo, le 15 Juillet 1719.

Monsr,—C'est avec bien du plaisir que j'ai receu l'honneur de la votre par la derniere Poste. Je suis faché d'apprendre le bon succes des Enemies, et Je crains fort pour St Sebastien, puis que le Roy n'a pas assez des troupes pour s'opposer a leurs operations.

Je suis bien aise qu'avez [sic] tant de deserteurs, mais vous ne faites aucune mention s'il y a des officiers parmis. J'ai fait vos compliments a sa Majesté, qui est bien sensible de votre zele

---

[1] Literally 'under the ferule.'

pour son service. Il m'a ordonné de vous bien remercier de sa part, et de vous assurer de son estime. Je vous prie, Monsr. d'estre persuadé de ma reconnoissance pour ce que vous avez la bonté de vous interesser en ce que me regarde, et que je m'estimerai heureux, si je pouvois avoir des occasions pour temoigner l'estime que j'ai pour votre Personne et combien j'ai l'honneur d'estre, etc.

[To the Marquis de Franclieu. *Lugo, July* 15, 1719.

Sir,—It is with great pleasure that I have received the honour of your letter by the last post. I am sorry to hear of the enemy's success, and I fear much for San Sebastian, since the King has not enough troops to oppose their operations.

I am glad that you have so many deserters, but you do not mention if there are any officers among them.

I have presented your respects to His Majesty, who is very sensible of your zeal for his service. He has directed me to thank you cordially on his behalf, and to assure you of his regard.

I beg you, Sir, to be assured of my gratitude for your kindness in interesting yourself in what concerns me, and that I shall consider myself fortunate if I can have opportunities of showing my regard for you, and how much I have the honour, etc.]

CXLVIII

To LADY ARTHER

Lugo, the 15th July 1719.

Madam,—I did not think that I shou'd so soon have an occasion to trouble you with another letter, but being informed from Sir Timon Connock of your Ladyship's generous behaviour, relating to the affair between Mr. Joyes and I, it is impossible for me not to express how sensible I am of your goodness, and that I can never forget it, but shall be impatient to find occasions to shew how much I am penetrated with this goodness of yours, and to shew how much I am with great truth, Mad^m, etc.

CXLIX

To SIR TIMON CONNOCK, p^r express

Lugo, the 12th July 1719.

S^r,—This moment I receiv'd the favour of yours, and

acquainted our Master of your renew'd and continued professions, of your duty and zeall for his service. He has order'd me to give you his thanks, and to remember him kindly to you. I am very sorry to find by your's that your affairs are in so bad a posture, that there is no likelyhood of your putting a stop to the Enemie's operations. This is very bad both for his Majesty's, and our Master's affaires.

I hope you will be able to send me some account of Kelly, that may be of service. Mons. de Silly[1] is to be the active man in the Duke of Berwick's army. I think he is a particular friend of his Graces. I am extremly pleased with the assurances you give me of the Cardinal's Friendship. I will endeavour to preserve it.

My respects to his Eminence, and be assured of the perfect esteem, and true friendship I have for you, being, Sir, etc.

p. 131.

P.S.—I am obliged to you for what you mention concerning the passes. I have receiv'd an account from the Coruña that a Lieutenant with 30 Spaniards, soldiers, are come on board an English ship, to be exchanged.[2] They were made Prisoners in the Highlands. No news of the rest, or of any Body else.

CL

A MONS^R CASTLEBLANCO[3]

Lugo, 21 July 1719.

Mons^R,—C'est avec bien du plaisir que j'ay recu l'honneur de la votre du 4e du Cour^t avec l'agreeable assurance de la parfaite retablissement de votre santé, dont je m'interesse autant que personne, aiant tout l'estime et respect pour vous qui est possible, et vous prie de me continuer l'honneur de votre

---

[1] Jacques Joseph Vipart, Marquis de Silly, commanded the French army on the Spanish frontier before the arrival of Berwick. He is mentioned in Berwick's *Mémoires* as a distinguished officer, but is best known by his liaisons with Madame de Staal. He committed suicide in 1727.

[2] The prisoners taken at Eilean Donan. See Introduction, p. xlvii.

[3] Don Jose de Rozas, Count of Castelblanco. He married Lady Mary Drummond, daughter of the first Earl of Melfort. Bolingbroke speaks of him as 'a Spaniard who married a daughter of Lord Melfort, and who, under that title, set up for a meddler in English business.' See p. xxxv, note 4.

K

amitié. Il faut esperer que nous aurons plus de bonheur si l'occasion se presente. Je suis bien en peine pour nos Messrs qui sont en Ecosse, Dieu veuille qu'ils en revient. Faites moy la justice d'estre bien persuadé que j'ai l'honneur d'estre tres parfaittement.

P.S.—Il vient d'arriver 30 soldats Espagnoles avec un Lieu^t, mais point d'autre nouvelles.

[To M. CASTELBLANCO. *Lugo, July* 21, 1719.

SIR,—I have received with much pleasure the honour of your letter of the 4th current, with the agreeable assurance of the complete restoration of your health, in which I am interested as much as any one, as I have the utmost possible esteem and respect for you, and beg that you will continue to honour me with your friendship.

We must hope for better fortune if the opportunity occurs. I am very anxious about our gentlemen who are in Scotland. God grant that they may return.

Do me the justice to believe, etc.

P.S.—There have just arrived thirty Spanish soldiers with a lieutenant, but no other news.]

CLI

To SIR TIMON CONNOCK, P^R MR MORGAN

p. 132.

LUGO, THE 23^D JULY.

SIR,—It is by the King's commands that I send you this, by Mr Morgan. He is accompanied by a Gentleman, that carries a letter from his Majesty to the Cardinal, and the King desires that you will get him introduced to his Eminence. This is all I can say to you on his account, but I must desire you to endeavour to do Mr Morgan all the Service you can. The King sends the Cardinal a Memorial of his, which I wish may be answer'd to his satisfaction, or at least some part of it. He is a very great sufferer on the King our Master's acc^t, and is indeed ruin'd, if he has not some relief from your Court, for you know how unable our Master is to help or relieve any one that has been a great sufferer on his account. I have known him some years, and can answer for his being an honest Gentleman, and his sufferings shews enough how zeallous he has been, and is

for the King's Interest. I am sure that you will do all you can to serve him, therefore will say no more on this subject. *p.* 133
Mr Talbot is on the List as Lieutenant Colonel. He would have gone to the army some time ago, but that his Majesty wou'd not give him leave, having so few Gentlemen here to waite on him, but I hope that this will not be any prejudice to him, for I do assure that he has been for some time very impatient to go to the Camp. He is a great sufferer, and a very honest brave Gentleman, and one for whome I have a particular value and friendship. Tho' the Protestant Gentlemen cannot be employed, yet I hope they will receive half pay as they are on the List. The King is dayly expecting Mr Willoughby back, or at least some account of him. Believe me with great truth, S^r, etc.

P.S.—Pray assure his Eminence of my Respects. Since I begun this the King has order'd me to tell you that he wou'd be glad that there was orders sent to St Andero that whatever persons arrives there with letters for him, that they shou'd not be stop'd and embarrased as Mr Morgan was at his coming there, but to forward them to his Majesty.

CLII
To SIR TIMON CONNOCK

p. 134.

Lugo, the 24th July 1719.

Sir,—I forgot to let you know that the Compagnion of Mr Morgan desires our Master to have one to reside at St Andere, to receive letters from him, or messengers that are to come to the King; but untill you know from him how he is receiv'd, and treated by his Eminence there is no need of mentioning this to the Cardinal, for if his Eminence do's not enter into correspondance with him, the King wou'd not have any thing of this matter mention'd. Believe me most affectionately your, etc.

CLIII
Au MARQ^s de RISBOURG

Lugo, le 24 Juillet 1719.

C'est avec bien du plaisir, Monsr, que je me serve de cette occasion, pour vous assurer de mes respects et en meme temps de vous prier de la part de sa Majesté Britanique, que vous voulliez bien avoir la bonté de laisser partir le petit Vaisseau qui s'appelle La Ste Marie, et de donner un Certificat comme elle a esté retenu par force, et de voulloir encore l'assister de ce que dependra de vous.

p. 135. Sa Majesté Britanique m'a chargé de vous faire ses complimens. Je n'ai rien appris de nouveau, les premieres lettres du Camp nous apprendront que la tranché est ouverte devant St Sebastien, il ne paroit pas qu'on est en Estat de la secourer, on dit que la Place est bonne, et qu'elle ne manque rien, il faut donc s'attendre a une bonne deffense. Faite moy la justice d'Estre bien persuadé que j'ai l'honneur d'estre avec bien du respect, etc.

[To the Marquis de Risbourg. *Lugo, July 24,* 1719.

Sir,—It is with much pleasure that I avail myself of this opportunity to assure you of my respect, and at the same time to ask you on behalf of His Britannic Majesty to be so good as to allow the little vessel called the *Sainte Marie* to leave, and to give a certificate how she was detained by force, and also to give her assistance so far as that depends on you.

His Britannic Majesty desires me to send you his compliments. I have no news; the first letters from the camp will tell us that the trenches are opened before San Sebastian. It does not look as if we were in a condition to help (the town), they say it is a strong place and well supplied, so we must expect a good defence.

Do me the justice to believe, etc.]

CLIV

Au CARD. ALBERONI, p^r Monsr le Franc

Lugo, le 26^le Julliet 1719.

La lettre de votre Eminence j'ay eu l'honneur de recevoir hier matin, sa Majesté Britanique est tres sensible de l'amities de leurs Majestez Catholicque, et des attentions que V.E. a pour tout ce que luy regarde ; comme sa Majesté ecrit a V.E. vous serez informé des resolutions qu'il a prises pour faire le Voyage, il y a des risques de toute manière, et cestoit a luy d'en faire le jugement.

p. 136. Permettez moy de vous prier tres humblement de me mettre aux Pieds de leurs Majestez, et tres reconnaissant a V.E. de

toutes ses bontès recevant tous les jours des marques de son
Amitié. Je tascherai de la conserver par la plus parfaite reconnaissance possible. V.E. a la bonté de me dire que je parle
a Coeur ouvert et de vous informer de ce que je desire, je vous
obeÿ et comme je ne va pas avec le Roy Je souhaiterai de
pouvoir rester en Espagne jusque on voÿ quelle plie les affaires
prendront, car etant a Rome je ne puis pas etre d'aucune
Utilité au Roy mon Maitre, si V.E. a rien a dirè contre ce
que jai l'honneur de desirer il aura la bonté de me la fair
scavoir. Je resterai icy huit ou dix Jours après le depart de
sa Majesté Britanique qui part demain et jai desein d'aller a
petites journées a Valladolid et d'attendre la les ordres de V.E
aux quelles je me conformerai avec plaisir. Permetté moi de
vous feliciter des bonnes Nouvelles qui vient de Sicile, plut
au Bon Dieu que les affaires auront le succès que Je les souhait. Jai l'honneur d'etre avec la plus parfaite respect et un
Attachment a toute Epreuve de votre Eminence, etc.

[To CARDINAL ALBERONI, per M. LE FRANC.
Lugo, July 26, 1719.

I HAD the honour to receive your Eminence's letter yesterday morning.
His Britannic Majesty is very sensible of the friendship of their Catholic
Majesties, and of the attention which your Eminence gives to all that
concerns him. As His Majesty is writing to your Eminence you will be
informed of his decision as to making the journey. In whatever way it is
made there are risks, and it was for him to judge of them.

Allow me to beg you very humbly to place me at their Majesties' feet.
(I am) very grateful to your Eminence for all your kindness, receiving
every day marks of your friendship. I shall try to retain it by the most
perfect gratitude possible. Your Eminence is good enough to tell me to
speak frankly and to tell you what I want. I obey you, and as I am not
going with the King I should like to be able to remain in Spain until it
appears what turn affairs are to take, for at Rome I can be of no use to
the King my Master. If your Eminence has no objection to what I desire
have the goodness to let me know. I shall remain here eight or ten days
after the departure of His Britannic Majesty, who leaves to-morrow ; and
I intend to travel by easy stages to Valladolid and there to await your
Eminence's orders, which I shall obey with pleasure. Let me congratulate
you on the good news from Sicily.[1] God grant that affairs may turn out
successfully as I wish.

I have the honour, etc.]

---

[1] This probably refers to the defeat of the Austrians under Count Merci, by
the Spanish troops under De Lede, at Franca Villa, on June 27, 1719.

CLV

To SIR TIMON CONNOCK, by Monsʀ le Franc

p. 137.

Lugo, Jul. 26ᵀᴴ.

I have had yᵉ favour of yours of yᵉ 13ᵗʰ, and am sorry it is not in your power to send me good News. I am sure you will do all you can to serve Meagher and Smith, but I am of your Opinion that in yᵉ bad Circumstances the affairs are in, these just demands must be made with great Caution and in a proper juncture. What you propose concerning Meagher, I think, is very just: he shall be informed of it. I fear yᵉ taking of Pampelona will be the end of your Campagne. It is not impossible, but of yᵉ War also since you are not in a Condition to oppose the Enemy in the Field. I am glad so many of yᵉ Prisoners have made their Escape. What you say of yᵉ Duke of Berwicks character is agreed on by all yᵗ know him. Kelly has not made any discovery that is of consequence; it may be that he is but a poor Spie. The King goes from hence towards Valladolid tomorrow. I hope to goe to that place very soon, designeing if it please God to leave this place in a week after the King, where I shall be glad to hear from you. I have made your Compliments to our Master in yᵉ most respectfull manner. He bid me assure you of his Esteem. Believe me most sensible of your Friendship which I set a true vallue on, and am with great truth, etc.

[1] Since I made up my letter yᵉ King has order'd me to desire you to know if yᵗ yᵉ Gentlemen yʳ are Protestants and sent on the List shou'd go to the Army and serve as volunteers since they cannot have employment. This you will let me know.—I am, etc.

CLVI

To the DUKE of MAR

p. 138.

Lugo, yᴱ 26ᵀᴴ Jul.

My Lord.—I am very sorry to hear of your Graces misfortune in being stopp't,[2] but I hope that before this time you

---

[1] These five lines in the first hand.

[2] Mar was arrested at Geneva on May 22 while on his way to the waters o Bourbon. For an account of his curious negotiations with Stair at this time, see Mrs. Thomson's *Lives of the Jacobites*, vol. i. pp. 204 *et seq.*

are at Liberty, and that this will find you in perfect health, and that it will please God to restore his Majesty after all the dissapointments he has met with. I am sure we shall all of us do our Endeavours, and desire you to believe that I am, with truth, Your Graces, etc.

My most humble service to her Grace.

CLVII

To Mr. MURRAY

Lugo, Jul. ye 26th, 1719.

S^r,—This is to Congratulate you on your good fortune in the accomplishing what you were employed.[1] I have not heard from you this great while, which I attribute to ye great distance and ye loss of Letters. I hope you will soon have ye honnour and satisfaction of kissing our Masters hand. I shall be very impatient to hear of his safe arrivall. I am, with great truth, etc.

CLVIII

To the KING, by Mr. Willoughby

Zeky,   *Ezekiel Hamilton.*

Lugo, the 29th July 1719.

Sir,—I was very glad to hear from my servant that you left Galliegos in perfect health, pray God keep you so.

Zeky came hither last night at eleven, and I have the honour to send your Majesty the full powers in good latine as I believe. It is now near twelve, and Mr Willoughby is ready to go from hence. Pray God send you a good journey, and a safe and quicke voyage.—I am, with the greatest respect, Sir, your, etc.

p. 139.

P.S.—I send your Majesty the Earl Marishalls Commission with his Instructions.

---

[1] See Introduction, p. lvi, and p. 15 note 3.

CLIX

To the QUEEN

Lugo, 29ᵗʰ Juillet 1719.

Madame,—C'est avec la plus respectueuse reconnoissance que je reçois l'honneur que Votre Majesté m'a faite par sa lettre du 17ⁱᵉ de Juin, Je la supplie tres humblement d'estre bien persuadée que je ferai toujours tout ce que dependra de moy pour tacher de meriter l'honneur de sa protection, ne souhaitant rien au monde tant, que d'avoir les occasions pour lui temoigner comme bien j'ay l'honneur d'estre avec la plus grande veneration et la plus profonde respect, Madam de V.M., etc.

[To the Queen. *Lugo, July* 29, 1719.

Madam,—I receive with the most respectful gratitude the honour which your Majesty has done me by your letter of the 17th of June. I very humbly beg you to believe that I will do all that is in my power to try to deserve the honour of your protection, as there is nothing on earth that I desire so much as to have opportunities of showing how much I have the honour to be, etc.]

CLX

To Mr. HAYE[1]

Lugo, 29ᵗʰ July 1719.

Sir,—The reason I give you this trouble is to desire you to present the Inclosed to the Queen, with my most profound respect. I wish you a good journey and a prosperous voyage. I am very much, etc.

---

[1] John Hay of Cromlix, third son of the sixth Earl of Kinnoul. He accompanied Mar to Scotland in 1715, and was forfeited. He succeeded Mar as Secretary of State to James, who created him titular Earl of Inverness. Hay married Marjory, third daughter of the fifth Lord Stormont, and sister of James Murray and of Lord Mansfield. The insolence with which Princess Clementina was treated by the Hays was the main cause of the estrangement between James and the Princess. Lady Inverness was said to be James's mistress, a doubtful story. See Mahon, vol. ii. pp. 88 *et seq.*

CLXI

To the KING[1]

p. 140.

Lugo, July 30th, 1719.

This Moment Mr. Kennedy is arrived. He has a letter for you, and I send him away Immediately that he may overtake you before you Gett to the Latitude of Valladolid. I have the honour to send your Majesty a letter I received from my Lord Marechal of a very old date. I also send you, Sir, an Abstract of one I received from Sir Edmund.[2] This is all I have to trouble you with at present. Pray God continue you in health, and give you a good voyage. I am with all Imaginable respect, etc.

CLXII

To the KING

Lugo, July 31st, 1719.

As I was sending away Mr. Kennedy Sr John Healy came to me and desired that I wou'd beg of your Majesty to gett an Answer from the Cardinal concerning his Affair on which depends his all, for if that he has not justice done him he says he must be forced to endeavour to get his bread in some other service. I hope you will pardon me giving you this trouble. I am.

CLXIII

To SIR TIMON CONNOCK

Lugo, July 31st, 1719.

I have very little to say to you but to acquaint you that the King left this place last Thursday, which I believe you may have known from the Cardinal. Pray make him my Compliments in the best Manner. I hope to leave this place on Friday or Saturday next for Valladolid, where I hope to hear

---

[1] Here the first hand begins again.
[2] Sir Redmond Everard?

from you and his Eminence. I wish to God that it may be in your power to send me some Good News, but I much fear it as things are now.

I wrote to you last night but not with my own hand, which I hope you will excuse. The Gentlemen mentioned have been very zealous in the King's cause, they are on the list, and I hope you will do them what service you can. Believe me, etc.

CLXIV

A MONS^r DE CLANKASTROOM

Lugo, Aout 4^{eme,} 1719.

p. 141.   Je suis tres Impatient de scavoir que vous etez arrivé en bonne santé, et quelle reception vous aviez eu de son Eminence, J'espere qu'elle a été a votre satisfaction, et que vous partez tres content de votre visite, Je vous envoye Monsieur le Chifre, et souhaite que vous auriez occasion de vous en servir pour les Interets de votre Maitresse et de mon Maitre et de nos Pais. Sa M. Britannique partit d'icy la semaine passé pour la Castile, J'auray l'honneur de vous ecrire par la premiere Poste plus au longue, le Porteur vous informera de ce qui se passe ici depuis votre Depart. Je vous souhaite un bon Passage, et vous prie de me donner de vos Nouvelles. Je vous supplie d'etre bien persuadé que Je suis, etc.

Souvenez vous s'il vous plait qu'Astorga est le nom que vous etez convenu de vous en servir dans l'autre Chifre.

[To M. de Clancostrum. *Lugo, August 4, 1719.*

I am very anxious to know that you have arrived in good health and what reception you have had from his Eminence. I hope that it has been to your satisfaction, and that you are leaving well satisfied with your visit. I send you the cipher, and I hope that you will have occasion to use it in the interests of your Mistress and my Master and of our countries.

His Britannic Majesty left here last week for Castile. I shall have the honour to write to you at greater length by the first post. The bearer will tell you of what has happened here since you left. I wish you a good passage and beg you to send me your news.

I beg you to rest assured that I am, etc.

Please remember that Astorga is the name which you agreed to use in the other cipher.]

CLXV

To MORGAN

Lugo, Aug. 4th, 1719.

I HOPE this will find you safely arrived where you design to Embarque, and y* you and your Companion are satisfyed with your visit, if not, I fear there is little hopes of doing anything for the Common Cause.

The King left this place last Week for to go to Castile. You have your Instructions from the King and therefore will follow them exactly. I wish you a safe voyage and a quiet arrival. I suppose you will have had Orders about your Nephew, if not, I think the best he can do will be to go to the Camp, being he is on the List as Captain, and I will do all that I can to serve him. Pray believe me to be. *p. 142.*

CLXVI

To GENL. ECHLIN[1]

Lugo, Aug. 4th, 1719.

I THANK you for your's and am glad to find by it y* you were then in Good health, as I hope in God you are now.

Had not the bad Weather Separated and Disabled the fleet we might have Mett in our own Country but I hope yet for all these Disappointments y* it will please God to give us an occasion to endeavour to restore our King, which Opportunity offering you shall have timely Notice, for I shou'd be glad of your Company at all times, but more at such a Juncture when you would have an opportunity of doing the King service.

The King bad me remember him kindly to you. If you have not yet received the Arrears of Pension due to you, Mr. Dicconson[2] has orders to pay them.

---

[1] General Echlin was one of the officers of the '15. Along with Lord Duffus, Threipland of Fingask, and others, he made his escape to the Orkneys, and succeeded in reaching France.

[2] William Dicconson, for many years treasurer and comptroller of the household at St. Germains.

CLXVII

Au Marquis de Risbourg

Lugo, Aout 6^{ieme}, 1719.

J'ay dessein Monsieur de quitter ce Lieu Demain pour aller a Valladolid, mais Je ne pouvois partir sans vous prier d'etre bien persuadé que Je suis tres sensible de toutes vos honnetetez et tres reconnoissaut, et qu'en quel lieu ou Je me trouve J'en Conserveray toujours le resouvenir.

Je vous suis infiniment obligé pour les Asseurances que vous avez la bonté de me donner par la lettre que J'ay l'honneur de recevoir hier au soir de la continuation de votre Amitié, J'en fais tout le cas que Je dois et y Corresponderay avec bien du plaisir.

Je vous suis bien obligé pour ce que vous faites Mention a l'egard du petit batiment de Monsieur Smith, J'espere que la Cour aura quelque Consideration pour lui. J'ay eu des Lettres du 22eme du mois passé du Camp que Disent qu'on n'avoit point d'avis certain que la Tranché fut ouverte, mais à l'heure qu'elle est Je croy le siege formé Je suis faché que la ville n'est pas en meilleur Etat, Je plains la personne qui y doit Commander. J'espere que vous me faites la Justice de me croire que J'ay l'honneur d'etre, etc.

[To the Marquis de Risbourg. *Lugo, Aug. 6, 1719.*

Sir,—I mean to leave this place to-morrow to go to Valladolid, but I could not leave without begging you to believe that I am very sensible of all your kindnesses, and very grateful, and that wherever I may go I shall always preserve the remembrance of them.

I am infinitely obliged to you for the assurances which you have the goodness to give me, by the letter which I had the honour to receive last night, of the continuance of your friendship. I value it as I ought, and will respond to it with much pleasure.

I am much obliged to you for what you mention as to Mr. Smith's little vessel. I hope that the Court will have some consideration for him. I have had letters of the 22nd of last month from the camp, which say that there was no certain news that the trenches were opened, but now I believe the siege is formed. I am sorry that the town [1] is not in a better condition. I regret the person who is to be in command.

I hope you will do me the justice to believe that I have the honour, etc.]

---

[1] San Sebastian.

CLXVIII

Au CARDINAL ALBERONI

LAGOS, AOUT 7, 1719.

JE prens la liberté d'envoyer à V. E. les Incluses Sa M. Britannique m'ayant ordonné d'envoyer toutes les lettres Addressées pour lui à V. E. J'ay quitté Lugo ce Matin pour me rendre à Valladolid où J'attendray les ordres de V. E. J'ay l'honneur, etc.

[To CARDINAL ALBERONI. *Lagos, August* 7, 1719.

I TAKE the liberty of sending the enclosures to your Eminence, His Britannic Majesty having ordered me to send you all letters addressed to him. I left Lugo this morning to go to Valladolid, where I shall await your Eminence's orders.]

CLXIX

To MR. CAMMOCK

VALLADOLID, AUGUST 18TH, 1719.

I RECEIV'D your's from Madrid, and am very glad y^t you were so well recover'd as to be able to take so long a Journey in the heat of the Weather. I hope what you are design'd for will turn to your advantage; and that it may in some Measure make you amends for the great loss you have suffer'd in your last voyage.

As to what you mention of the King's having Blank Commissions to fill up as he shou'd think fitting, I do assure you that you are misinformed. I had indeed several, but had orders not to deliver any but after our Landing, and I assure you I have not disposed of one, as for Col. Fitzgerald I know nothing of him, or of his having a Colonel's Commission untill I saw him near the Groyn, he being a stranger to me. The Bearer you are acquainted with; he was with the King when his Majesty went from Dunkirk to Scotland, and is recommended very strongly by the King to the Cardinal. He is order'd to Cadix to be provided for. He carryes a letter from Monsieur de Patino. The King wou'd have you to do him all the service you can, therefore it is useless for me to say any thing to you on his account. I have no News to send you, but you will have heard of the King's leaving Gallicia, and of his Journey. I shall be glad to hear from you. Wishing you all Imaginable success, and am.

CLXX

Au CARDINAL ALBERONI

VALLADOLID, AOUT 19, 1719.

LA Lettre de V.E. du 7^{ieme} J'ay eu l'honneur de recevoir ce Matin et suis tres sensible des Marques que V.E. a eu la bonté de me donner de la Continuation de Son Amitié et de sa Protection, J'en ay toute la reconnoissance Imaginable, et la meriteray par une sincere Attachement a votre personne. V.E. me mande de vous ecrire en toute sorte de Confiance, J'obeis avec plaisir, et comme J'ay eu l'honneur d'ecrire à V.E. Je souhaite de pouvoir rester en Espagne pour voir comment les affaires de l'Europe se tourneront, il me semble qu'elles ne pourroient pas durer dans la situation qu'elles sont à present, et quand V.E. le trouvera bon Je souhaiteray d'avoir l'honneur de vous pouvoir parler. J'espere qu'il n'y aura point d'inconvenient, et Je suis pret de la faire de la maniere que V.E. Jugera le plus à propos, et en le tems et lieu que vous m'ordonnerez, en attendant J'ay dessein de demeurer icy puisque V.E. me laisse la Choix de ma Demeure. J'ay peur qu'il n'y a que peu d'esperance du coté du Nord. J'ay l'honneur d'envoyer a V.E. une Lettre pour le Roy mon Maitre comme il m'avait ordonné de faire de toutes celles qui sont addressées pour lui. J'ay l'honneur, etc.

[To CARDINAL ALBERONI. *Valladolid, August* 19, 1719.

I HAD this morning the pleasure of receiving your Eminence's letter of the 7th, and am very sensible of the marks which your Eminence has been good enough to give me of the continuation of your friendship and protection. I have all possible gratitude for them and will deserve them by a sincere attachment to your person.

Your Eminence tells me to write to you in all confidence. I obey with pleasure, and as I had the honour to write to your Eminence, I wish to be able to remain in Spain to see how the affairs of Europe turn out. It seems to me that they cannot remain long in their present situation, and when your Eminence finds it convenient I should like to have the honour of being able to speak to you. I hope there will be no objection to this, and I am ready to do it in whatever way your Eminence thinks most suitable, and at whatever time and place you direct. In the meantime I intend to stay here, as your Eminence leaves me the choice of my residence. I fear there is but little hope from the North.

I have the honour to send to your Eminence a letter for the King my Master, as he ordered me to do with all those addressed to him.

I have the honour, etc.]

CLXXI

To the King [1]

Abraham, *Mr. Menzies.*

VALLADOLID, AUG. 19TH, 1719.

I HAVE had the honour of your two letters of the First and 3d, and am infinitely glad that the heat of the Weather has had no ill effect on your health, which God long preserve and Continue to you as I wish it.

I arrived here the 17th, and have receiv'd the full powers from the President. I wish there may be occasion to make use of them; if there be, I will use them with all the prudence that I am master of. I shall be very uneasy and in pain untill I hear that you are safely landed. I am sorry that Mr. Hay's Letters were open'd, but they were not read, and I only took a letter y^t was for me from my Lady Arthur, and one for me Enclosed from Mr. Creon—there is two letters for Mr. Hay, one of them has an Enclos'd in it which may very probably be for me, but I wou'd not open the letter since I receiv'd your's, wherein you were pleas'd to give me a Caution concerning the opening of any letter. I shall obey your orders concerning Sr John Healy. I find y^r Majesty has changed your mind concerning Mr. Kennedy. I wish y^t Mr. Oglethorp and Abraham may have sent you any thing y^t is of Consequence, but I much fear the Contrary. I am glad you are pleased to approve of my Instructions to Lord Marechal. I am, etc.

p. 146.

---

[1] Original in Stuart Papers.

CLXXII

To Sʀ TIMON CONNOCK

VALLADOLID, AUGUST 19, 1719.

I HAVE not had the Satisfaction of hearing from you for some time. You have nothing agreeable to write, and that I believe is the reason of your Silence, however pray let no Excuse of that kind hinder me from the pleasure of knowing that my friend is well. Believe me.

CLXXIII

To Mʀ. HAY

VALLADOLID, AUGUST 19, 1719.

I AM obliged to you for your's from Lavanjez, and for the care you promise to take of my Letter to her Majesty, and for your Civilitys, which I shall return on any occasion. I am very glad you gott well so far on your Journey after enduring so great heats.

I send you by Kennedy the accounts of the money that the King left at Lugo, and also Sʳ Peter Stafford's accounts. As soon as I hear that his Majesty is embarked I'l send away Jolly to the most convenient place for his Embarkation.

CLXXIV

Au BARON WALEF

VALLADOLID, Aout 19, 1719.

JE vous suis bien obligé Monsieur pour la votre du 25 du Juillet que J'ay receu le 9. à Villa Franca, Je suis tres faché d'apprendre que les eaux ne vous ont point soulagé, et que vous eutes les facheux accidens dont vous faites mention, mais Je suis bien aise qu'elles n'ont pas eu des Suites. J'ay toute la reconnoissance imaginable a son Eminence pour ce que vous me mandez touchant un pension que vous dites que sa M.B. a ecrit à son Eminence en ma faveur. Je suis bien

p. 147.

faché que les Affaires se tournent comme elles sont pour l'amour de ce qui regarde son Eminence aussi bien que pour les Interets de mon Maitre. Je suis arrivé icy le 17eme, et Je croy que Je resteray. Je seray bien aise d'avoir l'honneur de vos Nouvelles, et vous prie d'etre bien persuadé que J'ay, etc.

[To Baron Walef. *Valladolid, August* 19, 1719.

Sir,—I am greatly obliged to you for your letter of the 25th of July, which I received on the 9th at Villa Franca. I am very sorry to hear that the waters have given you no relief, and that you had the annoying accidents which you mention, but I am very glad that they have had no bad consequences.

I feel all imaginable gratitude to his Eminence for what you tell me about a pension, as to which you say that His Britannic Majesty has written to his Eminence in my favour. I am very sorry that things are turning out as they are, for the sake of what concerns his Eminence as well as for the interests of my master.

I arrived here on the 17th and I think I shall remain. I shall be very glad to have the honour of your news, and beg you to believe that I have, etc.]

CLXXV

To SIR TIMON CONNOCK[1]

Valladolide, ye 23° August 1719.

S^r,—By yesterdays Post I receiv'd from Lady Arther the favour of three of your obliging letters. They were of the 2^d, 12, and 16th Inst. I am most sensible of y^r Friendship in the care and trouble you have taken, to endeavour to comply with what I have desired of you, and I am very sure that what has not been complied with was not for want of your solicitation. I am very sorry to see the Posture of affaires, which must necessarily produce a Peace before the next Spring, but what kind of a Peace God knows. It must be very mortifying to the Cardinal, I am heartily sorry for it on his account, as well as for the cause, for I shall be allways sincerely his friend and humble servant for his civilities and friendship to me; what you mention of the Parma Envoye is very probable and I am of your Opinion, that the Duke of Berwick will hardly

---

[1] Here the second hand begins.

p. 148. undertake the Siege of Pampeluna, considering the season of the year is so far advanced, and the place so well provided. We hear that the Castle of St Sebastien has capitulated, but I suppose it is not true.[1] I am sorry the Gentleman that was with Mr Morgan could not be of use, his having no Credentials, nor nothing to propose from his Court, made his journey down very unnecessary, for I fancied his Em. would not enter into engagements with him. I know no more of him, then what Mr. Dillon says of him, but I believe he is very well inclined to serve the cause. He and Mr Morgan are extreamly satisfied with your Civilities, and endeavours to serve them, the Second must be contented with what he can get. You tell me the Cardinall did not seem pleas'd with the last resolutions of our Master, but considering the situation of affaires, I do not see what he cou'd do, for he would not have been permitted to have stay'd in this Country any longer than the War lasted, and what condition the Allies wou'd have insisted on, as to the Place that he shou'd go to, I cannot guess at, but to be shure they would have hinder'd him from meeting with the Queen. I hope he has not left this Country too soon. I am very glad you have been so serviceable to Mr Talbot, he deserves as much as can be done for him. I am very much
p. 149. pleas'd with what you mention concerning the Protestant Gentlemen, who are all a going to the Camp, since there will be no questions asked, but am sorry that the Gentlemen on the List are not to receive pay but on their arrivall. I am infinitely pleased to see that his Majesty distinguishes you, by frequent commissions of consequence. I hope he will reward y^r merit. I am very glad that my Lady Arther is satisfied with my gratitude for her civilities; I can never forget her generous behaviour. Sr John Haley, Mr Talbot, and Mr Willoughby leave this place in a day or two, to go to joyn the Camp. I keep Mr Lesley with me, but if he cannot be allow'd his pay without being in the Camp, I will send him thither. He is very usefull to me in my little Family, but I wou'd not keep him to his Prejudice. I need not say anything of the two that go with Sr John, you know them both, they

---

[1] The citadel of San Sebastian capitulated on August 17.

are Persons for whom I have a particular regard. I have quite tired you, I believe, but will only add that it's impossible to esteem any one more than I do you, and that you will allways find me with great truth, sr etc.

CLXXVI

Au CARD. ALBERONI

p. 150.

Dutton, *Dillon.*

VALLADOLIDE, LE 23^{LE} AOUST 1719.

J'AI l'honneur d'informer V.E. que j'ay receu une lettre de Dutton, qui me mande qu'il est asteur[1] en liberté, Je supplie V.E. de me faire sçavoir, si vous continuez en les mêmes sentiments envers Dutton que vous estiez quand j'ay eu l'honneur de vous parler de lui, affin que si V.E. ait les mêmes bontez pour lui, je luy le pourray le faire sçavoir. J'ai l'honneur d'envoyer a V.E. une Pacquete pour sa Majesté Britanique, Je suis et serai en peine, jusques a ce que Je suis informé de son arrivée, J'attends des Lettres de sa Majesté de l'endroit de son Embarquement. J'ay l'honneur d'estre avec bien de respect de V.E. etc.

[To CARDINAL ALBERONI. *Valladolid, August* 23, 1719.

I HAVE the honour to inform your Eminence that I have a letter from Dutton, who tells me that he is now at liberty. I beg your Eminence to let me know if you continue to have the same feelings towards Dutton as you had when I had the honour of speaking to you about him, so that if your Eminence has the same kindness for him I may be able to let him know.

I have the honour to send to your Eminence a packet for His Britannic Majesty. I am and shall be anxious until I hear of his arrival. I expect letters from His Majesty from the place of his embarkation.

I have the honour, etc.]

CLXXVII

To LADY ARTHER

VALLADOLIDE, Y^E 23^D AUGUST.

MADAM,—I am extreamly obliged to your Ladyship for the favour of your's of ye 19th with the Packets from Sr Timon

---

[1] A cette heure.

Connock. I hope you do me the justice to believe that I am with a great deal of respect, Madam, etc.

CLXXVIII

To the KING [1]

p. 151.

VALLADOLIDE, THE 23ᴅ AUGUST 1719.

SIR,—I am impatient to hear that you are gotten safe to the Water side, and shall be as impatient to hear the good news of your safe Landing, which God grant. I have no news to send you. I wish your Majesty all imaginable happyness, being with great respect and submission, Sir, your Majesty's, etc.

CLXXIX

HIS Grace writ to the Prince of Campo Florido from Lugo the 5th August, in answer to his letter of the 30th June and acquents him that directions were given to supply his servant at the Coruña according to his desire, etc. Nta this letter was sent from Valladolide the 26th August 1719.

CLXXX

Au CARD. ALBERONI

VALLADOLIDE, LE 30ᴇ AOUST 1719.

LA lettre de V.E. du 24ie J'ay eu l'honneur de recevoir hier au Matin, et j attendray vos Ordres pour avoir l'honneur de vous faire la reverance, quand V.E. m'avertira du temps et le lieu qu'Elle aura fixée. Je suis fâché qu'il y a si peu d'apparance de Coté du Nord, Les Nouvelles qu'on voit dans les Gazettes touchant la Prusse, n'est guerre bonne, non plus que celle qu'on dit de larmement qu'on fait en Angleterre, et en France, ce qui est sens doute destinée contre ce Royaume, Il faut avoir l'œil a Cadix, les Nouvelles ne marquent pas les Lieux on Les Francois doivent s'embarquer. Il ne parroit pas par les nouvelles que Le Czar et la Suede sont prest a faire la Paix, mais pendant que S.M. Czariene garde Mons. de

p. 152.

---

[1] Original in Stuart Papers.

Lawles, il y a quelque peu d'Esperance que les affaires de ces Pais peuvent changer pour le mieux, Elles ne pourront estre pires.

J'ai l'honneur d'envoyer a V.E. un autre Pacquet des lettres pour S. M. Brittanique, J'ay eu l'honneur de recevoir une d'Elle du 12^{ie}, Le Roy devoit s'embarquer le 14^{ie} a Binares, J'espere qu'il pourroit estre debarqué a Present, Je seray fort en peine jusques a ce que je sache son arivé. J'ay l'honneur d'estre avec bien de reconnoissance et de respect de V.E. etc.

[To CARDINAL ALBERONI. *Valladolid, August 30, 1719.*

I HAD the honour of receiving your Eminence's letter of the 24th yesterday morning, and I shall await your orders, so as to have the honour of paying my respects to you when your Eminence tells me of the time and place which you have fixed.

I am sorry that there is so little appearance from the North. The news which one sees in the Gazettes about Prussia is hardly good, any more than the rumours about the armament which they are preparing in England and in France, which is doubtless directed against this kingdom.[1] An eye should be kept on Cadiz; the news does not mention the places where the French are to embark. It does not appear from the news that the Czar and Sweden are prepared to make peace, but so long as his Czarish Majesty keeps Mr. Lawless there is a little hope that the affairs of those countries may change for the better. They could not be worse.

I have the honour to send your Eminence another packet of letters for His Britannic Majesty. I have had the honour to receive from him one dated the 12th. The King was to embark on the 14th at Vinaros, I hope that he may now be landed. I shall be very anxious until I hear of his arrival.

I have the honour, etc.]

CLXXXI

To THE KING [2]

p. 153.

Amorsley, *Alberoni.* Dutton, *Dillon.*

VALLADOLIDE, THE 30TH AUGUST 1719.

S^R,—I have had the honour of your Majesty's letter of the 12th, and am glad to find by it that you are got safe to the

---

[1] A British squadron, under Lord Cobham, sailed from Spithead on September 21. Cobham captured, at Vigo, a large quantity of arms and stores which had been prepared for Ormonde's expedition. He also sacked Redondela and Pontevedra.

[2] Original in Stuart Papers.

place you mention. I hope you are safely arrived and that this will find you in perfect health.

I have the honour to send you some letters that I receiv'd from Lady Arther. I am to see Mr Amorsley in a little time, and shall obey your Commands. I am sending away Jolly by the way of Vallencia, where he is to embarke. I hope he will go safe. He could not go to Catalonia without an Escorte which must have been an Expense, and it was thought best not to ask for one, since their Troops have Bussiness enough. I shall know what Mr. Amorsley will do concerning Mr Dutton, he, Dutton, being desirous to leave the bad Company he is in, who he informes me have used him inhumanly, as soon as I have an Answer from Amorsley I will acquaint Dutton with it.

You will have heard of the great preparations from England, France, and the Emperour, this poor Country is to be pittied. I shall be in pain untill I hear you get safe to Rome. Give me leave, Sir, to put myself at the Queen's feet. I am with all submission and respect, Sir, etc.

p. 154.

CLXXXII

To Mr. CAMMOCK

VALLADOLIDE, ye 1st SEPTEMB{r} 1719.

Sr,—I trouble you with this to recommend Mrs Tullohs to your Protection. You know them better than I do, their Character is so much to their advantage that I am sure you will have a Pleasure in endeavouring to serve them. I wish I cou'd send you any agreeable news. Pray let me hear from you, and believe that I wish you success in all you undertake, being, etc.

CLXXXIII

To CARD{l} ALBERONI, pr Mr DRUMMOND.

VALLADOLIDE, ye 2d SEPT{r} 1719.

J'ESPERE que V.E. me pardonera la Liberté que je prends, de vous recommender le Porteur, qui aura l'honneur de vous presenter cette lettre. C'est une Personne qui a esté plusieurs fois employé par sa Majesté Britanique, et qui s'est bien acquité de son devoir. Il souhaitera d'avoir l'honneur de servir dans la

Marine, Il a un Ami qui est Capt de Vaisseau dans le service de sa Majesté, Monsr le Duc de Perth qui aura apparament l'honneur de vous faire la reuerance, le connoit mieux que moi, estant de ses Parents. J'attends la reponse de V.E. a ma lettre touchant Dutton, Il sera bien aise de sçauoir a quoi j'attendre affin qu'il prend son parti. J'ai l'honneur d'envoier a V.E. une lettre pour sa Majesté Britanique. J'ai l'honneur d'estre avec bien de respect et plus que Personne de V.E., etc.

p. 155.

[To Cardinal Alberoni per Mr. Drummond.
Valladolid, September 2, 1719.

I hope that your Eminence will pardon me the liberty which I take in recommending to you the bearer, who will have the honour to deliver this letter to you. He is a person who has been several times employed by His Britannic Majesty, and who has discharged his duty well. He desires to have the honour of serving in the navy. He has a friend who is captain of a ship in His Majesty's service. The Duke of Perth, who will have the honour of paying his respects to you, knows him better than I, being of his kinsfolk.

I await your Eminence's reply to my letter about Dutton. He will be very glad to know your decision so that he may decide as to his course.

I have the honour to send your Eminence a letter for His Britannic Majesty.

I have the honour, etc.]

CLXXXIV

To LADY ARTHER

Valladolide, the 2^D Septemb^R 1719.

To thank her for her Present of Tea and Snuff, etc.

CLXXXV

To the DUKE of PERTH [1]

the 2^D Septemb^R 1719.

In answer to his letter from Madrid by Mr. Drummond, the Copy in a Paper apart.

---

[1] James, Lord Drummond, eldest son of the fourth Earl of Perth, Chancellor of Scotland. Lord Drummond was out in the '15, and accompanied James in his flight. He was attainted, but his estate was saved by his having executed a disposition thereof in favour of his eldest son, which was sustained by the Court of Session in 1719 (affirmed by the House of Lords, 1720). The Chancellor had been created titular Duke of Perth by the exiled James II. in 1696, and on his death in 1716, Lord Drummond assumed that title. He died at Paris in 1730.

CLXXXVI

Au CARD^L ALBERONI[1]

VALLADOLIDE, LE 5^{LE} SEPTEMBRE 1719.

J'AI receu hier apres dinné la lettre de V.E. du 3me du Cour^t et je suis tres sensible a l'honneur que sa Majesté m'a faite, dont j'en ai toute la respectueuse reconnoissance imaginable, et aussy de la confiance que V.E. a de mon zèle pour les Interets du Roy. Je suis prest a en donner toutes les marques qui dependeront de moy, et a entreprendre aucune chose, ou il y a la moindre apparance du succes; Je scai la consequence de garder le secret, et puis que V.E. croit que mon Voiage a Madrid pourra faire du Bruit, Je me soumeterai a votre Opinion, mais s'il n'y avoit point d'inconvenient, Je souhaiterai forte d'avoir l'honneur de m'aboucher avec V.E. affin d'ajuster tout ce qui est necessaire de ce cotté icy, pour la grande affaire, et même je supplie V.E. de considerer, s'il n'est pas tres necessaire que je m'abouche avec le Deputé qui est arrivé, affin que je puis savoir l'Estat de la Province, a l'égard des Armes, des Munitions, et Artilerie, et aussy pour estre informé des Lieux les plus propers a debarquer, et pour estre jointe le plutost par les gents du Pais. Si V.E. continue dans la même resolution que je ne dois pas aller a Madrid, Je souhaite avoir votre Permission de vous envoyer une Personne de confiance d'ont je reponderay comme de moy même, V.E. a bien veu par le passé, que ce que m'a esté confié a esté bien gardé. J'ay la commission de Capt General d'ont sa Majesté m'a honoré, mais apparam^t V.E. trouvera a Propos de m'envoyer une declaration, et des Instructions appropriez pour le service auquel je suis destiné. Comme l'affaire est de tres grande importance et que V.E. dit qu'on ne demande que deux Battalions avec de L'argent, J'espere qu'ils sont bien assurez qu'il y aura du Monde suffisant prest a se joindre a si peu de Troupes, Il sera necessaire de fournir une bonne somme d Argent affin que l'affaire ne manque pas de ce cotté la. A l'Egard de l'humeur de ce Peuples, Je suis assuré qu'ils ne seront pas mecontents de ma maniere de vivre avec

---

[1] Letters CLXXXVI, CXCIII, CXCVIII, CC, CCI, CCII, CCIII, and CCVIII relate to the expedition to Brittany mentioned in the Introduction, p. lv.

eux, et puis qu'ils aiment la bonne Chere, j'espere que V.E. me donnera les moyens de les satisfaire sur cet article. Je crois que ce sera a propos que je fasse croire icy, que je dois bien tost suivre sa Ma. Brit. en Italie.

Si V.E. trouve a propos que j'envoye une Personne a Madride, Il ne verra que ceux que vous ordonerez et pour eviter le Bruit, Il ne prendra pas la Poste. Je croy que je pourrois voir le Deputé sans difficulté a quelque lieux d'icy, Je prendray le pretext d aller a la chasse aux Perdrix, et avec les Instruc- *p. 158.* tions que V.E. luy donnera. Et les precautions que je prendray cela se peut faire aisement, et sans bruit, car il est tres necessaire que Je luy parle.

Si V.E. luy donnera Et les precautions que je prendray cela se peut faire aisement, et sans bruit, car il est tres necessaire que Je luy parle.

Si V.E. le trouuoit a propos, Je serai bien aise d'avoir Monsr de Connock avec moy.

J'ay l'honneur de vous envoyer un Pacquet pour sa Majesté Britanique par la post d'hier, j'ai reçu une lettre de Dutton, Il me mande que le Regent leve beaucoup de Monde, Dutton est tres impatient d'avoir ma reponse, affin qu'il peut prendre son party, Il me mande qu'il a esté inhumainement traité par le Regent. J'avois commencée ma lettre hier mais elle ne parte que ce soire. Faite moy la justice d'estre persuadé que Je suis plus que personne, et avec bien de respect de V.E., etc.

[To CARDINAL ALBERONI. *Valladolid, September 5*, 1719.

YESTERDAY after dinner I received your Eminence's letter of the 3rd inst., and I am very sensible of the honour which His Majesty has done me, for which I feel all the respectful gratitude imaginable, and also of the confidence which your Eminence has in my zeal for the King's interests. I am prepared to give every proof of it which depends on me, and to undertake anything in which there is the least appearance of success. I know the importance of keeping the secret, and since your Eminence thinks that my travelling to Madrid might cause talk, I shall submit to your opinion, but if there is no objection, I should much like to have the honour of an interview with your Eminence, in order to arrange all that is necessary on this side for the great enterprise, and also I beg your Eminence to consider whether it is not very necessary that I should have a meeting with the deputy who has arrived, in order that I may know the state of the province with regard to arms, stores, and artillery, and also be informed as to the places most suitable for landing and for being joined as soon as possible by the people of the country.

If your Eminence is still of opinion that I should not come to Madrid, I wish to have your permission to send you a person of trust, for whom I will answer as for myself. Your Eminence has seen well in the past that what has been intrusted to me has been well kept.

I have the commission of Captain-General with which His Majesty has honoured me, but surely your Eminence will find it advisable to send me a declaration and instructions suitable for the service for which I am intended. As the affair is of very great importance, and as your Eminence says that only two battalions are required, with money, I hope that they are well assured that there will be plenty of people ready to join so small a body of troops. It will be necessary to supply a good sum of money if the enterprise is not to fail on that side. As to the humour of those people, I am assured that they will not be displeased with my manner of life among them, and as they love good cheer, I hope that your Eminence will give me the means to satisfy them in this respect.[1]

I think that it will be advisable for me to give out here that I am soon to follow His Britannic Majesty to Italy.

If your Eminence thinks it advisable that I should send some one to Madrid, he will only see those whom you direct, and in order to avoid talk he will not travel post.

I think I could see the deputy without difficulty at various places here. I will make the excuse of going partridge-shooting, and with the instructions which your Excellency will give him and the precautions which I will take, the thing can be done easily and quietly, for it is very necessary that I should speak to him.

If your Eminence thinks it advisable, I should be very glad to have Sir T. Connock with me.

I have the honour to send you a packet for His Britannic Majesty. By yesterday's post I have received a letter from Dutton. He tells me that the Regent is raising large levies. Dutton is very impatient to have my answer, so that he may decide as to his course. He tells me that he has been inhumanly treated by the Regent.

I had commenced my letter yesterday, but it is not going till this evening.

Do me the justice to believe, etc.]

CLXXXVII

To the KING

VALLADOLIDE, Y^E 6TH SEPT^R. 1719.

S^R,—I have had account by yesterdays post from Capt. Petite, that you were embarcked the 14th of last month at

---

[1] Swift, in the *Journal to Stella*, describes Ormonde as 'an expensive man.'

Vinares, that the Winde had continued fair, and that he hoped your Majesty was safely landed before this time. God grant that you be so. I have the honour to send you some letters. I shall be, and am impatient to hear of your being arrived in good health. I am, with great submission and respect, etc.

CLXXXVIII

To Mr. ROWLEY[1]

Rowley,   *Bishop of Rochester (Atterbury)*.[2]
Mrs. Franklin?

VALLADOLID, SEPT^R. 8, 1719.

It is a great while since I have had the satisfaction of hearing from you. You shou'd have heard oftener from me had I any thing to inform you of that could have been agreeable or diverting to you. You will have heard of what Concerns our little Domestick affairs from Mrs. Franklin when it is not troublesome to you. I shou'd be glad to hear from you. Pray believe that I am.

CLXXXIX

Au CARDINAL ALBERONI[3]

(*Not sent*)

VALLADOLID, SEPT^R. 9EME 1719.

J'ay l'honneur d'ecrire à votre Eminence par le Porteur Monsieur de Magny, il arriva icy hier au soir, Je n'ay le veu que ce matin, J'espere que V.E. aura egard de ce qu'il a souffert pour la bonne Cause. Il perd beaucoup, et Je puis Asseurer V.E. qu'il est homme d'honneur et de Probité, vous pouverez etre asseuré que Je ne lui ait pas fait Mention du secret Directement ni indirectement, mais Je suis assuré qu'on peut

---

[1] Here the first hand begins again.

[2] Francis Atterbury, Bishop of Rochester, the best-known of all Jacobite plotters, banished under a Bill of Pains and Penalties in 1723. Dubois wrote to Craggs that the secret of Ormonde's expedition had not been communicated to Atterbury: 'parcequ'il ne favorise pas volontiers ce qu'il n'a pas lui même imaginé,' March 8, 1719, Appendix, No. 21, p. 225.

[3] This letter is crossed through in the manuscript.

s'y fier. Il est venu un Gentilhomme Ecossois avec lui qui souhaiteroit d'etre Employé, il a eté dans l'affaire du Duc de Mar en Ecosse, Monsieur le Duc de Perth le Connoit et informera V.E. de son Caractere. J'attends les ordres de V.E. et suis avec bien du respect.

[To Cardinal Alberoni (*not sent*). *Valladolid, September* 9, 1719.

I have the honour to write to your Eminence by the bearer, M. de Magny. He arrived here last night. I only saw him this morning. I hope that your Eminence will have regard to what he has suffered for the good cause. He loses much, and I can assure your Eminence that he is a man of honour and probity. You may be sure that I have not mentioned the secret to him directly or indirectly, but I am sure he might be trusted.

A Scottish gentleman has come with him, who would desire to be employed; he was in the Duke of Mar's affair in Scotland. The Duke of Perth knows him, and will tell your Eminence about his character.

I await your Eminence's orders, and am with much respect, etc.]

CXC

Au BARON WALEF

Valladolid, Septr. 9, 1719.

Je voy par vos deux Lettres dates le 22 et 30eme d'Aout que vous n'aviez pas receu la mienne daté le 19eme d'Aout en reponce de la votre que J'avois receu à Villa Franca, Je l'avois mis sur une Couverte Addressé à Monsieur Connock apparement vous l'auriez receu à present. Je suis faché que son Eminence vous oublie, par votre premiere J'ay cru que vous etiez content de lui.

A l'egard de ceque vous desirez touchant le Patent que vous souhaitez que Je vous envoye, Je vous prie de m'excuser, car Je ne Croy pas que Je le puis faire, et suis mortifié de ne pouvoir pas vous satisfaire sur ce sujet, car J'aurois toujours beaucoup de plaisir a vous pouvoir rendre service.

Je suis faché que vous avez raison d'etre Mecontent des personnes que vous en faites mention, J'espere que ca ne vous fera point du tort, Je croy que Cette Lettre vous trouvera à Madrid ou J'espere que vous aurez raison d'etre Content de votre reception du Cardinal. Croyez moy, etc.

[To Baron Walef. *Valladolid, September* 9, 1719.

I SEE by your two letters, dated the 22nd and 30th of August, that you had not received mine dated the 19th of August,[1] in answer to yours which I received at Villa Franca. I put it under cover addressed to Sir T. Connock; doubtless you will now have received it.

I am sorry that his Eminence is forgetting you. From your first letter I thought you were satisfied with him.

As to what you desire about the commission which you wish me to send you, I beg you to excuse me, for I do not think I can do it. I am sorry that I cannot gratify you in this matter, for I should always have much pleasure in being able to do you a service.

I am sorry that you have reason to be dissatisfied with the persons whom you mention. I hope that this will not do you harm. I suppose this letter will find you at Madrid, where I hope you will have reason to be satisfied with your reception by the Cardinal.

Believe me, etc.]

CXCI-CXCII

His G. wrote to the Duke of Perth Septr. 9th by Mr. Areskine, and to Captn. Esmonde.

CXCIII

Au CARD. ALBERONI[2]

VALLADOLID, LE 9^{IE} SEPT^{RE}, 1719.

J'AI l'honneur d'ecrire a V. E. par le Porteur Monsr le Marq^s de Magny, qui arriva icy hier au soir. Il a de l'impatience a vous rendre ses devoirs, V. E. a esté informé de son zele pour la bonne Cause, qui lui coute cher, car il perde beaucoup, Je le connois pour estre un tres honeste homme, a qui on on se peut fier, et j'espere que V. E. aura egard a ce qu'il a souffert, V. E. peut estre asseuré que je ne lui ai parlé du secret directement ou indirectement, mais je crois qu'il pourroit m'estre utille dans le Projet, estant de la Nation et aiant des biens dans la Normandie qui est joignant comme V. E. scait du Pais de quoy il est question. J'attendrai la reponse de V. E. sur cecy, *p. 161.*

---

[1] Letter CLXXIV.
[2] Here the second hand begins again.

et vos ordres, que je tacherai d'executer le mieux qu'il me sera possible. Il y a un Gentil homme qui est venu avec Monsieur de Magny, qui a esté dans l'affair du Duc de Mar en Ecosse, Il souhaite de pouvoir avoir de l'Employ, Monsr le Duc de Perth le connoit et peut rendre conte de ses services, J'ay lhonneur d'estre avec bien de respect de V. E., etc.

[To CARDINAL ALBERONI. *Valladolid, September 9*, 1719.

I HAVE the honour to write to your Eminence by the bearer, the Marquis de Magny, who arrived here last night. He is impatient to pay his respects to you. Your Eminence has been informed of his zeal for the good cause, which is costing him dear, for he loses everything. I know him to be a very honest man, who may be trusted, and I hope that your Eminence will have regard to what he has suffered. Your Eminence may be sure that I have not spoken to him of the secret, directly or indirectly, but I think he might be useful to me in the enterprise, being of the nation and having property in Normandy, which, as your Eminence knows, is adjacent to the country concerned. I shall await your Eminence's answer as to this, and your orders, which I shall try to carry out as well as I can.

There is a gentleman who came with M. de Magny, who was in the Duke of Mar's affair in Scotland. He wishes to get employment. The Duke of Perth knows him and can tell you of his services.

I have the honour, etc.]

CXCIV

To SIR TIMON CONNOCK

VALLADOLIDE, LE 9^{IE} SEPTEMB^R 1719.

S^R,—This morning I have received the favour of yours, which is of a very old date. I am very glad that the Gentlemen you mention are to be provided for as you mention. Before this time you will have severall of my letters, from Mr. Talbot and his friends. I hope I shall have the satisfaction to hear from you often. I am obliged to you for presenting of Mr. Owen, and the rest of ye Gentlemen you mention, to his Eminence. I thank you for what you wou'd have done for my late Servant. Pray give my humble service to Genl Crafton and to Sr John. Believe me sincerely, etc.

CXCV

Au CARD^L ALBERONI

p. 162.

VALLADOLEDE, LE 13^{IE} SEPTEMB^R 1719.

J'AI l'honneur d'envoyer a V. E. la Patente que vous m'avez envoyé pour estre donné a Monsr de Healy aprez estre embarqué. Sa Majesté Britanique m'a dit qu'il avoit ecrit a V. E. en sa faveur, et m'a ordonné d'en faire resouvenir V. E., esperant que vous aurez la bonte a sa recommendation de rendre la patente au Chevalier, C'est un Officier plein de zele pour le service de sa Majesté, il en porte les marques et a esté a ce qu'il m'a dit honoré de votre Estime, mais il aprehende qu'il y a des Gens qui lui ont rendu des mauuaises offices aupres de V. E., Il jure qu'il ne se sente pas coupable d'avoir jamais manqué de respect a V. E. et qu'il a pour votre personne toute la veneration et atachement possible, et qu'il est prest a en donner des temoignages quand il plaira a V. E. de lui donner les occasions, Apres ce que S. M. en a ecrite a V. E., il ne faut pas que je pretend a en parler, mais si V. E. veut avoir la bonté de donner cette Patente au Chevalier, vous le tirerez du desespoir ou il est, et lui rendrez s'il est possible plus devoüee a votre personne qu'il est a present. Pardonnez la liberté que je prends et faite moy la justice d'estre bien persuadé que j'ay l'honneur d'estre avec bien de respect de V.E.

[To CARDINAL ALBERONI. *Valladolid, September* 13, 1719.

I HAVE the honour to forward to your Eminence the commission which you sent me to be given to Sir John Healy after embarking. His Britannic Majesty has told me that he has written to your Eminence in his favour, and has commanded me to remind your Eminence of this, hoping that you will have the goodness to give the knight the commission. He is an officer full of zeal for His Majesty's service; he bears the marks of it, and, according to what he has told me, he has been honoured with your esteem; but he understands that there are some people who have done him a bad turn with your Eminence. He swears that he cannot accuse himself of having ever failed in respect for your Eminence, that he has all possible veneration and attachment for your person, and that he is ready to give proofs of this when your Eminence shall please to give him opportunities. After what His Majesty has written to your Eminence I must not presume to speak of the matter, but if your Eminence would have the goodness to give the commission to the knight you would relieve him from his present despair and render him if possible more devoted to your person than he now is.

Pardon the liberty which I take, and do me the justice to believe, etc.]

p. 163.

CXCVI

To the KING

| Monsr. de Tonniere, | *Marquis de Magny.* |
| Amorsley, | *Alberoni.* | Dutton, | *Dillon.* |

VALLADOLIDE, THE 13TH SEPTR 1719.

Sʀ,—I hope this will find your Majesty safely landed, and in good health, after your voyage; I am impatient to be assured of it. I have nothing new to acquaint you with, only that Monsʳ de Tonniere came hither last friday night late. He parted for Madrid on Sunday morning; he had a letter from the Queen to your Majesty. I have the honour to send your Majesty a packet which I receiv'd from Lady Arther. From the Coruna I hear that there are five or six english ships, cruising between Cape Ortegall and the Isles of Sissargue;[1] once in four or five days they looke into the Coruna, which has allarm'd the peaple of that Place, they expecting to be atack'd when the English Squadron with their Transports comes to sea.

I have no answer from Amorsley relateing to Dutton, which I wonder at. God grant you good health, and all the happyness you can desire.—I am, with all submission and respect, Your Majesty's, etc.

p. 164.

CXCVII

To SIR JOHN HALEY

VALLADOLIDE, 13TH SEPTR 1719.

Sʀ,—I have writ to his Eminence in as pressing termes as I could, and that you could wish. I should be extremely glad that my letter might have the Effect I wish; and am ready to endeavour to serve you when in my Power. I have not heard from you since your arrivall in the Camp. Pray let me know what you are doing, and what is become of the french

---

[1] The Sisarga Islands, three uninhabited islets off Cape S. Adrian, about twenty-four miles west of Corunna.

Army; we have quite lost them. Some say that they are gone into France, others that they are going thro' France to come into Rousillon, and so to Catalonia; and we have every day a new report, without any ground, as I believe. A thousand lyes come to this Town, or are made here, but you will inform me of the situation of your Enemies.

Pray make my Compliments to Mr Crofton and to your Companions, and believe me very sincerely, etc. If Sr Timon be with you, make him my Compliments.

CXCVIII

Au CARDINAL ALBERONI[1]

VALLADOLID, SEPT^R 16, 1719.

La lettre de V.E. du 14e J'ay eu l'honneur de recevoir hier au soir, et ce Matin celle du 13e, Je suis ravi que sa Majesté soit content des offres que J'ay fait de mes services, Elle pourroit etre assurée de ma bonne volonté en tout ce qui regarde ses Interets.

Puisque V.E. est d'opinion que mon voiage à Madrid feroit du bruit, et qu'il est inutile d'envoyer une personne J'attendray, avec impatience l'arrivée du Deputé a fin que Je puisse etre informé du detail des Affaires de cette Province. *p.* 165.

J'espere que ces Messieurs ne manqueront pas à ce qu'ils ont promis au Roy, Je leurs suis bien obligé de la Confiance qu'ils ont en moy, Je feray mon possible pour Conserver leur estime, et de gagner leur Amitié en faisant de mon mieux pour le service de sa Majesté, ce qu'est inseparable de leurs Interets.

Nonobstant ce que les Messieurs disent touchant les Magazins, Je crois qu'il sera tres necessaire en cas d'accident d'avoir a notre Debarquement quelques pieces de Campagne et des Chevaux de frize si cela se peut et aussi de poudre avec une bonne quantité de Grenades qui ne peuvent qu'etre Utiles.

La Marche des Deux Battaillons ne peut Donner d'ombrage, et l'arrivée du Deputé ne peut Causer aucun soupcon de la Maniere que V.E. me le mande.

---

[1] Here the first hand begins again.

M

Je trouveray beaucoup de Difficulté à sortir d'icy sans bruit, car c'est un lieu où les Gens sont extremement Curieux, et si J'avois pu imaginer qu'il y auroit eu quelque affaire qui me regardoit, Je n'aurois pas choisi cet endroit pour ma Demeure, mais Je feray tout ce que Je peux pour cacher ma route.

Je suis bien obligé a V.E. pour ce que vous avez dessein de m'envoyer par le Courier, (Je m'en Serviray pour les Interets de sa Majesté) et aussi de la bonté que vous avez de m'envoyer Monsieur de Connock, Monsieur de Walef me sera toujours agreable.

p. 166.

J'espere que V.E. aura la bonté d'informer le Roy mon Maitre des raisons que Je ne puis pas l'avertir que J'ay l'honneur d'etre employé par sa Majesté a fin qu'il ne soit pas pas Mecontent de Moy.

J'avertis Monsieur Dutton par la Poste D'hier qui va a Bilbao de ce que V.E. m'a mandé a son egard, Je crois qu'il viendra en Espagne, Dieu veuille que les affaires tournent de la Maniere qu'il pourroit etre utile en ce pais. A l'egard de Monsieur de Magny Je suis seur qu'il est homme d'honneur, à qui on peut se fier, Je scais qu'il n'a Jamais eté au service, mais Je croy qu'il me pourra etre tres utile ayant des amis dans la Province Joignant, mais Je Soumetts a l'opinion de V.E.

Je prens la liberté d'envoyer une liste de ce que Je crois etre necessaire pour Embarquer avec nous si cela se peut, et J'ay l'honneur d'etre, etc.

Six Pieces de Campagne de huit ou de six livres.
Des Balles, des Boulettes à proportion.
Des Chevaux de frise autant qu'ont peut trouver.
Mille ou quinze cens Grenades, et Mille Quintaux des Poudre et une Bonne Quantité des Pierres à fusil.
Deux ou trois Mille Armes avec Bayonets nous seroit utile.

P.S.—[1] Je rends tres humbles graces a V.E. de l'attention que vous avez a ma recommendation p^r le Monsr qui doit estre employé en la Marine.

J'espere que le Deputé n'a pas esté connu a St Andere.

---

[1] These four lines are in the second hand.

[To Cardinal Alberoni. *Valladolid, September* 16, 1719.]

Last night I had the honour to receive your Eminence's letter of the 14th, and this morning that of the 13th. I am delighted that His Majesty is satisfied with the offers which I have made of my services. He may rest assured of my willingness in all that concerns his interests.

Since your Eminence is of opinion that my journey to Madrid would cause talk, and that it is useless to send any one, I await with impatience the arrival of the deputy in order that I may be informed in detail of the affairs of that province.

I hope these gentlemen will not fail in what they have promised to the King. I am much obliged to them for the confidence they have in me. I will do what I can to retain their esteem and to gain their friendship by doing my best for His Majesty's service, which is inseparable from their interests.

Notwithstanding what these gentlemen say about the magazines I think it will be very necessary in case of accidents to have at our landing some field-guns and if possible chevaux-de-frise, also powder, with plenty of grenades, which cannot but be useful.

The march of the two battalions cannot cause suspicion, nor can the arrival of the deputy cause suspicion in the way which your Eminence suggests to me.

I shall find much difficulty in leaving here quietly, for it is a place where people are extremely inquisitive, and if I had been able to imagine that there would be any affair which would concern me I should not have chosen this place for my residence; but I shall do what I can to conceal my route.

I am much obliged to your Eminence for what you propose to send me by the courier (I shall make use of it for His Majesty's interests) and also for your kindness in sending me M. de Connock. M. de Walef will always be welcome to me.

I hope that your Eminence will have the goodness to inform the King my master of the reasons, which I cannot tell him, why I have the honour to be employed by His Majesty, so that he may not be displeased with me.

I informed M. Dutton by yesterday's post to Bilbao of what your Eminence has told me concerning him. I think he will come to Spain. God grant that affairs may so turn out that he may able to be useful in this country.

As to M. de Magny, I am sure that he is a man of honour who may be trusted. I know that he has never been in the army, but I think that he might be very useful to me, having friends in the adjoining province. However, I defer to your Eminence's opinion.

I take the liberty of sending a list of what I think necessary to put on board with us if possible, and I have the honour, etc.

Six field-guns, 8 or 6 pounders.
Bullets and roundshot in proportion.

Chevaux-de-frise, as many as can be found.

1000 or 1500 grenades, 1000 quintals of powder, and a good supply of gun-flints.

Two or three thousand muskets with bayonets would be useful to us.

P.S.—I offer my humble thanks to your Eminence for your attention to my recommendation on behalf of the gentleman who is to be employed in the navy.

I hope that the deputy was not recognised at Santander.]

CXCIX

To PETER

Peter,   *The King.*   Dutton,   *Dillon.*

p. 167.   VALLADOLID, SEPT. 20, 1719.

I AM in continual expectation of hearing of your being safely landed, and of your being arrived in Rome.

I have no News to send you, but enclose a letter which I believe is from the Duke of Mar to your Majesty. The Cardinal has desired me to send to Dutton, and to let him know that he shall have the termes that were promised when first I writt to him on this subject.

I thought I shou'd have seen the Cardinal soon, but am not like to do it yet. The Duke of Perth has been at Madrid this fortnight. I had one letter from him; he desired to know if that you had left with me any orders for him. I Answer'd him that your Majesty told me that you believed that he might come into this Country, and when that he heard you were gone back it was your Majesty's opinion that he wou'd follow you. I have not heard from him since, which I wonder at. I hope your Majesty will find the Queen in Good health. I wish y^r Majesty's all imaginable happyness. I am with great, etc.

CC

Au CARDINAL ALBERONI

VALLADOLID, SEP. 20, 1719.

J'AY l'honneur d'envoyer à votre Eminence un Paquet pour sa Majeste Bretanique. V. E. aura la bonté de vous souvenir d'ecrire au Roy D' Angleterre pour lui dire les raisons que Je ne l'ay pas informé du Projet. V. E. se souviendra de me Donner le pouvoir de Donner des Patentes, la Patente que J'ay ne m' autorise pas en cette Matiere, apparemment Je les auray dans les Instructions. J'ay l'honneur d'etre, etc.

[To Cardinal Alberoni. *Valladolid, September 20, 1719.*

I have the honour to send your Eminence a packet for His Britannic Majesty.

Your Eminence will have the goodness to remember to write to the King of England to tell him the reasons as to which I have not informed him of the project.

Your Eminence will remember to give me power to grant commissions; the commission which I hold gives no authority to do so; presumably I shall receive it with my instructions.

I have the honour, etc.]

CCI

Au. CARD. ALBERONI par un exprès[1]

p. 168.

Vall.^{dd,} le 22 S^{tr,} 1719.

Les trois Lettres de votre Eminence datés du 19 Jai eu l'honneur de recevoir hier après dinner. Quand je fis la demande des pieces de Campagne et des Grenades Jai crue qu'on en pouroit trouuer a St. Andere.—V. E. m ayant dit qu'il y avoit la une fabrique des Canons et jai crue quil y pourroit avoir des Magazins, Le Deputé m assure qu'ils en ont douze pieces mais point des Grenades. J ay aussi demandé des Chevaux de Frise en cas qu ils s'en trouueroient a L'endroit de l'embarquement des Troupes.—Je suis ravi que le Roi aura la bonté d' informer sa Majesté Britanique des raisons qui m'empechoient de lui avertir de cette affaire. Il sera bien difficille de cacher ma route etant obligé de me servir des Voiturines d'icy, mais je ferai tout ce que je puis pour couvrir ma marche en faisant courrir le bruit que je dois aller a Rome. —Jay dessein de partir d'icy le dimanche au soir, mais comme V. E. marque que mon depart donneray l'alarme Je souhaiterois de scavoir le jour que V. E. veuille que je part, etant pret en n'attendant que vos ordres, car si j arrive quelque tems avant les Vaisseux sa pourroit causer trop de bruit.—Jai receu

---

[1] Here the second hand begins again.

les 500 Pistoles et j attendrai le reste a St. Andere dont j aurai toute la Reconnaissance possible. Je promet a V. E. que ces Messieurs ne manqueront pas a boire pendant que sa dure.—J'attendrai les Pattentes et les instructions a mon Arrivée a St. Andere.—Jai la declaration du Roi signé par sa Majesté promettant une retraite en Espagne en cas de Malheur a ceux qui auroient pris les Armes, mais cest approprié pour L'angleterre ne seroit y pas necessaire qu'il y auroit une autre signé de sa Majesté.—Je suis du sentiment de votre E. qu'on doit attaquer le Coeur aussitot qu'on pourra, et nous tascherons de faire la Guerre auec L'espée et la Plume et par toutes les Moyens qu'on trouvera necessaires.

p. 169.

Jay receu beaucoup de satisfaction du deputé qui me paroit un homme de bons sens et qui Connoit bien son Pais, J'espere que ses Amis ne manqueront pas a ce qu'ils ont promis. Jai l'honneur de vous envoyer l'inclus a l'egard du tems qu'il propose que le peuple prend les Armes, j'en Convienne pour les raisons quil marquoit, Je lui avois dit que si par malheur L'Escadre etoit separé ou aucun autre Accident qui pourroit empecher les Vaisseaux d'arriver, que ses pauvres gens seroient sacrifié, mais il m'a dit que je ne deverois pas me mettre en peine de sa, car ils etoient resolus de prendre les Armes meme sils navoient point de Secours. A l'egard des trois milles pistols qu il demande je souhaiterois scavoir l'opinion de V. E. il y a de risque a les envoyer de la maniere quil le propose mais il dit que il est tres necessaire de les envoyer comme il le propose. Jai ecris a Dutton par une bonne Chifre et Je me suis servis dune addresse sure. Je suis bien obligé a V. E. de la bonté que vous auez de me donner un Personne qui eit tant de merite que Don Blaze de Loya. J attendrai avec impatience les ordres de V. E. par un Courrier et suis avec bien de respect, etc.

p. 170.

P.S.—Ne seroit y pas necessaire d'avoir des Lettres de sa Majesté pour le Parlement de Paris et de Rouen aussi bien que que pour le lieu destinée.

[To CARDINAL ALBERONI, by an express messenger.
Valladolid, September 22, 1719.

YESTERDAY after dinner I had the honour to receive your Eminence's three letters dated the 19th.

When I asked for field-guns and grenades I thought that they could be found at Santander. As your Eminence had told me that there was a gun-factory there I thought that there might be stores. The deputy assures me that they have twelve guns but no grenades. I also asked for chevaux-de-frise in the event of there being any at the place of embarkation of the troops.

I am delighted that the King will have the goodness to inform His Britannic Majesty of the reasons which prevented me from telling him of this affair. It will be very difficult to conceal my route, as I must make use of drivers from here, but I shall do all I can to conceal my journey by spreading a rumour that I am going to Rome.

I mean to leave here on Sunday evening, but as your Eminence points out that my departure will give the alarm, I should like to know on what day your Eminence wishes me to leave, as I am ready and only await your orders; for if I arrive some time before the ships that might cause too much talk.

I have received the 500 pistoles and shall await the remainder at Santander, for which I shall be as grateful as possible. I promise your Eminence that these gentlemen shall not lack something to drink while this affair lasts.

I shall expect the commissions and the instructions on my arrival at Santander.

I have the declaration signed by the King promising a retreat in Spain in case of mishap to those who have taken up arms, but this applies to England. Would it not be necessary that there should be another signed by His Majesty?

I am of your Eminence's mind that we should attack the heart as soon as possible; and we shall try to make war with sword and pen and by all means which may be found needful.

I have received much satisfaction from the deputy, who seems to me a man of good sense, and who knows his country well. I hope that his friends will not fail in what they have promised.

I have the honour to send you the enclosed regarding the time at which he proposes that the people should take up arms; I agree with it, for the reasons which he notes. I have told him that if by ill-luck the fleet should be separated, or any other accident should prevent the ships from arriving, these poor people would be sacrificed; but he tells me that I need not distress myself about that, for they were determined to take up arms even if they had no assistance.

As to the 3000 pistoles for which he asks, I should like to have your Eminence's opinion. There is risk in sending them in the way which he proposes, but he says that it is very necessary that they should be sent as he proposes.

I have written to Dutton in a good cipher, and have made use of a safe address. I am much obliged to your Eminence for your goodness in giving me a person of such merit as Don Blas de Loya. I shall await with impatience your Eminence's orders by a courier, and am with much respect, etc.

P.S.—Would it not be necessary to have letters from His Majesty for the Parliaments of Paris and of Rouen, as well as for the intended place?]

CCII

Au CARDINAL ALBERONI [1]

VALLADOLID, SET^R. 23, 1719.

J'AY receu la lettre de V.E. du 20e ce Matin et Cette après Diné celle du 22. J'attends les ordres de V.E. pour le Jour de mon depart, et suis bien aise que le Courier m'a trouvé icy car cela auroit fait du bruit d'etre resté a cinque lieux d'ici sur le Chemin de S^t. Ander. M^r. Lambert m'avoit dit que V.E. lui avoit dit que Je pouvois partir le Samedy qui est aujourd'huy, mais n'ayant pas vos ordres par votre Lettre du 19e m'a fait envoyer le Courier qui apparement est arrivé a Madrid cet après Midy pour Sçavoir le Jour que V.E. vouloit que Je parte d'icy, mais par votre Lettre du 22 Je vois qu'il faut que Je reste jusqu'a ce que V.E. ait des Nouvelles de la sortie des Vaisseaux, le Courier est allé ou il a eté ordonné. Il n'etoit pas Necessaire de le retenir puisqu'il m'a trouvé icy, Je ne Doute pas que Monsieur Chacon ne fera son possible pour sortir aussi tot qu'il pourra, J'attendray les Ordres de V.E. et Je feray tout mon possible pour les suivre avec, etc.

[To CARDINAL ALBERONI. *Valladolid, September* 23, 1719.

I RECEIVED your Eminence's letter of the 20th this morning, and after dinner, that of the 22nd. I await your Eminence's orders as to the day of my departure, and am very glad that the courier found me here, for it would have caused talk to have stopped five leagues from here on the Santander road.

Mr. Lambert had told me that your Eminence had said to him that I might leave on the Saturday, which is to-day, but not having your orders by your letter of the 19th made me send the courier, who evidently reached Madrid that afternoon, to know the day on which your Eminence wished me to leave here, but by your letter of the 22nd, I see that I should stay here until your Eminence has news of the ships having put to sea.

---

[1] Here the first hand begins again.

The courier has gone where he was ordered; it was not necessary to keep him since he found me here. I do not doubt that M. Chacon will do what he can to get to sea as soon as possible.

I await your Eminence's orders, and will do what I can to follow them, being, etc.]

CCIII

A DON BLAS DE LOYA[1]

VALLADOLID, CE 26 SEPT. 1719.

JE me sers de cette Occasion par le Porteur de celleci pour vous temoigner la satisfaction que j'ay de scavoir par son Eminence que Je dois avoir l'honneur de vous avoir a mes Ordres dans le Dessein Projetté, Je lui suis infiniment obligé de m'avoir donné une personne de votre Merite et de votre Caractere, et je puis vous asseurer qu'en toutes Occasions Je tacheray de vous donner des Marques de l'estime que j'ay pour votre Personne et Merite etant tres parfaitement, etc. Je me remets au Porteur pour ce que nous avons eté D'accord.

[To DON BLAS DE LOYA. *Valladolid, September* 26, 1719.

I MAKE use of this opportunity by the bearer to express to you the satisfaction which I have in learning through His Eminence that I am to have the honour of having you under my command in the projected expedition. I am infinitely obliged to him for having given me a person of your ability and character, and I can assure you that on all occasions I shall try to give you proofs of the regard which I have for your person and your merit, being, etc.

I refer to the bearer for what we have agreed upon.]

CCIV

To THE KING

VALL^D., SEPT^R. 26, 1719.

THIS Morning I had the agreeable News of your Majesty's safe arrival at Leghorn on the 25th of the last Month. I thank God for your safe passage, and beg leave to congratulate you

---

[1] Don Blas de Loya was intrusted with the preparations for the expedition to Brittany, and its subsequent utter failure was attributed to his incapacity and lack of energy. St. Philippe says of him that 'he had no great reputation for valour among the troops.'—*Mémoires*, vol. iii. p. 366.

on your being now with her Majesty. May you be bless'd together with many years and may heaven grant you a numerous posterity, wch is the hearty prayer, etc.

CCV

A la REINE

V^all^D., Sept^R. 26, 1719.

p. 172. Votre Majesté me permettra de temoigner ma Joye sur l'heureuse Arrivée de sa Majesté, que le bon Dieu vous Comble de ses Benedictions, et vous rende aussi heureux que Je vous souhaite, et que vous puissiez vivre bien des Années ensemble, et de laisser a vos sujets des Princes qui pourroient les rendre heureux. Je suis avec toute la soumission et tout le respect possible.

[To the Queen. *Valladolid, September* 26, 1719.

Your Majesty will permit me to express my joy at His Majesty's happy arrival. May God crown you with His blessings; may He render you as happy as I desire; may you live many years together, and leave to your subjects Princes who will make them happy.

I am with all possible submission and respect, etc.]

CCVI

To Mr. HAY

V^all^D., Sept^R. 26, 1719.

I give you many thanks for the agreeable account you send me of the King's arrival at Leghorn. You cou'd not have sent me a more agreeable News except that of a Restoration. Pray do me the favour to putt me at her Majesty's feet and to present her the Enclosed. Pray make my Compliments to your Lady and to M^r. Murray. My Compliments to my friends if you please.

CCVII

To SIR TIMON CONNOCK

V^all^D., Sept^R. 26, 1719.

This morning I receiv'd the favour of your's of the 14th from Huesca and send this by the Bearer to be given into your own hands, believing that he will find you at S*t*. Ander. I do not know how soon I may see you there but shall be glad of an opportunity to assure you by Word of Mouth how sensible I am of your friendship and to return you thanks for all the trouble you have taken in what I have recommended to you.

I can send you the Good News of our Master's being landed the 25th of last Month at Leghorn, and of his being then in Good health. Pray God keep him so. I am sorry the Gentlemen have not as yet their Commissions, but hope that Mr. Crafton will have credit enough with Monsieur Patino to gett them provided for without delay.

I am Glad my friends came to you before you had the Cardinal's Orders to leave the Camp. You give me but a Melancholy account of the Condition of the Army. I fear the News from Sicily will not mend Matters. The Gazettes that came in this Morning mentioning the taking of Messina, and of all the Castles, except the Citadel,[1] and I believe you will soon if that you have not already heard of the besieging of Rozes. I cannot see how it is possible for the Cardinal to hold out, especially if that the Troops Embarked in England are Designed for to make a Descent in Spain, as it is most probable, tho' the West Indies is talked of. I have tired you with this long Epistle, so will Conclude with assuring that I am with great truth and friendship, etc.

p. 173.

CCVIII

Au CARDINAL ALBERONI.

VALL^D SEPT. 27, 1719.

VOTRE Eminence aura appris par le Dernier ordinaire que sa Majesté Britannique arriva en bonne santé à Livourne le 25eme du Mois Passé, J'ay l'honneur de vous envoyer un Paquet pour sa Majesté.

Apparemment Monsieur de Chacon que la Lune sera passée a fin que par l'obscurité du Nuit il pourra plus facilement eviter les Vaisseaux Anglois qui Croisent devant la Corogne, le Deputé partit ce matin pour St Ander ou il se tiendra de la Maniere

---

[1] The citadel of Messina surrendered to the Imperial troops on October 18.

de n'etre pas Connu ce qu'il n'auroit pas pu faire icy sans donner quelque soupcon aux Gens Curieux dont il n'en manque pas ici, il a Dessein d'envoyer sa Barque en son Pais pour leur donner de ses Nouvelles et pour en avoir la leurs, en cas que l'embarquement fut retardé par les vents Contraires, ou par aucune autre Cause.

p. 174.   V.E. aura veu Monsieur le Baron de Walef, c'est icy le chemin de St Ander, mais Je croy qu'il est Mieux qu'il ne vienne pas en cette ville, mais qu'il se Detourne un peu pour eviter aucun soupcon. J'ay l'honneur, etc.

[To CARDINAL ALBERONI. *Valladolid, September 27,* 1719.

Your Eminence will have learned by the last post that His Britannic Majesty arrived at Leghorn in good health on the 25th of last month. I have the honour to send you a packet for His Majesty.

Apparently M. de Chacon (is waiting) till the moon is past in order that in the darkness of night he may the more easily escape the English ships which are cruising off Corunna.

The deputy left this morning for Santander, where he will conduct himself so as not to be known. He could not have done so here without arousing some suspicion in the inquisitive, of whom there is no lack here. He intends to send his vessel to his own country, to give them his news and get theirs, in case the embarkation should be delayed by contrary winds or by any other cause.

Your Eminence will have seen the Baron de Walef. He is here (on) the way to Santander, but I think it is better that he should not go into that town, but should turn aside a little so as to avoid any suspicion.]

KEY TO CIPHER NAMES.*

		PAGES			PAGES
Peter,	the King.		une personne, etc.,		
Simon,	duke of Ormonde.			Ez. Hamilton.	21
			mon Secretaire,		
Elmore,	Emperour.			Ez. Hamilton.	
Barnaby,	El^r of Hanover.		Dutton,	Dillon.	23
Sorrell,	Spain.		Melchior,	Monsr Seminati.	
Dutton,	Mr Dillon.		Stamfort,	Ez. Hamilton.	24
Otway,	the Regent.		seigneur Ecossois,		
Herne,	El^r of Hanover.			Ld Mares^l.	
Ker,	K. of Spain.	1	un de mes Parens,		
Martel,	Ld Mar.			Sr Red^d. Everard.	25
Paul, Phillis,	the King.		mon secretaire,		
Martilla,	Duchess of Mar.			Dav. Kennedy.	26
Belson,	D. of Berwick.		mon secretaire, Ligne II.,		
Egan,	Sr R. Everard.			David Kennedy.	27
Panton,	Paris.		Robinson,	Card^l Alberoni.	36
Amorsley,	Alberoni.	2	un Gentilhomme, etc.,		
Andrew,	the Queen a Prisoner.			Toby Mathews.	
			the Major,	Ez. Hamilton.	37
Evans,	England.	4	Binet,	Ez. Hamilton.	38
Mrs. Onslow,	D^{ss} of Ormonde.		Philips,	Ld Mareschal.	40
Simson,	d. of Ormonde.		Walton,	Captn Morgan.	
Kemp,	King of Sweden.		Obadiah,	Mr Wright.	
Digby,	Mr. Dillon.	5	Plunkets Clerk,		
Charpentier,	Ld Mareschal.	6		Monsr Clancostrum, the King of Swedens Agent.	41
Gregory,	K. of Sweden.	7			
14/a,	Card^l Alberoni.				
21/l,	Sr Patrick Lawless.				
			Posadas,	Inns in the Spanish Language.	52
507,	Sweden.				
249,	Elector of Hanover.		Zeky,	Hamilton.	69
			Egan,	Sr R^d Everard.	
496, 497,	K. of Spain.	9	Allen,	Ld Arran.	
165,	England.		Fisher,	D. of Ormonde.	105
475,	Scotland.		Tobacco,	money.	106
9/m,	Ld Mareschal.		Abraham,	Mr Menzies.	145
14/e,	Brig^r Campbell.	10	Amorslie,	C. Alberoni.	153
23/b	Mr Bagnal.		Dutton,	Mr Dillon.	153
Elmore,	Emperour.		Rowley,	Bp. of Rochester.	159
Morpeth,	Jam. Murray.	11	Monsr de Tonniere,		
Maitre Pierre,	le Roy.			Marquis de Magny.	163

* See p. vii, note. The pages referred to in the Key are those of the Manuscript, indicated on the margins of this volume.

APPENDIX

THE following documents, with the exception of No. 86, have been selected from the Stuart Papers at Windsor, the State Papers and Home Office Papers in the Public Record Office, and the Stowe Manuscripts in the British Museum. They are arranged in two series, viz.:

I. Papers relating to events abroad (pp. 194 to 268);
II. Papers relating to events in Scotland (pp. 269 to 297).

FIELD MARSHAL JAMES KEITH.

I

PAPERS RELATING TO EVENTS ABROAD

No. 1.

THE DUKE OF ORMONDE TO JAMES STUART

(*Stuart Papers. Received at Bologna, October* 31)

The names in italics are interlined in the original in another hand.

OCTOBER Y^E 3, 1718.

SR.,—I have received yours of the 9th of Sep^{tbr} with the inclosed for Mr Rig (Atterbury), and the others which shall be sent to them by ye first conveniency. I am very glad to see in Rig's that parte that concernes Elmore (*the Emperor*); it is all could be expected of him att this time. I hope Mr Andrew (*the Princesse*) is by this time very near his journeys ende. I long impatiently to hear that he is arrived. What is mentioned concerning Lesly (*the Parliament*) is very right, and, I hope, may have good effect.

Letters from Kers house (*Spain*) says that Evanes (*England's*) wvvwygh (*effects*) are hprbx (*seized*). I wish this may be a good omen, and that Sorrele (*Spain*) may shew his frendship to Mrs Philis (*the King*). A litle time must shew what Peter (*the King*) is to expect from Amersly (*Alberoni*). Simon (*D. Ormond*) wishes with all his hearte that he may have the satisfaction of waiting on Mr Paule (*the King*) att Kers (*Spain*). Simon (*D. Ormond*) thinkes it most for Peters (*the King's*) service to staye some where in this country untill he sees what Mr Amersly (*Alberoni*) does in his Law suite.

Yesterday I received a letter for Mrs Philis (*the Princess*) from Mrs Simones (*Dss. of Ormond*), which I enclose, and am very sorry she cannot be so happy as to waite on Mrs Philis (*the King*) for the reasones that she mentiones, giue me leave refer to her letter.

I wish you may finde Castle to your minde, tho I hope Mrs Peterson (*the King*) will not stay there long.

I have seen Scravemore (*Southcoat*), and inclose what he has answered. I here inclose allso a letter of Hooker's (*Jerningham*) to fennele, in this. I am sorry to see that Colman (*the Czar*) and Kemp (*K. of Sweden*) were not[1] likely to agree so soon as was expected.

Mrs Phillis (*the King*) will give me leave att the request of an old servante of hers, to recomende him to her. Mr Nugent is the persone; he is a man of merite and valued by every body that knowes him. I hope Mrs Phillis (*the King*) will be mindefull of him, and forgive Simon (*D. Ormond*) the liberty he takes in mentioning of him.

I wish Mr Person (*the King*) all happiness, and am,

S^r,

Your most faithfull humble Servant,

L. SIMONES.

Merepoix (*Magny*) is most faithfully Mrs Philliss (*the King's*) hm^ble servant.

No. 2.

THE DUKE OF ORMONDE TO THE EARL OF MAR

(*Stuart Papers. Received at Bologna, Oct.* 31)

Names in italics interlined in original.

OCTOBER Y^E 3, 1718.

S^R.,—I have yours of ye 10th Sept^b, and shall take care to have the inclosed sent to the persones they are directed to. It is saide the Spaniardes have seized the English merchantes effectes, a little time will shew if that the King of Spain will refuse the offers the Englishe will make them. If Alberony

---

[1] 'Not' inserted in another hand.

oes not submitte, there may be some good to be hoped for. I have reade Cadogan the copy of the paper to Cobler, I wish it had produced the desired effect.

I have the names you mentione. I wish Andrew (*the Queen*) were with you. I hope she may be in a little time.

I am very glad Morpethe (*Mr. Murray*) is in so faire a way of recovering, my compliments to him, if you please. Egan (*Sr. Edmond*) is your most humble servant. I wish wee may mette at Mr Soreles (*Spain*) in our way to Mr Evanes (*England*). I realy doe not know yett where Simon (*D. Ormond*) will staye for some time. Mr Allen (*Ld. Ar—n*) shall know the favour you doe him. It is strange wee doe not hear what becomes of the affairs in Sicily. I hear Martilla (*Ds. of Mar*) is come to Pantones (*Paris*).

S^r, believe me,
Your most faithfull hum^{ble} Servant,
L. SIMONES.

No. 3.

THE DUKE OF ORMONDE TO THE EARL OF MAR

(*Stuart Papers. Received at Bologna, Nov. 7*)

OCTOBER Y^E 17TH, 1718.

SR,—I have very little to trouble you with, having wrote to Mrs Paule, which I must refer to.

I am sorry there was no account of Mr Andrew when you wrotte to Dutton but hope by this time that he is come to his relation. If Ker does not show his friendeship to Paule very soone, I much fear the good success of the Law suite, and if it be not begune in Mickelmas terme, or at farthest in Hillary terme, I feare wee shall have but little hopes of success.

I hope Ker has not neglected Colman and Kemp. I have had a letter from Payton of ye fourth, he has wrotte to you, att the same time, so have nothing to say on that matter, but wish his power will prove true. I had one from Jerry (Jerningham) of the 16th Sep^{tbr} which does not say much, to be sure you hear from him punctually. I hope there is no doubte of Colman and Kempes agreeing.

I am sorry I could not have the honour of waiting on Martilla, but my circumstances would not permitte. She is by this time pretty far on her Journey. I wish her safely arrived. Doe me the favour to make my complimentes to my friendes. I congratulate Morpethe on his recovery, and am,

   S^r,
     Your most faithfull humble Servant,
             L. SIMONES.

No. 4.

THE DUKE OF ORMONDE TO JAMES

(*Stuart Papers. Received at Bologna, Nov. 7*)

OCTOBER Y^E 17, 1718.

S$_R$,—I am sorry to see in Marteles to Dutton of ye 24th Sep^{tbr} that your friende was not then sett out, att least, that there was no news of his being on the Roade, but by this time, I hope he is with his relation Mr Peters.

We have no certaine account of the affairs in Sicily, some pretende to say that the Spaniardes are masters of the Citadell of Messina, but this seemes only reporte, people talke very diferently of what measures the Courte of Spain will take. Simon told me (*i.e.* Ormonde himself thought) that he believed that courte would not come to any resolution untill they sawe what the Parliament of England would doe, and then to take their measures.

Onslow hopes that Paule presses Amorsley to be his friende, and to shew that he is realy so, this is a time *that* will shewe what is to be depended on. I owne, I feare what Simon told me, but I am sure Mrs Phillis ought to press him to helpe her in her Law suite, for should Ker and Evanes be made friendes, Peter would be a greate sufferer, and but little prospect of his gaining his suite.

I hope Amorsley is in friendeship with Colman and Kemp. Kers mantle would be of greate use to those poore Merchantes, and if Ker be kinde to them, he may finde it may turne to his accounte and Mrs Phillis might be the better for it. Dutton has told me, that he has mentioned this to Soreles factor. I hope Meredethe is a friende to Mr Paule and that Percy will not shew any kinde of goodwill to Ker. If Sorele is truly a friende to Peters, and does intende to shew it, Evanes ought to be acquainted time enough that he may see the Lawyers and that they be ready att the terme. I fear if that we lose Hilliary terme, that it will be very prejudiciall to our cause.

I must recomende to Mrs Phillis a friend of hers, that is att Mr Stiel, Mrs Charlote. She is a very[1] object of charity, a poore widow.

I have seen Mrs Camp. She is very much Mrs Phillises devoted humble servant, and has refused her friende Evaneses offers for Mrs Phillises sake.

I am, with all respect,
S^r,
Your most faithful humb^{le} servant,
L. SANGSTON.

No. 5.

THE DUKE OF ORMONDE TO JAMES

(Stuart Papers. Received at Bologna, Nov. 14)

SR,—I am not able to express the joy I have att the reading of the Duke of Mars to Mr Dillon informing of him, of the Princesses being on the roade, and that your Majesty was to meet her on the 15th. I hope before this time, S^r, that you have finished what has been so much desired by your friendes and subjects. May heaven give you, and the Queen all the blessings of this life, and that you may see a numerous posterity, is what I heartely pray for.

I hear it reported that the Spanish Ambassador is recalled. I have no other newes, nor shall trouble yow more, S^r, att this time, but to wish you all the happiness imaginable.

I am with all the duty imaginable,
S^r,
Your Majesties
most dutifull subject and most Obedient Servant,
ORMONDE.

October ye 12th, 1718.

---

[1] Word apparently omitted.

No. 6.

JAMES to WILLIAM DICCONSON

(*Stuart Papers*)

Bologne, Nov^{er} 2^{d}, 1718.

Yours to S^{ir} William, to Nairne and to my self of the 3^{d} of October require but little answer, and what is necessary I shall put down here myself. I hope my letter to Pere Galliand will have had good effect, and am very glad the gentlemen you mention to have stood their tryal in England came off so well. I shall be far from disapproving anybody's making application for subsistance to the court of France. Would to God they could gett bread any where, and I should be very well pleased. By what you say I am in some hopes that the Collonells List may still continue. You did well to stop all under servants coming to Urbino. But for hindering wives from going to their husbands that is an Imperial prerogative I do not pretend to. As to what you mention of the confectioner, an old field bed, and some other useless trumpery, do with them what you think fitt. Give poor Mr Bryerly something to buy cloaths, for I could strip my self to cloath modest people. The misery that so many are in is a most affecting thing, but where we do all we can we must trust to Providence for the rest, and as long as you have any thing left you must not lett people starve, tho considering that, and the slowness of the french payment, it will no doubt diminish the remnent of the arreares, but for that there is no remedy.

If I'm not mistaken there is in one strong box several seals, pictures, etc., which box I directed to have come with Mr Sheldon, but that now failing, I would have you send it to Rome by the first saffe occasion. I shall say nothing to you of my melancolly situation here, nor of the occasion of it, which will have made noise enough in the world.[1] One must still hope well, but in the meantime one is uneasie enough.

James R.

---

[1] Princess Clementina's arrest.

No. 7.

JAMES TO THE DUKE OF ORMONDE

(*Stuart Papers*)

BOLOGNA, Novr 2ND, 1718.

MARTEL being gone for a few days to meet his wife, I make Morpeth acknowledge to Dutton the recepts of the letters we receiv'd from him last post, and which came only on munday late, so that I have not much leisure to write to you this post, having been a good dale taken up since with Andrews (Princess Clementina's) affair. I have at last heard from him; he and his relations are as firm as a rock, and tho patience may be still necessary, I have little reason to doubt but that all will end well at last, and probably soon, so much for your comfort, for further details would, I think, be useless.

Pray return my kindest compliments to Mrs Onslow (Duchess of Ormonde), her letter is so handsome and so kind, that it makes me yet more regrate the want of her company, especially on the account which deprives me of it, but I hope in God better dayes and circumstances will come in which friends and honest people will not be forced at so great a distance from one another. After this, as things stand, I cannot but approve your determination of staying some time longer where you are, for it cannot be imagin'd but that Ker must soon absolutely take his party. I find that one Sr Peter Redmond hath a great vocation to be my man in those parts. I am sure I never promis'd him he should be so, and tho I think few people more honest, I know few more unfitt, all things consider'd, for such a nice bussiness. I expect every post to hear from Ker, and I hope my accounts may be satisfactory, of which you shall be inform'd. Jerry's letter hath good and bad in it, and Scravenmore's will, I hope, be soon follow'd with the mantle.

We have had such rains as I never saw. Mme Chigi is with us for some dayes, and an Opera begins to'night to which I am neither in humour to go, nor could I in decency do it. I thank God I keep my health well, which is a wonder, but I trust in God I shall be soon easie. I send you a ffrench paper of Inspruch news in which there is no Secrets, and I think the matter cannot be too much publish'd. Adieu. I send this open to Dutton that it may Serve for you both. I stay here till I see what becomes of the affair of my Marriage. Horsly Scap'd worse usage by being treated only as a follower of Andrews, and tis not known or not minded that he belongs to me.—Truely Yours.

No. 8.

JAMES TO THE DUKE OF ORMONDE

(Stuart Papers. Answer to Letter I.)

ROME, Nov^{er} 27th, 1718.

You will easily believe what a surprize it was to me to find by yours of the 4th the jurney you were going to begin, and your saying so little on the subject did the more embarrasse me that I received att the same time the enclosed note from Cardinal Aquaviva which I here send you, and by the contents of which you will see it was impossible for me to avoid declaring that you had made that jurney without my precise order. But I turned the matter att the same time in such a manner, and the present conjuncture is such that I cannot but hope that this jurney of yours will turn to account. You have been all along acquainted with all my proceedings in relation to Spain, and that you may have a clearer insight into those matters, I send you the very copie of the letter I write to Cardinal Aquaviva to be sent to Spain, which may indeed serve as a sorte of Instruction for your self [and the Memoire also mentioned in it shall also be sent you as soon as it is finished].[1] On the whole 'tis certain I am very much in the dark as to the King of Spains resolutions, but I hope you will be able to see clearer into them, and even to determine them on the right side. After this you cannot certainly keep your self too private in Spain, and on the footing I am with Cardinal Alberoni, you must in great measure be guided by his advice. He is a man that must be taken in his own way, and tis in vain to think one can force him to do what he will not do of himself. In fine I heartily wish you success where you are, and as I am sure your zeal for

---

[1] The passage in brackets is deleted.

my service carryd you there, so I should be the more concerned did you meet with any disagrement on that account. Sir Peter Redmond is a perfect honest man, but I cannot but caution you that I think him very unequal for great affairs, and not capable of nice manadgements which will be your great business.

You will be surprized att the date of this letter, but after what has happened att Inspruck, all my friendes in these parts advised me to come here where alone they thought my liberty could be secure. And I have taken care that my friendes in England should be advertised of the true reason of my coming to this place. I know no more as to the Princesses at Inspruck; they are still prizoners there, and where that matter will end God knows. When I know anything new on the subject, you shall be sure to be acquainted with it. This is all I have to say att present, but to assure you of all the kindness I am capable of.

Since whats above, I have heard from the person about whom I cautioned you; he's certainly very indiscreet, and not fitt to be trusted with secrets, which I could not but hint here, the rather that I perceive by himself that he is not very well with Ammersly.

Enclosed Note.

The dispatch which your Eminence received from your friend is just come to my hands, to whom you may make it known that I have no want of any confident of his or of any Instructions. Your Eminence may tell your said friend that he needs only think of preserving his health, since he has another who thinks of his Interest and advantages, which is all I can say to your Eminence in answer to this particular.

October 24th.

This is a translation of what Cardinal Alberoni writes to Cardinal Aquaviva in answer to the proposal made by the King of sending a person into Spain to manadge his affairs att that Court, and sent to the King by C. Aquaviva.

No. 9.

The EARL OF MAR to the DUKE OF ORMONDE

(*Stuart Papers*)

Rome, Dec^R. 22^D, 1718.

Sir,—The enclos'd is a duplicate of what was sent you t'other day by another canal, but this seeming to be a sure one, I hope it will come safe to your hands.

I wrote to Simon th' day before I left Bologna all that occur'd to me then, and to Mr Dutton since, who, I presume, will give you an account of it so that I may be the shorter now.

I heartily wish Sam good success where he is gone, but unless he had some certain and good encouragement before he went, for the reason I wrote to Dutton, I much fear his not having so good a reception as I could wish. I shall be overjoyed to be mistaken, and I wish that Amorslie may have some project to putt suddenly in execution which requir'd Sam's presence, and that he gave him privately an invitation of encouragement to go thither. Dutton refers to you for an account of his Journey in two I have had from him since I came here, and in the last he sayes you was to write fully when you came to Mr Boston's, where we'll long to know you are got safe, which I hope we soon shall, but I suppose your stay there will not be long, and may you soon be where it will be more agreable to you than it was with M^r ffraser.

I had the pleasure of yours of the 3^d of October, and deliver'd that for Peter as soon 's I mett with him. I wish Andrew had been there that I might have given him that for him too, but we know nothing more about him as yet, and since the Determinations about him seem to depend on the returns Elmore is to have from Evans, I much doubt of his being with us soon, tho' I hope he will at last, but even that in my humble opinion must not be too long waited for.

Mr Oldcorn, I hear, is come to Panton's. I had a note from him on his road thither, by which, as well as some other letters, I see it is about some business, but what it is I know not as yet, tho' I suppose I shall next post, and when I do I shall give you an account of it, but whatever it be I own I have no expectation of great good from thence.

I do not at all dread Simon's being wearie of the place where he had been for some time and gladd to change it, and it was very natural for him to think of Sorrels, where I wish him all the pleasure he can wish himself, and that there may be soon a good occasion for our meeting with him there.

Peter having nothing further to say at this time than what you will be informed of by the enclos'd, does not write, but desires I may make you his compliments. He is very well.

Martila is very much oblidged to you for your kind enquiry after her. She and her little one are very well, and had a very good Journey.

17^d. is still uncertain about his own affair, so we wait to hear further of it from himself, his being remov'd from thence would be a very great loss, and I scarce see how it could be made up.

Perhaps he has given you an account of a fine pamphlet which is far from spareing Peter more than others.[1] It could not have been done without the assistance at least of some who might have been thought to have had more regard for Peter, but their private resentment has it seems got the better of their Duty. They have shewn their malice by it, but it is too simple to do much hurt or give uneasiness to those it was aim'd against.

I hope to have soon an address how to write to you safely, and shall not fail of letting you know from time to time what occurs with us. I'll trouble you no further at this time, but you shall ever find me affectionately and ffaithfully,

Yours, etc.

It is odd enough that Amorslie did not come in to the project which your friend C——k made to Wright in Aprile last, of which Dutton would informe you. There was no time lost in laying it before Amorslie, but he gave little or no answer to it, and without him nothing could be done. Perhaps he repents it e're now, but ther's still time for it, as C——k wrote to me t' other day.

Amorslie is putt in mind again of it, and one would think

---

[1] See Letter XVI. and note.

that he will not neglect a thing which may prove so much for their Service. The papers in relation to it have been ready ever since a little after it was first proposed, but there was no finishing of them or sending of them to C——k till we should have a positive answer from Amorslie, which I hope now Samuel may have an opportunity of forwarding.

There came a letter to my hands some dayes ago from C——k to Sam, which I forwarded to Dutton. I find C——k and poor R——y McD. are fallen out, which I am sorry for.

I am to write one of these dayes to C——k, wherein I'll tell him of his letter being forwarded, but I'll say nothing till I hear from you again of Sams Journey.

No. 10.

The EARL of MAR to the EARL MARISCHAL

(Stuart Papers)

ROME, DECEM^R 6TH, 1718.

MY LORD,—The King has orderd me to acknowlege the letter you wrote him of the 28th of September wh^{ch} had been sooner done had I not been longer o' coming to this place than His Majesty. He approves of your Lop^s design of going to serve in Spain, if a war break out w^t the Elector of Hannover, but in that case he hopes there will be more of us in that country. A litle time will now show what will be in that matter, and your Lop shall be informd what further Resolutions His Ma^{ty} takes in that event.

I wrote to your Lop, as I remember, the begining of Octo^r, and since that time yow would hear of the unlucky accident (of the) Princess being stopt at Inchsprug by the methods of her coming wch were given and prest by the King not being followd, but her ffriends, trusting to the ffriendship as well as Relation of those who had stopt her, could not be perswaded that there was any thing of that kind to be apprehended, so lost more time in setting out and on the road, besides the great noise they made with their journey, than might have finish'd the affair w^{t}out any danger of its being prevented, and to say truth what has happen'd is so barbarous and w'out example that it is the less wonder they did not think it possible to be so used, but they were mistaken, and see now too late the need there was of the precautions given them from hence. By the last account we had the Princess and her Mother were still at Inchsprug, and were in hopes that they would still be allow'd to come on their journey, so that we must have patience for some time, hoping the best, but it cannot be expected that the King can stay longer than in honor he's obliged, to do what is so necessary for his intrest and that of his people, as the pains his Enemies have taken to prevent this marriage sufficiently show. There are more women in the world, and tho' this match, both upon account of the princess herself and many other motives, be the most desireable, yet the impracticableness of it, or too long delay, wch is near as bad, must not keep him from looking about elsewhere, and one where or other completeing what his ffriends and faithful subjects so much desire, and if he should match below his quality, what has now happen'd in this affair takes off any objection there might be to a thing of that kind. I would fain hope tho' that this as desireable an one, wch was so far advanced, may yet do, in spite of all the contrivances of his Enemies to stop it.

The King is very well in his health, and designs to continue in this place all winter, Castello being found to cold, w'out chimneys as it mostly is, if something do not happen to require his presence elsewhere, wch I wish may be the case. It is a much better quarter than we had last winter, but the Wine by no means agrees w^t us.

Your Lop would hear the disagreeable account of the Regents having declared that he is not to continue the pension the late Queen had longer than the time of her death, and they are very slow in paying up the arrears of it, wh^{ch} is the occasion that the allowances His Ma^{ty} gave to his people have been of late so ill payd, that being the only fund he had for it. The straits those honest worthy Gentlemen are in and still further likly to be put to is a great grief to the King. So long as the arrears last and are payd up, he has orderd the allowances to his people to be continued, that will not tho' last long, and what will become of them afterwards, if things do not take some lucky new turn, God only knows, but I hope in his providence he will give His Ma^ty success in what he is endeavoring to get done for their relief, till better days come, and that he have it in his power at home to do for them.

Lord Wm Drummond tells me that your Lop designs to pass this winter at Avignon w^t the Duchess of Melfort and Monsr Castleblanco, and that he beleives you are now there; but not being sure of that, I chose to send this to Paris, from whence it will be sent you whereever you be. If your Lop be w^t that good company, I beg you may do me the favor to make my compliments to them, no body being more their humble Servant, and I am particularly obliged to them for the civility they show'd to My Lady Mar as she past throw ffrance.

I long to know if Mr. Keith went where he intended, or if it is answering his expectations, which I heartily wish it may, and all that was possible to be done from home to make it so was carefully done.

Our Master orders me to make your Lop his kind compliments, and I am with all truth, My Lord, your Lop^s Most Obedient and most humble Servant, *Sic sub^t* Mar.

No. 11

The EARL of MAR to LORD PANMURE

(*Stuart Papers*)

Arrest of Mar and Perth at Voghera and their detention at Milan. See Introduction, p. xxxiii.

Rome, March 21st, 1719.

My Lord,—I hope you have not misinterpreted but have forgiven my long silence. I was unwilling to write to you about the time I left this place, since I could not then tel you of the real designe the King was about, but I intended to have wrote to you from Genoa, had I been so luckie to get there. You will have heard our story in generall long before this comes to y^r hand, but beliveing that you'll be desirous to know the particulars of it, I will now give you them and with much the better will that I have reason to hope that the King our Master has long e'er now got to his intended post, and that the Duke of Perth and I have got out of our confinement.

The King finding that it was no longer fitt for him to be in Italie, resolved to leave it, but some adress was necessary to make his passage out of it practicable and safe. He determind to go by sea and w^t only a very few of his servants who attend his person. He was pleased to order that the Duke of Perth and I should go togither by another rout and endeavour to join him at a place appointed. His Majesty toke the advice of those who he thought fittest to advise with as to the way he was to go, and also as to the rout for the Duke of Perth and I, both wch were followed accordingly. The rout we went was once thought of for his Majesty, but happie it was that he chose the other, as you'll see by what happend to us. After the Kings choseing to go the other way it was thought that our going off about the same time he did in chairs by the way of fflorance and so to Bologna, as if intending to meet the Princess (the reason wch was given out for the kings leaveing of Rome) was the way to blind the publick and prevent for some time the discovery of his real designe, so that his Majesty sett out from Rome towards the cost the 8th of ffeb. very airly and imbarkt and sailed that evening in a shipe that was reddy prepaired for him. The Duke of Perth and I about two hours after his Majesty sett out in three chairs w^t our servants on purpose to make it appear as if the King had been in the company and the bite toke as you'll see. We continued our journie to Bologna without endeavouring to make great heast, as was concerted, in case his Majesty had not got saild so soon as he intended. When this rout was proposed for our going to Genoa I mentioned a passport, wch was likly we might find occasion for, and I hopt might be got in other names than our own without giving any light into our business, but it was thought it wou'd be dangerous to endeavour getting it for fear of giveing suspicion, and that there was no occasion for it, every body comeing hither from ffrance dayly and returning thither throw the Milanese without any passport.

A Courier past us on the road twice, who we suspected had

some eye upon us. We made our servants speak to him, and he said he was sent from Naples to Milan to heaston on the march of the troops. This added to our suspicion, wch we find since was not ill grounded, he being a servant to Count Gallass, who he had sent on purpose to dog us, beliveing the King to be in the company, and to give an account of us to the Comanders at Mantua and Millan, haveing sent another to give the like accounts at Trent, Inchburg, and Vienna, and he wrote the same to Naples, of wch there were accounts returned here soon therafter.

Notwithstanding of our suspecting this Courier we had no way to help our selves, and it was but suspicion, nor did we see or hear any more of him after we passed Bologna. We stay'd a night at Bologna, being impossible almost to avoid it in the way we were traveling, but we were so well known to most of the people there, that there was no thinking of our passing undiscovered. We came there late at night and went away next morning by daybreak. We saw there one of the King's people who has for some time lived in that toun, and is well knowen to most of the best people and all our acquentance in it. We made him belive the story of our being so farr on our road to meet the Princess, that we were going towards Trent by Mantua, and that the King was gone by the other rout by fferrara, wch past very well at that time both w^t him and some of our friends there to whom we fancied he might mention us. So we desired he might make our compliments to them and excuse our not seeing them til our return.

ffrom Bologna we went the rout that had been given us towards Genoa by Modena, Parma, and Piacensa, and when we came two posts further to Vogera on fryday morning, 17th of ffeb., a post short of Tortona, where there is a German garison, and where we apprehended difficulty if we met w^t any. We were told at the posthouse that we could have no horses without an order from the Majestrats of the toun. As we were thinking upon this what was next to be done, The Podesta of the Toun as they call the chife Majestrat for the Emperour, an Italian, and a German Livetenant Colonel came into the room where we were and askt if we had a passport, and whither we were a going, and who we were, we told that we were going for ffrance by Turin, that one of us was a ffrench man, Mr. Le Brun (the name the Duke of Perth went by), and the other two English, Mr. Johnston and Robertson (the names for me and Paterson), that we had mett at Rome where we had been for severall months for our diversion and curiosity, and were now a returning to our own countrys, that we did not know a passport to be necessary, haveing had none when we came into the country and knew of severall of our acquentances, who had o' late gone back for ffrance without any. Then said they we cannot help stoping you here til we give an account of you at Millan since we have received orders about fifteen dayes ago to let no body pass w^{t}out a passport, and so they desired that we might go along w^t them.

I had not many papers of consequence along w^t me, but some few I had and others I should not have liked falling into their hands, and as the most secure way I thought for them, was keeping them in my own pockets, where they then were. We told those who came to look after us that we shou'd go immediatly along w^t them since they wou'd have it so, after eating a little sup that was geting reddy for us in the next room where they might be present, wch they agreed to. The Duke of Perth caried them to the court yard, and then into the next room, wch gave me and Paterson time to destroie any papers that I was uneasie about without any observation, and that done I was easie since neither the Kings service nor any of his friends could suffer by any discovery by what was about us. When we came along w^t the officers to the gate we found a gard on our chaises and baggage. We desired that our servants might be alow'd to wait on our things, but were answered that they must go along w^t us, and that our things should be taken care of and answered for, so on we were caried to the Podesta's house wch is in the toun house, and there we were keept til Sunday morning the 19th under a gard of ten or twelve souldiers. The Podesta, who is a very civil man, entertained us very well, but he had but one room for us all, where there were two beds and a Matlass on the floor, and when we went to them or even to a necessary affair the door was not alow'd to be shutt, but two sentries keept at it looking at us. Our things were all put into the same room, but

o

not then sealed, by wch I had an opportunity of takeing some papers out of my strong box in the night time tho they were of no great consequence. An express was immediatly sent upon our comeing into the Podesta's house to Millan w^t an account of us, who they assured us wou'd be back nixt morning, and they did not doubt of there being orders for our release. They lookt much at us the time they were writeing their letters, and particularly at the D. of Perth, by wch we imagind they belived the King to be in the company.

On saturday forenoon they told us that the express was returnd and that we wou'd soon hear what it brought, and some time therafter the Podesta came and told us that the express was not returnd, and that it was only two officers friends of his who were a passing by that way, but that he expected the express very soon. After dinner these two officers came to see us; one of them proved to be the Secretary to the late Governour of the Milanese, and the other the Ajutant-Generall of the troops in that country; the first spoke ffrench, Italian, and German, but the other, tho' a civill, wellbredd, modest man in appearance, spoke nothing but German, his own country language. The first told us that he was sorry for the accident of our being stopt, wch he toke care to say was occasioned by orders given fifetien dayes before. That the warr being now declaird oblidgd them to be more circumspect than useuall, but that we might make ourselves reddy to be gone to morrow morning, but that it must be very airly. We were not a little glade at this, so made our compliments upon it, and askt if we might not have a passport to prevent our being stopt again at Tortona, but that they said they had no power to give. The Podesta was not in the room when these two gentelmen spoke to us, but came in a little therafter, and seeing the D. of Perth and I standing by ourselves came and told us that he was sorry we were to be caried for Millan. We told him what these two gentelmen had said to us, so that he must be mistaken, w^t wch he was surprised, and seemd not well pleased, thinking they had imposed on him, but, says he, I shall clear that just now. So he went to them at a little distance, where we heard him ask why they told one thing to him about us and another to us. If we were to be caried to Millan, why did they not tel us now, and not do it by surprise to morrow; and if we were alow'd to go on our journie, why had they said otherways to him? They went away togither upon this, and Podesta told us that he wou'd soon return and let us know how it was. He accordingly did so, and told us there was no help for it, and that we must go to Millan to morrow. Upon our asking him why those gentelmen had spoke as they did to us, by wch we belived that we were alowed to proceed on our journie, he said he could not account for it, and that he did not approve of the way they had taken, but that they were to cary us along w^t them. A little after this our boxes and things were scaled up, and next morning airly we were caried from thence under a guard of Husars, and those two gentelmen went along w^t us in a chaise. When we came near Pavia these two went before us into the toun where we thought we should have stopt to dine, but we were caried out at another port as soon as we entred, and so round the toun w^tout to the port for Millan. There we were made to halt above an hour til our guard was changed. We sent to our two governours to desire that something might be sent us out of the toun to eat since we were not alowd to stope in it, but had word sent us that there was an Hoslaria some miles before where we might eat. We were keept after this waiting for our two Governours, and wearying by their not comeing soon we sent again desireing that the gard might be ordred to go along w^t us to the Hoslaria, where we should wait their comeing. Upon this we were ordred to march, but when we came to the Hoslaria our governours not being come up the Captain of the Husars wou'd not stope, so hungrie enough we were before we got w^t their slow march to the nixt post where we were to change horses, and before we came to it our two governours past us without speaking and stopt at the post til we came, and then told us that they were keept at Pavia by some officers friends of theirs to dine, wch made them be so long away from us, and until the horses were got reddy we might eat a bit there, wch we did, and then advanced on our march towards Millan. We arived at the port when it was darkish, and were caried a privat back way within the walls of the toun to the Castle, where when we came these two gentelmen deliverd us to the

Deputy Governour, a German who speaks a little Italian. He caried us to a lodging wch he told us was calld the casa nuda, and so it was indeed, where all our things were brought, save our strong boxes, wch our fformer Governours had we belived keept. The Deputy Governour told us that the Marischall, the Governour of the Castle, Colmenero, a Spaniard, and who was chefe de Concill in the absence of the Governour of the Milanese, was not then in the Castle, and that it wou'd be late before he came in, so that our accomodation wou'd not be good that night, but that next day we shou'd get better, so that he hopt we wou'd excuse it. He sent for beds and some chairs for us, and got us something to eat. There came but two beds at that time, but just as we were going to them the Governour sent us his own field bed. We heard nothing from them all nixt day, and our things all being seald up we could not get clean linning, wch made us send on tuesday morning to desire that they would be so good to let us have the use of our own things, but had no answer then to it. We had our dinner and supper sent us from the Governours every day all the time we continued there, wch was very good, and drest after the ffrench way, and beside the wine of the country we had at each meal a fflask of Ranish wine and two when we desired it. On wednsday we were sent to desireing that our servants might be sent to the Deputy governour w^t our things and the keys to see them and our boxes opned. I told that I had some papers in my boxes wch belong'd not properly to me, and therfore could not trust the seeing of them opned to our servants, that they were in their handes as we were; the keys we gave them, so if they had a mind they might open them as they pleased, but if any of us were to see them opned I desired it might be ourselves and not our servants. This was refused, and our servants and our things ordred to be caried along, wch was done accordingly. Our things were all opned and lookt over, our papers and writing boxes were put up and sealed before our servants wth the seals of the two gentelmen who brought us and that of the Deputy governours as we belived, and the rest of our things were sent back to us. At our comeing into the Castle we had given the same account of our selves that we had given at Vogera, and wrote down as we were desired the names we went by. Our swords were never taken from us, nor were our pockets ever searcht.

Generall Broun, who has been long in the German service and was accidentaly in the toun, came to see us on wednsday along w^t the Li^{vt} Governour. We had never seen other before so that he could not know us. He askt our names and an account of us, wch we gave as formerly, and then we fell a talking of other things in comon discourse, amongst wch he told us that who he calld ye King of England was gone from Rome privatly, nobody there knowing whither save the Pope, wch gave ground for many speculations, and a little after said, Well, Gentelmen, whoever you be, there is no dishonour done you; upon wch I askt him who they toke us to be, and sure they did not take us for the Pretender; no, God forbid, sayes he, and then left us. We belived he had been sent to see if he knew us and if the King was of the company, but we never saw him again nor heard more of him.

We sent to the Deputy Governour to beg we might be alow'd to see the publick newspapers, and were told that they should be sent us, but they never were, all the time we stay'd, save once an old Mantua Gazet, in wch there was nothing. Nobody was alowd to speak to us but when the Agutant of the Garison was bye, nor was our servants alowd to go abroad, but any thing we wanted, as we did some cloaths, were sent for from the toun by that Agutant. We askt liberty to write to some acquentances at Rome wch should be shown them before it was sent, but were denyd it, and were only alowd to walk abroad in the Castle w^t the Agutant attending us. I was a good deal out of order one day and had occasion for a vomitt, some doses of wch was in my writeing box, wch made me send to beg it, but was answered that it could not be opned til they had a return from Vienna, where they had given an account of us by an express, and this made me conclud that our papers were sent thither.

We had severall times compliments sent us by the Governour Colmenero, but after our things were opend, the Deputy Governour left us off and seem'd to avoid us when we chanced to see him at a distance when we were walking round the open gallary in the Castle.

On sunday the 5th of March the new Governour of the Milanese Coloredo came to Millan, and on wednesday morning the 8th the Marischall Colmenero sent the agutant to desire us to speak w^t him in the Gallary. The Agutant being most acquented w^t M^{sr} Le Brun (the D. of Perth) came only to him, so he went alone, but we first agreed that he should say nothing to the Marischall upon what he should say to him til he should once come and aquaint me what the Marischall had said. When Ld Perth mett w^t the Marischall he told him that he thought that he wou'd have brought M^{sr} Le Brun along w^t him; to which he answerd that he was that person, and that the Agutant had only spoke of his comeing and not of Mr Johnstons. The Marischall said he had desired to speak to both, but that it was the same thing, since he wou'd give his companion an account of it. Then he said that tho he had been chefe de Consill in the absence of the Governour, yet he could not take it upon him to set us at liberty, but that now the Governour was arived, and had had time to hear the account we had given of ourselves, had taken it upon himself to set us at liberty, even before the return of the courier from Vienna and that it was a *coup fort hardi*. How farr this was realie so, there being then full time for the courier to return, I shall not take upon me to determine, but since we came here we find that our being prissoners at Millan was left a secret everywhere than at Millan. He askt M^{sr} Le Brun what road we intended to take, for we might go where we pleased, but at the same time mentioned that of Genoa, to wch M^{sr} Le Brun (the D. of Perth) answered that he could say nothing as to that til once he spoke to his companion, so to me he came directly and told what had past. We had intelligence by a certain canale that Mr Davinantt, the English Resident at Genoa, was in watch for us on all the wayes to that place, and our storie haveing made so much noise we thought it was impracticable to get off from thence, or, indeed from any place since we could not go throu ffrance, until once we should cast up in some place where it might be reasonablie supposed we were to make some stay and by that might be forgot and out of the publick talk, so we resolved to return to Rome. Upon wch the D. of Perth went back to the Marischall and told him as we concerted, that by our being stopt so long the business we were going about was dissapointed and that we had some friends at Rome who wou'd think we were lost by their being so long o' hearing from us and that our journie to france did not now so much press, therefore we resolved to return towards Rome. The Marischall told him that the sooner we went the better, and that all should be ordred for our setting out that very night after it was dark, and after som compliments they parted.

We got our things reddy, and about eight oclock the Deputy Governour came to us w^t a coach and told us that our chairs were sent out alreddy, that he had brought a coach to carie us and our bagage to the place where they were, about half a mile out of toun. So we got into the coach and were caried out at the postern gate of the Castle to the place where our chaises were, where in a like time the two Gentelmen who had brought us to Millan came to us and brought us our writeing boxes and all our papers seald up wch they delivered to us. We did not look into them at that time, but when we did afterwards, it did not appear to our servants who had seen them seald up that they had been opned. We got into our chairs about 9 at night, these two gentelmen our former Governours going along w^t us, and leading our way. They caried us quit round the toun without the walls til we came to the road for Piacensa, wch we continued all night without stoping save to change our horses till we came to the bounds of the Emperours territorys, and there our Governours told us that we might go where we pleased and gave us a passport from Marischall Visconti who commands the Emperours troups in Lombardi in case we should have occasion for it. Thus we parted w^t a great deal of pleasur from our Governours and came on our journie to this place by Bologna and fflorance at neither of wch places we made any stope further than was absolutly necessary, and arived here on thursday last the 16th to the no little surprise of our friends who knew little or nothing certain about us. When we shall find a way of going to our Master is more than we yet know, but we are once at liberty again wch is by no means disagreeable, and we hope the King nor his cause will not suffer by the accident wch happned to us without our fault. The loss is ours by our not haveing the pleasur of attending him and giveing him all the assistance in our power, but we hope to hear soon of his Majestys being well and in a good way, wch heavens grant.

These are all the particulars that I can now tel you and I hope you 'll forgive and excuse this tedious account.

I 'll be glade to hear soon from y^r lop. and pray give any of our friends who want a particular detail of our story, an account of what I have now wrote to you.

I have troubled you too long alreddy to say any more now, but I shall write again when anything occurs, so adieu.

No. 12.

JAMES to POPE CLEMENT XI.[1]

(*Stuart Papers*)

James bids farewell to the Pope—Apologises for his hasty departure—Commends Princess Clementina to the protection of His Holiness.

7 Fev. 1719.

Tres Saint Pere,—C'est avec la plus grande confusion que je me trouve obligé de notifier a Votre Sainteté par ecrit seulement mon depart de ses Etats. Une necessité pressente et indispensable m'y a obligé et il etoit de la plus grande importance pour moy que mon voyage fut accompagné de la plus grande promtitude et du plus rigoureux secret, et quoiq'il n'y en devoit point avoir pour V.S. je suis persuadé qu'Elle ne prendra pas en mauvaise part d'avoir été privée jusq'ici d'une connoisance qui auroit pû l'embarrasser sans luy avoir pû etre utile. Du reste Elle jugera aisement de la juste douleur qui m'afflige, de me trouver reduit a quitter Rome dans le tems que j'y attendois la Princesse mon Epouse ; mais pour la consoler je luy ay laissé en partant les temoignages les plus forts de ma constance et de ma tendresse. Et comme je luy mande de faire son possible pour être au plutot dans cette ville comme l'endroit le plus convenable a sa liberté et a sa seureté j'ose la recommender a vos bontés avec tout instance possible vous suppliant

---

[1] Giovanni Francesco Albani.

T. S. P. de reunir en sa personne tout ce que vous avez de tendresse paternelle pour nous deux separement, et d'etre son soutien et sa consolation durant le tems que je la laisserai sous votre protection. Son merite personelle et sa constance heroique envers moy me la rendant uniquement chere et j'ose le dire digne des soins et des attentions de V.S. Je la suplie de nous donner a l'un et a l'autre sa benediction Apostolique et de recevoir ici mes très humbles actions de graces pour toutes les bontés dont V. S. m'a comblé pendant mon séjour dans ses Etats, bontés qui ne s'effaceront jamais de ma memoire et qui me serveront toujours d'un nouveau motif pour lui prouver en toute occasion ma soumission inviolable, mon respect infini, et l'attachement singulier et quil me soit permis de le dire tendre que je conserverai pour sa personne sacrée jusqu'au dernier moment de ma vie. C'est avec ces sentimens que vous me trouverez toujours.

Tres Saint Pere,

De Votre Sainteté,

Le tres devot fils.

Je suplie V.S. de vouloir permettre a ma famille de demeurer dans la maison qu'elle a eu la bonté de me donner pour ma demeur dans cette ville jusqu'a ce que je sois en etat de leur envoyer mes ordres et d'informer V.S. de mes demarches ulterieures.

No. 13.

JAMES TO WILLIAM DICCONSON, at St Germains

(*Stuart Papers*)

GIRONNE, MARCH 11, 1719.

SR,—I desire you will do me the favour to lett' Mr. Dutton know that I am gott thus farr on my way.—I am sincerely yours,   PETER KNIGHT.

No. 14.

JAMES TO WILLIAM DICCONSON

(*Stuart Papers*)

SARRAGOSSA, MARCH 22, 1719.

SR,—I desire you will do me the favour to inform Mr. Dutton that I am in good health in this place, and that I reckon to be on Munday next at Madrid; I am very much made of in this country, and in a short time hope to be able to write more fully to you,—I am, Sr, sincerely yours,

P. KNIGHT.

No. 15.

THE KING OF SPAIN (PHILIP V.) TO JAMES

(*Stuart Papers*)

Welcomes James to Spain—Willingness to help him.

A MADRID 16^E MARS 1719.

J'AY appris l'arrivée de Vostre Majesté en Espagne avec autant de plaisir que j'ay eu d'inquiétude sur les dangers qu'elle a eu a courir dans son voyage et je m'en fais aussi un très grand de pouvoir l'asseurer moy mesme de mon amitié.

Je me regarde comme bien heureux davoir trouvé l'occasion de vous en donner un marque en vous mettant a couvert des insultes de nos ennemys communs et je me le regarderai encore bien plus si Dieu bénissant mes desseins je puis vous rendre de services plus essentiels. Vostre Majesté peut estre asseurée que si elle regarde nos interests comme communs je pense aussi de mesme qu'elle et que je me ferai toûjours un très grand plaisir de pouvoir luy faire connoistre la sinceritè de mes sentiments et le fondes qu'elle peut faire en tout temps sur mon amitié.

PHILIPPE.

No. 16.

THE QUEEN OF SPAIN (ELIZABETH FARNESE) TO JAMES

(*Stuart Papers*)

Welcome to Spain.

A MADRID CE 16^E MARS 1719.

VOSTRE Majeste me fait beaucoup de justice d'estre persuadée que son heureuse arivée en Espagne m'ha[1] causé un sensible

---

[1] *Sic.* An Italian word occasionally slips into Elizabeth's French, also into Alberoni's.

plaisir, apres les allarmes, que nous avons eu pour sa persone. Vostre Majesté peut croire, que c'est pour moy une très grande consolation, que Le Roy aie pu Luy donner un asile dans ses etats, et La mettre en seureté dans son Royaume contre les trahisons de ses ennemis, qui sont en mesme temps les nostres, et que deshormais nos interets seront communs. J'attendray avec impatience l'arrivée de Vostre Majesté icy, afin de Luy pouvoir marquer de vive voix l'estime tres sincere que jay pour son merite.   ELIZABETH.

No. 17.

CARDINAL ALBERONI TO THE DUKE OF ORMONDE

(*Stuart Papers*)

Departure of the Cadiz Fleet on March 7—James's arrival in Spain—Secret of Expedition apparently unknown in London on Feb. 24—James's Voyage: his Misadventures—Arrest of Mar—No reason to despair of success, notwithstanding delay in sailing of Fleet—Departure of Earl Marischal from San Sebastian on March 13—News from Sweden.

A MADRID CE 18ME MARS 1719.

PAR monsieur Macdonnell V.E. aura apris le depart de L'Escadre de Cadix le 7me du Courant de sorte que je ne scais pas si la presente trouvera V.E^{xce} a la Corogne. Par autre Courier que je vous ai depesché Lundy passé 13 de Mars vous aurez appris aussi comme Le Roy Jacques avoit debarqué a Roses, et aujourdhuy je crois qu'il partira de Barcellone pour venir a Madrid ou il n'arrivera que le 25 ou 26 du courant, de sorte que je tiens pour infaillible que si vous avez un Vent favourable vous aurez fait votre debarquement en Angleterre ou en quelque autre part, supposé que vous trouviez des difficultez en Angleterre a cause que le Ministere aura les Moyens promptes pour y accourir et peutetre vous prendres toujours le partie d'aller en Ecosse. Vous verrez par les Gazettes icy jointes que le 24. Fevrier on ne parloit point de notre Expedition, qu'on vivoit a Londres fort tranquil, et même le Gazette d'Holande dit que le Duc D'Ormonde avoit solicité auprès du Roy d'Espagne de Commander son armée en Cattalogne, vous voyez qu'on nous meprisse beaucoup.

Le 4me du Courrant entrerent quatre Vaisseaux anglois avec la Pacquet boat a Lisbonne, un etoit de 60 pieces de Canons deux de 54 et l'autre de 40 sur lequel etoit embarque le Fils de L'Amirall Bing pour passer a Naples. Le Vaisseau de 60 pieces a besoin de reparation pour avoir essuyee une furieusse Tempête, il y en a autres onze de Transport chargés de toute sorte de municions pour Mahon et Gibraltar. Le Roy Jacques a courrus risques de se perdre cent fois a cause des Bourasques qu'il a essuyé. Il a demeure trois jours en Marseilles cache chez le Patron du Battiment sur lequel il sétoit embarque, il fut Saigné a cause d'une Grand Fievre, il fut obligee des e refugier bien caché a Villefranche 24 heures. Il fut obligee de se relascher aux Isles des Hieres proche de Toulon sur un miserable et Epouvantable Cabaret ou il y avoit une foulle de Canaille, il fut obligee quoique incommodé de la Mer de danser avec la Maitresse du Cabaret etant le jour de Carneval. Il a ete poursuivi par deux Vaisseaux Anglois.—On a arrêté plusieurs personnes sur le Chemin entre lesquels on dit le Duc de Mar et autres personnes attachés au Roy Jaques. D'abord qu'on sceut le depart du Roy Jacques de Rome Le Comte de Gallas depescha de tous Cotés des Courriers. Celui qui arriva a Paris obligea Stairs a avoir une Conference de trois heures avec le Regent après laquelle on depescha dix ou douze Courriers et je veux bien croire que quelques uns sera arrivé a Londres. Le jour de la depeshe fut le 22 ou le 23 de Fevrier, cependant je m'imagine que le Ministere de Londres se trouvera embarrassé et qu'il ne pourra pas donner si promptement comme il voudroit, les moyens necessaires; d'autant plus que je crois qu'il y aura bien du murmure dans le Pays et même dans Londres; Enfin quoyque L'Escadre est partie plus tard de ce qu'on croyoit, il ne faut pas desesperer l'affaire, le grand point est d'avoir en Espagne le Roy Jacques, car toutes les Lettres d'Italie et de France [1] qu'il a eté arresté sur l'Etat de Milan et je ne scais si veritablement les Ministres Imperiaux out débité un pareille nouvelle avec Artifice, ou si veritablement ils ont crus.

Monsieur le Marischall partit de St. Sebastien le 13 du

---

[1] *Sic.* Word omitted.

Courrant avec un Vent tres favorable. Il y a apparence d'une Rupture entre la Pologne le Czar et le Roy de Prusse, ce qui pourroit bien entraisner d'autres Puissances, si cela se trouve vray le jeune Duc d'Holstein n'a pas voulu se retirer en Moscovie comme on avoit ecrit de Suede. Les Deputés des Etats netoient pas tous assemblés a Stockholm le 10 de ce mois ni la Reine Coronée. On n'ecrit rien de particulier de ce pays la. Le Comte de Raventlau Min^{tre} du jeune Duc d'Holstein n'est pas allé en Angleterre comme on avoit dit pour traiter d'un Marriage pour ce Prince, il a passé en Suede pour se rendre auprès de son maitre avec Passeport de Danemarck; on poursuit vigoureusement le Baron de Gortz et le Comte de Vandernat qui sont fort häis des Suedois. Voila les Nouvelles du Nord que mande Monsr Laules. Je suis de V. E^{xce} avec la plus parfaite Amitie et tout le respect possible,

Le Card^L Alberoni.

Le Roy Jacques m'a depesha Monsieur O'brien qui arriva avanthier et qui partit le jour après pour aller trouver Sa Ma^{te} avec la reponse. Voicy une lettre de sa Ma^{te} pour V. E.

No. 18.

JAMES to WILLIAM DICCONSON

(Stuart Papers)

MADRID, MARCH 31, 1719.

You might naturally expect I should from hence send you some directions as to pensioners and mony matters, but that is Impossible; my being in this country cannot have hindered the Regent from paying arrears which were not due to me, and of which neither my person nor my affairs will any more profitt, but I hope they will at least keep people from starving till such time as I can inform you of my intentions, directions, and abilities, which I hope I shall be soon able to do, and will neglect nothing that lies in my power for the support of so many brave subjects and old servants. It is my Intention that all such as are my domestick servants should not think of removing or joining me till my further order, I allways except Sheldon out of general rules, but even as to him I cannot as yet give any directions. And this is all I can say at present, JAMES R.

No. 19.

CARDINAL ALBERONI TO THE DUKE OF ORMONDE

(Stuart Papers)

News from London—Reported alarm of English Ministry, and requests for help from France—Jacobite sympathies of French troops—Landing to be effected in England if possible, in Scotland only as a last resource—Is it advisable to risk James's person?

A MADRID, LE 4 AVRIL 1719.

DEPUIS ma derniere que j'ai escrit a V. E. il est arrivé un de nos Emissaires de Londres, d'ou il partit le commencement du passé, et il nous dit qu'il y avoit une confusion et un desordre si grand que le ministere croyoit tout perdu, que la crainte essoit tres grande nonseulement pour un debarquement qu'on croioit en Angleterre, mais aussy en Ecosse, que le d^t Ministere avoit demandé des Trouppes au Regent, mais que le François qui sont en Flandres disoient hautement que si ils alloient en Angleterre ce seroit pour servir le Roy Jacques. Une nouvelle aussy certain, et d'un homme plein de probité et d'esprit, donne motif a S. M^{te} Cat. d'ordonner a V. E. de faire tous les efforts possible pour faire la descente en Angleterre, mais si le malheur vouloit qu'elle se rendoit tout a fait impossible S. M^{te} veu absolument qu'on aille en Ecosse, bien entendu que ce sera la derniere ressource, et en cas que la descente en Angleterre deviene tout a fait impossible. On a consideré que l'honneur de Sa M^{te} Cat. ne veut pas qu'il sacrifie tant des honnetes gens en Ecosse qui auront a l'heur qu'il est pris les armes pour le Roy Jacques ; car on sçait deja que bien des personnes sont partis de plusieurs endroits pour se rendre en Ecosse. Comme on a cru que peut etre a l'arrivé de ce Courrier V. E. peut etre seroit party, on a fait des duplicates des lettres en Espagnole que portent la contenue de cette lettre, et on a donné des ordres a Mr de Risbourcq de vous les faire tenir par la voye de plusieurs batimens en cas que vous soiez party.

V. E. a bien fait de prendre le Chirurgien et Elle n'a qu'a prendre tout ce qu'elle jugera apropos pour la bonne issue de l'Expedition. On replique l'ordre a M⁽ʳ⁾ de Rissebourcq de donner la main a tout ce que V. E. demandera. A l'Egard du Roy Jacques S. M. Cat. ne Scauroit prendre sur soy même ce qu'il doit faire, puisque sa personne est de la derniere importance a la conserver ; car ses Enemies ne souhaitent sinon qu'il fasse un coup de desesperé, et alors ils auront gagné le proces. Monsieur le Duc vous estes sage et prudent, et je crois que vous ne voudries pas vous exposer que le monde dit que vous l'aviez risqué mal a propos. Je crois que votre personne, et votre credit, sachant vos Amis et le party du Roy Jacques, que le Roy d'Espagne veut soutenir la gageure que vous trouuerez des facilites a mettre les affaires en bon train, et alors vous aurez toujours le temps de faire venir le Roy. Enfin, Mons⁽ʳ⁾ Le Duc vous estes sage et prudent, et tout le monde est bien persuadé que vous avez de l'attachement pour votre Roy.

On ordonne a M⁽ʳ⁾ Le Marq⁽ˢ⁾ de Risebourcq de mettre ensemble sur le champ Quarante Mille Escus, et on songera apres les moyens de vous envoyer les autres soixante Mille. Je prie le bon Dieu qu'il nous fasse sçavoir bien tot des nouuelles de notre Escadre. V. E. cependant ne doutera point que personne au Monde n'a pour Elle ny plus d'Amitié n'y plus de respect que,

(Signé)   Le Card. Alberoni.

Les Nouvelles notre Emissaire les a appris le 8⁽ᵉᵐᵉ⁾ a Paris, meme sur le debarquement ; la confusion et le tumulte il l'a vus a Londres au commencement du mois de mars. Le 13⁽ᵉᵐᵉ⁾ du mois on parloit point a Londres de Notre Escadre.

No. 20.

The ABBÉ DUBOIS to SECRETARY CRAGGS

(*Extract. State Papers, Foreign, France*, 358)

James's Journey to Spain—Reports as to Ormonde's movements—
Alberoni to supply 6000 men and 15,000 muskets.

Paris, 16 Jan. 1719, n.s.

. . . Le Pretendant devoit aller en Espagne où le Duc d'Ormonde estoit deja arrivé, et de là l'un et l'autre avec plusieurs Officiers devoient passer en Irlande et y faire soulever les Irlandois. . . . On avoit resolu d'abord que le Duc d'Ormond resteroit à Madrid, mais il s'est embarqué depuis peu a Bilbao, et on a envoyé une autre personne de Madrid à Barcelone pour porter au Pretendant l'approbation de toutes les mesures qu'on avoit proposé de prendre. Le Ca¹ Alberoni devoit fournir six mille hommes qui devoient s'embarquer à la Corogne et fournir 15,000 fusils.

No. 21.

The ABBÉ DUBOIS to SECRETARY CRAGGS

(*Private. Craggs Papers, Stowe MSS.*, 247, ff. 35-39 b.
Received in London, Feb. 28, O.S.)

Alberoni's plans—Lawless's mission to Sweden—James gone to Spain—Information as to preparations in Spain for invasion of England.

A Paris, le 8 de Mars 1719.

Monsieur,—J'ai esté si agité depuis quelque tems, qu'il m'a esté impossible d'avoir recours à la principale consolation que je puisse trouver dans mes peines, qui est cette de vous ouvrir mon cœur et à Mylord Stanhope.

Mylord Stanhope vous communiquera, Monsieur, ce que j'ai l'honneur de lui ecrire touchant les affaires du Nord. Ce qu'on vous avoit dit de nos Negociations avec le Czar, sont des fables ; et nostre unique attention avec ce Prince, avec la Suede et avec le Roi de Prusse a esté de les tourner à prendre des sentimens qui pussent convenir au Roi de la Grande Bretagne. La mort du Roi de Suede n'a pas osté au Cardinal Alberoni la pensée de prendre des liaisons avec la Suede ; et Don Patricio Laulés qui est à Hambourg, a ordre de passer à Stockholm pour suivre les projets dont il estoit chargé. Ce n'est pas un mechant acteur que ce Laulés. Comme il estoit le depositaire des entreprises qui se devoient faire contre le Roi de la grande Bretagne, il seroit à souhaiter qu'on pût l'enlever et le mettre dans le premier chasteau appartenant au Roi de la grande Bretagne. La nouvelle qu'on nous avoit ecrite touchant l'arrest du Pretendant, n'est pas encore assés eclaircie. Il y a plus d'apparence pourtant, que les gens qui ont esté arrestés à Voghera et conduits dans le Chasteau de Milan, sont les officiers de sa maison à qui il avoit fait pretendre cette route, pour donner le change dans le tems que lui personellement ou s'embarquoit à Civita Vecchia pour aller en Espagne, ou prenoit un chemin opposé pour joindre la Princesse qu'il a epousée par procureur. Nous avions plusieurs avis qui faisoient croire que mesme depuis le nouvelle de la mort du Roi de Suede on l'attendoit en Espagne.

Nous avons decouvert un homme[1] qui estoit dans la confidence du premier projet des Jacobites avec l'Espagne, et qui pretend que malgré la mort du Roi de Suede, ils doivent encore faire une tentative dans peu.

Il nous a dit que le premier projet d'une descente en Angleterre avoit esté dirigé par le Comte d'Oxfort qui avoit reglé où et de quelle maniere on devoit entrer en Angleterre où l'on trouveroit tout disposé. Le Port où l'on devoit descendre, estoit vers Bristol. On ne jugea pas à propos de Communiquer ce detail a l'Evesque de Rochester, parce qu'il ne favorise pas volontiers ce qu'il n'a pas lui mesme imaginé. On vouloit envoyer le detail du projet au Roi d'Espagne par Prior ; mais ou il s'en deffendit sur sa mauvaise santé, ou on jugea qu'il s'en deffendroit ; et on confia ce projet au Sr Eon, Directeur pour les Espagnols de la Compagnie de l'Assiento, qui estoit pour lors à Londres, qui l'a porté et sur le rapport duquel on agissoît.

Nostre homme nous assûre qu'ils veulent encore suivre une partie de leur projet, et qu'on doit faire une descente en Angleterre dans moins de six semaines ; Que l'Espagne doit fournir cinq ou six bataillons Irlandois et des armes ; Que la descente se fera toujours à un Port du costé de Bristol, où les soldats, qui ont esté licentiés, et beaucoup de la petite Noblesse d'Angleterre munis de tout ce qui est necessaire, se joindront à eux, et peuvent faire ensemble jusqu'à 26/m hommes ; et que leur dessein est de marcher droit à Londres. Le Pretendant ne doit pas y passer dabord, mais le Duc d'Ormond ; et cet homme assûre qu'il y a environ trois semaines qu'il vint un homme qui devoit passer en Espagne, qui portoit des souscriptions de gens conjurés, dont quatre feüilles de papier estoient remplies.

Cet avis nous a fait faire attention à ce qui nous revient de

---

[1] Possibly Walef. See p. 25, note.

plusieurs costés, qu'on achete ou loüe pour les Espagnols tous les bastimens de charge que l'on peut trouver ; et qu'on prepare en diligence à Cadix des Vaisseaux de guerre et des bastimens de charge avec des troupes prestes à embarquer, et qu'on y arrestoit tous les Bastimens François qui vouloient prendre parti pour une expedition. On nous a mandé de Hollande en mesme tems, qu'il estoit arrivé depuis peu un homme de la part de l'Espagne à Amsterdam, pour presser l'envoi des munitions qui avoient esté embarquées, et pour faire emporter des armes. Ayés la bonté, Monsieur, de faire sur cela toutes les considerations que vous jugeres à propos. Je suis persuadé qu'il y a beaucoup de vrai dans ce qu'on nous a dit, et j'en ai crû la substance assés serieuse pour n'epargner rien pour engager cet homme à s'en aller auprès du Duc d'Ormond qui a de la confiance en lui, pour tacher de nous donner des nouvelles plus positives de ce qu'on auroit envie de faire. Comme je ne connois pas assés cet homme pour estre assûré de sa fidelité, j'ai voulu tacher de l'assûrer par interest, et j'ai fait consigner deux mille pistoles à son Banquier, pour lui estre delivrées si il nous donne de bons avis ; et je lui ai assûré que si il rendoit quelque service important, il auroit une pension considerable de la France et du Roi de la grande Bretagne. Il est parti aujourdhui pour aller chercher le Duc d'Ormond.

S. A. R. a laissé à M. le Marquis de Senectere le choix d'aller incessament à Londres pour suivre ensuite le Roi de la grande Bretagne à Hannover, si sa Majesté Britannique a agreable qu'il l'y suive ; ou d'aller d'ici droit à Hannover. Elle a nommé M. Destouches secretaire de l'ambassade qui suivra M. de Senectere à Hannover ; et je compte de laisser à Londres pendant le voyage du Roi, M. de Chammorel, pour cultiver la correspondance que vous me permettrés d'avoir avec vous. Si vous aimés mieux que je choisisse quelque autre personne, je vous prie de me le marquer naturellement, et j'en choisirai quelque autre avec toutes les convenances que je pourrai trouver. Je suis tres parfaitement Monsieur de Vostre Ex^{ce}
Tres humble et tres obeïssant serviteur.

DUBOIS.

P.S.—Nous avons, Monsieur, des avis qui me paroissent certains que le Pretendant est parti de Civita Vecchia pour aller en Espagne sur un bastiment que le Cardinal Aquaviva et Patigno lui avoient preparé ; et je crois que nous devons compter sur cela.

Gozzani qui est à Amsterdam pour l'Espagne, fait embarquer actuellement des agrets et des munitions de guerre.

Un parent du Duc d'Ormond a joint Patricio Laulés à Hambourg. Ils doivent s'embarquer à Lubeck ou à Rostock pour aller en Suede. Comme il y a sur les chemins de Hambourg à ces deux Ports, des troupes du Roi de la Grande Bretagne, si l'on pouvoit prendre ces deux hommes, ce seroit une bonne capture.   D.

No. 22.

The ABBÉ DUBOIS to SECRETARY CRAGGS

(*Craggs Papers, Stowe MSS.* 247, *ff.* 64-64 *b.*   *Received in London, March 7, O.S.*)

Further information as to Cadiz fleet—Offer of help from France.

A Paris, le 11e Mars n.s. 1719.

Monsieur,—On continue a nous donner des avis de tous costés que l'embarquement qu'on fait à Cadix en toute diligence est considerable. Presque touttes les lettres portent qu'on embarque treize bataillons, ce qu'il est difficile de croire, quelques lettres mesme font mention de mille hommes de cavallerie scauoir 500 avec leurs chevaux et 500 a pied. J'ay l'honneur de vous enuoyer des coppies des lettres que nostre Conseil de marine a receües. Par tout ce qui nous est revenu on compte plus sur ce qui doit se revolter en Angleterre que sur les secours etrangers. S. A. R. veillera a tout ce qui poura emaner de ce pays cy ou il faut se defier non seulement des jrlandois mais de beaucoup d'autres, et elle offre au Roy de la Grande Bretagne tout ce qui peut dependre d'elle, non seulement pour remplir ses engagemens, mais generallement pour tout ce qu'elle peut faire pour donner au Roy de la Grande Bretagne et a son ministere les preuues les plus fortes qu'elle ne fait point de difference entre ce qui les regarde et ce que la touche person-

nellement, ie ne puis qu'aplaudir a ces sentimens, et ie vous prie destre persuadé que ie suis avec un attachement particulier.
Monsieur,
De V^e Ex^{ce}
très humble et très obeïssant seruiteur,
Dubois.

No. 23.
REPORT from ST. MALO to the CONSEIL de MARINE

(*Craggs Papers, Stowe MSS.* 247, *f.* 66. *Enclosed in No.* 22)

Information as to preparations at Cadiz.

Lettre ecrite a M. le Marechal d'Estrees[1] de St. Malo le 3 Mars 1719.

M.,—Nous aprenons par nos lettres de Cadix par un vaisseau qui a passé a Brest en onze jours que les Espagnols arment tous leurs vaisseaux de guerre au nombre de sept ou huit, et ont arretés quarante a cinquante bâtimens pour le transport des troupes, sans qu'on ait pû penetrer leur dessein, on dit cependant que c'est pour la coste de Catalogne, ou pour Messine. Il y a plusieurs Bâtimens François entr'autres le Vaisseau Le Grand Comte de Toulouse de 54 a 60 canons appartenant a M. Danican, il ne faut pas douter que les Espagnols n'arretent tous les Vaisseaux François qui iront a Cadix retirer leurs effets sous pretexte de s'en seruir pour le transport de leurs troupes. J'aurai l'honneur de vous informer de tout ce qui viendra a ma connoissance.

No. 24.
REPORT from MARSEILLES to the CONSEIL de MARINE

(*Craggs Papers, Stowe MSS.* 247, *f.* 68. *Enclosed in No.* 22)

Further information as to preparations at Cadiz—Ships being impressed as transports.

Autre Lettre ecrite de Marseille a M. le Marechal d'Estrees.

le 26 Feb^r 1719.

M.,—Il arriva hier au soir un Navire de Marseille, qui est

---

[1] The Maréchal d'Estrées was President of the Conseil de Marine.

entré ce matin dans le Port ; il est parti depuis onze Jours de Cadiz d'ou il rapporte beaucoup d'Argent. Le Capitaine nommé Gasqui dit avoir eu de la peine a se sauver par ce qu'on arrêta tous les vaisseaux pour le Transport de treize mille hommes, avec de l'Artillerie ; on ne sçait point pour quel Païs ces Troupes sont destinées. Il y a 50 Batimens de Transport escortés par 8 navires de Guerre qui étoient déjà sortis du Pontal.

No. 25.
The EARL of STAIR to SECRETARY CRAGGS
(*State Papers, Foreign, France*, 353)

Information received from Regent as to preparations at Cadiz—Offer of French sailors—Small squadron cruising between Scilly Isles and Ireland will probably suffice to prevent Spaniards landing—Force of Expedition probably much exaggerated—Stair thinks the whole project absurd, but due precautions should be taken—Dillon has been dismissed from his command in Dauphine—Ormonde's departure from Madrid—James's journey from Rome.

A Paris, le 11 Mars 1719.

Monsieur,—Depuis que Je Vous ay escrit ce Matin, J'ay eu l'honneur de voir Monsieur Le Duc d'Orleans, qui m'a dit Qu'il avoit des Avis certains que l'embarquement à Cadiz estoit destiné contre l'Angleterre ; Il y a un Vaisseau françois arrivé à Marseilles, et un autre arrivé à St. Malo, partys de Cadiz le 16e Fevrier, qui disent, Que les Espagnols avoient huit Vaisseaux de Guerre dans le dit Port, et cinquante Vaisseaux de Transport ; Et qu'il y avoit treize Bataillons et un Regiment de Dragons prêts à s'embarquer. L'Epine d'Alicant, fameux Negociant de St Malo, s'est plaint à Monsieur Le Duc d'Orleans, que les Espagnols avoient forcé, dans le Port de Cadiz, un Vaisseau a Luy de soixante pieces de Canon de s'engager avec eux, pour servir dans la dite Expedition ; Je croy que la force n'a pas été grande car ledit l'Epine d'Alicant a été mêlé dans toutes les enterprises du Prétendant, et même le Prétendant a esté logé dans sa maison quand Il estoit à St. Malo.[1] Monsieur Le Duc d'Orleans m'a fait l'honneur de me dire, que si Le Roy ne trouvoit pas d'abord le nombre des Matelots suffisant pour mettre une Escadre en Mer, il offroit à Sa Majesté tel nombre de

---

[1] See Bolingbroke's Letter to Sir William Windham. *Works*, vol. i. p. 47.

Matelots françois que Sa Majeste pourroit souhaitter ; Je dis à S. A. R. que Je ne manquerois pas de faire sçavoir au Roy l'Offre obligeant que S. A. R. faisoit, mais que J'etois persuadé, qu'on trouveroit dans la Tamise assez de Matelots pour equipper l'Escadre dont on pourroit avoir besoin.

Monsr le Maréchal d'Estrées est venu me voir le soir. Il m'a confirmé les Nouvelles de Cadiz que S. A. R. m'avoit dites. Le Maréchal m'a dit, Qu'il avoit de la peine à croire que les Espagnols voulussent s'hazarder dans cette saison de faire le tour de l'Irlande pour venir debarquer du côté de Bristol, et qu'il Luy paroissoit, qu'il leur seroit difficile d'executer leur dessein tel qu'il puisse être, pourvû que nous eussions une Escadre de huit ou dix Vaisseaux qui croisât entre les Isles de Scilly et l'Irlande, parce que, si les Espagnols faisoient le tour de l'Irlande, l'Escadre seroit toujours à temps de les empêcher de debarquer, pourvû qu'on prît soin d'etre averty du Mouvement des Espagnols.

Pour moy J'ay la peine à croire que l'Embarquement des Espagnols puisse être aussy fort que les avis qu'on a icy le portent. Vous verrez par la Lettre de Monsr Davenant, qu'un Vaisseau party de Cadiz le 17e Fevrier, arrivé à Gènes le 28e, le fait beaucoup moins considerable ; Et Nous n'avons ouy parler icy que des Troupes Irlandaises qui devoient être employées à cette Expedition, dont il n'y a que cinq Battailons et un Regiment de Dragons en Espagne. Le Projet qui devoit s'executer de concert avec la Suede ne portoit que six mille hommes de la part de l'Espagne, Et Monsr Le Duc d'Orleans m'asseure, que par l'avis qu'Il a de cette affaire, My Lord et ses Amis qui avoient formé le Projet ne demandoient pas davantage, Disant qu'avec une telle teste de Troupes réglées, Ils levroient en peu de temps vingt six mille hommes, et qu'Ils avoient pris des mesures pour engager les Soldats licenciez en dernier lieu. My Lord Oxford avoit fait assûrer le Pretendant, qu'il auroit une Reconnoissance eternelle du Service que le Pretendant Luy avoit rendu dans l'Affaire de son Procez.

Tout ce beau Projet me paroît bien Chimerique, Les Espagnols viennent de très loin, tres incertains d'arriver, et ne sont sûrs de rien quand ils arrivent ; mais ce seroit bien pis pour Eux s'il est vray, comme il y a beaucoup d'apparence, que le Prétendant est dans le Château de Milan, Pourtant Je crois que vous serez de mon Avis, qu'il ne faut pas negliger de faire les Dispositions necessaires. Cela coute peu de chose, et dans une Affaire aussy importante, il faut laisser au hazard le moins qu'on peut.

J'auray soin de vous envoyer des Courriers toutes les fois quelque chose d'Importance parvient à ma Connaissance.

Monsieur Le Duc d'Orleans vient d'ôter à Monsr Dillon, le Commandement qu'Il Luy avoit donné en Dauphiné. J'ay dit à S. A. R. que cela auroit un mauvais effet, si on laissoit Monsr Dillon à Paris pour y faire les Affaires du Pretendant ; S. A. R. m'a dit, qu'elle y mettroit bon Ordre. J'ay raison de croire, que si les Espagnols debarquent en Angleterre, Dillon a dessein d'y passer. Tous les Anglois et Ecossois qui estoient repandus par les Provinces de France se sont eclipsez, On croit qu'Ils sont passez en Espagne.

Le 12^E Mars 1719.

J'ay voulu sçavoir les Nouvelles que la Poste d'Espagne avoit portées avant que de vous depecher mon Courrier, J'ay veu des Lettres de l'Espagne qui confirment les mêmes choses qui vous trouvez dans ma Relation, touchant l'Armement à Cadiz ; Tout le monde est persuadé à Madrid, qu'il est destiné ou contre L'Irlande ou contre l'Angleterre, Le bruit s'etoit même repandu à Madrid, qu'il avoit fait voile, mais cela ne peut pas être vray. Car l'Abbé du Bois m'a dit aujourd'huy, que le Duc d'Ormond n'a pris congé de la cour que le 24e, et n'a party de Madrid que le 25e, luy et toute sa suite pour Cadiz, et il luy faut plusieurs jours pour y arriver ; De sorte que quand tout seroit prêt, la Flotte ne pourroit être partie que le 5 on 6e de ce mois au plustot.

. . .

Les Jacobites icy paroissent fort en peine du Prétendant ; Il est seur qu'ils n'ont aucune nouvelle de ce qu'il est devenu. Le Pretendant en sortant de Rome a laissé une espece de Manifeste contenant les raisons de son depart, Il dit, qu'il ne S'estoit pas cru en seureté à Urbino et ensuitte à Bologne, à cause du Voisinage des Troupes Imperiales ; Que pour cela il S'etoit retiré à Rome, et que voyant que la Liberté de l'Italie etoit entirement opprimée, par le grand nombre de Troupes que l'Empereur y avoit fait passer, et que voyant qu'il avoit tout a apprehender pour sa personne, par la Violence injuste que l'Empereur avoit exercée contre la Princesse Royale Sobiesky, il avoit été obligé de prendre la Resolution de quitter Rome meme, pour Se mettre en Seurété ; Cet escrit montre assez que le dessein du Prétendant etoit de passer en Espagne, et qu'il croyoit qu'il ne seroit plus obligé de garder aucunes Mesures avec l'Empereur. On m'a promis ce Manifeste pour demain Matin, Si l'on me tient parole, je Vous l'enverray. . . .

Je suis avec une estime parfaicte,
    Monsieur,
        Votre très humble et très obeissant Serviteur,
            Stair.

No. 26.

The EARL of STAIR to SECRETARY CRAGGS

(*Extract from Private Letter. Craggs Papers, Stowe MSS. 247, f. 76*)

Paris, March 15, 1719.

My d^r Craggs,—Press ye fitting out of y^r Ships, raise as many troops as you (can) and send to ye Dutch to have their troops ready. The Spaniards could not sail before ye 7 or ye 8 of this month. I hope our squadron will be ready in time.

I think ye D. of Orleans is heartily in earnest to help us, but it is good not to want french assistance.[1]

No. 27.

The EARL of STAIR to SECRETARY CRAGGS

(*State Papers, Foreign, France,* 353)

James's departure from Nettuno confirmed—Arrest of Mar and Perth—Friendliness of the Regent to England, preparations to send over French troops—Jacobites in France believe expedition to sail from Corunna—Departure of Seaforth and others from Paris—Rumours as to James's arrival in Spain and sailing of the fleet.

Paris, le 18e Mars 1719.

Monsieur,—Les Lettres d'Italie nous portent la confirmation de toutes parts que le Pretendant est parti de Neptune,

---

[1] See Introduction, p. xxxviii, note 5.

Monsr l'Abbé du Bois m'a fait voir la Lettre d'un homme de Rome du 28º qui avoit eu audience du Pape le 27e, dans laquelle Audience le Pape Luy avoit dit, Qu'il estoit vray que le Pretendant etoit party de Neptune, pourtant Monsr Davenant continue toujours à croire qu'il est dans le Château de Milan, et je vous avoue, que ses raisons paroissent si fortes qu'on le croiroit tout comme Luy. Je vous enverray sa Lettre par mon Courrier que je depescheray ce soir ou demain, quand j'auray vû les Nouvelles d'Espagne, par l'Ordinaire qui arrive ce soir. Il est presque seur que les Lords Mar et Perth sont dans le Château de Milan ; Ils ont été le 14e à Boulogne. Gordon le Banquier icy a une Lettre de Milord Mar de Boulogne, laquelle est veritablement escrite de là ; On les a veus le 16e à Piaccenza, de sorte que c'est presque seur que c'est Eux ; qu'on a arrêté le 17e à Vogera. Le Maréchal Colmanero continue à faire le mysterieux sur le Chapitre de ces Prisonniers.

J'ay veu Monsr le Duc d'Orleans hier, qui m'a parlé avec toute l'affection possible pour les Interêts du Roy ; Il prend l'Invasion projettée contre l'Angleterre extremement à cœur, et il m'a dit qu'il avoit nommé Monsr le Comte de Sennecterre pour commander les Secours, si Le Roy en a besoin en Angleterre—Je Vous envoye incluse la Repartition des Regiments, dont le dernier arrivera au Port de Mer destiné, le 25e de ce mois ; de sorte que si l'affaire pressoit, vous les pourriez avoir en Angleterre en deux fois 24 heures de temps. Je vous enverray par mon Courrier les noms de Regiments. Monsr de Sennecterre a pour Maréchaux de Camp avec Luy, le Marquis de Belleisle et le Comte de La Val.

Nos Jacobites icy sont persuadez que c'est à la Corogne que les Troupes embarqueront. Les Espagnols n'ont que trois Batallions Irlandois en Espagne et un Regiment de Dragons, dont le Regiment de Liria est à Gironne.—Tout le monde est d'accord que leur Infanterie est quelque chose de très pitoyable.

On a donné des Ordres icy, que personne ne passera aux Ports du Mer, sans un Passeport de l'Abbé du Bois. On prend soin de Monsr Dillon, et, de tous les Irlandois.

My Lord Seaforth et les Montagnards Ecossois qui étoient icy à Paris, sont partis, il y a quatre jours, pour s'embarquer à Dieppe. Les Jacobites pretendent que les Espagnols en passant doivent jetter quinze cents hommes en Ecosse pour mettre le feu partout. Ils pretendant avoir Nouvelles, que le Pretendant est arrivé à Barcelone, et que les Troupes Espagnolles ont fait voile la nuit de 26ᵉ ou 27ᵉ, mais ce sont des Rêves sans aucun fondement.

Je suis avec une estime parfaicte
Monsieur,
votre très humble et très obeissant Serviteur
STAIR

Je n'ay aucun lettre d'Angleterre
par les dernieres postes.

No. 28.

SECRETARY CRAGGS TO THE EARL OF STAIR

(*State Papers, Foreign, France,* 351 *a*)

WHITEHALL, 9ᵀᴴ MARCH 1718/19, O.S.,
(MARCH 20, N.S.)

H. E. THE EARL
   OF STAIR
     MY LORD

. . . .

I come now, My Lord, to your last Dispatches wherein you give the King an account of the intended Invasion against us. I cannot say His Maj^{ty} is extreamly alarmed about it. However, it will be necessary to take the proper Precautions. His Maj^{ty} will go to-morrow to the House and acquaint them with it. He has avoided it hitherto, because he was afraid of the run such a story might bring upon the Credit and was willing to wait till the second Lottery was filled up, which I hope was done this morning. If I do not dispatch this messenger till tomorrow, Y. E. shall have Copys of the Kings speech and the Addresses of both Houses to him upon it. In the meantime four Battallions and eighteen Squadrons are marched and marching towards the west, where My Lord Cadogan will go and command them if it be necessary. Sr John Norris went last Saturday to Portsmouth where there is a Squadron ready of seven good ships, which will sail & cruize off the Landsend, and I do not doubt be able to give a very good account of a dozen Spanish ships, should they meet with them. He has orders and is resolved notwithstanding any inequality of numbers to attack them, and my Ld. Berkeley will in eight or ten days more be able to sail with eight good ships either to join Sr John Norris, or make a separate Squadron as shall be judged proper; and the Seamen do all agree that both these Squadrons will be ready before it is possible for the Spaniards to make the Coast of England. Notwithstanding these preparations I am persuaded the Parliament will enable His Maj^{ty} to increase his Land and Sea forces as he shall think fit. My Lord Stanhope has already sent to Holland to ask four Batallions of the Dutch and Monsr Penterridter has dispatched an Express to the Marquis de Prie to hold six more in a readiness to pass over from Ostend. Upon this occasion Y. E. must in the most obliging and friendly terms express the King's thanks to the Regent for his kind Offer of fifteen hundred Seamen, and the Disposition he is making to keep twenty Batallions along the Sea Coast. His Maj^{ty} does not refuse his Offer, but will not immediately make use of it, unless he finds a greater necessity than he apprehends at present. Y. E. will therefore only entreat H. R. H. to keep up the same disposition till you hear further from me,

      I am etc.

        J. CRAGGS.

P.S.—10 Mar. 1718/19.

His Maj^{ty} would have Y. E. let the Regent know that the most effectual succour H. R. H. can give him at present is to order as soon as possible the French forces to begin their Operations against Spain itself. I leave it to Y. E. to enlarge upon the necessity of such a service in this Juncture. The King has also this day in Council resolved to accept 5 or 600 of the French Seamen only as a proof that he can trust them, but still paying them himself at the English rates which far exceed the French ones, and will no doubt reconcile them to His Maj$^{ty's}$ Service. Of this Y. E. will be pleased to acquaint H. R. H., and that when he lets the King know at what Port they are ready he will send for them. I enclose to you His Maj^{ty's} Speech and the Addresses of both Houses with Extracts of Mr. Worsleys Letters of the 7th Inst. from Lisbon, which arrived this morning, J. C.

No. 29.

EXTRACT FROM REPORT BY HENRY WORSLEY, British Envoy at Lisbon, of which a copy was enclosed in No. 28.

(State Papers, Foreign, Spain, 163)

TRANSLAT^N OF INTELL^CE FROM MADRID, 20 FEB^RY 1719, N.S., TRANSMITTED BY MR. WORSLEY IN HIS OF 7 MARCH 1719.

THE Frigate of War named Hermione is gon from the Port of Cadiz after having embarked Provisions for the Ships Company for three months. There was a Packet on board which the Captain was to open 40 miles at sea, and it is not known what course they steered.

There were also ready at Cadiz 4000 men and good Horse, which are thought to be bound for Barcelona, tho their orders are not made publick, by reason of the great Secrecy they observe in all their dispositions.

At this very time it is said *extrajudicially* that this Squadron of 7 Ships of War, which was ready at Cadiz, is departed, and has on board the 4000 men and 900 Horse; and that they are going to England; it being added that the D. of Ormond went before in the frigate which sailed first, in order to prepare the minds of the people against the time when the Troops will arrive.

No. 30.

THE EARL OF STAIR TO SECRETARY CRAGGS

(State Papers, Foreign, France, 353)

News arrived that Ormonde has sailed from Passage on March 12 (obviously a mistaken account of the Earl Marischal's expedition)—Stair had heard of Ormonde's going to Corunna, but did not believe it.

À PARIS, LE 22^E MARS 1719.

MONSIEUR,—Aujourd'huy à deux heures, J'ay veu Monsieur Le Duc d'Orleans, qui M'a fait l'honneur de Me dire, qu'Il venoit de recevoir une Lettre du Maréchal de Berwick, dattée le 17ᵉ ce Mois, par laquelle le Maréchal Luy mande, Que le Duc d'Ormond S'etoit embarqué le 12ᵉ au Port de Passage, avec quatre Compagnies de Grenadiers, sur deux Fregattes que les Espagnols prisent aux François l'Année passée, aux Indes Occidentales. Il y a apparence que la Duc d'Ormond S'est embarqué là, pour joindre la Flotte d'Espagne, ou à la pointe d'Oushant, ou au Cape Finisterre, car il n'y a nulle apparence qu'il veuille envahir l'Angleterre avec ses quatre Compagnies de Grenadiers.

J'avois en avis, que le Duc d'Ormond alloit à la Corogne, et non pas à Cadiz, et que la Flotte Le viendroit prendre là, et y embarquer d'autres Troupes, et Je ne le croyois pas, à cause qu'il ne me paroissoit pas vraysemblable, que la Flotte partiroit sans avoir à son bord le General qui devoit commander les Troupes; et de plus Je croyois, qu'Ils auroient évité toute chose qui pouvoit retarder leur voyage, dont le succès dependoit de la Surprise. . . . STAIR.

No. 31.

SECRETARY CRAGGS to the EARL of STAIR

(State Papers, Foreign, France, 351a)

WHITEHALL, MARCH 16, 1719.
(27TH N.S.)

My Lord,—Since my Letter of the last Post I have received Yr Exᶜʸˢ Dispatch of the 20th Inst. by your Servant, as likewise that of the 22nd by Mr. de Genes, with two more of the same date by the Common Post.

The Wind is so fair for us at present, that in all probability our Ships will be able to get to the Station they are ordered to, and as it is to be presumed their number will be sufficient for the Service they go upon, Yr Exᶜʸ need not press any further the sending those two French Frigats, which you proposed should join them. As for our Preparations by Land, I have already acquainted Yr. Exᶜʸ what measures we have taken therein; and you will have heard that both the Dutch and Imperialists are very well disposed to assist us with their forces if there should be any occasion for them.

Yr. Ex^cy will omit no opportunity of thanking the Regent in the King's Name, and assuring him in the civilest Terms of the Sense His Maj^ty preserves of the readiness H. R. H. has shewn on his part by the disposition of his Troops for our Assistance; but I cannot help repeating to Yr. Ex^cy with what surprise we observe, that while the Regent is giving us these marks of his good intention to do us Service, the way of serving us most effectually is defeated by withdrawing the Troops, as we hear they do, from the Frontier of Spain, where a vigorous Push would certainly make the most important Diversion, and quickly defeat all distant Projects. Even the so long projected Enterprize upon Port Passage is neglected for reasons which the King does not apprehend to be strong enough against the execution of it; and the late Duke of Ormond's embarking there with four Companys of Grenadiers is a Circumstance that makes us the more regret its having been retarded. Another Point which His Maj^ty thinks necessary to be taken notice of to H. R. H. is, that such numbers of Jacobites are permitted openly to embark in the Ports of France in order to disperse themselves over our Provinces, and to resort at their ease and wth convenience to their Places of Rendezvous, when at such a Juncture nothing should excuse France from publickly seizing and confining them; and I can see no reason why Dillon himself should not be arrested or sent to his Post.

. . . . . .

J. CRAGGS.

No. 32.

THE EARL OF STAIR TO SECRETARY CRAGGS
(*State Papers, Foreign, France*, 353.)

News as to sailing of Cadiz fleet, contradictory as to details—News that Earl Marischal and Tullibardine have sailed from Passage, and that Mar and Perth are going to Scotland through France—Orders given for their arrest.

A PARIS, LE 2^E D'AVRIL 1719.

MONSIEUR,—J'ay attendu tout aujourd'huy, pour estre en etat de vous mander quelque chose de certain touchant l'Armement de Cadiz, mais Je ne trouve que de l'Incertitude; Les

Avis venus à l'Ambassadeur de Portugal disent, que l'Armement fit voile le 6° de Mars, de Cadiz, composé de 2 Vaisseaux de Guerre, et de vingt Vaisseaux de Transport, et qu'il prenoit la route de la Gallice, ou, à ce qu'on croyoit on faisoit un autre Armement, à cause qu'on avoit arresté tous les Vaisseaux qui se trouverent aux Ports de la dite Province, entre lesquels il y avoit 6 Vaisseaux Portugais.

Les Avis de l'Ambassadeur d'Hollande portent, que l'Armement avoit fait voile le 7ᵉ au matin avec un bon vent, faisant route vers la Côte de Barbarie, composé de vingt six Vaisseaux tant gros que petits; On comptoit qu'il y avoit quatre mille hommes de Troupes.

Monsʳ l'Abbe du Bois m'escrit un Billet pour me dire, qu'il avoit veu une Lettre escrite de Cadiz du 13ᵉ, laquelle dit, que l'Armement estoit party ce jour là, faisant route vers la Côte de Barbarie, composé de 26 Vaisseaux tant gros que petits; On compte qu'il y a quatre mille hommes de Troupes d'embarquez. Il n'y a aucune Nouvelle des Côtes de Gallice. Tous les Avis de Madrid confirment, qu'on y attendoit le Pretendant en deux ou trois jours. Il a debarqué à Roses le 8ᵉ. Il a passé au bord d'un Vaisseau François avec Pavillon Genois.

Tout ce qu'il y a à conclure de l'Incertitude de ces Avis touchant l'Armement d'Espagne est, qu'il est peu considerable, et que selon les Apparences, il ne Nous fera pas grand Mal.

Monsʳ le Maréchal d'Estrees m'est venu voir cet aprèsdiner, et m'a dit, que le Conseil de Marine n'a aucune Nouvelle de Cadiz, touchant la Flotte; Ils ont bien de Lettres de Cadiz du 6ᵉ et du 7ᵉ, mais elles ne parlent point de la Flotte. Il m'a dit qu'il est arrivé à Marseille le 28ᵉ, un Vaisseau venant de la Martinique, qui avoit passé devant Cadiz le 4ᵉ ou le 5ᵉ, où il avoit veu devant le Port, vingt cinq ou vingt six Vaisseaux; que dans la Mediterranée il avoit trouvé l'Amiral Byng le 15ᵉ, qui croisoit avec onze Vaisseaux de Guerre, à la hauteur de Cap de Gatte, et Qu'il avoit ensuitte passé à Port Mahon, où il n'y avoit qu'un seul Vaisseau de Guerre.

Il est certain que c'est le Lord Tullibardine et le Lord Marishall qui se sont embarquez au Passage, Ceux-là peuvent fort bien être arrivez en Ecosse. J'ay eu Avis hier, que les Lords Marr et Perth devoient passer par la France pour se rendre en Ecosse ; J'ay communiqué cet Avis à Monsieur Le Duc d'Orleans et à Monsʳ l'Abbé du Bois ; On a envoyé des Ordres sur toutes les Routes, et aux Ports de Mer, de les faire arrester, s'ils entreprennent de passer par la France ; On a envoyé au même temps la Description de leurs Personnes.

Je suis tres parfaictment,
Monsieur,
votre très humble et très obeissant Serviteur,
Stair.

No. 33.

CARDINAL ALBERONI to JAMES

(*Stuart Papers*)

No news of fleet—News from Paris—Alarm of English ministry—Requests for French aid—Jacobite sympathies of French troops—Movements in Scotland—Favourableness of the opportunity—Anxiety for James's safety.

Sire,—Ce mattin a dix heures j'ay reçeu un Courrier de la Corogne sans la moindre nouvelle de L'escadre. Les Lettres sont dattées du 31 du passé. On a receu aussy des autres nouvelles de Paris par lesquelles on aprend que Le ministerre de Londres était dans une grande confusion et dans un grand allarme, qu'il demandoit a cor et a cris des trouppes au Reggent, et que les Francois qui devaient aller en Angleterre disoient hautement et publiquement, qu'ils iroient pour servir le Roy Jacques. Les mêmes nouvelles disent qu'il y avoit beaucoup de mouvement en Escosse, et selon Les apparences a L'arrivée du Comte Maréchal il mouvement se fera general ; que de tous cotes Les bons Escossois partoient pour se rendre dans Leur Pays. Par toutes les dites nouvelles on voit bien que la prnte situacion est assez favorable pour faire quelque tentatif ; aussi S. Mᵗᵉ Cat : a jugé de son honneur et du service de V. M. d'hazarder ses trouppes, plus tot qu'on dse qu'il a sacrifie tant des braves gens, et qu'enfin on Leurs a donné ce secours qui a été possible. S. Mᵗᵉ espere que V.M. apreuvera une telle resolution, et qu'elle ne produira qu'on bon effet pour L'auenir, et qui ne sçauroit qu'être estimée de toutes les gens de bien. Le tems icy est tres mauvais et si a Valladolid il est de même, V.M. aura bien a soufrir. Leurs Mtes. me chargent de dire a V.M. de leurs part d'aller a petites journées, et de ne pas parler de si grandes matières. Je diray franchement que le jour que V.M. est party de Madrid elle n'avoit pas bon visage. La vie de V.M. est très précieuse, et sans elle tout ce qu'on fait ne serviroit a rien. Il faut donc penser a se conserver, et croire que les ennemis de V.M. seroient ravis si elle même vouloit finir le proces. J'ay L'honneur d'etre avec un tres respectueux attachement de V. M^{te}.

Le très humble et très obeisant serviteur,
Le Card^l Alberoni.

Madrid, ce 4e Avril 1719.

No. 34.

The KING of SPAIN to JAMES

(*Stuart Papers*)

No news of fleet—Anxiety regarding it.

Au Buen Retiro ce 9e Avril 1719.

J'ay reçu avec beaucoup de plaisir la lettre de Vostre Majesté du 6e de ce mois et suis aussi sensible que je le dois aux nouvelles asseurances qu'elle veut bien m'y donner de son amitié que j'ose dire que je mérite par les sentiments que j'ay pour elle. Je suis très aise que vous continuassiez vostre voyage heureusement et je souhaitte de tout mon cœur que vous l'acheviez avec un bonheur parfait de toutes manières. Cela paroistroit presque seur si les bruits qui continuent a courir de la descente en Angleterre et qui y adjoutent mème des circonstances tres fauorable se trouuoient vrays, mais on ne peut pas y adjouter une foy entière, puis qu'il faudroit supposer que l'auis qu'on avoit enuoyé de la flotte au duc d'Ormond pour l'auertir de la venir joindre eust péri, ou eust ésté pris par quelque bastiment ennemy. L'ignorance ou nous sommes de la destinée de cette flotte dont on n'a point du tout entendu parler non plus sur les costes de Portugal peut cependant faire penser toutes sortes de choses et donner quelque rayon d'espérance touchant les brüits qui se sont répandus, puisque si il estoit arrivé quelque malheur, ou que les vents contraires fissent seuls du retardement il n'est guères naturel qu'on ne sceust depüis tant de jours quelque chose de la flotte sur les costes d'Espagne ou de Portugal. Vostre Majesté me rendera, jespère, la justice de croire que j'en attends des nouuelles auec bien de l'impatience, ses interests m'estant fort chers. Comme elle m'a marqué estre bien aise de sçauoir les nouuelles qui pouroient venir je luy enuoye des gazettes a la main du dernier courier de France et je la prie encore une fois de bien compter sur la sincérité de mon amitié pour elle. PHILIPPE.

No. 35.

THE QUEEN OF SPAIN TO JAMES

(Stuart Papers)

The Queen's hopes for the success of the enterprise—Assurances of friendship—Compliments to James on his Italian.

BUEN RETIRO, LI 9 APRILE 1719.

CON infinita mia soddisfazione ricevei ieri il foglio di V.M. del 6 del presente nel quale si compiace significarmi il suo felice arrivo a Beneuento, e di continuarmi li contrassegni della sua memoria verso di me. Ho sentito pure con sommo mio giubilo che V.M. sia contenta della risoluzione che ha preso il Re può essere certa che il Re non pensa ad altro che alli di lei maggiori vantaggi, dal canto mio spero ch'ella sarà persuasa quanto desidero che l'intrapresa rieschi bene, e quanto m'interesso, e interesserò sempre in tutto quello che la riguarda: Spero che V.M. sarà persuasa della sincerità dei miei sentimenti, e frattanto pregandola di volermi continuare la sua amicizia mentre l'assicuro della mia. ELISABETTA.

V.M. mi permetta che Le faccia li miei complimenti sopra la sua Lettera così ben scritta in italiano, pare che sia stata cent' anni in Italia. La prego perdonarmi la libertà che mi prendo, e di raffermarle la mia speranza.

No. 36.

REPORT AS TO THE DISPERSION OF THE SPANISH FLEET

(*Stuart Papers*)

Report by Captain of frigate *La Galera de España*—Course of fleet on leaving Cadiz—Dispersion by storm off Cape Finisterre—On April 3, in lat. 41°, had met ship belonging to fleet, which reported that of 24 horses on board only 8 were alive—Both ships short of water and provisions; were separated by storm on night of April 6; *La Galera de España* reached Corunna 9th—Had met Bristol ship; news from England—Guevarra believed to be about lat. 41° or 42° trying to collect fleet—Strength of fleet.

RELATION DONNÉ LE 9·ME D'AVRIL.

Le Capitaine de la Fregatte la Galera de España qui est un Vaisseau de la Flotte, Dit que la Flotte a été au Ouest accompagnant le Vaisseau St Francois de Bayonne qui va aux Indes avec une Balandre du Roy qui porte des Lettres pour Cartagene, et après cinq jours de Navigation ayant laissé les dits Vaisseaux a la hauteur de L'Isle Taburon appartenante aux Canaries, le Commandant de la Flotte Monsr Guevarra ordonna qu'on fit voile au Nord Nord-Est afin de prendre la hauteur du Cap Finisterre ce que toute la Flotte a fait degrèz, les gros vents de Nord-Est ont Separé les Vaisseaux, chacun prennant la Route qu'il a pû, et après trois jours que la Tempête a duré sans qu'on pût se mettre une demi jour a la Cape il n'a pu voir aucun Vaisseau jusqu'au 3me du Courrant etant a la hauteur de 41 degrez il recontra une Prise Anglois qui etoit de la Flotte, et ayant parlé au Capitaine il luy dit qu'il navoit plus que huit Chevaux de 24 qu'il avoit a son bord, et qu'il ne luy restoit que pour Six jours d'eau, et qu'il n'en donnoit que la demie ration, la même chose qui arrivoit a la Galera. Ces deux Vaisseaux ont restés ensemble trois jours voulant prendre la hauteur de 45 degréz, et furent separés la Nuit du 6me par un gros Vent et depuis il n'a rien Veu jusqu'a son arrivée dans ce port le 9me Avril ou il se trouve avec quelques Petites

Voiles et quelques Cordages de moins, et sans provisions pour les deux Compagnies d'Infanterie qu'il a a son bord, ayant eté obligé de partager les propres vivres avec les Soldats les derniers jours de sa Navigation.

Ce Capitaine ajoute que le 2e Courrant il a rencontré un Vaiseau de Fabrique Angloise mais avec un Capitaine et Passeports Francois come aussi la plus part de l'Equipage et l'ayant obligé de venir a Son Bord pour voir s'il netoit point Anglois il a veu ses factures et toutes ses papiers et qu'il alloit a la Martinique, et comme le Cap^{no} de la Galera feignoit de venir d'une longue Voyage il luy demanda d'ou il venoit et quelles nouvelles il avoit, il luy repondit qu'il sapelloit Jordan et quil y avoit huit jours qu'il etoit Sortie de Bristoll ou tout etoit dans une grande Confusion par l'attente du Prince de Galles, et que dans toute L'Angleterre on se pressoit extremement a oter quelques Gouverneurs des Places et de changer d'autres, mais qu'il ne scavoit pas qu'il etoit sorti aucun Vaisseau de Guerre si ce n'est quelques uns qui suivoient la route vers le Portugal, mais il nest pas certain si c'etoient des Vaisseaux de Guerre ou Marchandes.

Le dit Capitaine ajoute qu'il croit que Monsieur Guevarra se sera detenu a la hauteur de 41 ou 42 degréz, pour y ramasser les Vaisseaux de Transports et pour continuer sa Navigation, et que si celuy cy ne l'a point rencontré, cest que dans l'incertitude ou il etoit il est monté a la hauteur de 46 degrés pour venir de la a ce port sans tombre entre les mains des Ennemis, depuis qu'il s'est separé de la Flotte il n'a pas eu un seul jour de beau tems. Sa Flotte et composée de deux Vaisseaux de Guerre, une petite Fregatte de 24 pieces de Canon, 23 Vaisseaux de Transport grands et petits, une Tartane un Bregantin et un Bregantin Anglois qu'on a pris deux jours avant la Separation, et il ajoute que cette Flotte netoit pourveue de vivres et d'eau pour les Soldats de Transport que pour trent jours.

No. 37.

REPORT as to the DISPERSION of the SPANISH FLEET, dated April 10, 1719

(*Stuart Papers*)

Reports by Captains of four ships which reached Corunna April 10—The storm—Flagship dismasted, and lost most of her guns—Sufferings of the troops—Out of 15 companies on board the *Comte de Toulouse*, 8 men dead and 40 sick.

EXTRAIT DES RELATIONS DES CAPITAINES DES QUATRE VAISSEAUX QUI SONT ENTRÉS DANS CE PORT LE 10. AVRIL.

La Flotte est partie de Cadix le 7° Mars et a continue sa Navigation Sans accident jusqu'au 27. quelle a eté dispersée par un gros vent de Nordest, et chacun a flotte n'a eu que pour 30 jours de vivres et d'eau, tous les Capitaines auront pris le parti qui leur aura paru le plus convenable pour prendre port et ne point mourir de Faim et de Soif, ils n'ont donné que la demie ration aux Soldats et aux Chevaux se voyant desja presque au bout de leurs Vivres, les Chevaux sont fort defaits, et des 57 qu'on avoit Embarqués dans ces Vaisseaux il n'en est morts que trois.

Deux de ces Vaisseaux n'ont rencontrés aucun Batiments de la Flotte les deux autres Le Comte de Toulouse et la petite Fregatte la Rebecca ont veu L'Amiral, le Capitaine du premier dit qu'il avoit perdu tous ses Mats hors le Grand Mat et l'autre assure l'avoir veu quand il etoit entierement dematé, et qu'il avoit jette la plus part de son Artillerie dans la Mer cependant qu'il avoit trouvé le moyen de mettre une petite voile avec la quelle il faisoit route au Nord il etoit accompagné d'une Tartanne chargée de vivres et d'eau.

Un de ces Vaisseaux est en mauvais etat faisant beaucoup d'eau, et il faudra le decharger entierment pour le raccommoder.

Les Soldats ont Souffert extremement et sont dans un Etat pitoyable, des quinze Compagnies qu'il y a abord le Comte de Toulouse il y en a huit de morts et 40 malades.

Voicy en Substance tout ce qu'on Scait de la Flotte il a fait un gros Vent hier au Soir du Nord qui aura eloigné les Vaisseaux qui auront pu etre a portée d'entrer dans ce port. Mais aujourdhui le Vent est tourné favorable.

No. 38.

REPORT as to the DISPERSION of the SPANISH FLEET, dated April 13, 1719

(Stuart Papers)

Reports from ships which reached Vigo April 9, 10, and 11—Sufferings of the troops; want of food and water; loss of horses—British squadron has left Lisbon to look for the fleet.

EXTRAIT DES RELATIONS ENVOYÉES DE VIGO A MONS^R LE MARQUIS DE RISBOURG, RECEUS A LA COROGNE LE 13^{ie} AVRIL 1719.

Le 9^{ie} est entré dans le port de Vigo le vaisseau nommé le Mercure, avec 200 Soldats de transport qui ont souffert infiniment, n'aiant eu ni vivres ni eau les 4 derniers jours de leur navigation, de quoi plusieurs Soldats sont tombes malades.

Le 10^{ie} Sont entres dans le même porte les deux vaiss^x nommes le Guadaloupe, et la Fregate el Rosino, les quels ont abord Sept compagnies d'Infanterie, et trois de Grenadiers, dont il y a quelques Malades : le Guadaloupe est le vice Admiral, qui a a Son Bord l'Intendant, le Tresorier et 14000 pistoles, le tout est debarque.

Le 11^{ie} Sont arrives dans le port de Muros deux Vaisseaux nommés la Susanne Marie, et le Vedon, qui portent quelque Infanterie, et 13. Chevaux en tres mauvais estat, ils en ont jetté neuf a la mer, qui ont crevé faute d'eau. La Susanne Marie est en mauvais estat et fait beaucoup d'eau. On nâ encore aucune nouvelle du reste de notre Flotte. Mais ont écrit de Portugal qu'ne Escadre Angloise est sortie de Lisbone pour la chercher.

No. 39.

CARDINAL ALBERONI to JAMES

(Stuart Papers)

News of the Fleet—Four ships have arrived at Cadiz and four at Lisbon, much damaged—Orders have been given to furnish supplies for refitting as soon as possible—James had better remain at Corunna—A ship should be sent to let the Earl Marischal know of the disaster and that the fleet cannot now be ready for several months—General Gordon and 40 officers have left Bordeaux in two Swedish ships.

SACRA REAL MAESTÀ.

Dopo havermi consegnato queste Mta le due ingionte

mi commandarono sospendere la missione del Corriere lusingandosi che d'un giorno a l'altro si sarebbe ricevuta qualche nuova della Squadra. Alla fine hieri arrivarono Corrieri di Cadice e di Lisbona con avviso che nel pmo Porto erano arrivati q̄ro Legni molto mal trattati e nel Secondo altri quatro comprendendo gli uni e gli altri da tre mila Soldati con alcune reliquie di Cavalli che sono amazzati dal furore della grand^{ma} burrasca. Oggi pure arriva il Corriero della Corogna con l'avviso di quanto era colà arrivato come ha veduto. V. Mta, questi sono di que colpi della mano di Dio, a quali conviene rassegnarsi con sincera sommissione. Ho spedito a Cadice e a Lisbona perche con tutta la celerità possibile si inviano alla Corogna tutto il bisognevole per andare al riparo dei danni sofferti, però come si crede che La Capitana sia del tutto diarborata, il minimo degli alberi solo portera seco da quaranta giorni, aggiungasi il tempo che sarà necessario per comprarli in Lisbona e inviarli alla Corogna. Doppo essersi date queste provvidenze quali mirano al raccomodare la squadra si anderano osservando quali sarano le providenze che daranno i nemici e secondo quelle si regoleremo le nostre. Intanto pare più che necessaria la dimora di V. M^{ta} in cotesto luogo la quale non può che produrre nella pnte sittuat^{ne} delle Cose, che un buon effetto.

Il Duca d'Ormonde prima che havesse inteso la succeduta borasca, mi proponeva di scrivere in Olanda a D. Patricio Laules, perchè facesse passare armi in Scozia, come stava già da me progettato; però oggi le cose mutano di faccia e parmi che non ci sia altro che fare se non Spedire il Legno di S. Sebastiano che propone il Duca d'Ormonde, a fine d'avvisare Marescial del contratempo successo alla nostra squadra acciò possi prendere le sue misure, avvertendolo che quando non trovassimo impedim^{to} alcuno per parte degli Inglesi, che La nra Squadra non può porsi alla vela se doppo molti mesi; questa parmi l'unica e necessaria diligenza che può praticarsi con Maresciale, e tutta la sua Comp^a, sapendo di più che il Gnale Gordon con quaranta uffiziali si era imbarcato a Bordeaux sopra dua fregate Svedesi, una da lui Comprata, L'altra presa a nolo, sopra le quali haveva imbarcato alcuna porzione di polvere e viveri.

All' Intend^te si invia ordine perche assista cotesti uffiziali a conto di quello che donerà, di alcun soccorso. Il med° Intend^te ha bastante danaro in mano per supplire a tutto il bisognevole senza che abbia da porre mano in quello che sia sopra La Hermione. Questo è quanto per hora posso dire a V. M. riserendomi di ragguagliarla da quanto anderà succedendo e arriverà a mia notizia. Faccio alla M. V. umilissima riverenza.

di V. M.
Umiliss^mo devot^mo Servit^re
G. CARD. ALBERONI.

Madrid, li 16 Aprile 1719.

Quando non bastassero per le spese da farsi delle 24/m scudi, il S. Intend^te ha preso delle rendite reali all' hora potra prevalersi delle sette mila doppie che stanno sopra La Hermiona. Con Corriere che arriva in questo punto si sa essere arrivato in Cadice D. Baltasar Guevara con la Capitana disalberata seco non poco tempo (fa) però si sono datti li ordini piu pressanti per La maggiore sollecitudine. Per quello che riguarda la persona di V. M. non ho che riportarmi ai giusti e savi sentimenti di S. M^ta Cat. però non mi pare per hora che siamo nel caso di fare alcuna dichiarazione, ma bensi riservarla a migliore congiuntura e quando si presenterà il caso. Si e fatta riflessione che si potrebbe dare il Caso che Mr Mareschal havesse bisogno d'armi e munizioni scrivo al Duca d'Ormonde che dandoli L' avviso del suo contratempo li dica che quando havesse bisogno di d^te armi e munizioni l'ambasiat^e Cat^lo che sta in Hollanda ha ordine di fornirli. Oltre Le due p^me lettere di queste Maestà ne sono ingiunte altre due con la data d'oggi.

No. 40.

THE KING OF SPAIN TO JAMES

(Stuart Papers)

All diligence will be used to refit the expedition—Difficulty of getting arms over from Holland—The King's desire to help James; his anxiety for James's person.

AU BUEN RETIRO, CE 25^E AURIL 1719.

Nous venons de receuoir la Reyne et moy la lettre que Vostre Majesté nous a escrite par Connok et je réponds dans le moment pour ne point perdre de temps comme elle le souhaitte a ce dont elle l'a chargé. Vous pouuez estre asseuré qu'on travaille et travaillera a remettre tout en estat pour l'expédition auec toute la diligence et tout le soin possibles et je donnerai auec grand plaisir tout ce que vous me demandez pour cela. Il n'y a que la quantité d'armes qu'il sera difficile d'avoir, c'est a dire pour les faire sortir de Hollande car pour l'argent qui est nécessaire il ne manquera point. Ce m'est une si grande satisfaction de pouuoir contribüer au bonheur de Vostre Majesté et a la remettre sur un throsne qui lüy est si injustement usurpé que je népargnerai certainement rien pour cela et il faut espérer que Dieu voudra bien bénir une cause aussi juste que celle la.

Mon amitié pour vous m'a vous representeé ce que je pensois sur les risques que vous coureriez en vous embarquant, mais aprés tout c'est a vous a prendre sur cela aprés y auoir bien fait réflexion la résolution que vous croirez la plus conuenable pour vous. Comptez cependant encore que vous ne sçauriez me donner une plus grande marque de vostre amitie qu'en prenant soin de vostre personne, la conservation de Vostre Majesté m'estant plus prétieuse que je ne püis le lüy exprimer par celle que j'ay pour elle qui est asseurement telle qu'elle peut la désirer. PHILIPPE.

No. 41

THE QUEEN OF SPAIN TO JAMES

(Stuart Papers. On same sheet as No. 40)

Assurances of interest and friendship.

POUR ne pas multiplier L'incomodité a Vostre Majesté puisqu'elle à bien voulu m'escrire ensemble auec Le Roy je prens la Liberté de Luy escrire aussi au mesme temps. Je suis fort sensible aux Marques que vous me donnez de vostre souvenir, et vous pouvez compter que je minteresse tres veritablement a tout ce qui vous regarde. Je ne m'etends point sur Le reste de La Lettre de Vostre Majesté parcequ' Elle le pourra voir dans celle du Roy. Il ne me reste plus qu'a La prier de me vouloir continuer son amitié pendant que je L'asseure de la sincerité de la mienne.

ELIZABETH.

No. 42.

CARDINAL ALBERONI to JAMES

(*Stuart Papers*)

Enterprise to be renewed, but Expedition cannot be ready till August—Necessary preparations—Cammock thinks things can be ready in eight days—The Cardinal's opinion of him—Attempt will be made to send help to Scotland—Difficulty of getting arms over from Holland—Progress of French war—Nothing to be expected from Sweden—Lawless at Amsterdam—If Mar and Perth arrive, Alberoni will send them to Corunna.

SIRE,—Hier a huict heures de soir arriva Mr Conok avec le paquet de V. M. Il me parla aussy sur le memoire qui traitte d' l'affaire en question. V. M. verra par la lettre que le Roy Cat. luy escrit la resolution qu'il a prise de tenter une seconde fois l'entreprise; cependant il est bon que V. M. sache que l'execution ne le pourra faire qu'au comencement du moy d'aoust prochain. La dessus V. M. Doit prendre ses mesures. Il n'y a pas un bien de biscuit, il faut du tems a le faire et Se laisser reposer. M. le Mis de Risbourg, mande que pour en faire mil cinq cens quintaux il faut deux mois de tems. Il faut raccomoder les arbres des Vaissaux ; Il faut ramasser des Vaissaux de transport, Il faut rassembler le tout pour marcher ensemble ; enfin après des longues discussions qu'on a fait icy et L'avvis de Mr Patino qui luy seul a fait les deux expeditions de Sardegne, et Sicile, sans compter celle de Mallorque, dit qu'on ne scauroit être pret pour se mettre a la voile qu'au comencement du moy d'aoust prochain. Camok gran Visionaire dit qu'on peut composer le tout en huict jours. J'ay bien connu après le peu de probité qu'il a que c'est un drol tres dangereux Il a tenu et tient continuellement des discours aussy insolents, que je ne sçais pas come je ne l'ay fait mettre dans un cachot. Il n'espargne persone ; c'est tout dire. Ses discours sont Publics.

Quant à l'Escosse on tachera, d'y envoyer ce que V. M. dit, et elle peut être sur qu'on tachera de faire de son mieux. Pour les cens mil pistolles on tachera aussy de les fournir, aussy bien que les Canons, La poudre et les vivres. La difficulté consiste de livrer les fusils d'Hollande. L'argent est en Amsterdam dans les mains du Banquier Cesar Sardi, nonseulment pour vingt mil fusils, mais pour cinquant mil s'ils étaient necessaires. Par le recit que j'ay L'honneur de faire a V. M. c'est a elle de prendre les meseures qu'elle jugera a propos avec les bons amis qui sont en Angleterre. Les mouvements des francois sono forts et grands et je ne sçais pas Si on peut se flatter de la prouver come bons amis Ils ont doné six assauts formidables au Chasteau de Beonia en Navarre, et il L'ont emporté. Quant a la Suéde on voit bien qu'on ne sçauroit faire aucun fondement sur elle. La nouvelle Reyne a beaucoup a faire pour regler le dedans de son Royaume. Il est naturel qu'elle veuille prendre du tems et voir come les affaires d'Europe Se mettent; Cependant V. M. ne fera que bien d'envoyer son plein pouvoir a son home pour tout ce qui peut arriver.

Laules sera a cette heure a Amsterdam, ou il auroit été tres util, en cas qu'on eusse fait la descente en Angleterre. C'est pour ca qu'on lui ordona de partir de Lubec on il etoit, pour passer en Hollande. En cas que les ducs de Mar et de Perth arrivent a la cour ie les envoyeray a la Corogne, et on aura toute L'attention possible pour ce qui regarde V^{re} Maj^{te}. Par la premiere occasion j'envoyeray a M^r Le Car^{al} Aquaviva le paquet de V. M.

J'ay L'honeur d'etre avec un respectueux attachement,

De V. M^{te}
Le très humble et très obéisant serviteur,
Le Card^L Alberoni.

Madrid, ce 26 Avril 1719.

Je part dans cet Instant, de sorte que je ne sçaurais escrire plus au long a V. M. Leurs M^{tes} sont deja partis il y a deux heures. Je repete a. V. M. qu'on a donne les ordres pour travailler, et qu'on ne perdra pas un moment de tems.

Mr Conok est arrive, et come presentem^t il y est pas necessaire aupres de V. M. aussy et qu'il sera retably je pense de le faire venir en Cattalogne.

No. 43.

SIR TIMON CONNOCK to JAMES

(Stuart Papers)

MADRID, Y^E 28TH OF APRIL 1719.

S^R.,—When I arrived here I found the Court in a great bustle preparing for their march ye next morning for Valencia, and from thence to Catalonia. In this conjuncture I coud not acquit myself to my satisfaction of the Commission your Majesty honored me with. However, I did all, the little time I could have with the Cardinal, and the favor I had upon me coud permit.

The dutch Ambassador came out of his Eminency's as I went in. Upon what footting this Minister's negotiation is, passes my penetration, but I fear the violent situation of this Kingdome may oblige his Ca. Majesty to take measures for his Security, contrary to his inclination for y^r Majesty's Service.

I was an half an hower with his Em. who, after reading, s^r, your letter fell a reasoning upon it, he said, Patinio told him that in less than three months, the fleet, etc., coud not be repaired, and that then it woud be too late to expect to succeed in that enterprise. I replyed that that depended on the situation Spain is in, that if the C. K. coud weather out the time necessary to dispose all things according to the memoire inclosed, your Majesty and the Duke of Ormonde did not doubt but all woud go well, and that for my part seeing the disposition in England, wh his Em. woud allso se by Stamfort's memoire, and the measures of y^r Majesty and the Duke woud take, I woud not question the happy event, and I begged his Emi. to be persuaded, that haveing the honour to be of the expedition, I am too near my self, to strive to induce the King of Spain to an undertaking where I must succeed or loose my life, if we had not a fair prospect. Then we fell upon the measures to be taken. I told him I believed the Ferol a fit port for ships to be sent there with all necessarys, and the imbarkment to be made there, but that Patinio being here, I did not question, but his Eminencys projects and commands woud be executed at an other rate, and that he might examin him and Camock upon the fitting out the fleet, as particularly the latter upon the probability of avoiding the English fleet, lett them take whatever measures they will. The Card. fleu into a fury against Camock, and said he had no principels as to God, or man, that he was mad, and coud not be trusted, and a great lyer, etc. I replyed that with all these ill qualitys, great use might be drawn out of him, and that his knowledge of his trade, and especially of all the coasts of England, woud be of vast service.

The King sending for the Cardinal, interrupted the conversation. His Eminency took all the papers, caryed them to his M., and bid me see his Em. next morning ere we parted, which I did, as he was a dispatching a Courier to y^r Majesty, and bid me write there in his room and tell y^r Majesty that all measures possible shall be taken to push on this great dissign, but that all was to be feared from the sinking condition Spain is in, and that the Ennemies woud not leave us time to finish the dispositions necessary for the interprise.

The Cardinal being in haste, I writ in a hurry to my Lord Duke what the Cardinal had ordered me, and now I find myself in the same circumstance, for the Courier is staying for my letter, and I dear not detain him too long.

His Em. ordered me to stay here to recover my health, and that he woud send me orders to join the Court in Catalonia, where I shoud stay while the dispositions were a making, and that then I shoud return to the Groine.

I begg y^r Majesty's pardon for this scrole.

I have the honour to be, with a most passionate Zeal and a most profound respect,

S^r,

Your Majesty's

most humble, most obedient, and most devoted Servant and Subject,

TIMON CONNOCK.

No. 44.

CARDINAL ALBERONI TO JAMES

(*Stuart Papers*)

News of Princess Clementina's escape.

SIRE,—Toutes les lettres veulent que La Princesse Clementine sé soit sauvée d'Inspruk. On mande qu'elle a logée a Boulogne et que de la elle soit allée a Rome pour se mettre dans un Couvent. Je me flatte que tout cela puisse être vray et j'en felicite V. M^{te}. Leurs M^{tes} Cat. continuent a se bien porter graces a Dieu. Elles partiront demain pour Pampelune et y attendent La confirmation de la nouvelle pour en faire leurs compliments a V. M^{te}. J'ay l'honneur d'être avec un attachement très respectueux.

De V. M^{te}
Le très humble et très obéissant Serviteur
Le Card. Alberoni.[1]

Tudela ce 7e Juin 1719.

No. 45.

The KING of SPAIN to JAMES

(*Stuart Papers.*)

Congratulations on Princess Clementina's escape.

A Tudela ce 8e Juin 1719.

J'envoye ce courier a Vostre Majesté pour luy apprendre que la Princesse Clémentine Sobieski s'est sauuée d'Inspruck. Outre les avis que je vous envoye qui rapportent cette agréable nouuelle elle est confirmée de tous costéz avec ces circumstances, qu'elle estoit allée a Bologne ou on la disoit arrivée et que de la elle devoit passer a Rome. Je m'en réjoüis de tout mon coeur avec Vostre Majesté la priant de croire que je m'intéresse très vivement a tout ce qui la regarde et en particulier a la satisfaction qu'elle ressentira dans cette occasion. Nous partirons demain d'icy, s'il plaist a Dieu, la Reyne et moy pour nous rendre en 3 jours a Pampelune ou l'armée s'assemble actuellement et ensuite de la nous approcher des Français et tascher de secourir Fontarabie qui se deffend avec beaucoup de vigueur. Je prie Vostre Majesté d'estre toujours bien persuadée de mon amitié et de vouloir bien me continüer la sienne qui m'est très prétieuse.   Philippe.

---

[1] Alberoni wrote again on the 8th confirming the news of the Princess's escape.

No. 46.

THE QUEEN OF SPAIN TO JAMES

(*Stuart Papers*)

Congratulations on Princess Clementina's escape.

TUDELA LI 8 GIUGNO 1719.

BENCHE V. M. intendeva della Lettera del Rè la nuova di essersi salvata la mia cugina d'Inspruch non ho voluto tralasciare di rallegrarmene ben vivamente con lei sapendo con quanta ansietà V. M. lo desiderava e quanto io m' interessi in tutto quello che la riguarda, e però gliene porto i miei più sinceri complimenti. Domani partiamo per Pamplona, e in qualunque luogo io sarò, sarò sempre pronta servire V. M. che prego darmi soventi nove della sua salute, che gli bramo sempre perfetta e di credermi, che sono e sarò sempre, a suoi cenni. ELISABETTA.

No. 47.

CARDINAL ALBERONI TO JAMES

(*Stuart Papers*)

Instructions to Ambassador in Holland—Negotiations with Northern Sovereigns fruitless—Expedition to Scotland only useful if landing effected in England—Ships cannot be sent (to Scotland) from Corunna as James wishes, but measures will be taken in Holland—Progress of French war—King of Spain cannot count on anything but good intentions from his French supporters.

SACRA REALE MAESTA,—Tre sono li umanissimi fogli di V. M. ricevuti nell'istesso tempo, cioè de 14. 15. e 16 del corrente, con le due lettere per queste Maestà da me poste nelle loro Reali mani. Savia è la risposta di V. M. data, e per questa parte non si è lasciato di dare all'Amb^{te} d'Olanda li ordini necessarii; anzi dal med^{mo} s'intende havere fatto pagare una soma di danaro.

Creda V. M. che non si è tralasciata diligenza alcuna per guadagnare i Prpi del Nort, e si è gettato a quest hora qualche soma considerabile di danaro; però fin hora ogni nrā practica è riuscita infructuosa; que' min^ti ricevono danaro da ogni parte e tradis cono gli Interessi de loro Principi giachè essi sono irresoluti nelle loro risolusioni osserverà che sono tre anni che si parla dei Prpi del Nord senza che si sia veduto ad effettuarsi la minima cosa.

S. M. ha ordinato a questo Seg^rio dela Guerra perche si prendi una regola e provisione p i legni e gente che costì si trovano.

In quanto alle truppe di Scozia sempre si penso che queste potessero essere utili in caso si facesse lo sbarco in Inghilterra e cosi parmi si siano dichiarati i med^mi Scozesi i quali dissero che ogni loro fondata esperanza consisteva nello sbarco che farebbe il Duca d'Ormonde. Nel resto compatisco la Maestà V.; ben conoscendo quanto sia la pena che prova nel fare vivere assieme gente di differenti massime interessi ed inclinazioni.

Rispetti alle due navi che V. M. dice di fare allestire alla Corogna, oltre il tempo longo che è necessario, il pericolo d'essere predate è evidente; Si prenderano altre misure in Olanda, ove la trascita è piu facile, e meno pericolosa.

Io non so quali ordini aspetta Mr. Mattallan; se mi havessé scritto le sue intenzioni, se li sarebbe a quest' hora risposto categoricamente sapendo essere homo habile e honorato.

Resta dato corso alle lett^e di V.M. e qui ingionte riceverà altre che si sono havute da pmp^ti.

I francesi faño la guerra da davero. Si accingono all' ascedio di S. Sebastiano, che verrà principiato dentro di questa settimana. Ben si conosce che il Re mio Principe non può far conto alcuno sopra la nazione francese, nella quale non si trova che quella buona volonta, della quale anche. L'Inferno n' è ripieno. Queste Maestà si sono presentate all esercito francese in distanza di solo tre leghe, e senza che abbia dato il minimo segno di vita. Faccio alla Mt V. umillis^a riverenza.

Umiliss^mo devot^mo Servit^re,

G. CARDL. ALBERONI.

Campo di Cirasso, li 28 Giug^o 1719.

No. 48.

CARDINAL ALBERONI to JAMES

(Stuart Papers)

Arrangements for James's return to Italy.

SACRA REALE MAESTA,—Si spedisce il pñte corriero, afine che se mai mancassero viveri o altro alle due Galere, cot° Intend^{te} del Regno di Valencia ne facci subito la provisione. Ha ordine il commandante delle med^{me} di servire V. Majestá per lo sbarco in quel porto d' Italia che più piacerà alla M. V. Iddio sia quello conceda a V. M. un felice viaggio, sopra il quale l'assicuro che ne starò sommamente inquieto fino al sentirla gionto in Porto. Faccio alla Maestá Vr'a umiliss^{ma} riverenza

Di Vr'a Maesta

Umiliss^{mo} deuotiss^{mo} Seruit^{re}

G. CARD. ALBERONI.

Coreglia, li 12 (*Aug.* 1719).

No. 49.

THE KING OF SPAIN TO JAMES

(Stuart Papers)

Farewell on his leaving Spain.—Hopes for a safe voyage.

A CORELLA, CE 15 AOUST 1719.

JE suis fort sensible aux nouvelles asseurances que Vostre Majesté m'a données de son amitié dans sa lettre du 1er de ce mois aussi bien qu'a son éloignement et je serai fort inquiet jusques a ce que sçache son voyage heureusement terminé, souhaittant de tout mon cœur que puisqu'elle l'a jugé nécessaire pour elle, dans un conjoncture que le rend sujet a tant de risques, il lüy soyt aussi heureux que mon amitié sincère, sur laquelle elle peut toujours compter, me le fait desirer.

PHILIPPE.

Mon fils est très reconnoissant des bontéz de Vostre Majesté et il l'asseure qu'il a pour elle toute l'amitié qu'il doit.

No. 50.

The QUEEN of SPAIN to JAMES

(*Stuart Papers*)

Farewell—Compliments to Princess Clementina.

CORELLA, Li 16 Agosto 1719.

Li novi contrassegni della solita bontà di V. M. verso di me ancora nella presente congiuntura della sua partenza di quà, mi danno motivo di renderlene vivissime grazie. Dio sia quello, che la conduca felicemente ov'ella ha voluto and are con tanto suo rischio. Prego V. M. di fare li miei più sinceri complimenti alla Regina sua sposa e già che non hò potuto hauere la sorte di vederla, spero, che mi vorrà dare almeno qualche occasione di poterla servire in queste parti, assicurandola che sono sempre pronta come V. M. ancora a farle conoscere che sono, e sarò sempre a loro cenni.

ELIZABETH.

No. 51.

CARDINAL ALBERONI to JAMES

(*Stuart Papers*)

Has received news of James's sailing from Vinaros on Aug. 14—Regrets that as James's voyage had to be kept secret, better arrangements could not be made for his comfort—Journey of King and Queen of Spain to Madrid.

SACRA REALE MAESTA,—Con corriero spedito dal Duca di S. Pietro Si è oggi inteso il felice arrivo di V. Maestà in Vinaros e nel med^{mo} tempo l'imbarco con vento favorevole con la particolarità che alle due doppo mezzogiorno de 14. si havevano perdute di vista le due Galere. Iddio sia quello facci giungere La m^{ta} V. in Livorno e fin a tanto che non se ne abbia la notizia assicuro V. M. che qui si starà con pena. Ha havuto rag^{uo}, La M.V. di credere che era arrivato contra tempo al Corriero da me Spedito perchè apunto fù trattenuto do foruscito: Il dolore mio è che non hauendo uoluto far confidenzà dell' affare al Comand^{te} delle Galere se inviava ordine p. alcune provisioni ed altro p. il comodo del viaggio, che sa come lo farei

V.M.—Il med° Segreto Si è guardato con il Duca di S. Pietro e l' Intend^te ai quali si dava l' avviso con d^to Corriero, e se ordinava al med^m altre cose conducenti al viaggio di V. M.

Queste Maestà proseguirono il viaggio a Madrid con felicità, ove non arriverano che a piccole giornate l' ultimo del corrente. La M^ta della Regina porta bene la sua grauidanza. Faccio alla Maestà Vra umilissimo reverenza.

Di Vra Maestà
Umilisso^mo deuotiss^mo Servit^re
G. Card. Alberoni.

Inososa, Li 20 Agosto 1719.

No. 52.

JAMES to the KING of SPAIN

(*Stuart Papers*)

James back in Italy—His Marriage to Princess Clementina.

A Montesfiascone, 5 le Sep. 1719.

L'interest que Votre Ma^te a bien voulu prendre a l'accomplissement de mon mariage m'oblige encore plus a lui apprendre que vendredi dernier la Reine arriva ici, ou aussitot la ceremonie en fut faite par l'Evêque de cette ville. Je me trouve dans le derniere impatience de scavoir des nouvelles de l'Espagne et de la bonne santé de Vos Matés, et je me flatte que vous etes bien persuadé que mon attachement, ma reconnoissance et mon amitié n'auront d'autres bornes que celles de ma vie.

Jacques R.[1]

No. 53.

JAMES to the DUKE of ORMONDE

(*Stuart Papers*)

Montefiascone, 5 Sept. 1719.

I writt to you from Legorn a letter which was to return with the Spanish gallys, and at the same time I made John[2]

---

[1] An Italian letter, in similar terms, from James to the Queen of Spain, written along with No. 52, mentions his intention of immediately returning to Rome.

[2] Probably John Hay. See p. 152 note.

write to you by the french post, easily believing you would be impatient to know of my safe landing, and I have now the pleasure of letting you know that the Queen arrived here on fryday night, and we were immediately marry'd by the Bp. of this place, without any regard to the ceremony performed at Bolonia, for my orders and intentions in that respect had been so nicely observed, that upon examination it was found to be no mariage at all, but only a solemn confirmation of the Contract and a necessary step in me by which the Queens escape was authentically approvd by me, and she intitled in the eye of the world to take my name upon her.

It is no more my business now to publish the Queen's praises, but to a friend with whom I have no reserve, I cannot but say once for all, that she has surpassd my expectation, and that I am happy with her.

Having not heard since I came in to this Country either from Spain or England, I have nothing of business to entertain you with at present, but I am very impatient to have some comfortable news from your Card[1] as to mony matters. The heats are here in a manner over, but I shall not go to Rome till the middle of next month at soonest.

The Queen will write to you, if she can, with this post. I thank God my health is very good, as I hope this will find yours. May happiness be as inseparable from you as my kindness, and you'l have no reason to complain, wch is all I have at present to say, and that I am Intirely yours.

Pray remember me kindly to Dick Butler, and make my compliments to your good Vicepresident, with whom I suppose you now are.

No. 54.

PRINCESS CLEMENTINA TO THE DUKE OF ORMONDE

(Stuart Papers)

Thanking him for his letters and assuring him of her regard—Feeling towards Britain; Hopes for a restoration—Compliments to Duchess of Ormonde.

DE MONTEFIASCONE, 11 SETT^{RE} 1719.

MON COUSIN,—J'ay reçu avec plaisir depuis je suis icy vos

lettres de 4[1] et 22 Juillet ; votre merite distingué auprès du Roy, et votre attachment singulier pour sa personne, ne me rendent point douteux vos sentiments a mon egard, et vous doivent etre des gages assurés de ceux que j'ay et conserveray tojours pour vous. Il est vray j'ay eu quelques travers et fatigues a essuyer depuis quelque tems mais je m'en trouve suffisement recompensé par le bonheur present dont je jouis, et je serois trop contente s'il ne falloit que les renouveler pour rendre heureuse une nation, pour laquelle j'ay toujours eu un si haute estime, et que je regarde a present comme ma propre patrie. Mais j'espere que apres tant de malheurs, zele indefatigable pour un si juste fin, et qu'ayant eu la gloire de le perfectioner vous en partagiez les avantages et le douceurs avec nous. J'appris avec satisfaction, la distinction que le Roy vouloit faire La D^{sse} d'Ormonde, en la mettant seulle aupres de moy avec lettre de charge, et le mauvaise estat de sa sante me fait d'autant plus de peine que je croye quelle ne me plaie pour un temps de la Compagnie la quelle en pouvoit que m'est aussi avantageux. Je vous prie de luy faire un millier de compliments de ma part, et d'etre persuadés l'un et l'autre qu'on ne pouroit rien adjouter a l'estime parfait et a l'amitie sincere dont je suis penetree a vos egards estant

Votre affectionee Cousine,
CLEMENTINE R.

No. 55.

JAMES TO CARDINAL ALBERONI

(Stuart Papers. There is a copy of this letter in the Carte Papers, Bodleian Library, vol. 308, f. 322.

James thanks Alberoni for the trouble taken about his voyage—Urgent need of money—No assistance to be hoped for from the Pope—The 4000 pistoles received from the King of Spain by James all that he has for the maintenance of his household—Debts—Friendliness of Cardinal Acquaviva.

A MONTEFIASCONE, CE 14 SEP^{BRE} 1719.

J'AY receu ce matin vos lettres du 12, du 17, et du 20 Aoust,

---

[1] Letter CXXXVIII. The letter of July 22d does not appear to have been copied.

et vous suis sensiblement obligé des attentions que vous avez bien voulu avoir a l'egard de mon voyage. Vous en aures deja sceu l'heureuse fin et que l'accident arrivé a votre Courier n'a rien retardé ni derangé, car pour tout le reste nous avons eté a merveil abord des galeres. Comme dans uos trois lettres vous ne me dites pas un mot ni de Monsr le Franc, ni des paquets dont je l'avois chargé pour vous, je crains positivement que quelque accident ne lui soit arrivé, et c'est pourquoy je vous envoye ici une Duplicate des dits paquets, auxquels je n'ay pour le present rien a adjouter, si non de vous conjurer de faire quelque attention au Memoire, car nous n'avons rien a esperer du coté du Pape, et sans un prompt secours je ne scais ce que deviendra meme le peu de monde que j'ay a Rome, puisque les quatre mil pistoles que le Roy m'a donné en partant est tout ce qui me reste au monde pour les subsister. Je dois meme quelque peu d'argent dans ce pais cy, et sans les 3000 Ecus que le Cardinal Acquauiua prit sur luy de faire toucher a Monsr Murray, c'auroit eté encore pire.

Il me coute bien de toute sorte de manieres de vous dire ces verités, mais la necessité n'a point de loy, et je ne ferois pas meme mon devoir si je ne m'addressois ou je puis seul trouver du secours en faveur de ceux qui ont tant souffert et tant perdu pour moy, et je ne scaurois m'empecher d'adjouter que le mal presse et demande un prompt remede. J'ose m'y attendre de la bonté et de la generosité du Roy, et je m'asseure qu'après avoir eté si essentiellement de mes amis, vous le seres encore efficacement dans cette occasion.

La bonne santé de leurs Ma^{tés} me rejouit infiniment, il seroit a souhaitter que tout le reste y repondit, et vous ne doutes je crois de mes voeux ardents a cet effet.

J'ay eu le plaisir de voir hier a Viterbe le Cardinal Acquauiua rempli de zele pour ses maitres et d'amitié pour moy, et je me flatte que vous luy scaurés bon gré de toute celle qu'il nous a temoigné a la Reine et a moy. Continuez moi je vous prie la votre, et soyez persuadé que la mienne pour vous augmente s'il est possible tous les jours.

No. 56.

JAMES to the KING of SPAIN

(Stuart Papers.)

Refers to preceding Letter to Alberoni—Philip now James's only resource—Assurances of devotion.

Je recois ce matin la lettre dont V. M. m'a honnorée du 15 du passé et me trouve penetré de la bonté dont Elle me comble, j'en ay receu tant et de si grandes preuves que je ne pourrai jamais douter ni de sa sincerité ni de Sa constance, et aussi y ay je une confiance entiere dans un tems ou je me trouve necessité de l'importuner, et sans resource que dans Elle. Je ne repeterai pas ce que je mande au Card^l sur ce sujet, et je ne doute nullement que V. M. n'y donne quelque attention, et ne laisse agir en cette occasion sa sagesse et sa generosité ordinaires. De mon coté Elle me trouuera toujours prest de la servir avec plaisir en tout ce que je luy pourrai etre bon a quelque chose, et j'ose l'assurer avec verité que ma reconnoissance et mon attachement sinceres pour elle n'auront d'autres bornes que celles de ma vie. La bonne santé de Vos Mat^{es} et l'heureuse grossesse de la Reine me font un sensible plaisir, fasse le Ciel que mes voeux soient exaucés, et vous aures l'un et l'autre tous les bonheurs que uous merites.

Jacques R.

No. 57.

PRINCESS CLEMENTINA to the QUEEN of SPAIN

(Stuart Papers)

Gratitude for all her kindness.

De Montefiascone, ce 14^m Sett^{re} 1719.

Je suis trop sensible aux expressions obligeantes dont V. M^{te} eu bien voulu se servir a mon endroit, dans sa lettre au Roy pour ne luy en pas temoigner moy meme ma sincere et parfaite reconnoissance. Le Roy n'ose pas importuner V. M^{te} si souvente luy meme par ses lettres, mais il me charge de l'assurer que ses sentiments pour V. M^{te} repondent entierement aux bontes dont elle nous comble l'une et l'autre, et nous avons une confiance entiere qu'elle voudra bien nous en accorder la continuation dans un tems ou nous n'avons d'autres ennemis que ceux de V^{os} Majestiés, n'y d'appuy et de consolation veritable que dans elles, envers qui notre attachment et notre amitié dureront a jamais.

J'ay cru que V. M^{te} trouveroit bon que je luy escrire desormais sans cerimonie Je la supplie d'en user de meme envers moy et de me regarder comme une parente qui luy est sincerement devouée.

No. 58.

JAMES TO THE DUKE OF ORMONDE

(*Stuart Papers*)

MONTEFIASCONE, SEP^{TER} 14TH, 1719.

THO' it was scarce possible I could yet hear from you, you'll easily believe how impatient I am to do so. I have not att present any thing material to say to you, but I would not however miss this occasion of letting you know we are all well, as I hope this will find you. I'm in pain for poor le Franc for I dont find your Cardinal has received the letters I writ by him and so I send him now duplicates of them, and I wish I may have a speedy and favourable answer, for the truth is we are in a terrible way as to money matters and the more that the Pope dos, I may say, behave ridiculously towards us, in which he certainly dos himself more dishonour than real hurt to us, for that I'm sure he will not do, and for the rest we slight it very much.

I have had yet no fresh accounts here of the D. of Mar, but I cannot but hope he will gett his liberty when it is once known I am in this Country. Our people at Rome easie again now, and I believe I shall find them so when I go back there. I believe Wogan gives an account to his friend Talbot of himself and his three companions,[1] I'm sure I have reason to be pleased with them, and they are modest enough to be it with

---

[1] See Introduction, p. lvi.

me. I say nothing to the Cardinal of some of them refusing the Spanish Commissions, because it is always good to have that in store in all events, and if they are useless att last, I can easiely return them. I had a letter from D——n returned me now from Spain, he refers me to you for particlurs for want of a cypher with my self, but I hope by this time he has gott that which I sent him, and when he knows where I am I shall to be sure hear fully from him. Pray remember me very kindly to poor Maigny who dos not I'm sure want my recommendation to make you do all what lyes in your power where you are for him. Tho' I have had three letters this day from your Cardinal I am n'ere the wiser for them, which makes me fear there was nothing good to be writ. I thought I had nothing to say when I begun my letter and yet I have made a shift to make it a long one. To which I have nothing now to add but that I am sincerely yours.

No. 59.

JAMES to the DUKE of ORMONDE

(*Stuart Papers*)

MONTEFIASCONE, 3 OCT. 1719.

I THINK it an age since I had the satisfaction of hearing from you, but I hope I shall not be now long depriv'd of it for I reckon tho' you should have even nothing to say you will however give me often the pleasure of hearing from you. I shall make Murray or Nairne write a line to you at least once a fortnight by Paris that you may know we are alive, but as for business it is not to be venturd any other way but by sea. A felouca parts every fortnight and by that occasion you shall never miss hearing from me.

Your servant parted some time ago, and will I hope be safe with you before this. I sent you by him a little snuff wch I hope will come safe. Will. Gordon the marchands son is gone into Spain. Pray do what can to get him into the Spanish service for he is a pretty young man, and the father deserves well of me.

I am curious to know what reception your Card^l made to

the stranger I sent to him from Lugo, if what we hear be true, I fear there is little good to be expected at present from that branch of our hopes. In the meantime I am endeavouring to discover the sentimens of your northern Landlord, of wch you shall be informed when I am it myself. I dare say the good will is not wanting, but which way it can be applyd in our favour is the question. D. of Mar is still at Geneva and has not as yet so much as leave to go to the waters, which his health very much requires. I cannot think it possible but that he will be at least allowd to return to me, and till I see more clearly in to the contrary I shall not torment myself about it. In the meantime I shall be my own Secretary for which I am not like to stand in need of much help, not at this time that our affairs are in a manner all at a stand. Tho' I had nothing now to mention to your Card[1] I have writt to him to keep up that correspondence from this Country. I have nothing now to tell you, but that the Queen and I are, thank God, very well, and still resolvd to go to Rome the beginning of next month, and when we come there I'l send you her picture which you will not I believe be sorry to have. I expect Card. Gualterio here in a few days, who is a worthy honest man, as you know, and a true friend to us. I am very impatient to have a return from Spain on the Memoire about mony, for we are almost quite aground at present. As occasion offers you will do well to press the Card[1] on that head. D——n informs you I suppose about Brig. Campbel, if he has not sent him to you. It is pitty so many zealous people should be at present useless, but I see no remedy nor any other party they have to take but to return and wait in Spain for a more favorable opportunity. I write to this effect to D——n, who has not yet received the new Cypher, so that till I know 'tis safe in Engl^d and with him it is in vain to make use of it. I have nothing at present to add but that my kindness and best wishes neither don or ever will fail you.

Postscript.—I keep your letter to D. Mar till we meet to give it him myself, but have taken care he should not be ignorant of your kind sentiments towards him.

No. 60.

JAMES TO THE DUKE OF ORMONDE

(*Stuart Papers*)

MONTEFIASCONE, OCTOBER 14TH, 1719.

HAD I any thing material to inform you of att present, I should be a good dale perplexed, for there is no more writing to you by sea, as I am informed by my friend at Rome, tho he dos not tell me the reason of it, and not being as yet able to make use of the cypher we have, I have no other way to send my letters but through France. I received some days ago yours of the 19th, 29th, and 30th of August all together.[1] I am glad you are gott saffe to Valladolid, which tho' but a melancoly place, is, I beleive, att best better than Lugo. Mrs Ogilthrops and Abrahams letters contained nothing att all, but a great deal of self justification or old storys. I made Kennedy acknowledge the receipt of them, not being very fond of corresponding *en droiture* with all sort of honest people. Pray tell Da. Kennedy that I am very well pleased with his brother. I have employed him a little already for writing, and am likely to continue to do so.

I perceive that the D. of Mar has little or no hopes of his liberty for this winter; he has sent for My Lady to him, whom I expect here in a few days; but I cannot but hope by Spring he will one way or another be able to return to me. You will have heard to be sure of Brigadeer Campbells being come from Scotland. I heartily wish his companions were it, and in the mean time have writ to him, that both he and they cannot do better than go to Spain, where they cannot but be well received, and where you will, I doubt not, do all in your power for their assistance. You may remember I wrote about them to the Cardinal before I left Spain in a letter of which I left a copy with you. You do well to send Jolly to Valencia, for it was not worth asking an escorte for him, especially since the troops in Cattolagina [*sic*] have, I fear, but too much work on

---

[1] Letters CLXXI, CLXXVIII (?) and CLXXXI; '29th' should perhaps be 23rd.

their hands. You mention a friend of yours being desirous to quit the bad company he is in,[1] but I think there is *pro* and *con* to be said in the matter, the decision of which I have left entirely to himself, for he may no doubt be useful to his friends in both places. Our news from Sicily is very irregular and very uncertain, so I shall say nothing of it here. We have had a prodigious quantity of rain of late, which makes this a very melancoly place; however, we must have patience for three weekes longer. The Queen is, thank God, very well, and returns you her kind compliments. I have att present no more to add, but that my best wishes and constant kindness ever attend you.

I heard some time ago the D. of Perth was gone to Spain. If he should be there when this comes to you, pray facilitate his return to Rome, whether I would have him return immediatly, and lett him know as much with my kind compliments.

---

[1] This probably refers to Dillon.

II

PAPERS RELATING TO EVENTS IN SCOTLAND

No. 61.

The MARQUIS of TULLIBARDINE to the EARL of MAR

(Stuart Papers)

Islandonan, April 29th, 1719.

My Lord,—Tho' we have gone through a good dale of uneasiness since my last at imbarquing neare Hanfleur, yet can add little heare, only refer to whats inclos'd at present, tho I must say that my Lord Marischall has been very teasing, particularly by keeping a fifth part of the little money was sent for his Majestys services, which its possible may incommod us, but I hope things will mend or a way be found to prevent rash measures for the future. I'm sorry that Brig^r Campble seems to run headlong into the most violent proceedings, which I am afraid will appeare to much at this occasion, a litle time will make all plaine, we are in great paine how to behave without instructions in case there be not quickly a landing in England. Your Grace will soon perseve our precarious condition, so shall insist no farther, being with the utmost respect, faithfully,

My Lord, your Graces Most Humble and Most Obedient Servant,   Tullibardine.

No. 62.

The MARQUIS of TULLIBARDINE to the EARL of MAR

(Stuart Papers)

My Lord,—Since what I write by Mr Douglas, there has been no means untryed to get people together so as to keep life in the affair till we should have some certain accounts of the expedition from Spain, or else the Kings commands, which would enliven every body and make things go right, in expectation of that with a great deal adoe a few of the Clans were prevailed on to send some small assistance, which was gathering, that we might be able to keep together when their came accounts of the Enemys march from Inverness with above twelve hundred horse and foot. On the fifth Lochiel came first up with near one hundred and fifty men, and finding others could not soon enough join us, so as that we might be in a condition to fight the Ennemy, we went about three miles from Glenshell to view the narrow passes in the little Glen, hoping to maintain the Rough Ground till people that were expected should come up on the seventh. My Lord Seaforth met us and told me he had brought to the Crow of Kintaile about five hundred of his men who, it was thought, would heartily defend their own Country. On the eight Rob Roy's son brought a Company of men who, with some volunteers, made up near Eighty. That night we got accounts the enemy were removed from Gilly whining[1] to the Braes of Glenmoriston, which made us march early next morning, till that part of the pass at Glenshellbegg, which every body thought the properest place for defence, in which we posted our selves the best way we could. In the evening one hundred of Mr Lidcoats[2] people came to us, and the same night my brother George who was on the outguard sent word that he saw the Enemy in Camp at the end of Loch Clownie, within four or five miles of us. Next morning he sent again to inform us they were decamp'd and moving slowly forward. About ten a Clock fifty men joined us, and at twelve McKinnin came with fifty more which were the last, for tho' several men that were to been with us [were] on the top of the mountains on each side, yet they did not descend to incorporat with the rest. I suppose because they thought the Enemy too near us, who as they advanced Lord George retyrd, keeping all the way about half a mile from them till they came in our sight, which was at two a clock in the afternoon. They

---

[1] Cilla-chuimein, 'the church of Cumin,' the old Gaelic name of Fort Augustus. It is spelt in a great variety of ways.

[2] See Introduction, p. l. note 2.

APPENDIX 271

halted at near half a miles distance to make there disposition for the attack, which was between five and Six a clock at night. We had drawn up to the right of our main body on the other side of the water upon a little Hill about one hundred and fifty men, including the Companys of my Lord Seaforths, besides above four-score more were allotted for that place who was to come from the top of the Hill, but altho' they sent twice to tell they were coming, yet they only beheld the action at a Distance. This party was commanded by Lord Geo. Murray, the Laird of McDougal, Major Mcintosh, and John of Auch, ane old officer of my Lord Seaforths people; at the pass on the other side of the water were first on the right the Spanish Regiment which consisted of about two hundred men, about fifty more of them were left behind with the Magazine, several of them being Sick. The next in the Line was Locheill with about one hundred and fifty. Then Mr Lidcoat's and others, being one hundred and fifty, twenty volunteers, next fourtie of Rob Roy's, fiftie of McKinnins, and then two hundred of my Lord Seaforth's men Commanded by Sr John McKenzie of Coul; on the left of all at a considerable distance on a steep hill was my Lord Seaforth posted with above two hundred of his best men, where my Lord Marshall and Brigadeer Campble of Ormondell Commanded with him, Brigadier M'Intosh commanded with the Spanish Colonel, Brigadeer Campble of Glenderwell and myself commanded in the center, where we imagin'd the main attack would be, it being by far the easiest Ground, besides the only way thro' the Glen. However, it happen'd otherways, the Enemy placed there horse on the low Ground, and a battalion of them on there left, with there Highlanders on the fare side of the water, all the rest of there foot was on a rising ground to there Right. The first attack they made was on our men with Lord George on the Right, by a small detachment of Reed coats and there Highlanders, who fired several times at other without doeing great damage, upon which they sent a second and third detachment that made most of those with Lord Geo. run to the other side of a steep Burn where he himself and the rest were afterwards obliged to follow, where they continued till all was over, it being uneasy for the enemy to pass the hollow Banks of that Burn. When they found that party on our Right give way there Right began to move up the Hill from thence, to fall down on our left, but when they saw my Lord Seaforths people, who were behind the steep Rock, they were oblig'd to attack them least they should been flank'd in coming to us, upon which the Laird of Coul (most of whose men began to goe off on the seing the enemy) mov'd up with his Battalion to sustain the rest of the McKenzies, which oblig'd the Enemy to push the harder that way, on which on my Lord Seaforth sent down for a Reinforcement, and immedately after Brigadier Campble of Ormondell came likewise, telling it was not certain if there main body would not just then fall upon our Centre, which made Rob Roy with the M^{c}grigors and McKinnin the longer of drawing off to there assistance, but seeing them give way he made all the dispatch he could to join them. But before he could get up, so as to be fairly in hands with the Enemy, Lord Seaforths people were mostly gone off, and himself left wounded in the Arm, so that with difficulty he could get out of the place. Rob Roy's detachment, finding them going off, began to retyre. Likewise, that made us still send off fresh suplys from our left, so that Mr. Lidcoats men and others, seeing every body retire before them, did also the same, and the enemy, finding all give way on that hand, they turn'd there whole force there, which oblig'd us to march up the Camerons, who likewise drew off as others had done; at last the Spaniards were Called and none standing to Sustain them, they likewise were oblig'd to draw up the hill on our left, where at last all began to run, tho' half had never once an opportunity to fire on the Enemy, who were heartned on seeing some of ours once give way, and our oun people as much discourag'd, so that they could never be again brought to any thing. But all went off over the mountains, and next morning we had hardly any body togeither except some of the Spaniards. I then proposed to my Lord Marshall, Locheill, Brigadier Campble and all present, that we should keep in a body with the Spaniards and march thro' the Highlands for some time till we could gather again in case of a Landing, or else should the King send instructions, the Highlanders would then rise and soon make up all that was past. But every body declar'd against doing any thing further, for as things stood they thought it impracticable, and my Lord Mairshall with Brigadier Campble of Ormondell went off without any more adoe or so much as taking leave. The Spaniards themselves declared they could neither live without bread nor make any hard marches thro' the Country, therefore I was oblig'd to give them leave to Capitulate the best way they could, and every body else went off to shift for themselves; so that all we could make of My Lord Marishalls ill concerted expedition is to be now shamefully dispers'd at last. However if a Landing happens soon in England the Highlanders will still act their part. But if the Expedition be retarded our being brought away so very unreasonably will I'm affraid ruin the Kings Interest and faithful subjects in these parts; seeing we came with hardly any thing that was realy necessary for such an undertaking or the Kings immediat Instructions how to behave on all events that might happen, which was absolutely necessary; seeing otherwise nothing could be done to purpose among the people at Home without a Landing in England, I and some others with the Clans concern'd will endeavour to keep private till we know how affairs are like to go.

Your Grace has here a full account of what has happen'd since my last, by which you'l see to what a miserable condition we are now reduc'd, and his Majestys affairs in these parts are infallibly at the brink of ruin unless there be some speedy succour at Hand. It is not to be imagin'd how much people are dispirited at the manner of our Coming and there has not been as yet so much as one word sent us from any that have the manadgment of affairs. But hopeing there will be ere long good accounts I 'le say no more, being,

My Lord,

Your Graces most Humble and most Obedient Servant,

TULLIBARDINE.

Glen G(arry), 16th June 1719.

No. 63.

THE EARL OF SEAFORTH TO JAMES

(*Stuart Papers. Received at Rome Dec. 22, 1719*)

SIR,—Your Maj^{ties} I received by Captain Barkley, and am most sencible of the regard, and kindness, you are pleased to honour me with. I read the two letters of May ye 1st and june the 9th you ordered to be communicated to me, and regrates from the bottom of my hart the unlucky situation of circumstances, not upon mine, but your Maj^ties account.

I will not pretend, Sir, to give you a detaile of things here, since you have not honoured me with the trust of any, only to assure your Maj^tie that as there was no men engag'd in the late action of Glenshell but mine, and those but few (tho a great many standing by) so there are non more reddy on all occasions to shew there zeale for your service, when opportunity offers.

I am sorry I am forc'd to acquaint your Maj^tie that your affairs here are brought to so low an ebb (by whose fault I wont say) that there nothing remains but every one to shift for him self, and y^t by ye advise of him you honour with your commands, I still made it my studdy (upon which account I suffer most of any) to serve your Maj^tie to ye utmost of my power, and tho I be once more oblig'd to leave my native country, as in all probabilty I must, to wander abroad, in what ever place fortune alots my abode, I shall always beg leave to subscrive my self, with the proundest regret,

    Sir,
      Your Maj^ties most dutifull subject
        and most Obedient humble servant,
                          SEAFORT.

Aug. ye 10th, O.S., 1719.

No. 64.

GENERAL LORD CARPENTER, COMMANDING IN SCOTLAND, TO **CHARLES DELAFAYE,** SECRETARY TO THE LORDS JUSTICES.

(*Home Office Papers, Scotland, Bundle* 14, *No.* 58)

                              EDINBURGH, 27TH JUNE 1719.

SIR,—Last night at 9 I received yours of the 23^d, with their Excellency's orders to send the Spanish prisoners under a sufficient guard to Plymouth, and I write by this opportunity to Mr. Treby, for appointing guards to receive them on the

Borders, my routs being good no farther, whose answer will be here before those prisoners can come to this place.

Lord Justice Clerk and I are endeavouring to discover what persons of note, being his Majesty's subjects, were engag'd in this Rebellion. I suppose you have writt the same to Mr. Wightman in your letter, that I have this morning early forwarded to him; however, I have writt to him to the same purpose.

Hearing he had taken one Arnott, a Rebell Doctor or Surgeon, I writt to Mr. Wightman on the 22d, to send him hither by the Dragoons, or first Troops that march this way, giving the Commanding officer a strict charge to take care he do's not make his escape. No doubt but he can tell us of all persons of any consideration who were with the Rebells, or had engag'd to join them.—I am,

      Sir,
    Your most humble Servant,
        CARPENTER.

Charles Delafaye, Esqr.

No. 65.

LORD JUSTICE-CLERK COCKBURN[1] TO CHARLES DELAFAYE.

(Home Office Papers, Scotland, Bundle 14, No. 57)

        EDINBR., 27TH JUNE 1719.

SIR,—As has been done hitherto, so shall it be continued to give the Clergy all encouragement to come in and take the oaths, tho' they had not the opportunity before the first of June; Shirreffs have been written to, that they should admit the Clergy to qualifie whenever they applye, and severalls have appeared before the Court of Session and taken the oaths. As

---

[1] Adam Cockburn of Ormiston, appointed Lord Justice-Clerk in 1692, dismissed from all his offices on the accession of Queen Anne, reappointed 1705. He was superseded as Lord Justice-Clerk in 1710 by James Erskine of Grange, but retained his seat on the bench as an ordinary Lord of Session till his death in 1735. In the papers of 1719 he is frequently referred to as 'Lord Justice-Clerk,' though not actually holding the office at the time.

to the Recusants, who is to put **the Laws** in execution? I'm affrayed without a special direction for that effect, there **shall** be no prosecution either **of** these of the established Clergy or these for the Episcopall meeting houses. What their Excellys. **comand as** to the procuring ane exact List of all his Majys. subjects of any note who are engadged in the present Rebellion, wt the proper evidence to convict them, My Lord **Carpenter** and I had both of us written North to the same purpose, but in Regard there are so few prisoners, we apprehend ane exact List will be very difficult, and will require some **time**. But nothing shall be omitted to give yr Excellys **satisfaction** is in the power of him who is in great truth,

Sir,

Your most obedient and most humble Servant,
AD. COCKBURNE.

No. 66.

MAJOR-GENERAL WIGHTMAN TO CHARLES DELAFAYE

(*Home Office Papers, Scotland, Bundle* **14,** *No.* 60)

INVERNESS, JUNE THE 30TH, 1719.

SIR,—I had the Favour of yours of the 23d Instant, and am infinitely obliged to their Excellencies the Lords Justices, and have a very gratefull Sense of the particular Honour they have been pleased to do me, by approving of my services to my King and country, and in a most humble manner Return them my Thanks for their kind Recommendation of me to **his** Majesties Favour. I shall always endeavour so to discharge my Duty as I hope will **ever meet** with their Excellencies Esteem and aprobation.

I have used all possible means **to put a** Dread upon those who have been more immediately concerned in this late unnatural Rebellion, and by all Just Accounts am assured the Rebells are totally dispers't.

I have sent to His Grace of Roxburghe to Comunicate to their Excellencies the exactest list I can obtain of the persons of note and numbers of those who have been in this Rebellion. **But it** will be hard to find evidence against them, since (I **am** sorry to say) that most of the Gentlemen of this Country who profess to be in His Majesties Interest, think their Tyes of Affinity and Consanguinity such obligations that they will not be the evidence their Excellencies expect.

The Spanish Prisoners march't from this Town on the 27th towards Edenburgh in Order to proceed to Plimouth.

Capt. Abercrombie (who lies ill wounded at this place) acknowledges with gratitude the Honr. their excellencies the Lords Justices have conferred upon him, in Recommending him for the Company in Mountagues Regim^t now vacant by the Death of Capt. Downs.

Please to recommend my Duty most humbly to the Lords Justices, and give me leave to assure you I am with great truth and esteem,

Sir,
Your most Obedient humble Servant,
J. WIGHTMAN.

Honble. Charles Delafaye, Esq.

No. 67.

LORD CARPENTER TO CHARLES DELAFAYE

(*Home Office Papers, Scotland, Bundle* 14, *No.* 61)

SIR,—I have rec'd this evening your letter of the 30th, with the Lords Justices orders relating to the Spanish Prisoners, and disposition of his Majesty's Troops in this Country for guarding the building of Barracks, and for preventing Robery's and depredations, which shall be obey'd in the best manner I can. The 2 Regiments of foot that their Excys. have order'd hither will make all easy. 'Twould have been impossible to have attended those Services well without them.

I am, Sir,
Yr. most humble and obedient Servant,
CARPENTER.

Edenburgh, July 4, 1719.
Charles Delafaye, Esqr.

No. 68.

LORD CARPENTER TO CHARLES DELAFAYE

(*Home Office Papers, Scotland, Bundle* 14, *No.* 68)

EDENBURGH, JULY 7, 1719.

SIR,—On Sunday night late I rec'd your favour of the 2, with the Lords Justices orders to keep the Spanish Prisoners here, and to let them have money on the chief Officers bill if he shall desire itt nott exceeding their Pay.

Their Excys. do me great hon. in leaving to my discretion the making dispositions for preventing Robbery's, Seizing Rebells, and disarming the Highlanders; I will certainly do my best for all three, butt the 2 latter will require much better Judgement than mine to make them effectuall. Att the first confirmation of the Rebells being beaten and dispers't I desir'd a meeting of the lord Justice Clerk, Mr. Dundass,[1] the Kings Sollicitor, Brigadier Preston, and my self, to consult what measures could be taken to forward his Majesty's Service and the Security of his Government, perticularly in the above points; and if anything could be done immediately att that Juncture; accordingly they all came to my house, but we could nott forme any scheme that would answere those ends. It is impossible to catch any Rebell Highlanders with Party's of Regular Troops, and any sort of orders from the Civill or Military here to bring in their Armes would signify nothing. Such orders by proclamation or otherwise must come from those who have Power to promise that all Common People who will bring in their armes by a day prefixt and returne home to live peaceably shall nott be molested; and for the others who pay nott obedience to that order, their houses shall be burn't and their stocks taken away; which last may be putt in execution in the Winter, butt in this season they are on the mountains with their Cattle, and will be able easily to avoid any Parties of the Troops that might be sent to take them or their Cattle.

Whatever orders the Lords Justices are pleas'd to send me

---

[1] Robert Dundas of Arniston, who was raised to the Bench as Lord Arniston in 1737, and in 1748 succeeded Duncan Forbes of Culloden as Lord President.

I will putt them in execution, and use my best endeavours to make them answere the purposes they are designed for.

I am, Sir, Yr. most humble and obedient Servant,

CARPENTER.

Charles Delafaye, Esq.

No. 69.

LORD CARPENTER to CHARLES DELAFAYE

(Home Office Papers, Scotland, Bundle 14, No. 65)

SIR,—Being indisposed, and the London post coming in late on Saturday, I could not that night answer your favour of the 14th. I never thought of proposeing a Generall Indemnity, but only a promise to such persons as would bring in their arms, take the oaths, and promise to live peaceably at their habitations, that they should not be molested; and for others who do not submitt to that order, and lay hold on such ane advantage, that their houses and corn should be burnt, and their stocks taken. None of these common people have power to cause bring in more than their own arms. The heads of the Clans and chieftans only can oblige others to it. In a letter I had the honour to write to the Duke of Roxburgh[1] of the 2^d instant, I took the liberty to mention my opinion that 'twould be impossible to get the arms from the Rebells and Highlanders without ane act of parliament to make it Fellony for any person to have in his house or possession any fire arms, or even swords, except such as shall be licenc'd to have them, and that the parishes in which any arms are found shall be fin'd in a good sum to be levied on them. All which is most humbly submitted. Collonel Monro, at my desire, came yesterday to me, and I offer'd him such partys as he would require for the security of his and other good subjects tennents in those parts. He told me he had not lately heard of any Cattle taken from his tennents, but will come to me with the first letters he receives, and whatever he desires shall be comply'd with; as also every other order that the Lords justices have been pleas'd to send me,

---

[1] John Ker, fifth Earl and first Duke of Roxburghe, Secretary for Scotland from 1716 to 1725.

tho' full partys cannot be sent everywhere, till the two Regiments from New Castle, that are passed here, can arrive at Inverness and Elgin.

      I am, Sir,
    Yr. most humble and obedient Servant,
             CARPENTER.

Edinburgh, July 21*st*, 1719.
Charles Delafaye, Esqr.

No. 70.

LORD CARPENTER TO CHARLES DELAFAYE

(*Home Office Papers, Scotland, Bundle* 14, *No.* 69)

         EDINBURGH, JULY 28TH, 1719.

SIR,—By yours of the 23^d, I have the Lords Justices order to write to Glengarry, which I will do to-morrow morning, and their Excellencys shall know his answer, if he sends any. I am inform'd he do's not keep at home, which is an ill sign. However, I will send my letter to his house, concluding they will forward it to him wherever he may be.

      I am, Sir,
    Your most humble and obedient Servant,
             CARPENTER.

Charles Delafaye, Esqr.

No. 71.

MAJOR-GENERAL WIGHTMAN TO CHARLES DELAFAYE

(*Home Office Papers, Scotland, Bundle* 14, *No.* 72. *Extract*)

      EDENBURGH, AUGUST THE 4TH, 1719.

JUST now a Leiv^t Col. of my acquaintance that arrived last night from Glasgow Informs me, that a very honest man, a

Master of a Ship that came from the Norward to that place, saw two or three boats with armed men near the Island of Orkneys, and spoke to them, who told him plainly they wanted to impress a Ship, But the Master stood on his Defence, so that the Boats durst not attempt him, however spieing two other ships they made towards them to seize them, in order as he Reports to carry off Lord Seaforth and Marshall with others for Spain, or where they can make a safe Retreat—who had been gone long ago had Seaforth been well of his wounds.

No. 72.

LORD CARPENTER TO CHARLES DELAFAYE.

(*Home Office Papers, Scotland, Bundle* 14, *No.* 76)

Sir,—I am concern'd at the difficultys to Secure Inverness, which in my opinion would be very usefull work, especially when 't would cost so little: had I a Commission for the constant command here, would lay out that small sum myself, and can do no more than represent matters and submitt them.

I send you a Coppy of my letter to Glengary, who not having answer'd it, I must conclude him guilty of the accusation against him, and that he absconds. I gave mine to a lawyer in this town, who brought Lord Justice Clerk and me our letters from Glengary; he engag'd to send it to him.

I go on Thursday next for Bath, where hope to be soon well, and ready for any commands the Lords Justices please to send me.—I am,

Sir, Yo. most humble and Obedient Servant,

CARPENTER.

Edenburgh, August 18*th,* 1719.
Charles Delafaye, Esq.

No. 73.

LORD CARPENTER to GLENGARRY

(*Enclosed in No.* 71)

COPPY OF A LETTER FROM LORD CARPENTER TO GLENGARY.

EDENBURGH, JULY 29TH, 1719.

SIR,—The very good opinion My Lord Justice Clerk and I had of you made us backward to beleive any information against you, and even after the party had been at your house, we concluded you would come hither to justify your conduct, but your delaying of it so long looks not well, and the longer will be the worse.

As to your having enemys, you know we are bless't with laws that do not suffer them to prevaill; but are very favourable to persons accus'd, and every man must be tryed by his peers, which is an absolute Security against the malice of our enemys: whoever is innocent of what is laid to his charge is sure to be clear'd. Our laws are so very mild that the guilty sometimes escape, but the innocent never suffer. Since the first party none has been sent in Search of you, for I expected to see you here. But if, in fourteen days from this, you neither come here, or write assurances of your coming in few days, all dilligence shall be us'd to seize your person, and, as far as the law admitts, your estate also, and this is the last notice you are to have of it; therefor hope you will not delay coming to clear your reputation, that your friends may without reproach or Censure own the good opinion they had of you, and shew you freindly civilitys, and that you may enjoy undisturbed liberty, which I heartily wish, and am, etc.

No. 74.

MAJOR-GENERAL WIGHTMAN to CHARLES DELAFAYE

(*Home Office Papers, Scotland, Bundle* 14, *No.* 78)

EDENBURGH, SEPT. 1ST, 1719.

SIR,—I have the favour of yours of the 25th, and am extreamly obliged to you for your friendly Sollicitations towards obtaining me leave for London, that which might proved an Obstacle to my Coming for London is now Removed, for the Dutch Brigadier has left this Country near a month, and is at New Castle with the Swiss Troops, and as I am informed designs soon for London. Therefore I earnestly intreat you to move their Excellencies the Lds. Justices to send an Order for Brigd^r Preston to Command here in my Absence. I shall wait with impatience your answer, and in the meantime shall be Regulating everything for the Kings Service.

The Spaniards begin to grow very sulky under their Confinem^t, and the money advanc't by Ld. Carpenter for subsisting of them is almost expended (wch I have already acquainted His Grace of Roxburghe with), and shou'd be glad to know what their Excellencies the Lords Justices designe to do with them. All things in these parts Remain perfectly quiet.

   I am with great Truth,
    Sir,
     Y^r most humble Servt,
            J. WIGHTMAN.

P.S.—Inclosed I send you a Genl Return of all the Regiments in North Brittain for the month of July 1719.

No. 75.—RETURN OF THE TROOPS IN SCOTLAND FOR JULY 1719

(*Enclosed in No. 74.*)

A RETURN of all the Regiments of Dragoons in North Brittain, for the month of July 1719, shewing the Number of Commission and Non Commission Officers and Effective private Dragoons present in each Regiment.

Regiments	Field Officers	Capts.	Lieuts.	Cornets	Quar. Mrs.	Sergts.	Corporals	Drums	Effective Dragoons present	Effective Horses	Horses dead	Horses disabled
Coll. Campbell's	3	3	5	6	6	6	12	6	150	158	3	13
Lord Carpenter's	3	4	5	5	6	6	12	6	150	161	2	11
Earl of Stair's	2	3	2	5	6	6	12	6	150	163	1	10
Totall	8	10	12	16	18	18	36	18	450	482	6	34

A RETURN of all the Regiments of Foot in North Brittain, for the month of July 1719, Shewing the number of Commission and Non Commission Officers and Effective private Centinels in each Regiment.

Regiments	Field Officers	Captains	Lieuts.	Ensigns	Sergts.	Corporals	Drums	Effective Centinels present	Men wanting to Compleat
Coll. Montagu's	3	6	7	8	20	30	10	350	0
Coll. Clayton's	3	6	8	9	20	30	10	320	30
Coll. Harrison's	3	8	9	9	20	30	10	313	37
Coll. Chomley's	3	7	9	8	20	30	10	342	8
Major-Genl Wightman's	3	8	9	7	20	30	10	350	0
Lieut.-Genl Macartney's	1	7	18	0	20	30	10	340	10
Totall	16	42	60	41	120	180	60	2015	85

No. 76.

MAJOR-GENERAL WIGHTMAN to CHARLES DELAFAYE

(*Home Office Papers, Scotland, Bundle* 14, *No.* 80)

EDINBURGH, SEPT. 17TH, 1719.

SIR,—I have the favour of yours of the 10th Instant, and wrote to His Grace of Roxburghe last post what will prevent my setting out untill the 28th, or thereabouts. Since which I have had the Commanding Officers of the Spaniards with me, and told them the substance of your letter directed to Brigadr. Preston, by order of their Excellencies the Lds. Justices, withall that they ought to be sensible the Governmt. had treated them with great humanity, which they all acknowledged with many thanks. I also told the Commanding Officers that they were to give their Bond for the expences the King has been at as well on Accot of those taken at Castle Donan for their Subsistance and Transportation. As for what subsistance those taken at Castle Donan have had they were willing to give their Bond, but for the charge of Transportation, they said they durst not by no means to do it, for that their master wou'd certainly Punish them very severely to pretend to Signe any expence of that kind, being not accustomed to any such thing, and it wou'd look as if they were impatient of their sufferings, and brought an unnecessary charge on their King. I also acquainted His Grace of Roxburghe that Brigadr Preston was by no means capable to gett credit for the money you wrote to him by their Excellencies orders to advance for the Spaniards, without ordering him to draw Bills for it, he being now out of Pockett a considerable sume for the Governments Service which he is threaten'd to be sued for,—therefore I hope you will communicate this to their Excellencies the Lds. Justices, that Directions be given as to this, and likewise to the Spaniards giving their Bond for Transportation, either to me or Brigadr Preston in my absence. I have advanc't the Spaniards fifty Pounds to Subsist them, and keep their men from starving, and have drawn my Bill on Ld. Lincoln[1] (the

---

[1] Henry Clinton, seventh Earl of Lincoln, was Paymaster-General of the Forces from 1715 to 1720.

money which Ld. Carpenter advanc't them being all exhausted).

I am with great Truth, and Sincerity,
Sir,
Yo. most obliged humble Servt,
J. WIGHTMAN.

Honble. Chas. Delafaye, Esqre.

No. 77.

LORD CARPENTER to CHARLES DELAFAYE

(*Home Office Papers, Scotland, Bundle* 14, *No.* 79)

BATH, SEPT. 12, 1719.

SIR,—By the last post I rec'd here the enclos'd from Glengary, in answere to that I writt to him of the 29 of July, by order of the Lords Justices, of which I sent you a Coppy.

I had also a letter by last post from the Earl of Ffindlater,[1] with the enclos'd paper of Intelligence, and another from Glenbucket, which I send you. I had desired he would write to me hither, and tho' I find he has a ffriendship for Glengary, yett have a very good opinion of his gratitude and duty to His Majesty. He is cheif Chamberlain to the Duke of Gordon, and has very great power with all the Dukes ffollowers and Tenants; he came to me soon after I gott to Edenburgh, and offer'd his Service, assuring me he had taken such care that nott one of the Dukes People would joyn or in any manner assist the Rebells, which wee found to be true; he will constantly lett me know every thing materiall from the Highlands, and being a Protestant, I have great confidence in him; I write to him to encourage his Correspondance, and if he sends me any intelligence of consequence, will enclose it to you to lay before their Ex^{cys}.

I am,
Sir,
Yr. most humble Servant,
CARPENTER.

Charles Delafaye, Esq.

---

[1] James Ogilvy, fourth Earl of Findlater, who was Chancellor of Scotland at the Union, and who, when the Scots Parliament rose for the last time, made the famous remark : 'There's the end of an auld sang !'

No. 78.

GLENGARRY to LORD CARPENTER

(*Enclosed in No. 77*)

INVERGARRY, AUG. 24, 1719.

My Lord,—As I had the honour to informe your Ldp formerly of my being upon the road to waite upon your Lop, and my Lord Justice Clerke, being advertised of a partie searching for me, I did returne instantly, having abundantly suffered imprisonments, though most innocent several tyms.

And it is most certaine, as your Lp. very well observes, that our laws are good and our King most clement and just, yet ye subjects does suffer both in person and means frequently, notwithstanding of which, be the being keept in gaole in Nth. Britain by the ruling power of a partie or a great man, and this, my Lord, and not any feare of guilte, and ye dying circumstances of my wife these many bypast months does impede me; alsoe your Lp. will be pleased to consider what ane hard task it is to any persone to vindicate their conduct or reputation, whereas they do not know what they are accused of, and I humbly begged of your Ldp. to be pleased to acquaint me whereby I might candidly and sincerely impart to your Lp. the trew matter of fact, there being some reasons I cannot well appear in that place without danger of imprisonment and inconvenience, for it seems their informing your Lp. designs the danger of my libertie in that manner, for your Lp. may easily perceive by what they suggest my innocence, being neither in armes or assisting to them with men by my self or others, though some of them might be with them, and yet I contributed to keep the peace in adjacent places, and hindred others from joyning of them, and assisted by my tenants to further and advance the Barrack of Kilichumen,[1] and anie intelligence one other thing demanded of me (excepting going to prison) was cheerfully obeyed; and I presume to assure your Lp. that none honours your Lps. merite and person

---

[1] The barrack at Fort Augustus was built in 1716.

or would be more obsequious to your commands than I should be, but what I have humbly represented to your Lp. will, I hope, excuse me and putt a stope to all trouble of yr forces to make search for me; being on the west coast your Lp.'s letter did not come to my hand but last night, otherwise an answer would be returned to your Lp. sooner be,

My Lord,

Your Lo. most obliged, most obedient, and most humble Servant,

ALEX. M'DONNELL.

No. 79.

ENCLOSURE FROM THE EARL OF FINDLATER TO LORD CARPENTER

(*Enclosed in No. 77*)

THE EARL OF FFINDLATERS LETTER IN WHICH THIS WAS ENCLOSED BEARS DATE THE 24 OF AUG.

MY LORD,—The week before last the attainted Lords and the Chiefs of the Clans hade a meeting in Knoidart in Glengary's country, where he went himself in disguise to concert measures for a new Rebellion. They hade no men with them but a hundred which Seaforth brought with him and a hundred of Clan Ronalds men which Tilliebardine hade with him, which they called their Guards. They give out for the reason of their meeting that some great man has come lately from the Southward to them with fresh assurances of a landing in England very soon. Whatever is in it, it is certain that they are very uppish just now, and that they have sent messages to severall people to be ready to join them, or to expect very bad usage.

No. 80.

GORDON OF GLENBUCKET TO LORD CARPENTER

(*Enclosed in No. 77*)

LETTER FROM GLENBUCKETT TO LORD CARPENTER, WHO LIVES NEAR RUTVEN OF BADENOCH, AND CALLS HIS HOUSE GORDON HALL.

MY LORD,—I had the honour of your Lops. last post, qrby

I am sorie to understand your healt obliges to goe to ye Bath, but I hope and heartily wish speedie recoverie.

As to ane meeting of the Rebells in Glengarie his intrest (?) your Losp. was justly informed, but not to ye numbers. I cane assure ther were not above six or seaven Gentlemen (and that of attented), with no doubt a few servants, Seaforth and Tillibardine being two of the number. The place of meeting was not within twentie milles of Glengarie's house, but it appears he still laboures under ye misfortune to be misrepresented, tho I cannot omit to informe your Losp that about later end of Jully or beginning augst Glengarie had certain accounts that some gentlemen had gone North and were askeing after Tillibardin, Seaforth, and others of the Rebells with letters and intelligence to them, and being certainly informed they had gone into Knodard he gave his bro^rs orders to apprehend them and send y^m to Inverlochie to Sir Robert polloch, wh. order his bro^rs put to executione and sent two gentlemen prisoners, but unluckilie were retaken by on McGriger of Downan within six mills of the Garissone; this I had yesterday frome ane good auther, and that Sir Robert pollock had sent his thanks, tho ye thing miscarried inclination was good. As I took leave by my last to acquant your Losp that these misfortunat people wants not incouragement, I continoue to assure your Losp so, tho I must own that its slyghtly grounded, and I take it to be aither from a set of people that wants to have ye Goverment at expenss to keep a great many troops on foot, or ye distructione of so many people that will be deluded and so blynded that they cannot or at least will not see. I know notwithstanding they are endeavouring to get abroad, wch against next post I believe I shall give your Losp. more particullar accounts of, and shall always beg ye honor of your Losp commands, and sincerlie continoue,

My Lord,
  Your Losp. most humble, obedient,
    and obliged servant,
      J. Gordon.

Gordon hall, 29 augst. 1719.

No. 81.

LORD CARPENTER to CHARLES DELAFAYE

(*Home Office Papers, Scotland, Bundle* 14, *No.* 87)

BATH, SEPT. 19, 1719.

SIR,—I have rec'd your ffavour of the 15th and wish I had sent you the Earl of Findlaters letter to me, which I shew'd here to the Duke of Kingstone,[1] and having answered itt I burn't itt. There was no assurances that the Intelligence was true, only that he had it from a good hand, and had sent me an exact Coppy of that part of the letter to him, for my acquainting the Lords Justices of itt if I thought proper.

His Lo^p living so farr north may probably have always good intelligence, and wee corresponded while I was in North Brittain.

If you please to write to him, may direct to his seat, Cullen house, in the Shire of Bamf.

Having no pain, only a great stiffness in the lower part of my back, of which I can yett onely think I am better, however if any disturbance should offer in Scotland, whether I recover or nott, will go strait thither from hence if the Lords Justices think I can be usefull there for his Majesty's Service.

I am,
Sir,
Yr most humble and obedient Servant,
CARPENTER.

Charles Delafaye, Esqre.

No. 82.

MAJOR-GENERAL WIGHTMAN to CHARLES DELAFAYE

(*Home Office Papers, Scotland, Bundle* 14, *No.* 82)

EDENBURGH, SEPT. 29TH.

SIR,—I have the honour of yours of the 22d instant signifying their Excellencies the Lds. Justices Directions that so much

---

[1] Evelyn Pierrepoint, first Duke of Kingston, Lord President of the Council, 1719-1720.

money shou'd be advanc'd the Spanish prisoners as shou'd not exceed the amount of their Pay, and that you have since Received their Excellencies Pleasure to write to the Lds. of the Treasury, that the Paymaster-General of His Majesties forces may enable me or the Commanding Officers of the Forces in this Country to Comply with these directions by answering our bills. Accordingly I have enclosed an Acco^t of what is due to the Spanish Prisoners to the 1st of next month which will be drawn for, and what I hope will be sufficient for them to pay all their debts, and imbarke them on board the ship when it arrives.

I am also favoured with two more of yours, both dated the 24th, the one signifying that the Lds. Justices thought it strange the Commanding Officer shou'd make a Scruple of being bound for the Repaym't of their Transportation, and that their Excellencies did not think of altering their Order of sending the Spaniards away, directing me at the same time to detain the Commander of the Spaniards as an Hostage for the Repaymn^t of the expences. Brigad^r Preston being just come to Town I sent for him as also the Commander of the Spaniards and informed him of the Lds. Justices Commands, and he returned his answer as before, that he cou'd not Submitt, and be content rather to remain a Prisoner as a Hostage, for he cou'd by no means answer Complying in giving a bond for any charge of Transportation, But only for that money he had or shou'd Receive on Acco^t of Subsisting the Spaniards. Brigad^r Preston hearing all that past intends to follow their Excellencies orders in every Point, only Desires their farther Orders as to the Colonel who is now a Prisoner on Parole, and in Case he persists in not Complying to Signe a Bond for the Charge of Embarkation, whither he must Confine the Colonel closer Prisoner or Continue him as he is. Your other letter of the 24th tells me their Excellencies ye Lds. Justices being informed of the Order I sent to Huffells Regiment to march from their Quarters at Coldstream and Kelso, to Dalkeith and Preston Panns, they are pleased to direct that the said Regim^t of Huffels shou'd not be removed so near Edenburgh; as to this I beg leave to inform their Excellencies it cannot be well avoided removing their Quarters, because Col. Campbells Regim^t

has laid up all their winter Stores of Forrage in the Quarters Huffells Regim^t now lyes in, and it draws near the time they take up their horses from Grass, and they were only quartered where they now are for that time, beleiving they might march more to the South before the Dragoons wou'd have occassion to Return, and there is no place near the Borders capable of Quartering them But Dalkeith and Preston Panns which is much the best Quarters in Scotland, except they were ordered to England—this I desire you will please to Communicate to the Lds. Justices, and Direct your next to Brigad^r Preston, who gives his humble Service to you, I intending to Sett out in two or three days for London.—I am with great truth,

Sir, Your most humble Servant,

J. WIGHTMAN.

No. 83.

ACCOUNT OF EXPENDITURE ON SPANISH PRISONERS

(*Enclosed in No. 82*)

To the Collonel p. diem . .	£0 10 9$\frac{1}{2}$
To five Captains at £0. 3. 10$\frac{2}{3}$ each p. diem	£0 19 5$\frac{1}{3}$
To five Lieuts. at £0. 2. 9$\frac{1}{4}$ each p. D°	£0 13 10$\frac{1}{4}$
To Six Ensigns at £0. 2. 2 each p. D°	£0 13 0
To Eleven Sergeants at 5$\frac{1}{2}$d each p. D°	£0 5 0$\frac{1}{2}$
To Eighteen Corporalls at 4d each p. D°	£0 6 0
To Six Drums at 3$\frac{2}{3}$d each p. D°.	£0 1 10
To 221 Soldiers at 3d each p. D°.	£2 15 3
To 273, being the number of the above persons for bread at 1$\frac{1}{2}$d to each p. diem is . .	£1 14 1$\frac{1}{2}$
	£7 19 4$\frac{1}{6}$

To Ditto officers, Sergeants, Corporalls, Drums, and private soldiers 110 days mere Subsistence as above from the 12th June to the 30th September 1719 at £7 19 4⅛ p. Diem . . £876 8 2⅓

1719
July 28 By Don Nicolas de Bolano y Castro, his bill on the Marquis de Berreti Landi payable to Lord Carpenter of this date. 200 0 0
Augst 19 By D° Don Nicolas's bill on D° Marquis payable to Do Lord Carpenter of this date 200 0 0

No. 84.—RETURN OF THE TROOPS IN SCOTLAND FOR SEPTEMBER 1719

(*Home Office Papers, Scotland, Bundle* 14, *No.* 82)

A RETURN of all the REGIMENTS of DRAGOONS in NORTH BRITAIN for the month of September 1719, Shewing the number of Commission and Non Commission Officers and Effective private Dragoons present in each Regiment.

Regiments	Field Officers	Capt^{ns}.	Lieuts.	Cornets	Qur. Mrs.	Serjts.	Corporals	Drums	Effective Dragoons present	Effective Horses	Men wanting Compleat	Horses wanting Compleat
Coll. Campbell's	3	3	5	6	6	6	12	6	150	174	...	...
Lord Carpenter's	2	4	5	5	6	6	12	6	150	174	...	...
Earl of Stair's	2	3	3	6	6	6	12	6	150	174	...	...
Total	7	10	13	17	18	18	36	18	450	522	...	...

A RETURN of all the REGIMENTS of FOOT in NORTH BRITAIN for the month of September 1719, Shewing the Number of Commission and Non Commission Officers and Effective private Centinels present in each Regiment.

Regiments	Field Officers	Captains	Lieuts.	Ensigns	Serjts.	Corporals	Drums	Effective Centinels present	Men wanting to compleat
Coll. Montagu's	1	6	8	8	20	30	10	350	0
Coll. Clayton's	1	5	7	9	20	30	10	328	22
Coll. Harrison's	1	3	6	7	20	30	10	309	41
Coll. Cholmley's		7	9	8	20	30	10	341	9
Major-Genl. Wightman's	3	7	9	8	20	30	10	350	0
Lieut.-Genl. Macartney's	1	7	18	0	20	30	10	339	11
Total	8	35	57	40	120	180	60	2017	83

Endorsed:—QUARTERS OF THE WITHIN REGIMENTS.—Coll. Campbell's, Dunss; Lord Carpenter's, Haddington, Linlithgow, Falkirk and St. Ninians; Earl of Stair's, Glasgow; Coll. Montagu's, Perth, Dundee and Montrosse; Coll. Clayton's, Sterling; Coll. Harrison's, Edenburgh; Coll. Cholmley's, Elgin, Aberdeen and Forres; Maj^r.-Genl. Wightman's, Inverness; Lt.-Genl. Macartney's, Fort William.

No. 85.

BRIGADIER PRESTON to CHARLES DELAFAYE

(Home Office Papers, Scotland, Bundle 14, No. 84)

Sir,—I was in the Country when I receiv'd your favour of the 13th instant, in which you signify'd to me their Ex^{cys} the Lords Justices pleasure, that I should accept of the Spanish Collonel's bill on the Marquis de Beretti Landi, specifying not only the Sum for which he draws, but the use for which the sum was advanced, which if he refuses to do, or to give some other note or acknowledgement by which it may appear that such sums have been advanced to him for the Subsistance of himself and the other Spanish Prisoners, I shall according to directions allow no more money to be laid out upon them, and shall order them to be confined in closs prison on bread and water. But I hope the Collonel shall comply with their Excys. indulgent temper.

S^r, my letter from the transport office of the same date informs me, that the Ship to carry the said Prisoners sail'd from the River of Thames the 9th instant, but she is not yet come to Leith. I am with great truth,

Sir,

Your most obedient humble Servant,

J. Preston.

Edenburgh, October 22d, 1719.

Charles Delafaye, Esqr.

No. 86.

BISHOP GADDERAR to BISHOP CAMPBELL [1]

(Episcopal Chest, Edinburgh)

HONBLE. SIR,—I have a letter from ye Bp. of E.[2] of ye 27th Octor., in wch he gives his humble Service to you, acknowledges ye receit of yours with yt from Mr C[ollie]r, expresses a due concern for your ill health, with his best wishes for your recovery, and yt we may live to see better days.

His Lōp. had ye good nature in stead of news to write me of ye Spanish Prisoners as follows, they were embarqued yt day for Sp. They were surprised with ye temperateness and kindlyness of our air at this season, and much more at ye gt heat of ye long sumer. Their Comander in chief told him, yt our weather would have been reckon'd hot even in Spain, and yt on June 4th as they march'd through a Glen, one of ye strongest and healthiest of their men, suffocated with ye heat, dropt down dead, and never recover'd. They left this place highly satisfy'd wt the dispositions of our people, wheresoever they came, and the civilities they met with, and I cannot say but they deserv'd ym, for they were exceeding mannerly, inoffensive and pleasant,

---

[1] James Gadderar, Bishop of Aberdeen from 1724 to 1733, was originally minister of Kilmaurs, Ayrshire. His friend and correspondent, Bishop Campbell, was a son of Lord Neil Campbell, second son of Archibald, eighth Earl and first Marquis of Argyll. He was Gadderar's predecessor in the See of Aberdeen from 1721 to 1724. See Russel's edition of Keith's *Catalogue of Scottish Bishops*, Appendix, pp. 530-532.

I am indebted for this letter to the courtesy of Dr. Dowden, the present Bishop of Edinburgh. Bishop Dowden writes: 'It is curious that Bishop Campbell, afterwards so pronounced a Jacobite, had been involved in Argyll's rebellion of 1685. Dr. Samuel Johnson said, "He afterwards kept better company and became a Tory" (Croker's *Boswell*, vol. v. pp. 100, 101, where other particulars will be found). He died June 16, 1744. His book, in folio, on the *Middle State* (1721), shows much learning, and is still sought after and fetches a high price.'

[2] Alexander Rose, son of Alexander Rose, Bishop of Moray, one of the Roses of Kilravock, was Bishop of Edinburgh from 1687 to 1720.—Keith's *Catalogue*, p. 64.

without stiffness or affectation, very unlike ye character comm̄only given of Sp—. One very com̄endable quality must not be forgot, gt temperance both in eating and drinking. . . . I ever am,

    Honble. Sir,
      Your most humble,
        obliged & affec°nate Servt,

Lond., Novr. 7th, 1719.   JA. GADDERAR.

Pray excuse the courseness of the paper which I had in the Coffee house. Vale.

INDEX

ABERCROMBIE, captain, wounded at Glenshiel, 277.
Aderhanon, liii n.
Alberoni, cardinal, xxii, xxiv, xxvi, xxxiv, xxxv, xxxviii, lv and n, lviii and n; sketch of his career, xxiv; supports a scheme for a Swedish invasion of Scotland in 1716-17, xxii; refuses to recall Spanish forces from imperial territory, xxv; resolves to assist a Jacobite invasion of England, xxvi; welcomes Ormonde to Spain, xxviii, 7, 8; agrees to provide men and war material for the landing in England, xxix, 15; invites James Stuart to Madrid, xxix, xxxi, 17; conspires against the Regent Orleans, xxx; promises men and arms for the expedition of the earl Marischal, xxxv; his opinion of admiral Cammock, 250, 253; his intentions known in England, xxxviii and n, 224; refuses to support the earl Marischal's forces in Scotland, lv, 125; his fall from power, and death, lvii, lviii and n; letters from, to Ormonde, 219, 222; letters from, to James, 240, 246, 250, 253, 255, 257, 258; letter to, from James, 261; letters to, from Ormonde, 4, 5, 10, 12, 14, 18, 22-24, 26, 29, 31, 34, 38, 41, 44, 47, 49, 52, 58, 60, 61, 68, 80, 85, 92, 97, 100, 103, 106, 111, 113-115, 117, 126, 129, 132, 137, 140, 143, 149, 157, 158, 163, 165, 167, 169, 172, 174, 175, 179, 181, 182, 184, 188.
Alcala, xxviii.
Amerongen's regiment at the battle of Glenshiel, l, lii n.
Amsterdam, 6 n, 86, 107-109, 117, 226, 227, 251.
'Andalusia' reaches Vigo, 113 and n.
Aquaviva, cardinal, xxvi n, 17 and n, 20, 201, 227, 251, 262.

Arnott, Dr., taken prisoner at Glenshiel, 275.
Arran, Charles Butler, earl of, 51 and n, 123, 195.
Arthur, lady, 135, 159, 161, 162, 166, 176; letters to, from Ormonde, 144, 163, 167.
Astorga, xxxv.
Atterbury, Francis, bishop of Rochester, 193, 225; letter to, from Ormonde, 171 and n.
Auch, John of, 271.
Avignon, xxi, 206.

BAGENAL, GEORGE, xxvii, xxx, 12, 15, 17, 19, 45, 49, 60, 86, 87, 126, 128.
Barcelona, xxv, 69.
Barkley, captain, 273.
Bar-le-Duc, xxi and n.
Bayonne, xxvii.
Bealach-na-Spainnteach, lii and n.
Belleisle, marquis de, 233.
Beretti Landi, marquis de, Spanish ambassador in Holland, xxviii, liv, 114, 117 and n, 293, 295.
Berkeley, lord, xxxix, xli n, 235.
Berwick, duke of, lv, lvi n, 3 n, 4, 142, 145, 150, 161, 237.
Betanzos, 113.
Bilbao, 27, 33.
Bolano y Castro, don Nicolas de, commander of Spanish troops at the battle of Glenshiel, l; surrender of, liii; a prisoner in Edinburgh, liv, 293.
Bolingbroke, viscount, xx and n.
Bologna, xxxii n, lvi, 207, 208.
Borlum. See M'Intosh.
Bourke, sir Toby, 4 n.
Boyle, captain, xlvi; attacks Eilean Donan castle, xlvii and n.
Brandy recommended for Scotland, 119.
Bremen bishopric, ceded to George I., xxi.

Bristol, 225.
Brittany, preparations for a Spanish expedition to, lv, 169, 174, 179, 181, 182, 184.
Brolas. *See* MacLean.
Broun, general, 213.
Bryerly, Mr., 198.
Burgos, 45, 128.
Butler, Ormonde's cousin, 135, 260.
Byng, admiral sir George, xxv, 19 and *n*, 20, 239; defeats the Spanish fleet at Cape Passaro, xxvi and *n*.

CADIZ, 25 *n*, 29, 54 and *n*, 83, 228, 230, 231; preparations at, for Ormonde's expedition, xxx, xxxvi and *n*, 22, 23, 92, 226, 227, 229, 232; departure of the fleet, xxxvi and *n*, 219, 239; its destination, xxxviii and *n*, 83, 229; dispersion of the vessels, xl, 119, 243, 245, 246.
Cadogan, earl of, 195, 234.
Cameron of Lochiel, xlii *n*, 38 *n*; his arrival in Scotland, xlvi; joins Tullibardine, xlviii, 270; at the battle of Glenshiel, l, 271.
Cammock, admiral George, xxxiii, 19 and *n*, 20, 30 *n*, 122; Alberoni's opinion of, 250, 253; letters to, from Ormonde, 157, 166.
Campbell, bishop, letter to, from bishop Gadderar, on the conduct of the Spanish prisoners in Edinburgh, 296 and *n*.
—— brigadier, of Ormidale, xlii, xlvi, 15 *n*, 16, 38 *n*, 266, 267, 269; at the battle of Glenshiel, l, 271, 273.
—— of Glendaruel, 38 *n*, xlii-xlv, 38 *n*, 54, 58, 62, 86, 94, 271; at the battle of Glenshiel, l.
—— colonel, 284, 291, 294.
—— James, sheriff-depute of Argyll, 70 *n*.
Campo Florido, the prince of, xlii, 32 *n*, 38, 45, 117, 164; letters to, from Ormonde, 33, 35, 36, 40, 43, 48, 50, 54, 56, 115, 130.
Cape Finisterre, 74, 84, 85, 87, 90, 117.
Cape Ortegal, 176.
Cape Passaro, battle of, xxvi and *n*, 19 *n*, 74 *n*.
Carpenter, general, lord, 284, 294; letters from, to Delafaye, 274, 277, 278, 279, 280, 281, 286, 290; letter to, from Glengarry, 287; letter to, from the earl of Findlater, 288; letter to, from Gordon of Glenbucket, 288.

Castaneta, Antonio de, defeated by Byng off Cape Passaro, xxvi and *n*.
Castelblanco, count of, xxxv *n*, 145 *n*, 206; letter to, from Ormonde, 146.
Castro, Pedro de, xli.
Catalonia, 252, 253.
Cellamare, prince of, Spanish ambassador at Paris, xxvii, xxviii, xxx, 4, 5 and *n*, 16, 23 *n*, 29, 31, 34, 35, 47.
Chacon, M. de, 120 *n*, 121, 124, 185, 188.
Chammorel, M. de, 226.
Charier, a surgeon, 101.
Charles VI., emperor, xxv, 2, 3, 4, 16, 17, 193; causes the arrest of the princess Clementina, xxvi, 232.
Charles XII. of Sweden, 6 and *n*, 7, 16, 195, 196, 224; reasons for his animosity towards George I., xxi; is ready to support an invasion of Great Britain, xxix; death of, xxxi, xxxiv, 41, 47.
Chigi, Mme., 199.
Chomley's regiment, 284, 294.
Clancostrum, M. de, agent of Charles XII., 54 and *n*, 55; letter to, from Ormonde, 154.
Clanranald. *See* MacDonald.
Clayton, colonel, l, li, 284, 294.
Clement XI., pope, xxxiii, 233; letter to, from James, 216.
Clementina Sobieski, princess, xxiii and *n*, 7, 16 *n*, 95 and *n*, 137, 216, 225, 258; arrested at Innspruck by order of the emperor, xxvii and *n*, 2 and *n*, 17, 193-195, 197, 198, 232; her escape, lvi and *n*, 253-255; her marriage to James, lvi-lvii and *n*, 259; letters to, from Ormonde, 137-138 and *n*, 152 and *n*, 186; letter from, to Ormonde, 260; letter from, to the queen of Spain, 263.
Clotau, M. de, 107, 108.
Cobham, lord, at Vigo, 165 *n*.
Cobler, 195.
Cockburn, Adam, of Ormiston, lord justice-clerk, 278, 281, 282; letter from, to Delafaye, concerning those engaged in the battle of Glenshiel, 275 and *n*.
Cohorn mortars, xlviii and *n*.
Colmenero, marshal, governor of Milan castle, 212, 213, 214, 233.
Connock, sir Timon, 57 and *n*, 58 and *n*, 64, 68, 83, 84, 86, 113, 114, 139, 170, 173, 179, 248, 251; letter from, to James, 252; letters to, from Ormonde, 62, 82, 83, 116, 129, 133,

INDEX

138, 140, 141, 144, 146, 147, 150, 153, 160, 161, 174, 186.
Corunna, xxxiv, 29, 54 and *n*, 55, 58, 74, 75, 84, 85, 109, 119.
Cottier, Mr., 296.
Crafton, general, xxvii, 4 and *n*, 5, 35, 39, 58, 62, 174, 187; letter to, from Ormonde, 62.
Craggs, James, secretary of state, letters from, to the earl of Stair, 234, 237; letters to, from the abbé Dubois, 223, 224, 227; letters to, from Stair, 229, 232, 233, 236, 239.
Crean & Company, bankers in Madrid, letter to, from Ormonde, 98.

DALKEITH, 291, 292.
Danican, M., 228.
Davenant, British envoy at Genoa, xxxiii, 214, 230, 233.
Delafaye, Charles, secretary to the lords justices, letter to, from Cockburn of Ormiston, 275 and *n*; letter to, from brigadier Preston, 295; letters to, from general Carpenter, 274, 277-279, 280, 281, 286, 290; letters to, from major-general Wightman, 276, 280, 282, 285, 290.
Destouches, M., 226.
Dicconson, William, 155 and *n*; letters to, from James, 198, 217, 221.
Dillon, general Arthur, xxxi, xliii, l *n*, 2, 3, 8, 13, 21, 31, 35, 38, 59, 68, 86, 162, 163, 166, 167, 170, 176, 179, 180, 183, 196, 197, 199, 202, 217, 231, 233, 238, 268 *n*; letters to, from Ormonde, 8, 11, 13; letters to, from James, 12 *n*, 48.
Douglas, Mr., 269.
Downes, captain, killed at the battle of Glenshiel, lii *n*, liii, 277.
Drummond, James, lord. *See* Perth.
—— lady Mary, 145 *n*.
—— lord William, 206.
Dubois, abbé, xxvii, xxx, xxxviii, 231, 233, 239, 240; letters from, to secretary Craggs, 223, 224, 227.
Duffus, lord, 155 *n*.
Dundas, Robert, of Arniston, 278 and *n*.

EAS-NAN-ARM, lii *n*.
Echlin, general, letter to, from Ormonde, 155 and *n*.
Eilean Donan castle, xlvi; garrisoned by Spanish troops, xlvi; taken by captain Boyle, xlvii; 145 and *n*.

Elizabeth Farnese, queen of Spain, letters from, to James, 218, 242, 249, 255; letter to, from princess Clementina, 263.
Eon, M., director of the Compagnie de l'Assiento, 225.
Erskine (Areskine), Mr., 173.
—— James, of Grange, 275 *n*.
—— John. *See* Mar, earl of.
Esmonde, captain, 35, 38, 60, 129, 134, 140-143, 173.
Estrées, marshal d', 239; reports to, on the preparations at Cadiz, 228 and *n*; is convinced of the futility of the attempt, 230.
Everard, sir Redmond, 3 *n*, 4, 35 and *n*, 38, 42, 47, 51, 153 *n*, 195; letter to, from Ormonde, 123.

FERROL, 71.
Findlater, earl of, 286 and *n*, 290; enclosure from, to general Carpenter, on a meeting of Jacobites in Knoydart, 288.
Fitzgerald, colonel, 134, 157.
Fraga, 54, 58.
Franca Villa, battle of, 149 *n*.
Francisco, chevalier, 139, 140, 142.
Franclieu, marquis de, 86; letter to, from Ormonde, 144.
Frederick IV. of Denmark, xxi.
Frederickshall, siege of, xxxi and *n*.
Frioch Corrie, li.
Fuentarabia, lv, 139 and *n*, 254.

GADDERAR, JAMES, bishop of Aberdeen, letter from, to bishop Campbell, on the Spanish prisoners, 296 and *n*.
Gairloch, xlv.
Gallas, count de, 137 and *n*, 208, 220.
Galliand, père, 198.
Galliegos, 151.
Gardi, Cesar, banker in Amsterdam, 251.
Gasqui, captain, 229.
Gaydon, major, lvi.
Geddes, captain, xxxiii *n*.
Genes, M. de, 237.
Genoa, 207, 208.
George I., 2, 15, 86 *n*.
Gillywhining, 270 and *n*.
Glenbucket. *See* Gordon.
Glendaruel. *See* Campbell.
Glengarry. *See* MacDonell.
Glenmoriston, 270.
Glenshellbeg, 270.
Glenshiel, sources of information relating to the battle of, xli *n*; description of the battlefield, xlviii; disposi-

tion of the forces, l; account of the battle of, li-lii and *n*, 270-273; list of casualties, lii *n*; difficulty of obtaining information as to those engaged at, 276.
Gordon, banker in Paris, 233.
—— duke of, 286; letter to, from Ormonde, xxxv, 63.
—— general, xlii and *n*, xliii, 38 *n*, 54, 58, 62, 247.
—— of Glenbucket, loyalty of, 286; letter from, to general Carpenter, on a meeting of Jacobites in Glengarry, 288.
—— William, 265.
Gortz, baron, minister to Charles XII., xxii, 6 and *n*, 47, 53, 221; his trial and execution, xxxi and *n*.
Gozzani, M., 107, 227.
Gualterio, cardinal, 266.
Guevarra, don Balthasar de, admiral of the Cadiz fleet, xxxvi, 74 and *n*, 75, 76, 77, 90, 243, 244, 248; letter to, from Ormonde, 75; dispersion of his fleet, xl, 111, 119, 243, 245, 246.
Gyllenborg, count, Swedish minister at London, xxii, xxiii *n*, 6 and *n*.

HAMBURG, 227.
Hamilton, rev. Ezekiel, 17 *n*, 18, 33, 38, 40, 45, 47, 48, 51, 54, 88, 97, 101, 113, 123, 134, 151, 152; letters to, from Ormonde, 50, 54.
Hardy's squadron, 110.
Harrison's regiment, l, li, 284, 294.
Hay, John, of Cromlix, 1 *n*, 259 *n*; letters to, from Ormonde, 152 and *n*, 160, 186.
Healy, sir John, 58 and *n*, 72-74, 77, 80-81 and *n*, 127, 153, 159, 162, 174, 175; letters to, from Ormonde, 118, 121, 124, 125, 128, 177.
Heighington, captain, lii *n*.
Hesse, the prince of, 53, 77 and *n*.
Hochkirchen, battle of, lix, 9 *n*.
Holland, 58, 62, 77, 251.
Holstein, xxi.
—— duke of, 221.
Hossack, provost, of Inverness, lii *n*.
Huesca, 186.
Huffel's Dutch regiment, 291; at the battle of Glenshiel, l, lii *n*.
Hungary water, 131.

INNSPRUCK, detention of princess Clementina at, xxvii and *n*, lvi, 199, 201, 205.
Inverness, xliv, xlvi, xlviii, 281.

JERNINGHAM, Mr., xxiii, 194, 195, 199.
Jolly, Mr., 160, 166, 267.
Jones, Mr., 118, 121, 125.
Jordan, captain, 244.
Joyce, Mr., 127, 129, 134, 138, 144; letters to, from Ormonde, 135, 141.

KAISERSLAUTERN, siege of, 1 *n*.
Kays, commander of ship, 120.
Keith, George. *See* Marischal, earl.
—— James, xlviii and *n*, 9 and *n*, 13 *n*, 19 *n*; his journey to Spain, xxxiv and *n*; warns the Jacobites abroad of the intended expedition to Scotland, xlii; joins the earl Marischal in the island of Lewis, xliv; his subsequent career, lix.
Kelly, 130, 133, 142, 145, 150.
Kennedy, David, secretary to the duke of Ormonde, 35, 36, 38, 117, 153, 159, 160, 267.
Kilichumen (Fort Augustus), building of barrack at, 287 and *n*.
Kingston, duke of, 290 and *n*.
Knoydart, meeting of Jacobites in, 288.

LAMBERT, ROBERT, 45, 184.
La Val, comte de, 233.
Lawless, sir Patrick, sent on a mission to Sweden to negotiate for an alliance with Spain, xxviii, 15, 17, 23, 27, 31, 38, 42, 47, 60, 86, 87, 108, 126, 165, 221, 224, 227, 247; at Amsterdam, 251.
Lawrence, lieutenant-colonel, l.
Lede, marquis de, xxvi, 149 *n*.
Le Franc, M., 149, 150, 262, 264.
Leghorn, arrival of James at, 185-188.
Lesley, Mr., 31, 40, 48, 54, 97, 162.
'*Letter from a gentleman at R(ome) to a friend at L(ondon)*,' 21 *n*.
'Lidcoat, Mr.,' l and *n*, li, 270-272.
Lincoln, earl of, 285 and *n*.
Liria, duke of, xxxv, 39 and *n*, 48 *n*; letters to, from Ormonde, 53, 130.
Loch Alsh, xlv, xlvi.
Loch Clunie, xlix and *n*, 270.
Loch Duich, xlvii, xlviii, xlix.
Loch Kishorn, xlvi.
Loch nan Corr, xlvii *n*.
Lockhart of Carnwath, xlv *n*.
Louis XIV., death of, xxi.
Loya, don Blas de, 183; letter to, from Ormonde, 185 and *n*.
Lubeck, 251.

MACARTNEY's regiment, 284, 294.
MacDonald of Keppoch, 38 *n*.

INDEX

MacDonald, Donald, of Benbecula, letter to, from Ormonde, inviting his support to Jacobite attempt, xxxv, 70 and *n*.
—— Ranald, of Clanranald, xlii *n*, xlvi, 71 *n*.
MacDonell, Alastair Dubh, of Glengarry, xxxv, l *n*, 280; general Carpenter suspects the loyalty of, 280, 281; letter of warning to, from Carpenter, 282; letter from, to Carpenter, in vindication of his conduct, 287; attends a Jacobite meeting in Knoydart, 288; his good intentions, 289; letter to, from Ormonde, 69 and *n*.
—— Mr., 41, 58, 69, 80, 85, 119, 219.
M'Dougall, the laird of, at the battle of Glenshiel, 271.
—— of Lorn, 38 *n*.
MacGregor, Robert, 'Rob Roy,' at the battle of Glenshiel, xlviii, l, li, 270-272.
M'Griger, of Downan, rescues two Jacobite prisoners, 289.
M'Intosh, brigadier, of Borlum, at Glenshiel, l, 271.
—— major, at the battle of Glenshiel, 271.
Mackay, ensign, l.
M'Kenzie of Avoch, 38 *n*.
—— sir John, of Coul, at the battle of Glenshiel, l, li, 271, 272.
M'Kinnon, the laird of, at the battle of Glenshiel, l, 270-272.
Maclaine, colonel, xx.
MacLean, Donald, of Brolas, letter to, from Ormonde, xxxv, 70 and *n*.
M'Mahon, Forman, letter from, to James, 11 *n*.
M'Pherson, Mr., 121, 129.
Magny, marquis de, 129 and *n*, 172, 174, 176, 179, 194.
Maine, duc du, xxx.
—— duchesse du, xxx.
Mantua, 208.
Mar, countess of, 2 *n*, 3, 21, 195, 196, 203, 206.
—— John Erskine, earl of, xx, xxiii, xxxi *n*, xxxii *n*, l *n*, 21 *n*, 102, 180, 197, 199, 239, 251, 264, 266, 267; arrested at Voghera, xxxiii and *n*, 206-216, 220, 233; letter from, to Ormonde, 202; letter from, to the earl Marischal on the imprisonment of the princess Clementina, 204; letter from, to lord Panmure giving an account of his arrest at Voghera, and imprisonment at Milan, 206-216; letter to, from Tullibardine, 269; letters to, from Ormonde, 2

and *n*, 21 and *n*, 87 and *n*, 194, 195.
Mari, rear-admiral, xxvi.
Marischal, George Keith, 10th earl, 13 *n*, 38, 54, 58, 60, 63, 68, 70 and *n*, 86, 87, 94, 97, 101, 107, 108, 114, 116, 153, 159, 220, 247, 267; selected as leader of the expedition to Scotland, xxix, 47; leaves Paris for Madrid, 35; his journey to Spain, xxxiv and *n*; sails with the expedition for Scotland, xxxv and *n*, xli, 239, 240; in the island of Lewis, xliv; at the battle of Glenshiel, l, 271, 273; escapes to the Continent, liv and *n*, 280; his subsequent career, lviii; letter to, from Mar, 204; letters to, from Ormonde, 9 and *n*, 69, 119, 120.
Marseilles, report from, on the preparations at Cadiz, 228.
Mary of Modena, death of, xxiv.
Mathews, Toby, 50, 51, 54, 55, 117; letter to, from Ormonde, 51.
Matillion, M. de, 68, 256.
Meagher, John, 107, 108, 114, 116, 127, 130, 131, 133, 138, 150.
Mecklenburg, affairs of, 103 and *n*.
Melfort, duchess of, 206.
Menzies, Mr., 159.
Mercy, count, 149 *n*.
Messina, 228; taken by Spaniards, xxvi, 187 and *n*, 196.
Milan, detention of Mar and Perth at, xxxiii, 208, 210, 211, 224, 231, 233.
Milburn, major, l.
Misset, captain, lvi.
Modena, 208.
Monro, colonel, 279.
Montagu's regiment, li, lii *n*, 284, 294.
Montefiascone, marriage of James at, lvii and *n*.
Monteleone, Spanish ambassador at London, recall of, xxvi.
Moor, captain, lii *n*.
Morgan, captain, 54 *n*, 55, 141, 142, 146, 162; letter to, from Ormonde, 155.
Munro, captain George, of Culcairn, li and *n*, lii *n*.
Muras, 110, 111.
Murray, lord George, xlviii-li, liii, 38, 270, 271.
—— the hon. James, lvi, 15 *n*, 17, 21, 195, 196, 199, 262, 265; letter to, from Ormonde, 151.
—— Marjory, daughter of lord Stormont, 152 *n*.

Navarre, 16.
Nettuno, xxxiii.
Norris, sir John, xxxix, 235.
Norway, 6.
Nugent, Mr., 89, 194.

O'Brien, Daniel, xxiii, 131, 221.
Oglethorpe, Fanny, 11 *n*.
—— Mr., 159, 267.
Ormonde, duchess of, 6 *n*, 7, 194, 199.
—— James Butler, 2nd duke of, his early career and character, xix, xx and *n*; mission to Sweden and Russia, xxiii; threatened with arrest in France, xxiv; invited to Spain, xxvii; interviews with Alberoni at Madrid, xxviii, xxix, 5-8, 15-17; intrusted with command of expedition against England, xxix; goes to Valladolid, xxx; invites the earl Marischal to Spain, xxxiv, 9, 13, 35, 47; meets him at Astorga, xxxv, 61; goes to Corunna and awaits fleet there, xxxv, 54, 55, 78, *et seq.*; reward offered in England for his arrest, xxxix; receives James at Corunna, 113; leaves Corunna, 118; employed in expedition against Brittany, lv, 168, 173, 174, 177, *et seq.*; his later years, lviii and *n*.
O'Toole, captain, lvi.
Owen, colonel, xxvii, 96 and *n*, 97, 174; memorial from, 142; letter to, from Ormonde, 125.
Oxford, lord, 225, 230.

Palamos, xxxiv.
Palermo taken by Spaniards, xxvi.
Pampeluna, 23, 150, 162, 254.
Panmure, lord, letter to, from Mar, giving an account of his arrest and imprisonment at Voghera, 206.
Parker, lord chancellor, 86 *n*.
Parliamentary debate on Spanish affairs, 10 and *n*.
Parma, 208.
Paterson, sir Hugh, letter to, from James, lvii.
Patino, don Jose de, 133, 142, 157, 187, 227, 250, 252.
Pavia, 211.
Payton, 195.
Penterridter, M., 235.
Perth, duke of, 102, 172-174, 239, 251, 268; arrested at Voghera, xxxiii and *n*, 206-216, 233; letter to, from Ormonde, 167 and *n*.
Petite, captain, 170.
Philip V. of Spain, xxi, xxxvi, 86, 107,
109, 183, 199, 200; letters from, to James, 218, 248, 254, 257; letters to, from James, 257, 263.
Philip, duke of Orleans, 2, 3 *n*, 4, 6, 62, 129 *n*, 143, 170, 205, 220, 231, 236, 240; his reasons for desiring the friendship of England, xxi; offers military aid in the event of a Spanish invasion, xxxviii and *n*, xxxix, 229, 232, 233, 235, 238; discovery of a conspiracy against his person, xxx, 23 and *n*.
Piacenza, 208, 215.
Pierrepoint, lady Frances. *See* Mar, countess of.
Pio, prince, of Savoy, xxxiv *n*.
Polignac, cardinal, xxx.
Pollock, sir Robert, 289.
Pontevedra, 89, 95, 97, 165 *n*.
Portocarrero, don Vincente, xxx.
Port Mahon, xxvi, 82, 83.
Port Passage, xxxv, xli, 237, 238; the arsenal destroyed by the French, lv, 124 *n*, 127.
Power, Mr., 131.
Prado, marquis de, 101.
Preston, brigadier, 278, 283, 285, 291, 292; letter from, to Delafaye, on the repayment of expenses incurred by the Spanish prisoners, 295.
Preston Pans, 291, 292.
Price, M., Swedish resident in Holland, 6.
Prie, marquis de, 235.
Prior, Matthew, 225.

Raventlau, count of, 221.
Reading, lieut.-colonel, l.
Redmond, sir Peter, 7, 8, and *n*, 20, 25, 28, 30; letters to, from Ormonde, 122, 136.
Redondela, 119, 165 *n*.
Regiments in Scotland in July 1719, 284; in September, 294.
Reports on the dispersion of the Spanish fleet, 243, 245, 246.
Risbourg, marquis de, viceroy of Galicia, xxxv, 63 *n*, 66, 68, 69, 76, 85, 87, 93, 94, 102, 107-111, 113, 121, 124, 125, 128, 222, 223, 246, 250; letters to, from Ormonde, 64, 65, 71-74, 77, 79, 81-83, 88, 121, 124, 127, 130, 131, 133, 134, 138, 148, 156.
Rocca, count, xxxvii *n*.
Rosas, James lands at, xxxvi, 86, 119, 219, 239.
Rose, Alexander, bishop of Edinburgh, 296 *n*.
Roussillon, xxvii, 16.

INDEX

Roxburghe, John, duke of, 276, 279 and *n*, 283, 285.

SADA, xxxv.
St. Aignan, duc de, French ambassador at Madrid, xxx.
St. Malo, report from, on the preparations at Cadiz, 228.
St. Mary, M. de, 102.
St. Paul de Leon, 62.
Salvador, Mr., 135.
Sampson and Sandilanes of Bordeaux, 98.
San Sebastian, xlii, lv, 27, 29, 45, 51, 66, 69, 93, 94, 107, 139, 142, 144, 148, 156, 162 and *n*, 256.
Santander, 141, 147, 183.
Santona, lv.
Sardinia, xxv, 250.
Sardy, M. de, 107.
Saunders, captain, xxvi.
Scottish exiles in France in 1719, 38 and *n*.
Scour Ouran, xlix, l, lii.
Seaforth, William Mackenzie, earl of, xlii, xliv *n*, 38 *n*, 120 and *n*, 288, 289; leaves France for Scotland, 233; joins Tullibardine with 500 followers, xlviii; at the battle of Glenshiel, l, 270, 271; wounded, liii; letter from, to James, on the defeat at Glenshiel, 273; escapes to the Continent, liv and *n*, 280 returns to Scotland, lviii.
Seminati, M., 32; letter to, from Ormonde, 134.
Senectere, marquis de, 226, 233.
Sheldon, Mr., 198, 221.
Sherlock, sir Peter, 45 and *n*, 110.
Sicily, xxv, xxvi, 148 and *n*, 187, 195, 196, 250.
Silly, marquis de, lv, 145 and *n*.
Sisarga islands, 176 and *n*.
Sleswick, xxi.
Smith, Mr., 138, 150, 156.
Somerset, lady Mary. *See* Ormonde, duchess of.
Southcoat, 194, 199.
Spaar, baron, Swedish minister at Paris, xxii.
Spanish soldiers with earl Marischal's expedition, xli and *n*; surrender of, at Glenshiel, l and *n*, lii and *n*, liii, 273; ordered to Plymouth, 274; marched to Edinburgh, liv and *n*, 277, 278; grow sulky in confinement, 282; the question of expenses incurred by them, 285, 291; account of expenditure on, 292; they embark for Spain, 296.

Spartman, Richard, xxxvi *n*.
Stafford, sir Peter, 121, 124, 125, 131, 133, 135, 160.
Stair's regiment, 284, 294.
—— John Dalrymple, 2nd earl of, British ambassador at Paris, xxiv and *n*, liv *n*, 220; letters from, to secretary Craggs, 229, 232, 233, 236, 238; letters to, from Craggs, 234, 237.
Stanhope, colonel William, xxv, lvi *n*.
—— earl, xxvii, 10 *n*, 47 and *n*, 224, 235.
Stirling, sir Henry, xxiii.
Stormont, lord, xlv *n*.
Stornoway, xliv.
Strachell, pass of, xlix *n*.
Strachlony, xlix *n*.
Stralsund, xxii.
Strathnaver, lord, l.
Strickland, abbé, 21 *n*.
Stuart, James Francis Edward, quarrels with Bolingbroke, xx and *n*; his want of prudence, 11 and *n*; goes to Italy, xxi, 14, 205; invited to Spain, xxix-xxxi and *n*, 17; arrangements for the journey, xxxii, 18, 20, 22; rumoured arrest of, at Voghera, xxiii, 224, 231; journey to Spain, xxxiii, xxxvi, 207, 220; lands at Rosas, xxxvi, 86, 119, 219, 239; reception in Spain, xxxvii and *n*, 85, 218; is opposed to the idea of an invasion of Scotland, xxxviii, 104; reaches Corunna, xl, 113; question of his accompanying the expedition, 107, 109; marriage by proxy to princess Clementina, lvi; reasons for his leaving Spain, lv-lvi and *n*; arrangements for his return to Italy, 257; reaches Leghorn, 185, 188; meeting with princess Clementina, lvii; letter from, to Alberoni, 261; letter from, to Clement XI., 216; letters from, to Dicconson, 198, 217, 221; letters from, to Philip v., 259, 263; letters from, to Ormonde, 199, 200, 259, 264, 265, 267; letter to, from Seaforth, 273; letters to, from Alberoni, 240, 246, 250, 253, 255, 257, 258; letters to, from Ormonde, 1 and *n*, 6 and *n*, 15, 19, 86, 93, 95, 101, 104, 108-110, 112, 151, 153, 159, 164, 165, 170, 176, 180, 185, 193, 196, 197; letters to, from Philip v. of Spain, 218, 241, 248, 254, 257; letters to, from the queen of Spain, 218, 242, 249, 255 258.

U

Sutherland, Mr., brother of lord Duffus, xlii, xliv *n*.
Sweden favourable to Jacobite schemes, xxi; arrest of the Swedish minister in London, xxii; negotiations for an alliance with Spain, 11, 15, 16, 49, 53, 87, 103, 224, 251.

TALBOT, lieut.-col., 147, 162, 174, 264.
Trant, Olive, 11 *n*, 12 *n*.
Treby, Mr., 274.
Threipland of Fingask, 155 *n*.
Trent, 208.
Tullibardine, marquis of, xlii, xliii, 38, 288, 289; sails for Scotland, 239; joins earl Marischal in the island of Lewis, xliv and *n*; assumes command of the expedition, xlv; in favour of a return to Spain, xlvi; endeavours to raise the clans, xlviii; defeated at the battle of Glenshiel, l-lii, 269-273; escapes to the continent, liv and *n*; death of, lviii; letters from, to the earl of Mar, 269.
Tullo, Alexander, 45, 68, 69, 80, 120, 121, 166.

UIST, 108.
Ulrica, queen of Sweden, xxxi, 77 *n*, 86.
Urbino, xxi.

VALENCIA, 107, 166, 252.
Valladolid, xxx, xxxv, 12-60 *passim*, 149, 150, 153, 156-188 *et seq*.
Vanbeque, M., 98.
Vandernat, comte de, 221.
Verden, bishopric of, ceded to George I., xxi.
Vienna, 208.
Vigo, 110, 111, 113, 119, 165 *n*, 246.
Vinaros, 165, 171, 258.
Visconti, marshal, 215.
Voghera, Mar and Perth arrested at, xxxiii and *n*, 87 *n*, 208, 224, 233.

WADE, general, xxii.
Walef, baron, 25 and *n*, 38, 41, 58, 85, 93, 124, 179, 188, 225 *n*; letters to, from Ormonde, 27, 66, 76, 78, 80, 82, 161, 173.
Walton, captain, xxvi *n*, 19 *n*.
Wightman, major-general, xlix *n*, l *n*, 275, 284, 294; marches from Inverness, xlviii; disposition of his forces, l; defeats the Jacobites at Glenshiel, li-lii and *n*, liii; letters from, to Charles Delafaye, 276, 280, 282, 285, 290.
Willoughby, Mr., 137, 147, 151, 162.
Wogan, Charles, xxiii, lvi, 264.
Worsley, Henry, British envoy at Lisbon, report by, on the preparations at Cadiz, 236.
Wright, Mr., 55, 123, 142.

Printed by T. and A. CONSTABLE, Printers to Her Majesty
at the Edinburgh University Press

REPORT OF THE NINTH ANNUAL MEETING OF THE SCOTTISH HISTORY SOCIETY

THE NINTH ANNUAL MEETING OF THE SOCIETY was held on Tuesday, October 29, 1895, in Dowell's Rooms, George Street, Edinburgh—The Earl of Rosebery, President of the Society, in the chair.

The HON. SECRETARY read the Report of the Council, as follows:—

During the past year the Society has lost fifteen members, seven by death, and eight by resignation. The vacancies have been filled up, and there remain forty-nine candidates waiting for admission.

Three volumes have just been delivered to members. *Scotland and the Commonwealth*, edited chiefly from the Clarke MSS. in Worcester College, Oxford, by Mr. C. H. Firth, belongs to the issue of last year, 1893-94. The other two volumes, *i.e.*, vols. 1 and 2 of *The Lyon in Mourning*, edited by Mr. Henry Paton, belong to the issue of the present year. The long-expected *Ormonde Letters*, which was also promised as one of the publications of this year, and which forms No. 19 of our series, numerically preceding *The Lyon in Mourning*, is already in type, and will be ready for distribution in a few weeks. It will bear the title: *The Jacobite Attempt of* 1719: *Letters of James Butler, second Duke of Ormonde, relating* to Cardinal Alberoni's project for the Invasion of Great Britain on behalf of the Stuarts, and to the Landing of the Earl Marischal in Scotland. The interest and originality of the contents will, it is hoped, fully compensate for the delay in publication, the editor, Mr. W. K. Dickson, Advocate, having recently been enabled, by the gracious permission of Her Majesty the Queen, to supplement the volume with some valuable documents preserved among the Stuart Papers at Windsor.

Early in next year members may expect the third volume of *The Lyon in Mourning*, which will contain an index to the whole work. It will be accompanied by a second volume of the *Minutes of the Commissions of the General Assembly* for the years 1648-1650; and by a volume of *Extracts from the Presbytery Records of Inverness and Dingwall*, prepared by Mr. William Mackay of Inverness. The complete text of these two last-mentioned works is already in type.

A list of other books in progress or in contemplation will be found printed at the end of the volumes now issued.

Further transcripts of Dutch papers at the Hague relating to the Scots Brigade have been obtained from Dr. Mendels, and arrangements are being made for their translation into English.

Mr. Firth has in preparation a volume, to be entitled *Scotland under the Protectorate*, which will form a sequel to his *Scotland under the Commonwealth*.

Mr. J. G. Fotheringham of Paris has offered to the Society for publication a translation which he has made of the secret correspondence of Jean de Montreuil with Cardinal Mazarin and others on Scottish affairs in the years 1645-1648. Montreuil was sent into England by the French Government on the proposal of the Scots that both nations should combine to secure the safety of the king. He thereupon entered into the negotiations, on the faith of which Charles left Oxford and put himself under the protection of the Scots army, then besieging Newark. Montreuil was with the king for some time at Newcastle, and subsequently, February 1647, went to Edinburgh, where he was accredited by the King of France, as resident French Minister, to the Scots Government. He returned to Paris in the autumn of 1648. The weekly news-letters, partly in cypher, which he despatched to France have remained hitherto unpublished in the French Foreign Office. In view of the importance of these Letters to Scottish historians, the Council, in accepting Mr. Fotheringham's translations and notes, determined to print with them the French originals. The greater part of the transcripts has already been made.

The Lord Provost and Magistrates of the City of Perth have kindly invited the Council to examine their municipal archives, and to select for publication any documents which may appear suitable for our Society. Mr. David Marshall, F.S.A., who had been engaged in arranging and cataloguing the archives on behalf of the city, has furnished the Council with a full report of their contents. They comprise, in addition to many documents of local interest, a collection of letters and papers relating to the rebellions of 1715 and 1745, the examination of prisoners, and depositions of witnesses, etc. There are papers of John Glas, 1650-89, sometime Lord Provost of Perth, and of John Mercer, 1670-1743, sheriff-clerk of Perthshire, with family pedigrees. There are also two account-books of prominent merchants, the Compt-book of Bailie Alexander Jamieson, merchant and shipowner, sometime treasurer of Perth, 1660-1673, and the Book of Accounts of Nathaniel Fyfe, 1705-1715. Mr. Fyfe was one of the magistrates appointed by Colonel Hay, governor of Perth under the Earl of Mar, in 1715. These mercantile account-books may perhaps, in due time, form a companion volume to the Diary of Bailie Wedderburne of Dundee, now being prepared for publication by Mr. A. H. Millar.

According to rule, Mr. Gregory Smith, Mr. Hume Brown, and Mr. J. R. Findlay retire from the Council. It is proposed that

Mr. Hume Brown and Mr. Findlay be re-appointed, and Mr. G. W. Prothero, Professor of History in the University of Edinburgh, be nominated in the place of Mr. Gregory Smith.

The accompanying abstract of the Hon. Treasurer's accounts shows that the income for 1894-95 has been £477, 10s. 11d., and the expenditure £569, 1s., an excess of expenditure over income of £91, 10s. 1d. There was a balance due by the bank in October 1894 of £175, 6s. 8d., leaving a balance in favour of the society at this date of £89, 1s. 7d., which includes 5 subscriptions for 1895-96 paid in advance.

There has been paid out of the Reserve Fund to Dr. Mendels, for transcripts from the Hague, the sum of £43, 10s., leaving the amount of that fund now at £178, 7s. 6d.

The HON. TREASURER (Mr. Jas. T. Clark) explained that three volumes had been issued last year, being one volume more than the usual number, and that the sum of £227 had been spent upon volumes not yet issued. Although the Council intended to issue three volumes next year, he fully expected that so much money having been already advanced, the income would cover the expenditure.

LORD ROSEBERY said—It affords me great pleasure to move the adoption of this Report, because the only flaw in it, which is the excess of expenditure over the income during the present year, has been removed by the explanation of Mr. Clark. May I, in the first place, express my great personal pleasure at being among you again? I regard it as a great privilege to be a Member of this Society—a privilege which I hope will not be extended by opening the gates to those who are panting to enter. Four hundred is a very suitable number for a society of this kind, and if we once begin to open the floodgates, who knows where our Society may stop, and we may have to degenerate as regards our publications to some extent in quality in order to meet the demand for quantity. Let us proceed on the safe and sure lines that have led us to such abundant prosperity, and do not let us seek to enlarge our Society by any concession to the candidates who are so properly anxious to come amongst us. If, then, I regard it as a privilege to be a member, I regard it as the greatest of distinctions to be the President of this Society; and though I do not know that I have any undue attachment to this distinction, I shall part with that distinction only with a struggle, which will be equivalent to the surrender of life itself. Now, gentlemen, I do not think there is any point of moment or act in the history of this Society which we can look back to with anything but satisfaction, and I doubt if there is any other society in the world of which that can be said. We have produced nothing but good practical work. It has not been a mere record of the reproduction of several antiquities, but each of our books has borne on it the marks of conscientious work, and will bear the test of utility, I think, in regard to every one of them. We have given special attention to the Jacobite risings of the last century, but I do not think any one can blame us, or consider that that attention has been superfluous or excessive. After all, we are still in the position of being a generation that has some hope, by sedulous care, of keeping in existence all that is in existence with regard to these most interesting events and epochs. Now, I declare to you, gentlemen, that if this Society in the nine or ten years of its existence had done nothing more than reprint *The Lyon in Mourning*, which we are producing now, it would have fully justified its existence. But we have already a list of those who took part in these risings, which is tolerably complete in itself. We have in contemplation, as the Secretary has told us, papers of great value relating to the abortive rising of 1719; we have papers from Perth coming to us with regard to the risings both of 1715 and 1745; and we have, above all, the prospect, which, I think, would justify a much greater excess of expenditure over income than has been declared to be the case, of the publication of the journal of Murray of Broughton, which I confess I look forward to with an avidity which I can hardly repress at this moment; and I may say, Mr. Law, I would have gladly seen some intimation in the Report of the approximate appearance of that publication. In one of the prefaces—I think it is the preface to *The Lyon in Mourning*—we are promised, as, I suppose, the result of that publication, an exact map of the young Prince's wanderings in the year 1746. My belief is, though I have not had an opportunity of seeing in detail the whole of *The Lyon in Mourning*, that it will be almost possible to produce from that, what Chambers, though he had *The Lyon in Mourning* in hand, has never given us—it will be almost possible to give an exact journal from day to day of where the Prince spent the day and the night. There are epochs which are left with the greatest blanks in Chambers's book, which is after all the most complete account of the wanderings of the Prince, and who drew largely on *The Lyon in Mourning* for his information; and these, I cannot help thinking—though I cannot speak with the authority of the editor of the book—might be cleared up by careful investigation of the evidence it affords. Well, gentlemen, after all, interesting as all this is, we have another encouragement in the work that we are prosecuting, and it is this, that not merely have we a library produced by the Society of the most abundant interest—and I confess that one of the pleasures of being out of office is in looking forward to being able to read up back volumes—not only have we a handsome library of volumes provided by the Society, but the work of the Society is bringing in offers constantly of valuable manuscripts and sources of information, which I believe, but for the Society, might have remained entirely lost and forgotten. Well, if only for that, I think Scotland has some reason to be grateful to us. But in effect, I think nobody who looks over the publications that are brought out in Scotland at the present time can fail to see that our work is prosperous, not merely because of the intelligence of the working officials like Mr. Law, and the editors of the papers, and Professor Masson, but also because it is part of the spirit of the times. I am immensely struck, wishing as I do to see all publications coming out in Scotland, with the enormous number of small family histories—I do not mean, of course, the great monumental works of Sir William Fraser, the appearance of which forms a sort of epoch itself, but I mean the smaller histories, of fifty or sixty pages—each of which come out apparently in response to some demand, which I cannot trace, but which come out in such abundance as to make it quite clear that the people of Scotland are determined not to lose any trace of their former local history. Let me give another instance. Every parish almost is now publishing its history—parishes, some of them, extremely obscure; but it is apparently a labour of love on the part of some one to publish such a history in the case of almost all parishes which have the faintest interest—no parish can be without any interest —and it is evidently also a labour of love to a certain number of people to acquire and read those histories. Therefore I say from the great abundance of the parochial and family histories, small in size but careful in workmanship, which are being turned out every day, we can appreciate the anxiety of the nation at large to preserve every record that can be possibly of the slightest interest with regard to its past history. Well, gentlemen, I hope, as we have provided wisely, we shall continue on the same track. There is one small departure I wanted to make, and I have consulted Mr. Law about it. As I have not seen him lately I do not know with what success; but I wanted to approach one of the most eminent of our antiquaries, who has made a special collection of travels in Scotland, ever since travelling in Scotland was known —to approach that eminent antiquary to ask him to furnish the Society with a catalogue *raisonné* of all such books. It is not in the ordinary scheme of our publications, which is usually limited to republication of ancient manuscripts; but this little book will be of such enormous and inestimable advantage to students of Scotch history, that I think it would be, although a departure from the letter, not a departure from the spirit of our constitution, and it is one which the Society at large would welcome. That is all I have to say, except to congratulate you most sincerely on your success, and myself on being once more in so congenial a scene.

The Rev. Dr. HUTCHISON, Leith, seconded the adoption of the Report, which was unanimously agreed to.

Mr. W. K. DICKSON, Advocate, moved that the thanks of the Society be tendered to the Council for their services during the year.

The motion was adopted with acclamation.

Professor MASSON, in replying for the Council, thought the result of their deliberations had been the production of a series of volumes creditable to the Society, and, perhaps, teaching the Scottish people new notions of what Scottish history might be.

SIR JOHN COWAN, in moving a vote of thanks to Lord Rosebery for presiding, spoke of the great interest of the list of the Jacobites who were out in the '45, which Lord Rosebery had given them. In his youth he was always trained to be a lover of the Stuarts. The word Pretender was never permitted in his home. His grandmother was one of those who were introduced to Prince Charlie at Holyrood; and he (Sir John) was very much aggrieved that in the list of the 'rebels' which Lord Rosebery presented to the Society, the name did not appear of his great-grandfather, who fled with his wife and daughter to France, and spent the remainder of his days there, a pensioner at St. Germains.

LORD ROSEBERY, in his reply, said he was particularly pleased to see his friend Sir John Cowan appearing in a novel character—that of a Jacobite of the strongest and most absolute leanings. If Sir John had any MSS. relating to these Jacobite ancestors, the Society would gladly add it to the volumes already published.

The proceedings then terminated.

ABSTRACT OF THE HON. TREASURER'S ACCOUNTS.

For Year to 26th October 1895.

I. Charge.

Balance from last year,	.	.	.	£175	6	8
400 Subscriptions for 1894-95, at £1, 1s., £420 0 0						
Less 3 for 1894-95, paid in advance (£3, 3s.), and 9 arrears for 1894-95 (£9, 9s.), 12 12 0						
				407	8	0
46 Libraries at £1, 1s., ...			.	48	6	0
Copies of previous issues sold to New Members,			.	16	5	6
Interest on Deposit Receipts, . . .			.	5	11	5
Sum of Charge,		.	.	£652	17	7

II. Discharge.

1. *Incidental Expenses—*

Printing Cards and Circulars,	.	£1	10	0	
,, Annual Report,	.	1	15	6	
Stationery (£1, 13s. 8d.), Receipt Book (18s.), . . .		2	11	8	
Making-up and delivering copies, .		22	7	0	
Postages of Secretary and Treasurer,		3	12	6	
Clerical Work, . . .	.	4	15	0	
Charges on Cheques, . .	.	0	3	0	
				£36	14 8

II. *Scotland and the Commonwealth—*

Composition, Printing, and Paper,	£90	8	6		
Proofs and Corrections,	.	25	8	0	
Binding and Back-lettering,	.	18	16	6	
Transcribing, . . .	.	27	12	10	
Indexing, . . .	.	4	0	0	
				166	5 10

Carry forward,		.	£203	0 6

Brought forward,			£203 0 6

III. *The Lyon in Mourning,* Vol. I.—
- Composition, Printing, and Paper, £81 3 0
- Proofs and Corrections, . . 17 14 0
- Binding and Back-lettering, . . 18 15 0
- Facsimile of Title-page, . . 1 6 6

                                                        118 18 6

IV. *The Lyon in Mourning,* Vol. II.—
- Composition, Printing, and Paper, ... £80 18 0
- Proofs and Corrections, . . 11 12 0
- Binding and Back-lettering, . 18 3 0

                                                        110 13 0

V. *Records of the General Assemblies,* Vol. II.—
- Composition, Printing, and Paper, ... £86 18 0
- Proofs and Corrections, . . 21 12 0

                                                     £108 10 0

- Less paid to account, October 1893, ... 37 18 0

                                                       70 12 0

VI. *The Jacobite Rising of 1719*—
- Composition, Printing, and Paper, ... £36 0 0
- Proofs and Corrections, . . 11 8 0
- Transcribing, ... 1 18 0

                                                     £49 6 0

- Less paid to account, October 1893, ... 16 14 0

                                                     32 12 0

VII. *Murray of Broughton's Journal*—
- Typewriting MS., ... 20 1 0

VIII. *Presbytery Records of Inverness*—
- Typewriting MS., . . . 9 0 0

                          Carry forward, .   £564 17 0

Brought forward,		£564	17	0
IX. *Lauder's* (*Lord Fountainhall*) *Journal*— Transcripts,		4	4	0
		£569	1	0
X. *Balance to next account*—				
Sum due by Bank of Scotland on 26th October 1895,	£89 1 7			
Less 5 Subscriptions, 1895-96, paid in advance,	5 5 0			
		83	16	7
Sum of Discharge,		£652	17	7

Reserve Fund.

As at 24th October 1894,	£221	17	6
Paid in terms of the Resolutions of Council—Dr. Mendels' further Researches and Transcripts at the Hague relating to the Scottish Brigade,	43	10	0
	£178	7	6
On Deposit Receipt, 25th October 1895,	£178	7	6

EDINBURGH, 16*th November* 1895.—The Auditors, having examined the Accounts of the Treasurer of the Scottish History Society for the year to 26th October 1895, and having compared them with the vouchers, find the said Accounts to be correct, closing with a balance in bank on General Account of £89, 1s. 7d., and in bank on deposit receipt, in respect of Reserve Fund, of £178, 7s. 6d. The subscriptions paid in advance, amounting to five guineas, will be included in next year's Account.

RALPH RICHARDSON, *Auditor.*
WM. TRAQUAIR DICKSON, *Auditor.*

Scottish History Society.

THE EXECUTIVE.

President.
THE EARL OF ROSEBERY, K.G., K.T., LL.D.

Chairman of Council.
DAVID MASSON, LL.D., Historiographer Royal for Scotland.

Council.
G. W. PROTHERO, Professor of History in the University of Edinburgh.
J. R. FINDLAY.
P. HUME BROWN, M.A.
J. FERGUSON, Advocate.
Right Rev. JOHN DOWDEN, D.D., Bishop of Edinburgh.
Professor Sir THOMAS GRAINGER STEWART, M.D.
J. N. MACPHAIL, Advocate.
Rev. A. W. CORNELIUS HALLEN.
Sir ARTHUR MITCHELL, K.C.B., M.D., LL.D.
Rev. GEO. W. SPROTT, D.D.
J. BALFOUR PAUL, Lyon King of Arms.
A. H. MILLAR.

Corresponding Members of the Council.
C. H. FIRTH, Oxford; SAMUEL RAWSON GARDINER, LL.D.; Rev. W. D. MACRAY, Oxford; Rev. Professor A. F. MITCHELL, D.D., St. Andrews.

Hon. Treasurer.
J. T. CLARK, Keeper of the Advocates' Library.

Hon. Secretary.
T. G. LAW, Librarian, Signet Library.

RULES

1. The object of the Society is the discovery and printing, under selected editorship, of unpublished documents illustrative of the civil, religious, and social history of Scotland. The Society will also undertake, in exceptional cases, to issue translations of printed works of a similar nature, which have not hitherto been accessible in English.

2. The number of Members of the Society shall be limited to 400.

3. The affairs of the Society shall be managed by a Council, consisting of a Chairman, Treasurer, Secretary, and twelve elected Members, five to make a quorum. Three of the twelve elected Members shall retire annually by ballot, but they shall be eligible for re-election.

4. The Annual Subscription to the Society shall be One Guinea. The publications of the Society shall not be delivered to any Member whose Subscription is in arrear, and no Member shall be permitted to receive more than one copy of the Society's publications.

5. The Society will undertake the issue of its own publications, *i.e.* without the intervention of a publisher or any other paid agent.

6. The Society will issue yearly two octavo volumes of about 320 pages each.

7. An Annual General Meeting of the Society shall be held on the last Tuesday in October.

8. Two stated Meetings of the Council shall be held each year, one on the last Tuesday of May, the other on the Tuesday preceding the day upon which the Annual General Meeting shall be held. The Secretary, on the request of three Members of the Council, shall call a special meeting of the Council.

9. Editors shall receive 20 copies of each volume they edit for the Society.

10. The owners of Manuscripts published by the Society will also be presented with a certain number of copies.

11. The Annual Balance-Sheet, Rules, and List of Members shall be printed.

12. No alteration shall be made in these Rules except at a General Meeting of the Society. A fortnight's notice of any alteration to be proposed shall be given to the Members of the Council.

PUBLICATIONS

OF THE

SCOTTISH HISTORY SOCIETY

For the year 1886-1887.

1. BISHOP POCOCKE'S TOURS IN SCOTLAND, 1747-1760. Edited by D. W. KEMP. (Oct. 1887.)

2. DIARY OF AND GENERAL EXPENDITURE BOOK OF WILLIAM CUNNINGHAM OF CRAIGENDS, 1673-1680. Edited by the Rev. JAMES DODDS, D.D. (Oct. 1887.)

For the year 1887-1888.

3. PANURGI PHILO-CABALLI SCOTI GRAMEIDOS LIBRI SEX. — THE GRAMEID: an heroic poem descriptive of the Campaign of Viscount Dundee in 1689, by JAMES PHILIP of Almerieclose. Translated and Edited by the Rev. A. D. MURDOCH.
(Oct. 1888.)

4. THE REGISTER OF THE KIRK-SESSION OF ST. ANDREWS. Part I. 1559-1582. Edited by D. HAY FLEMING. (Feb. 1889.)

For the year 1888-1889.

5. DIARY OF THE REV. JOHN MILL, Minister of Dunrossness, Sandwick, and Cunningsburgh, in Shetland, 1740-1803. Edited by GILBERT GOUDIE, F.S.A. Scot. (June 1889.)

6. NARRATIVE OF MR. JAMES NIMMO, A COVENANTER, 1654-1709. Edited by W. G. SCOTT-MONCRIEFF, Advocate. (June 1889.)

7. THE REGISTER OF THE KIRK-SESSION OF ST. ANDREWS. Part II. 1583-1600. Edited by D. HAY FLEMING. (Aug. 1890.)

PUBLICATIONS

For the year 1889-1890.

8. A LIST OF PERSONS CONCERNED IN THE REBELLION (1745). With a Preface by the EARL OF ROSEBERY and Annotations by the Rev. WALTER MACLEOD. (Sept. 1890.)

Presented to the Society by the Earl of Rosebery.

9. GLAMIS PAPERS: The 'BOOK OF RECORD,' a Diary written by PATRICK, FIRST EARL OF STRATHMORE, and other documents relating to Glamis Castle (1684-89). Edited by A. H. MILLAR, F.S.A. Scot. (Sept. 1890.)

10. JOHN MAJOR'S HISTORY OF GREATER BRITAIN (1521). Translated and Edited by ARCHIBALD CONSTABLE, with a Life of the author by ÆNEAS J. G. MACKAY, Advocate. (Feb. 1892.)

For the year 1890-1891.

11. THE RECORDS OF THE COMMISSIONS OF THE GENERAL ASSEMBLIES, 1646-47. Edited by the Rev. Professor MITCHELL, D.D., and the Rev. JAMES CHRISTIE, D.D., with an Introduction by the former. (May 1892.)

12. COURT-BOOK OF THE BARONY OF URIE, 1604-1747. Edited by the Rev. D. G. BARRON, from a MS. in possession of Mr. R. BARCLAY of Dorking. (Oct. 1892.)

For the year 1891-1892.

13. MEMOIRS OF THE LIFE OF SIR JOHN CLERK OF PENICUIK, Baronet, Baron of the Exchequer, Commissioner of the Union, etc. Extracted by himself from his own Journals, 1676-1755. Edited from the original MS. in Penicuik House by JOHN M. GRAY, F.S.A. Scot. (Dec. 1892.)

14. DIARY OF COL. THE HON. JOHN ERSKINE OF CARNOCK, 1683-1687. From a MS. in possession of HENRY DAVID ERSKINE, Esq., of Cardross. Edited by the Rev. WALTER MACLEOD. (Dec. 1893.)

For the year 1892-1893.

15. MISCELLANY OF THE SCOTTISH HISTORY SOCIETY, First Volume—
    THE LIBRARY OF JAMES VI., 1573-83.
    DOCUMENTS ILLUSTRATING CATHOLIC POLICY, 1596-98.
    LETTERS OF SIR THOMAS HOPE, 1627-46.
    CIVIL WAR PAPERS, 1645-50.
    LAUDERDALE CORRESPONDENCE, 1660-77.
    TURNBULL'S DIARY, 1657-1704.
    MASTERTON PAPERS, 1660-1719.
    ACCOMPT OF EXPENSES IN EDINBURGH, 1715.
    REBELLION PAPERS, 1715 and 1745.   (Dec. 1893.)

16. ACCOUNT BOOK OF SIR JOHN FOULIS OF RAVELSTON (1671-1707).
    Edited by the Rev. A. W. CORNELIUS HALLEN.
                                            (June 1894.)

For the year 1893-1894.

17. LETTERS AND PAPERS ILLUSTRATING THE RELATIONS BETWEEN CHARLES II. AND SCOTLAND IN 1650. Edited, with Notes and Introduction, by SAMUEL RAWSON GARDINER, LL.D., etc.
                                            (July 1894.)

18. SCOTLAND AND THE COMMONWEALTH. LETTERS AND PAPERS RELATING TO THE MILITARY GOVERNMENT OF SCOTLAND, Aug. 1651—Dec. 1653. Edited, with Introduction and Notes, by C. H. FIRTH, M.A.   (Oct. 1895.)

For the year 1894-1895.

19. THE JACOBITE ATTEMPT OF 1719. LETTERS OF JAMES, SECOND DUKE OF ORMONDE, RELATING TO CARDINAL ALBERONI'S PROJECT FOR THE INVASION OF GREAT BRITAIN ON BEHALF OF THE STUARTS, AND TO THE LANDING OF THE EARL MARISCHAL IN SCOTLAND. Edited by W. K. DICKSON, Advocate.

20, 21. THE LYON IN MOURNING, OR A COLLECTION OF SPEECHES, LETTERS, JOURNALS, ETC., RELATIVE TO THE AFFAIRS OF PRINCE CHARLES EDWARD STUART, by the Rev. ROBERT FORBES, A.M., Bishop of Ross and Caithness. 1746-1775. Edited from his Manuscript by HENRY PATON, M.A. Vols. I. and II.
                                            (Oct. 1895.)

For the year 1895-1896.

THE LYON IN MOURNING. Vol. III.

EXTRACTS FROM THE PRESBYTERY RECORDS OF INVERNESS AND DINGWALL FROM 1638 TO 1688. Edited by WILLIAM MACKAY.

RECORDS OF THE COMMISSIONS OF THE GENERAL ASSEMBLIES (*continued*) for the years 1648-49, 1649-50, Edited by the Rev. Professor MITCHELL, D.D., and Rev. JAMES CHRISTIE, D.D.

In preparation.

JOURNAL OF A FOREIGN TOUR IN 1665 AND 1666 BY JOHN LAUDER, LORD FOUNTAINHALL. Edited by DONALD CRAWFORD, Sheriff of Aberdeenshire.

JOURNALS AND PAPERS OF JOHN MURRAY OF BROUGHTON, PRINCE CHARLES' SECRETARY. Edited by R. FITZROY BELL, Advocate.

NOTE-BOOK OR DIARY OF BAILIE DAVID WEDDERBURNE, MERCHANT OF DUNDEE, 1587-1630. Edited by A. H. MILLAR.

SIR THOMAS CRAIG'S DE UNIONE REGNORUM BRITANNIÆ. Edited, with an English Translation, from the unpublished MS. in the Advocates' Library, by DAVID MASSON, Historiographer Royal.

A TRANSLATION OF THE STATUTA ECCLESIÆ SCOTICANÆ, 1225-1556, by DAVID PATRICK, LL.D.

DOCUMENTS IN THE ARCHIVES OF THE HAGUE AND ROTTERDAM CONCERNING THE SCOTS BRIGADE IN HOLLAND. Edited by J. FERGUSON, Advocate.

THE POLITICAL CORRESPONDENCE OF JEAN DE MONTREUIL WITH CARDINAL MAZARIN AND OTHERS CONCERNING SCOTTISH AFFAIRS, 1645-1648. Edited from the originals in the French Foreign Office, with Translation and Notes by J. G. FOTHERINGHAM.

SCOTLAND DURING THE PROTECTORATE, 1653-1659; in continuation of SCOTLAND AND THE COMMONWEALTH. Edited by C. H. FIRTH.

RECORDS OF THE COMMISSIONS OF THE GENERAL ASSEMBLIES (*continued*), for the years 1650-53.

REGISTER OF THE CONSULTATIONS OF THE MINISTERS OF EDINBURGH, AND SOME OTHER BRETHREN OF THE MINISTRY FROM DIVERS

PARTS OF THE LAND, MEETING FROM TIME TO TIME, SINCE THE INTERRUPTION OF THE ASSEMBLY 1653, ON THE PUBLIC AFFAIRS OF THIS DISTRESSED AND DISTRACTED KIRK, WITH OTHER PAPERS OF PUBLIC CONCERNMENT, 1653-1660.

PAPERS RELATING TO THE REBELLIONS OF 1715 AND 1745, with other documents from the Municipal Archives of the City of Perth.

THE DIARY OF ANDREW HAY OF STONE, NEAR BIGGAR, AFTERWARDS OF CRAIGNETHAN CASTLE, 1659-60. Edited by A. G. REID from a manuscript in his possession.

A SELECTION OF THE FORFEITED ESTATES PAPERS PRESERVED IN H.M. GENERAL REGISTER HOUSE AND ELSEWHERE. Edited by A. H. MILLAR.

A TRANSLATION OF THE HISTORIA ABBATUM DE KYNLOS OF FERRERIUS. By ARCHIBALD CONSTABLE.

DOCUMENTS RELATING TO THE AFFAIRS OF THE ROMAN CATHOLIC PARTY IN SCOTLAND, from the year of the Armada to the Union of the Crowns. Edited by THOMAS GRAVES LAW.

www.ingramcontent.com/pod-product-compliance
Lightning Source LLC
Chambersburg PA
CBHW051244300426
44114CB00011B/882